Bad News From Israel

Greg Philo and Mike Berry

THE RESEARCH GROUP
Greg Philo, Mike Berry, Alison Gilmour,
Maureen Gilmour, Suzanna Rust and Lucy West

Pluto Press
LONDON • STERLING, VIRGINIA

First published 2004 by Pluto Press
345 Archway Road, London N6 5AA
and 22883 Quicksilver Drive, Sterling, VA 20166–2012, USA

www.plutobooks.com

British Library Cataloguing in Publication Data
A catalogue record for this book is available from the British Library

ISBN   0 7453 2062 7 hardback
ISBN   0 7453 2061 9 paperback

Library of Congress Cataloging in Publication Data applied for

10 9 8 7 6 5 4 3 2 1

Designed and produced for Pluto Press by
Chase Publishing Services, Fortescue, Sidmouth, EX10 9QG, England
Typeset from disk by Stanford DTP Services, Northampton, England
Printed and bound in the European Union by
Antony Rowe Ltd, Chippenham and Eastbourne, England

Contents

Acknowledgements   vii
Preface   viii
Final Status Map   x

1 Histories of the Conflict   1
Introduction   1
Zionist Roots and the First Wave of Jewish Immigration
    into Palestine   2
Theodor Herzl and the Emergence of Political Zionism   3
The Second Wave of Jewish Immigration into Palestine   4
The Balfour Declaration and the British Mandate   5
American Politics and the Settlement of the Holocaust
    Survivors   13
The End of the Mandate   16
The United Nations Debates the Future of Palestine   17
The Unofficial War   18
The First Arab-Israeli War   20
Post-War Negotiations: Peace Treaties, Borders and Refugees   22
1956: The Suez Conflict   27
1967: The Six Day War   29
Resolution 242 and the War of Attrition   34
Settlement Building and Economic Integration   36
Military Occupation/Administration   41
Nationalism and the Rise of the Opposition Movements   42
1973: The October War   47
Conflict in Lebanon   48
Diplomacy and the Camp David Accords   52
1982: The Invasion of Lebanon   54
1987: The First Intifada   61
The Beginning of the Oslo Process   67
The Declaration of Principles   69
The Cairo Agreement and Oslo II   72
The Netanyahu Administration   76
The Barak Administration   81
The Camp David Final Status Talks   83
The Sharon Administration   88

2   Content Studies   91
   Introduction   91
   Content Analysis: Methods   94
   Samples and Results   99
   Sample One: 28 September to 16 October 2000   99
   Additional Content Samples: October–December 2001,
      March–April 2002   156
   Sample Two: October–December 2001   160
   Sample Three: March 2002   182
   Sample Four: Jenin, April 2002   192

3 Audience Studies   200
   Introduction   200
   Samples and Method   200
   Focus Group Methods and Questions Asked   202
   Qualitative and Quantitative Approaches   204
   The Questionnaires   207
   Results   209
      Memories, Images and Associations   209
      Sources of Information Used   210
      Origins, History and Causes of the Conflict   212
      The News Writing Exercise   225
      Beliefs About Casualties   231
      Cultural Identification and Empathy   236
      Understanding and Interest in News   240

4   Why Does it Happen?   244
   Factors in Production   244
   Claims that the Media are Biased Against Israel   250
   The US Connection   252

5   Conclusion   257
   Appendix 1: Answers to Questions on the
      Israeli-Palestinian Conflict by Student Groups   261
   Appendix 2: Answers to Questions on the
      Israeli-Palestinian Conflict by Focus Groups   270
   Appendix 3: Black Holes of History: Public
      Understanding and the Shaping of Our Past   276

Notes   286
References   300
Index   305

Acknowledgements

We would like to thank other members of the Glasgow University Media Group who helped us and gave advice and encouragement: John Eldridge, David Miller, Jacquie Reilly and Emma Miller. Thanks especially to Ruth Moore and Etta Gaskill who gave a great deal of time and energy to data preparation on the project. Thanks to Bernard Glancy for filming and also to Aidan Warner and Michelle Tonge for their help in preparing press reports. Thanks to others in the Department of Sociology: Andy Furlong, Ruth Madigan, Kathleen Ward, Lynn Campbell, Olive Kearns and Maureen McQuillan. Thanks also for help and advice to Avi Shlaim, Nachman Shai, David Ruben, Joy Wolfe, Ghada Karmi, Justin Lewis, Frank Webster, Lucretia Chauvel, David Morley, James Curran, Daya Kishan Thussu, Georgina Sykes, Mary Philo, David Anderson, David McLennan, Norman Finkelstein, Ian Lustick, Baruch Kimmering, Roane Carey, Gershon Shafir, Shaul Mishal and Geoffrey Aronson.

Many people helped in the development and setting up of interviews and focus groups. Thanks especially to Ursula Grimberg and to Lyndall O'Brien. Special thanks also to Anna and Iain Semple, Margaret and Andrew Dunn, Phillip Radcliffe, Claire Wood, Daniel Green, Phoebe Maine, Adele Cowie, Margaret and Keith Bradly, Gregor Mill, Mike Phillips, Jenny Owen and Sarah and John Philo.

Thanks also to all the journalists and media practitioners who spoke with us and who gave help and advice: George Alagiah, Brian Hanrahan, Tim Llewellyn, Lindsey Hilsum , Ken Loach, Adrian Monck, Gaye Flashman, John Humphrys, Sian Kevill, Chris Shaw, Gary Rogers, Fran Unsworth, Sue Inglish, Evan Davis, Paul Adams, Nik Gowing, John Underwood, Alex Graham, Sandy Ross, Paul McKinney , John Pilger, David Cowling, Robin Lustig, Marie Colvin, Rodrigo Va'zquez, Alan Hayling and Donald McLeod, and the staff at Pluto Press: Anne Beech, Robert Webb and other members of the production team. Finally thanks again to all those people who took part in producing this work and who gave so much of their time and energy so freely and with such good grace.

Preface

This is a study of TV news coverage of the Israeli-Palestinian conflict and of how this coverage relates to the understanding, beliefs and attitudes of the television audience. The work was undertaken with support from the Economic and Social Research Council whose help we would like to acknowledge. In producing this study our intention was not to 'monitor' the media or to criticise individual journalists. Our intention was to discuss the pressures and structures within which they work, to show the effects of these on news content and to examine the role of the media in the construction of public knowledge. It is a very extensive study with an audience sample of over 800 people and a detailed analysis of TV news over a two-year period. This work also raises a series of important theoretical issues in mass communications. The main focus in the book is on giving a clear exposition of our methods and results, but the theoretical concerns are latent and there is a more detailed discussion of them in other work by the Media Group.[1] We begin this book with an account of different histories of the conflict to illustrate the extraordinary range of conflicting beliefs and opinions which exist in this area. The second chapter of the book is a study of television news content. We analyse large samples of news from September to October 2000, at the outbreak of the intifada and then later samples from October to December 2001 and March to April 2002 – a total of 189 bulletins. We also look at other areas of television and the press for purposes of comparison. In Chapter 3 we examine processes of audience reception of how television viewers understood and responded to news about the conflict. For this, we questioned large groups of students from Britain, the US and Germany and also engaged in detailed discussions in focus groups. There were 14 of these groups whose participants were drawn from the population as a whole and 100 people took part in this way. This part of our work raised a number of issues such as the relation between viewers' understanding of news and their level of interest in it. We also looked at the role of television in informing mass audiences and asked the young people in our samples a range of questions on international issues in order to assess their levels of knowledge. We found sharp differences in this between those from different countries. In Chapter 4 we discuss the key factors which affect the production of news about the Israeli-Palestinian conflict including the impact of lobbying and public relations. Chapter 5 draws some conclusions from the study.

In bringing together the processes of production, news content and audience reception, this research developed into one of the most extensive studies ever undertaken in this area. We were given invaluable help in it by a large number of journalists and media practitioners, whom we interviewed and who gave us comments and sometimes detailed accounts of stories on which they had worked. Some also took part in the research by sitting in on focus groups and playing an active role in the discussions. This level of collaboration between academics and media practitioners is unusual in media studies and we hope that it points the way to further useful developments in the conduct of research. Academics and broadcasters certainly have much to learn from each other.

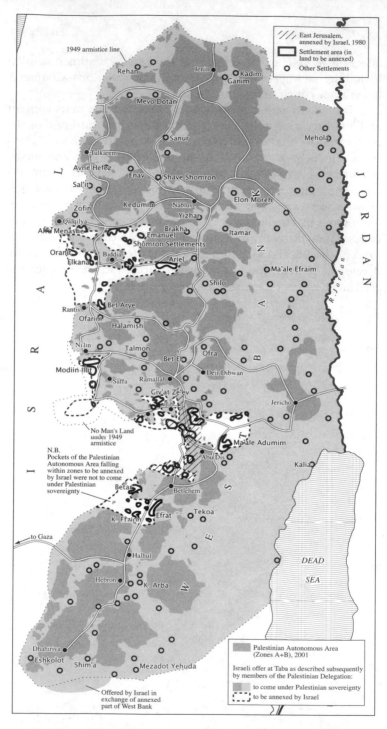

Final Status Map – Taba, January 2001 (Andras Bereznay, adapted
from Jan de Jong and the Foundation for Middle East Peace, 2001)

1
Histories of the Conflict

INTRODUCTION

The Israeli-Palestinian conflict is deep and long-standing. In all such conflicts the origins and history of particular events are contested by the different parties involved. Participants tell the story from their own point of view and often to legitimise their own actions. In the course of this study we interviewed a large number of journalists who had worked in this area. Several commented on the difficulties of reporting when the causes of the conflict are subject to constant debate, as one very experienced correspondent noted:

> Even describing the physical reasons why things happened or what happened in the Middle East you are on very tricky territory. The Israelis will say that the '67 war, that they were threatened, that it was a pre-emptive strike and the Arabs say that there was no question of attacking Israel, that they were too feeble, too disorganised that the Israelis had always wanted this territory. So there are two schools of thought always about the reasons. (Focus group interview, November 2002)

This makes the journalist's task very difficult. If there is no single account of what has happened which everyone accepts, then the journalist has to rely on the concept of balance and attempt to represent the range of views which exist. This is made more complex because there are not simply two sides in the conflict but there are actually divisions of opinion within each 'side'. Journalists therefore have to pick their way through the competing opinions and versions of events and to make clear if possible what is established as fact. In the Israeli-Palestinian conflict there is some agreed information but much is still disputed. In the following histories we will indicate this range of views and we will begin with the period leading up to the creation of the State of Israel in 1948.

ZIONIST ROOTS AND THE FIRST WAVE OF
JEWISH IMMIGRATION INTO PALESTINE

The American historian Howard Sachar (1977) traces the contemporary emergence of Zionist thought to the European Rabbis, Judah Alkalai and Zvi Hirsh Kalischer, who from the 1830s onwards stressed the need for Jews to return to the Holy Land as a necessary prelude to the Redemption and the second coming of the Messiah. Sachar argues that such messianic exhortations did not immediately or widely take root amongst European Jews. However, he suggests that by the 1870s societies generally known as Chovevei Zion – 'Lovers of Zion' – had formed across Russia, which viewed Palestine as a site for national renewal and a refuge from anti-Semitism.

In 1881, following the assassination of Tsar Alexander II, large numbers of Jews were killed in a series of Russian pogroms. By 1914 up to 2 million Jews had fled Russia to escape persecution. The vast majority sought sanctuary in the United States but 25,000 arrived in Palestine in two waves of immigration in 1882–84 and 1890–91. At the time the Jewish population in Palestine was small. The official Ottoman census of 1878 had put the total at 15,011 living amongst a combined Muslim/Christian population of 447,454 (McCarthy, 1990). Relations between the new Jewish immigrants and the native population were mixed. Jewish settlements were built on land that was purchased from absentee *effendi* ('notable') landlords. Often the locals who had tended the land were evicted with the help of Turkish police and this led to resentment and violence. Some Zionists such as Ahad Aham were very critical of the way the settlers gained control of the land and treated the local population. In 1891 he argued that the settlers 'treat the Arabs with hostility and cruelty, and unscrupulously deprive them of their rights, insult them without cause and even boast of such deeds; and none opposes this despicable and dangerous inclination' (1923: 107, cited in Hirst, 1977: 24). There was also evidence that the two groups were able to accommodate each other because the settlers also brought benefits. They provided employment opportunities, access to medical care, the loan of modern equipment and a market for produce. Sachar reports that in the 1890s the agricultural settlement of Zichron Ya'akov employed more than 1,000 Arabs working for 200 Jews. The former *Guardian* Middle East correspondent David Hirst (1977) argues that the beginning of the twentieth century brought a new, more militant type of settler to Palestine, inspired by the ideas of Theodor Herzl and determined to 'redeem the land' and 'conquer labour'. The Jewish National Fund, set up to manage Jewish land purchases, decreed in 1901 that all land it purchased could never be resold or leased to gentiles, and settlers began to boycott Arab labour (Hirst, 1977; Shafir, 1999).

THEODOR HERZL AND THE EMERGENCE
OF POLITICAL ZIONISM

Theodor Herzl, who is commonly regarded as the father of political Zionism, was a Jewish Austro-Hungarian journalist and playwright. He had been deeply affected by the virulent anti-Semitism sweeping across Europe, and as a journalist for the Vienna newspaper *Neue Freie Presse* had covered the notorious Dreyfus trial in Paris, where a Jewish officer was falsely charged with passing secrets to the Germans. Herzl felt that a central issue for Jews was their dispersal across the Diaspora and their existence as a minority in each country they inhabited. This, Herzl argued, led to a dependence on the host culture and a suppression of self-determination. Furthermore, Herzl believed that widespread anti-Semitism meant that complete assimilation into European society was an impossibility for most Jews. His solution as laid out in the 1896 *Der Judenstaat* (*The Jewish State*) was for Jews to create their own state, in which they would constitute a majority and be able to exercise national self-determination. In contrast to the 'practical Zionism' of the Jewish settlers who began to arrive in Palestine from 1882, Herzl adopted a political orientation, cultivating links with prominent imperial statesmen in an attempt to gain a charter for Jewish land settlement.

Herzl had two potential locations in mind for the prospective Jewish state, Argentina and Palestine. His diaries show that he was greatly influenced by the British imperialist Cecil Rhodes, and in particular the manner in which Rhodes had gained control of Mashonaland and Matabeleland from its inhabitants (Hirst, 1977). In his diaries he suggests that the settlers should follow Rhodes' example and 'gently' expropriate the native population's land and 'try to spirit the penniless population across the border by procuring employment for it in the transit countries, while denying it any employment in our own country' but that 'the process of expropriation and the removal of the poor must be carried out discreetly and circumspectly' (1960: 88, cited in Hirst, 1977: 18). In order to further this aim Herzl sought out an imperial sponsor prepared to grant a settlement charter. He canvassed Germany's Kaiser, the Ottoman sultan and Britain's Joseph Chamberlain, stressing to each the benefits that a Jewish state and Jewish capital could bring. In 1901 Herzl travelled to Constantinople and met the sultan. Herzl offered Jewish capital to refinance the Ottoman public debt in a failed attempt to gain a charter for the establishment of a Jewish Ottoman Colonisation Association in Palestine. Bohm (1935) claims that the third article of the proposed charter would have given the Jewish administration the right to deport the native population from Palestine. Herzl then switched his attention to lobbying British politicians. Hirst (1977) suggests that Herzl linked Zionist ambitions to British imperial interests, and argued that a Jewish homeland would lessen the flow into Britain of Jewish refugees fleeing pogroms. Herzl lobbied Lord Rothschild for the creation of Jewish colonies in Cyprus and the Sinai peninsula but the plans met with resistance from the Egyptian authorities. In April 1903 Joseph Chamberlain suggested to Herzl that the Zionists should consider Uganda as a homeland. The proposal received a mixed reception from Zionists and was firmly rejected by the Zionist Congress in 1905 which ruled that colonisation should be confined to Palestine and its immediate vicinity. Herzl died in 1904, and the task of forwarding political Zionism passed to Chaim Weizmann.

THE SECOND WAVE OF JEWISH IMMIGRATION INTO PALESTINE

1904 saw the beginning of another wave of Jewish immigration into Palestine, again in response to Russian pogroms. The Israeli historian Ahron Bregman estimates that 35,000 arrived, and argues that these settlers were different from the previous immigrants in that they sought to exclude Arab labour and were 'driven by a fierce sense of mission and bent on redeeming the land' (2003: 11). The Israeli sociologist Gershon Shafir argues that the struggle for the 'conquest of labour' transformed Jewish workers into 'militant nationalists' who 'sought to establish a homogenous Jewish society' (1999: 88). Some Zionists began to stress the importance of armed force in creating the Jewish homeland. Israel Zangwill, who had coined the Zionist slogan 'A land without people for a people without land', informed a meeting of Zionists in Manchester in 1905 that '[We] must be prepared either to drive out by the sword the [Arab] tribes in possession as our forefathers did or to grapple with the problem of a large alien population' (Zangwill, cited in Morris, 2001: 140).

The Palestinians, as a subject population under Ottoman rule, were initially deferential in their protests. Repeatedly during the 1890s, members of the Palestinian elite unsuccessfully petitioned their imperial overlords in Constantinople to limit Jewish immigration. The late nineteenth century was a period of growing pan-Arab awareness which had seen a renaissance in the appreciation of Arab literature and culture. Ovendale argues that both the Ottoman Empire and the spread of Zionism were seen as a threat to Arab development. He suggests that 'between 1909 and 1914 nationalist opposition in Palestine to Zionism grew: there were fears that if the Jews conquered Palestine the territorial unity of the Arab world would be shattered and the Arab cause weakened' (Ovendale, 1999: 12). In 1914 the Muslim intellectual Rashid Rida argued that the Palestinians had a choice. They could either come to an accommodation with the Zionists in which the Zionists, in return for concessions, would put a limit on their ambitions, or they could oppose them with arms:

> It is incumbent upon the leaders of the Arabs – the local population – to do one of two things. Either they must reach an agreement with the leaders of the Zionists to settle the differences between the interests of both parties ... or they must gather all their forces to oppose the Zionists in every way, first by forming societies and companies, and finally by forming armed gangs which oppose them by force. (Rida, cited in Hirst, 1977: 32–3)

THE BALFOUR DECLARATION AND THE BRITISH MANDATE

During the First World War the dissolution of the Ottoman Empire was widely anticipated and the Entente Powers began negotiating over contending territorial ambitions. In 1916 negotiations between Britain, France and Russia (later to include Italy) led to the secretive Sykes-Picot agreement which sought to establish 'spheres of influence' for the European Powers within the region. However, the agreement also accepted the realities of emergent Arab nationalism and specified the recognition of 'an independent Arab State' or 'confederation of Arab States' within the region. British assurances of Arab independence after the defeat of the Axis Powers (which had been pledged as a reward for Arab support during the First World War) can be found in the correspondence between Sir Henry McMahon, British High Commissioner in Egypt and Sharif Hussein, Emir of Mecca, who was recognised as the Keeper of Islam's most holy places.[1] However, these pledges by European Powers to strive for the recognition of Arab independence conflicted with British assurances given, at the time, to Zionist leaders that Britain would seek the establishment of a Jewish homeland in Palestine. Zionist leaders established close links with prominent British politicians including Lloyd George, Arthur Balfour, Herbert Samuel and Mark Sykes. In 1915, in a memorandum entitled 'The Future of Palestine' Samuel proposed 'the British annexation of Palestine [where] we might plant three or four million European Jews' (Weisgal, 1944: 131, cited in United Nations, 1990). British support for a Jewish homeland was made explicit in the Balfour Declaration of November 1917:

> His Majesty's Government view with favour the establishment in Palestine of a national home for the Jewish people, and will use their best endeavours to facilitate the achievement of this object, it being clearly understood that nothing shall be done which may prejudice the civil and religious rights of existing non-Jewish communities in Palestine or the rights and political status enjoyed by Jews in any other country.

The 'non-Jewish communities', which comprised the 89 per cent of the population who were Arab Muslims and Christians, were angered by the declaration.[2] They noted that it spoke only of their 'civil and religious rights' and made no mention of political rights. Conversely for the Zionists the declaration was regarded as a triumph. The Israeli historian Avi Shlaim, paraphrasing Chaim Weizmann, argues that it 'handed the Jews a golden key to unlock the doors of Palestine and make themselves the masters of the country' (Shlaim, 2000: 7). The legality of the Balfour Declaration has since been questioned by some legal experts (Linowitz, 1957; Cattan, 1973).

After the First World War Britain was assigned control of Palestine through the Mandates system governing the dismemberment of the Ottoman Empire. In 1921 the British divided the area in two with the sector east of the Jordan river becoming Transjordan and the area west of the river becoming the Palestinian Mandate.

The indigenous population of mandated Palestine feared mass Jewish immigration would lead to the further colonisation of their country followed by their own subjugation. This view was shared by some prominent British politicians such as Lord Curzon who, on 26 January 1919, commented to Lord Balfour:

I feel tolerably sure therefore that while Weizmann may say one thing to you, or while you may mean one thing by a national home, he is out for something quite different. He contemplates a Jewish State, a Jewish nation, a subordinate population of Arabs, etc. ruled by Jews; the Jews in possession of the fat of the land, and directing the Administration ... He is trying to effect this behind the screen and under the shelter of British trusteeship. (British Government, Foreign Office, 1919a, cited in Ingrams, 1972: 58)

Some members of the British establishment believed that by supporting the Jewish national home they were directly violating the terms of the mandate.[3] Others seemed less concerned about the opinions of the Arab population. Chaim Weizmann claimed that a British official had told him that in Palestine 'there are a few hundred thousand Negroes but that is a matter of no significance' (Heller, 1985, cited in Chomsky, 1992: 435).

Between 1919 and 1926 the Jewish presence in Palestine swelled with the arrival of a further 90,000 immigrants (Bregman, 2003). The community also became increasingly militarised, with the creation of what Shlaim describes as an 'iron wall' of impregnable strength designed to protect Jewish settlements from Arab attacks. The concept of the 'iron wall' had first been deployed by Vladimar Jabotinsky, the leader of the Revisionist movement.[4] Jabotinsky was convinced that the indigenous Arabs would not accept the Zionist project voluntarily and advocated the creation of an 'iron wall' that the local population would be unable to breach:

If you wish to colonise a land in which people are already living, you must provide a garrison for the land, or find a benefactor who will maintain the garrison on your behalf. Zionism is a colonising adventure and therefore it stands or falls by the question of armed forces. (Jabotinsky, cited in Masalha, 1992: 45)

The Zionists also substantially increased their land holdings. Agricultural land was purchased from absentee Arab landlords and the peasants who tended and lived on it, were evicted. The 1919 American King-Crane Commission, which had been sent to Palestine to assess local opinion, reported in their discussions with Jewish representatives that 'the Zionists looked forward to a practically complete dispossession of the present non-Jewish inhabitants of Palestine, by various forms of purchase' (British Government, 1947: 3, cited in Laqueur and Rubin, 1984: 29). The Zionists also increasingly boycotted Arab labour. The British Hope-Simpson Commission had criticised the Zionist Keren ha-Yesod employment agreements as discriminatory and pointed to Article 7 which stipulated that 'The settler hereby undertakes that ... if and whenever he may be obliged to hire help, he will hire Jewish workmen only' and Article 11 which stated that 'the settler undertakes ... not to hire any outside labour except Jewish labourers' (British Government, 1930, Cmd. 3686: 52–3, cited in United Nations, 1990). The tensions created by this labour exclusivism, the Commission reported, constituted 'a constant and increasing source of danger to the country' (British Government, 1930, Cmd. 3686: 55, cited in United Nations, 1990).

Throughout the 1920s Arab hostility to the Zionist project manifested itself in increasingly prolonged outbreaks of violence. In 1921 Arabs attacked Jews at Jaffa during a May Day parade and the violence spread to other towns and the countryside. By the time the British Army brought the situation under control nearly 200 Jews and 120 Arabs were dead or wounded. Britain set up a commission of inquiry to investigate the violence. The Haycraft Commission reported that the violence was spontaneous and anti-Zionist rather than anti-Jewish. The report blamed the Arabs for the violence, but also pointed to Arab fears that the mass influx of Jewish immigrants would lead to their subjugation. General William Congreve, the commander of the British forces in the Middle East, criticised Herbert Samuel's policy of trying to establish a Jewish national home in Palestine in the face of opposition from most of the indiginous population (Ovendale, 1999). Shortly afterwards the Arabs sent a petition to the League of Nations asking for democratic elections and independence for Palestine (Segev, 2001). In 1922 the British government published a White Paper which was intended to mollify Arab fears. It denied that the Balfour Declaration paved the way for a Jewish state, and that the Arab population, culture and language would be subordinated. It also proposed a legislative council made up of Jewish, Muslim and Christian representatives, a suggestion that was rejected by the Arabs. Hirst (1977) alleges that a large proportion (likely to give Jewish representatives a majority) of the council would have been directly appointed by Britain, and that the Palestinians feared that Zionist policies might be legitimised under a constitutional façade.

The 1920s and 1930s saw more violent disturbances followed on each occasion by Commissions of Inquiry dispatched by Britain to examine causes. After 1921 there was a period of relative calm before the next major outbreak of violence in 1929. The flashpoint for the 1929 violence was a dispute over sovereignty of an area containing important Jewish and Muslim religious sites. Tension had been brewing for some months over this issue, fomented by inflammatory rhetoric in the Arab and Hebrew press. In late August 1929 a group of armed Arabs attacked Jewish worshippers in Jerusalem, and in a week of rioting and violence 113 Jews and 116 Arabs were killed. In Hebron more than 60 members of a long-standing community of non-Zionist religious Jews were killed. In response the British set up the Shaw Commission of Inquiry, which concluded that the trigger for the violence was Jewish demonstrations at the Wailing Wall but that the underlying causes were economic and political grievances against the Mandate. An Arab delegation including the Mufti of Jerusalem met with British officials in London requesting a prohibition on the sale of lands from Arabs to non-Arabs, an end to Jewish immigration and the formation of a national parliament. The Hope-Simpson Commission dispatched by Britain shortly afterwards highlighted the problem of a growing population of landless Arabs and recommended controls on Jewish immigration and land purchase. These recommendations were carried through in the 1930 Passfield White Paper. However, these developments were regarded as a serious setback by Zionists who managed through lobbying to reverse the terms of the White Paper.

Sporadic violence ignited into a full scale Arab rebellion in the years between 1936 and 1939. Part of the revolt involved peaceful resistance, including a nationwide six-month strike and widespread non-payment of taxes. It also involved extensive violence in which Palestinians formed into bands and destroyed crops and trees, mined roads and sabotaged infrastructure and oil pipelines. They attacked and killed Jews, and also targeted Arabs who failed to offer support or who were suspected of collaboration. The historian Martin Gilbert claims that during this period 'most acts of Arab terror were met, often within a few hours, by equally savage acts of reprisal by the Revisionists' military arm, the Irgun' (1999: 92). The Arabs demanded democratic elections and an end to immigration. The British dispatched another commission of inquiry which in 1937 stated that the Mandate was unworkable and recommended partition. The Peel Commission proposed that the north-west part of Palestine, accounting for 20 per cent of the country though containing its most fertile land, would become a Jewish state, the remaining 80 per cent would become an Arab state linked to Transjordan. Jerusalem,

Bethlehem and a corridor to the sea would remain under British control. The proposal received a mixed reception amongst Jews. One group centred around Jabotinsky's Revisionists argued that a Jewish state should only be set up in the whole of Palestine and Transjordan. Another group, which included Weizmann and David Ben-Gurion, argued that this was a historic opportunity to create the Jewish state. The Israeli historian Simha Flapan suggests that Ben-Gurion accepted the plan as a stepping stone to Zionist control of all of Palestine, and points to comments he made before the Zionist executive in 1937 that 'after the formation of a large army in the wake of the establishment of the [Jewish] state, we shall abolish partition and expand to the whole of the Palestine' (Ben-Gurion, cited in Flapan, 1987: 22) The Israeli historian and *Ha'aretz* columnist Tom Segev (2001) suggests that for Ben-Gurion the proposal (inherent in the Peel recommendations) for the 'forced transfer' of the Arab inhabitants out of the proposed Jewish state, and the creation therefore of a 'really Jewish' state outweighed all the drawbacks of the proposal.

The Arabs categorically rejected the partition scheme, arguing that all of Palestine was part of the Arabian homeland and it should not be broken up. The partition plans were never carried through and the rebellion continued until the British finally quelled it. The rudimentary weapons of the Arab guerrillas were overwhelmed by vastly superior British military power. Hirst (1977) claims that during this period British forces took part in extensive acts of 'collective punishment'. They descended on Arab villages, undertook summary executions and destroyed possessions and dwellings. Segev (2001) claims that torture was also employed by the British authorities. The rebellion had cost the lives of 101 Britons and 463 Jews (*The Times*, 21 July 1938, cited in Hirst, 1977: 93). Palestinian losses were harder to gauge but Palestinian historian Walid Khalidi estimates that upwards of 5,000 were killed and approximately 14,000 injured (Khalidi, 1971: 846–9, cited in Hirst, 1977: 93).

The reasons for these increasingly serious outbreaks of hostility between the communities are contested. Some Israelis argue that the Zionist project was essentially beneficial to the Arabs of Palestine, and it was only Arab intransigence and xenophobia which prevented mutual accommodation. Cohn-Sherbok (2001), for instance, stresses the legal basis for settlement in the Balfour Declaration which was incorporated into the Mandate, and points to the Arab rejection of partition in 1937. He argues that Arab violence directed against the

Jews was 'incomprehensible' and that the Arabs were never prepared to compromise:

> Throughout this period the Arab community was unwilling to negotiate over any of the issues facing those living in the Holy Land. Jews, on the other hand, continually sought to find a solution to the problems confronting the native population while retaining their conviction that a Jewish national home must be established. (Cohn-Sherbok, 2001: 179)

Sachar (1977) argues that the Zionist enterprise developed the country, improved the material living standards of the Arab population and provided employment opportunities. The attacks on Jews, Sachar argues, were the result of incitement by xenophobic leaders such as the Mufti of Jerusalem and agitation by fascist infiltration from Italy and Germany. Joan Peters (1984) has claimed that the Zionist project was so beneficial to the Arab population that large numbers were drawn in from outside Palestine. She attributes the large rise in the Arab population during the mandatory period to illegal immigration from other Arab countries and argues that because of this the Jewish population in 1948 had as least as much right to the land as the Arab 'newcomers'. However, a number of British and Israeli reviewers have denounced Peters' thesis and most demographers attribute the Arab population rise to decreased mortality rates, due to improvements in sanitation and infrastructure.[5] Others provide different explanations for the revolt. Hirst points to economic resentment generated by peasant land evictions and the boycott of Arab labour:

> Driven from the land the peasants flocked to the rapidly growing cities in search of work. Many of them ended up as labourers building houses for the immigrants they loathed and feared. They lived in squalor. In old Haifa there were 11,000 crammed into hovels built of petrol-tins, which had neither water supply or rudimentary sanitation. Others, without families, slept in the open. Such conditions contrasted humiliatingly with the handsome dwellings the peasants were putting up for the well-to-do newcomers, or even with the Jewish working men's quarters furnished by Jewish building societies. They earned half or just a quarter the wage of their Jewish counterparts and Hebrew Labour

exclusivism was gradually depriving them of even that. (Hirst, 1977: 75)

Some Israeli academics such as Gershon Shafir (1999) have characterised twentieth-century Zionist settlement as similar to a form of European colonialism – the 'pure settlement colony' model which was imposed on societies in North America and Australia. This model 'established an economy based on white labour which together with the forced removal or the destruction of the native population allowed the settlers to regain the sense of cultural and ethnic homogeneity that is identified with a European concept of nationality' (Shafir, 1999: 84). Segev argues that '"disappearing" the Arabs lay at the heart of the Zionist dream and was also a necessary condition of its realization' (2001: 405). He also maintains that prominent Zionists such as David Ben-Gurion believed that the Arab revolt was a nationalist struggle designed to prevent their dispossession:

> The rebellion cast the Arabs in a new light. Instead of a 'wild and fractured mob, aspiring to robbery and looting,' Ben-Gurion said, they emerged as an organized and disciplined community, demonstrating its national will with political maturity and a capacity for self-evaluation. Were he an Arab, he wrote, he would also rebel, with even greater intensity and with greater bitterness and despair. Few Zionists understood the Arab feeling, and Ben-Gurion found it necessary to warn them: the rebellion was not just terror, he said; terror was a means to an end. Nor was it just politics, Nashashibi against the Mufti. The Arabs had launched a national war. They were battling the expropriation of their homeland. While their movement may have been primitive, Ben-Gurion said, it did not lack devotion, idealism and self-sacrifice. (Segev, 2001: 370–1)

In the wake of the revolt the British dispatched a further commission of enquiry, the result of which was the 1939 MacDonald White Paper. It proposed that 75,000 Jewish immigrants be admitted over the next five years, after which any further immigration would require Arab consent. The White Paper also proposed that land sales be strictly regulated and that an independent Palestine state should come about within ten years. The Zionists saw the White Paper as a betrayal that seriously threatened the creation of the Jewish state, especially in light of the increased persecution of Jews throughout Europe. The response was three-pronged. One element involved maintaining a flow of illegal Jewish immigration into Palestine. Gilbert (1999) claims that many of these Jews were trying to escape persecution in Nazi Germany and other parts of Europe. Another, which gathered pace from 1945 onwards, saw Zionist paramilitary groups launch attacks on the British using sabotage, bombings and assassinations. The third involved switching imperial sponsors from Britain to the United States. Zionists forged close links with American political leaders and used the Jewish vote to pressurise for policies that supported the continuation of immigration and the establishment of the Jewish state in Palestine.

AMERICAN POLITICS AND THE SETTLEMENT OF THE HOLOCAUST SURVIVORS

In May 1942 Zionists meeting in New York for the American Zionist Conference issued the Biltmore Resolution demanding the creation of a 'Jewish commonwealth' in mandatory Palestine, and began to pressurise American political leaders to support its terms. In 1941 Zionists had formed the American Palestine Committee. It included within its membership two-thirds of the Senate, 200 members of the House of Representatives and the leaders of the two main political parties and labour organisations (Ovendale, 1999). Unsuccessful resolutions were put before the House of Representatives and the Senate demanding free Jewish entry into Palestine and its reconstitution as a Jewish commonwealth. Zionist representatives also directly lobbied the two major political parties. The 1944 presidential election was a very close contest and because of this, Ovendale (1999) suggests, Zionist political leverage was considerable. America's 4.5 million Jews were concentrated in three key states (New York, Pennsylvania and Illinois) which could swing the election. The Republican Party adopted a platform calling for unrestricted Jewish immigration into Palestine, no restrictions on land ownership and the conversion of Palestine into a free and independent Jewish commonwealth. Roosevelt was under pressure to match this and in a private letter to Zionist leaders promised that if he were re-elected he would seek the 'establishment of Palestine as a free and democratic Jewish commonwealth' (Ovendale, 1999: 87).

The politics surrounding the settlement of Jewish refugees at the end of the Second World War are still highly contentious. The debate concerns whether the Holocaust survivors wished to settle in Palestine voluntarily or were left with little option because other potential refuges such as the United States were closed to them, with at least the tacit support of Zionist leaders. The debate remains emotive because tens of thousands of Holocaust survivors died in displaced-persons camps in Europe at the end of the war whilst US congressional legislation gave priority to accepting refugees from the Russian occupied states, including many Nazi sympathisers and SS troopers (Chomsky, 1999). At the time, Zionist leaders stressed the vital importance of Palestine as a sanctuary for the Jewish refugees in Europe who had survived the Nazi Holocaust. It was argued that only Palestine could provide a haven where Jewish refugees could rebuild their lives and avoid future anti-Semitism:

> They (the Holocaust survivors) want to regain their human dignity, their homeland, they want a reunion with their kin in Palestine after having lost their dearest relations. To them the countries of their birth are a graveyard of their people. They do not wish to return and they cannot. They want to go back to their national home, and they use Dunkirk boats. (Ben-Gurion, cited in Gilbert, 1999: 147)

Gilbert points to attempts by Holocaust survivors to reach Palestine aboard ships such as the *Exodus* as proof that most of the refugees were desperate to get there. The Israeli historian Yehuda Bauer (1970) agues that most refugees were keen to settle in Palestine, citing a 1946 Hebrew investigative commission that reported that 96.8 per cent of Jewish refugees languishing in European displaced-persons camps at the end of the war wanted to settle in Palestine. Avi Shlaim argues that 'few people disputed the right of the Jews to a home after the trauma' of the Holocaust and that the moral case for it became 'unassailable' (2000: 23–4). Other Israeli historians suggest a different picture. Segev argues that:

> There is ... no basis for the frequent assertion that the state was established as a result of the Holocaust. Clearly the shock, horror and sense of guilt felt by many generated profound sympathy for the Jews in general and the Zionist movement in particular. The sympathy helped the Zionists advance their diplomatic campaign and their propaganda, and shaped their strategy to focus effort on the survivors, those Jews in displaced-persons camps demanding

they be sent to Palestine. All the survivors were Zionists, the Jewish agency claimed, and they all wanted to come to Palestine. The assertion was not true. The displaced were given the choice of returning to their homes in Eastern Europe or settling in Palestine. Few were able or willing to return to countries then in the grip of various degrees of hunger, anti-Semitism or communism, and they were never given the option of choosing between Palestine and, say the United States. In effect their options were narrowed to Palestine or the DP camps. (Segev, 2001: 491)

Others such as Feingold (1970) and Shonfeld (1977) have been very critical of the conduct of the Zionist movement in Palestine and the US at the end of the Second World War. They argue that the Zionist movement should have mobilised to pressure the US administration to take in the Holocaust survivors, which would have saved the lives of many Jews who died in displaced-persons camps in Europe. Segev argues that the Ben-Gurion and the Labour leadership in Palestine saw the Nazi ascension in the 1930s as potentially 'a fertile force for Zionism' because it created the potential for mass Jewish immigration into Palestine (1993:18). He alleges that during the 1930s and 1940s the Labour leadership entered into *haavara* ('transporting') agreements with the Nazis whereby Jews were permitted to emigrate to Palestine with limited quantities of capital. He claims that Ben-Gurion's political rivals in the Revisionist movement opposed these agreements, and argued that rather than negotiate with Germany, it should be boycotted. Segev also suggests that after the *Kristallnacht* pogroms Ben-Gurion was concerned that the 'human conscience' might cause other countries to open their doors to Jewish refugees, a move which he saw as a threat to Zionism.

> If I knew that it was possible to save all the children of Germany by transporting them to England, but only half of them by transporting them to Palestine, I would choose the second – because we face not only the reckoning of those children, but the historical reckoning of the Jewish people. (Ben-Gurion, cited in Segev, 1993: 28)

The view that Jewish refugees were used as political leverage to create the Jewish state in Palestine was also shared by some prominent British and US State Department officials[6] who feared the effects on stability in Palestine and potential Russian penetration.[7] Roosevelt's successor, Harry Truman decided to press on with a policy supporting the settlement of Jewish refugees in Palestine. Ovendale (1999) suggests that this was primarily because of the 1945 New York election, in which the Jewish vote might be decisive. The American State Department official William Eddy claims that Truman had informed American ambassadors to the Arab world that 'I am sorry, gentlemen, but I have to answer to hundreds of thousands who are anxious for the success of Zionism; I do not have hundreds of thousands of Arabs among my constituents' (1954: 36).

THE END OF THE MANDATE

In Palestine Zionist paramilitary groups were gradually wearing down British morale. Towards the end of the Arab revolt the Jewish community had launched attacks against the Arabs. In July 1938 more than 100 Arabs were killed when six bombs were planted in Arab public places. The last of these, detonated in the Arab melon market in Haifa, killed 53 Arabs and a Jew (*Palestine Post*, 26 July 1938). Towards the end of the Second World War such tactics were turned on the British mandatory authority. Roads, bridges, trains and patrol boats were destroyed. British Army barracks were attacked and banks and armouries were looted. On a single day in 1946, Zionist paramilitary forces launched 16 separate attacks on the British Army, destroying many armoured vehicles and leaving 80 dead and wounded (Hirst, 1977). Lord Moyne was assassinated by the Stern Gang; British officers were captured, flogged and killed; and, in the most spectacular attack of all, the centre of British mandatory power in Palestine, the King David Hotel, was destroyed by 500 lb of explosives, leaving 88 dead including 15 Jews. Funding for the attacks was provided by sympathetic sources in the United States. The Hollywood scriptwriter Ben Hecht produced an article for the *New York Herald Tribune*, entitled 'Letter to the Terrorists of Palestine', in which he wrote:

> every time you blow up a British arsenal, or wreck a British jail, or send a British railway train sky high, or rob a British bank, or let go with your guns and bombs at the British betrayers and invaders of your homeland, the Jews of America make a little holiday in their hearts ... Brave friends we are working to help you. We are raising funds for you. (15 May 1947, cited in Hirst, 1977: 119)

The violence became so widespread that by early 1947 all non-essential British civilians and military families were evacuated from Palestine. Weakened by the Second World War, and demoralised by the attritional warfare, the British were unwilling to sacrifice more lives and money in Palestine. Gilbert (1999) suggests they were also wary of alienating Arab opinion because they were concerned to protect their oil interests in the region. In February 1947 the British decided to end the Mandate and hand the question of Palestine to the United Nations.

THE UNITED NATIONS DEBATES THE FUTURE OF PALESTINE

The UN dispatched a Special Committee to the region which recommended partition. Attention then switched to the diplomatic manoeuvring at the United Nations in New York. Arab representatives, called before the UN, questioned whether the Mandate was ever legal and whether the UN had the legal right to decide on the sovereignty of Palestine. They wished to see the issue referred to the International Court of Justice, and ultimately, they argued, it was the people of Palestine who should decide on the fate of the country, rather than an outside body.[8] Zionist representatives were sympathetic to the partition plan being debated by member states and lobbied to maximise the area that might be allotted to a Jewish state. On 29 November 1947 the partition plan was carried by a single vote after a last-minute change of policy by several nations, with a number complaining over the political and economic pressure that had been exerted on them.[9] Resolution 181 recommended the division of Palestine, with the Jewish state allotted 5,700 square miles including the fertile coastal areas, whilst the Arab state was allotted 4,300 square miles comprised mostly of the hilly areas. The proposed settlement would mean that each state would have a majority of its own population, although many Jews would fall into the Arab state and vice versa. Jerusalem and Bethlehem were to become a separate area under UN control.

For the Arabs the partition plan was a major blow. They believed that it was unfair that the Jewish immigrants, most of whom had been in Palestine less than 30 years and who owned less than 10 per cent of the land, should be given more than half of Palestine including the best arable land. The reaction of Zionists is disputed. Some historians such as Bregman (2003) argue that the partition resolution was seen as a triumph because it allowed for the creation of a Jewish state in an area three times that recommended by the Peel plan ten years earlier. Shlaim claims that the reaction was more ambivalent. He suggests that it was accepted by most Zionist leaders with a 'heavy heart' because they 'did not like the idea of an independent Palestinian state, they were disappointed with the exclusion of Jerusalem, and they had grave doubts about the viability of the State within the UN borders' (2000: 25). He notes that it was dismissed out of hand by Jewish paramilitary groups who demanded all of Palestine for the Jewish state. Gilbert suggests that the Zionist leadership realised that war was inevitable and that Ben-Gurion 'contemplated the possibility of fighting to extend the area allotted to the Jews' (1999: 149). Gilbert cites orders from Ben-Gurion that Jewish forces should 'safeguard the entire Yishuv [Jewish community in Palestine] and settlements (wherever they may be), to conquer the whole country or most of it, and to maintain its occupation until the attainment of an authoritative political settlement' (Ben-Gurion, cited in Gilbert, 1999: 149). Hirst (1977) suggests that the partition plan was accepted by the Zionists because they anticipated that they would quickly be able to militarily overwhelm the Arabs, and unilaterally to expand the borders of the Jewish state. He points to comments made at the time by the commander of the British forces in Palestine, General J.C. Darcy, who stated that 'if you were to withdraw British troops, the Haganah [Jewish fighting forces] would take over all Palestine tomorrow' and 'could hold it against the entire Arab world' (Crum, 1947: 220, cited in Hirst, 1977: 134).

THE UNOFFICIAL WAR

The UN partition plan did not solve the problems in Palestine. The Arab Higher Committee rejected it outright and called a three-day strike. The Mufti of Jerusalem announced a jihad or holy war for Jerusalem. Fighting between the two communities broke out in early December 1947 and the situation quickly deteriorated into civil war. The British, unwilling and unable to restore order, announced that they would terminate the Mandate on 15 May 1948. In the first stage of the conflict lasting up until Israel's Declaration of Independence on 14 May 1948, Jewish forces fought against Arab forces marshalled by three commanders. Fawzi el-Kawakji led the Arab League, Sir John Bagot Glubb and his 45 British officers led the Transjordian Arab Legion, and Abdul Qader al-Husseini led the Mufti's Arab forces in Jerusalem (Bregman, 2003). In the early part of this 'unofficial war' the Arab forces won some minor victories and for a time al-Husseini's forces cut the road between Jerusalem and Tel Aviv. In early April Zionist forces launched a major offensive codenamed Plan Dalet. According to Avi Shlaim, the aim of Plan Dalet was 'to secure all the areas allocated to the Israeli state under the UN partition resolution as well as Jewish settlements outside these areas and corridors leading to them' (2000: 31). Arab towns and cities were captured and their populations removed so as 'to clear the interior of the country of hostile and potentially hostile Arab elements' in anticipation of an attack by the combined armies of the neighbouring Arab states (Shlaim, 2000: 31). The operation involved the application of military and psychological pressure on the Arab population, who were reluctant to leave their homes. The Haganah, together with paramilitary forces, sprang surprise attacks on towns and villages, launching rockets, mortars and the Davidka, a device which lobbed 60 lb of TNT 300 yards into densely populated areas (Hirst, 1977). Psychological pressure was also exerted by spreading rumours via clandestine Zionist radio stations and loudspeakers mounted on army vehicles that Jewish forces were planning to burn villages and kill Arabs. An Israeli reserve officer recounts that:

An uncontrolled panic spread through all the Arab quarters, the Israelis brought up jeeps with loudspeakers which broadcast recorded 'horror sounds'. These included shrieks, wails and the anguished moans of Arab women, the wail of sirens and the clang of fire-alarm bells, interrupted by a sepulchral voice crying out in Arabic: 'Save your souls, all ye faithful: The Jews are using poison gas and atomic weapons. Run for your lives in the name of Allah'. (Childers, 1976: 252, cited in Hirst, 1977: 141)

In April and early May 1948 a number Arab towns and cities fell before the Zionist offensive, creating many refugees. The aims of Plan Dalet remain highly contested amongst historians. Some, such as Norman Finkelstein, Nur Masalha, Walid Khalidi and David Hirst, place the operation in the context of long-held Zionist plans to 'transfer' the native population out of Palestine.[10] They argue that the notion of transfer had been inherent in Theodor Herzl's plans for Palestine some 50 years earlier (see p. 3) and had remained an integral element of Labour and Revisionist strategy. Proponents of this perspective also point to the writings of Joseph Weitz, who was appointed by the Jewish Agency to head 'transfer committees' which encouraged the 1948 exodus by various forms of intimidation. In 1940 he confided in his diary that:

> Between ourselves it must be clear that there is no room for both peoples together in this country ... We shall not achieve our goal of being an independent people with the Arabs in this small country. The only solution is a Palestine, at least western Palestine [west of the Jordan river] without Arabs ... And there is no other way than to transfer the Arabs from here to the neighbouring countries, to transfer all of them; not one village, not one tribe, should be left ... Only after this transfer will the country be able to absorb the millions of our own brethren. There is no other way out. (*Davar*, 29 September 1967, cited in Hirst, 1977: 130)

This perspective is contested by Israeli historians such as Benny Morris and Avi Shlaim who contend that the expulsions were 'born of war not design', being part of military expediency rather than political planning. For these historians the expulsions were carried out as part of a military strategy that was spontaneous and instigated on an ad hoc basis by local commanders. Morris' conclusions have been subjected to a detailed critique by Finkelstein (2001), who argues that the evidence that Morris presents shows the expulsions to be more systematic and premeditated than his conclusions suggest. A third explanation, that the Palestinians left voluntarily in response to radio broadcasts from their leaders, was propagated by some Israeli historians after the 1948 war. However, although this version of events still has some currency across Israel's political spectrum (Pappe, 1999), it has become discredited amongst many historians.[11]

THE FIRST ARAB-ISRAELI WAR

On 14 May 1948, as the United Nations debated a truce and trusteeship arrangement for Palestine and the British were evacuating their troops, David Ben-Gurion declared the birth of the State of Israel in Tel Aviv, under a portrait of Theodor Herzl. Eleven minutes later, despite objections from the State Department and US diplomatic staff, America became the first country to recognise the new Israeli state. The following day the armies of five Arab nations entered Palestine and engaged Israeli forces. The motives of the various Arab armies and the military balance of power between Jewish and Arab forces are contested. The ex-Israeli prime minister Binyamin Netanyahu (2000) argues that the conflict was an unequal one involving a small Jewish force pitted against a larger and better-armed monolithic Arab entity determined to destroy the Jewish state at the moment of its creation. Others such as Shlaim (2000) dispute this and argue that Jewish forces significantly outnumbered the Arabs during all stages of the conflict, and during the final decisive phase by a ratio of nearly 2:1. The picture of a monolithic Arab force determined to destroy Israel is also disputed. Flapan (1987) suggests that the primary objective of King Abdullah of Transjordan (who had nominal control of all the Arab forces) was not to prevent the emergence of a Jewish state but to take control of the Arab part of Palestine, as part of a secret pact that he had made with Golda Meir in November 1947. Ovendale (1999) further suggests that the other Arab states involved were riven by competing territorial and political ambitions, in contrast to the Jewish forces that mostly fought with a united front.

In the first stage of fighting leading up to the truce on 11 June, Israeli forces consolidated their hold on a number of mixed Arab-Jewish towns, eastern and western Galilee and parts of the Negev. Jerusalem saw fierce fighting between Israeli and Transjordanian forces. During the first truce the Israelis took the opportunity to recruit more fighters and substantially re-arm. The UN appointed a mediator, the Swedish Count Bernadotte, who put forward a proposal for ending the conflict. It suggested a union between an Arab state linked to Transjordan and a Jewish state. Jerusalem would be part of the Arab state. The proposal was rejected by all sides. The Arabs rejected plans to prolong the truce and on 9 July battle recommenced. In nine days of fighting leading up to a second truce the Israelis took the initiative, capturing the Arab towns of Nazareth, Lydda and Ramleh. During the second truce Israel mobilised and trained more fighters, many of whom were newly arrived immigrants, and arranged the shipment of more weapons. They also consolidated their hold on the occupied territories and, according to Bregman, razed 'Arab villages to the ground so that their previous inhabitants who took what they believed to be a temporary refuge elsewhere would have nowhere to return to' (2003: 57). During the second truce Count Bernadotte put forward another proposal for settling the conflict. Territorially it was similar to his previous proposal, although Jerusalem would fall under United Nations control, and the Palestinians would decide their own political fate in consultation with other Arab states. The proposal was due to be debated by the United Nations General Assembly on 21 September, but on 17 September Count Bernadotte was assassinated in Jerusalem by members of a Jewish paramilitary group, the Stern Gang, under orders from a triumvirate that included Yitzak Shamir, who later became prime minister of Israel (Bregman, 2003). During this second truce Ben-Gurion proposed to the Israeli cabinet the launching of a major offensive to capture much of the West Bank, but failed to gain majority approval and switched his attention to a plan to push Egyptian forces back across the Negev into Egypt. At this time Shlaim (2000) claims that Israel received a peace proposal from the Egyptian government offering de facto recognition of Israel in exchange for Egypt's annexation of a portion of land in the Negev. He argues that Ben-Gurion ignored Egypt's proposals and persuaded the cabinet to authorise a series of military offensives designed to capture the Negev. These were highly successful, with the Israeli army driving the Egyptians out of the Negev and following them into Egypt proper. Eventually Britain intervened on the Egyptian side under the terms of the 1936 Anglo-Egyptian Treaty and, after forceful pressure from President Truman, Ben-Gurion agreed to withdraw his troops from the Sinai and accept a new truce.

POST-WAR NEGOTIATIONS:
PEACE TREATIES, BORDERS AND REFUGEES

The war ended on 7 January 1949. It had extracted a high price on all parties. Israel had lòst more than 6,000 lives, or 1 per cent of its population. It had, however, made huge territorial gains. UN Resolution 181 had recommended the Jewish state be established in 57 per cent of mandatory Palestine. By the end of 1948 the Israeli state had control of 78 per cent.

After the war the Israelis engaged in immediate nation building. Elections were held in January 1949 based on a system of proportional party lists. The Mapai Party won the most seats, with its leader Ben-Gurion becoming the nation's first prime minister, whilst Chaim Weizmann was installed as president. The Palestinians view the events of 1948 as so traumatic they are simply known as *Al Nakba*, 'The Catastrophe'. The refugees created prior to the start of the 'official war' on 15 May swelled during the conflict. The Israeli historian Illan Pappe claims that towards the end of the war 'several massacres were committed adding an incentive to the flight of the population' and in the final stages of the conflict 'expulsion was even more systematic' (1999: 51–2). The war ended with 520,000 Palestinian refugees according to Israel, 726,000 as estimated by the

UN, and 810,000 as estimated by the British government (Gilbert, 1999). The 150,000 Palestinians who were left in the new Israeli state were, according to Bregman, regarded by Israel as a 'dangerous and not-to-be-trusted potential fifth column' and were therefore placed under military rule:

> The military government operated in areas where Arabs were concentrated and its main task was to exercise governmental policies in these areas. It was a most powerful body hated by the Arabs, for it effectively controlled all spheres of their lives, imposing on them severe restrictions: it banned the Arabs from leaving their villages and travelling to other parts of the country without obtaining special permission; it detained suspects without trial and it also, frequently, in the name of security, closed whole areas, thus preventing Arab peasants access to their fields and plantations which was devastating for them for they were dependent on their crops for their livelihood. The military government also imposed curfews on whole villages and on one occasion, when the village of Kfar Qassem, unaware of the curfew, returned to their homes, the Israelis opened fire killing 47. (Bregman, 2003: 74)

During 1949, Israel, under the auspices of the UN, negotiated separate armistice agreements with all Arab states involved in the conflict. Jordan moved to annex the West Bank whilst Egypt moved to occupy the Gaza Strip, but unlike Jordan it made no effort to annex the territory. The name 'Palestine' had disappeared from the map, its territory having been absorbed into the Israeli and Jordanian states. In late April 1949 Israel met with delegations from Egypt, Jordan, Syria, Lebanon and the Arab Higher Committee in Lausanne to try to hammer out a peace deal. The two central sticking points were borders and refugees. The Arab delegation wanted to see borders based on the 1947 UN partition resolution, which they had previously rejected. The Israelis argued that the permanent borders should be based on the ceasefire lines with only minor modifications. No agreement was reached. On 11 December 1948 the United Nations General Assembly had passed Resolution 194 which resolved 'that the refugees wishing to return to their homes and live at peace with their neighbours should be permitted to do so at the earliest practicable date, and that compensation should be paid for the property of those choosing not to return and for loss of or damage to property'. This position on the repatriation of refugees, Pappe (1999) argues, was shared by the UN, Europe and the US. Israel rejected the return of refugees and the payment of compensation, arguing that the Arab states had created the refugee problem by attacking Israel and they should therefore settle the refugees in their own countries:

> We did not want the war. Tel Aviv did not attack Jaffa. It was Jaffa which attacked Tel Aviv and this will not occur again. Jaffa will be a Jewish town. The repatriation of the Arabs is not justice, but folly. Those who declared war against us will have to bear the result after they have been defeated. (Ben-Gurion, cited in Gabbay, 1959: 109)

From June 1949 onwards Pappe argues that Israeli leaders were committed to 'creating a fait accompli that would render repatriation impossible' (1999: 52). In that month Joseph Weitz wrote in a memorandum that there was a consensus among Israeli leaders that the best way to deal with the abandoned Palestinian villages was by 'destruction, renovation and settlement by Jews' (Weitz, cited in Pappe, 1999: 52). This plan, which Pappe claims Israel carried out 'to the letter', required the state 'to demolish what was left of abandoned Palestinian villages, almost 350 in all, so that the term repatriation itself, would become meaningless' (1999: 52). Pappe suggests that for Israelis the subject of the Palestinian refugees raises difficult questions about the nature of the Israeli state:

> Israelis – leaders and people alike – have a genuine psychological problem when faced with the refugee issue. This is indeed for them the 'original sin'. It puts a huge question mark over the Israeli self-image of moral superiority and human sensitivity. It ridicules Israel's oxymorons, such as the 'purity of arms' or misnomers, such as the 'Israeli Defence Forces', and raises doubts over the religious notion of the 'chosen people' and the political pretension of being the only democracy in the Middle East which should be wholeheartedly supported by the West. In the past it has produced a series of repressions and self denials as well as the promotion of unrealistic political solutions ... It was accompanied by an intellectual struggle against the Palestinians, epitomised by the official Israeli fabrication of the history of the land and the conflict. (Pappe, 1999: 58)

Although the armistice agreements had ended the military conflict, there were no formal peace treaties signed between Israel and its Arab neighbours, setting the scene for further sporadic clashes. This failure to negotiate comprehensive peace treaties is a contentious issue. Sachar, for instance, blames Arab intransigence, claiming that Israel repeatedly attempted to make peace but its efforts were rebuffed by Arab states: '[The] Arab purpose was single minded and all-absorptive. It was flatly committed to the destruction of Israel as an independent state' (1977: 430). Some historians claim the opposite. Shlaim argues that 'the files of the Israeli Foreign Ministry ... burst at the seams with evidence of Arab peace feelers and Arab readiness to negotiate with Israel from September 1948 on' (2000: 49).

In the years after 1948 the Arab world instituted an economic boycott against Israel, shut its borders and refused its aircraft permission to use their airspace. This period also saw a radical demographic shift in the Jewish population throughout the Middle East. In the nine years following the 1948 war, 567,000 Jews left Muslim countries and most settled in Israel, so that the population swelled from 1.174 million in 1949 to 1.873 million in 1956 (Ovendale, 1999). Sachar (1977) claims that in many of these societies, particularly Iraq and Egypt, the Jewish population had 'prospered mightily', but argues that in the 1940s they were subject to increasing levels of harassment and persecution. He claims that in Libya anti-Jewish riots in 1945 had left several hundred dead or wounded, and in Syria the Jewish population saw its property and employment rights curtailed. Gilbert (1999) maintains that Israeli officials were instrumental in facilitating these population transfers from Muslim countries, known in Israel as 'the ingathering of the exiles', because there was a shortage of manpower in Israel after 1948. It has been claimed that the methods employed were controversial. Gilbert (1999) and Hirst (1977) write that in Iraq, Israeli agents planted bombs in synagogues and Jewish businesses in an attempt to stimulate emigration to Israel.

Despite the stabilisation of the political and military situation following the 1948 war clashes along the armistice lines were a constant source of friction between Israel and its Arab neighbours. Displaced Palestinians in Arab states began to engage in what was known as 'infiltration'. Shlaim alleges that '90 per cent or more of all infiltrations were motivated by social and economic concerns involving persons crossing the ceasefire lines to retrieve property, see relatives or tend their land' (2000: 82). Many of the refugees had been separated from their homes and land and so had no employment and went hungry. The other 10 per cent of infiltrations involved acts of sabotage and violence directed against Israelis. Shlaim claims that the Israelis adopted a 'free fire' policy towards infiltrators which encouraged the Arabs to organise into groups and respond in kind. The British Major John Glubb argued that 'the original infiltrator was harmless and unarmed seeking lost property or relatives. Yet Jewish terrorism [i.e. shoot-to-kill and reprisals raids] made the infiltrator into a gunman' (cited in Morris, 1997: 51). Between the end of the 1948 war and the 1956 Suez War, the Israeli authorities estimated that 294 civilians had been killed by infiltrators from Jordan, Lebanon and Egypt (Morris, 1997: 97–8). Shlaim claims that in this period between 2,700 and 5,000 infiltrators, 'the great majority of them unarmed', were killed by 'trigger-happy' Israeli soldiers (2000: 82). Some Israeli historians argue that Arab leaders encouraged infiltration as an attempt to weaken and destroy the Israeli state. In contrast Shlaim claims that 'there is strong evidence from Arab, British, American, UN and even Israeli sources to suggest that for the first six years after the war, the Arab governments were opposed to infiltration and tried to curb it' (2000: 84). Israel adopted a policy of 'reprisals' directed against villages in Gaza and Jordan. Shlaim claims that 'all of these raids were aimed at civilian targets' and 'greatly inflamed Arab hatred of Israel and met with mounting criticism from the international community' (2000: 83). A specialist 'reprisal brigade', Unit 101 was created under the command of Ariel Sharon. It first major operation involved an attack on the village of Quibya in 1953, following the killing of an Israeli mother and two children by a hand grenade in Yahuda. Unit 101 reduced Quibya 'to a pile of rubble: forty-five houses had been blown up and sixty-nine civilians, two-thirds of them women and children' were killed (Shlaim, 2000: 91). A UN report found that 'the inhabitants had been forced by heavy fire to stay inside, until their homes were blown up over them' (Shlaim, 2000: 91). Shlaim claims that such acts were also carried out against Arab villages within the State of Israel:

> Periodic search operations were also mounted in Arab villages inside Israel to weed out infiltrators. From time to time the soldiers who carried out these operations committed atrocities, among them gang rape, murder and, on one occasion, the dumping of 120 infiltrators in the Arava desert without water. The atrocities were committed not in the heat of battle but for the most part against innocent civilians, including women and children. Coping with

day to day security had a brutalising effect on the IDF. Soldiers in an army which prided itself on the precept of 'the purity of arms' showed growing disregard for human lives and carried out some barbaric acts that can only be described as war crimes. (Shlaim, 2000: 83)

It was against this backdrop of border tensions that Israel became involved in a broader struggle between Britain, France and Egypt over control of the Suez Canal.

1956: THE SUEZ CONFLICT

In Egypt following a bloodless coup in 1952, Gamal Abd al-Nasser and his 'free officers' took power and turned the state into a republic. In 1954 Nasser became president and attempted to make himself the champion of a pan-Arabic renaissance, and the leader of the decolonisation movement across the Middle East and Africa. Ovendale (1999) suggests that the European colonial powers feared the effects of Nasser's Arab nationalism on their oil interests and geostrategic control of the Middle East and Africa. France was also hostile because of his support for Algerians fighting for independence. In July 1956 Nasser nationalised the Suez Canal after the US and Britain refused to fund the Aswan Dam Project, which Nasser saw as a means to develop Egypt as a modern nation. Britain and France, who were shareholders in the Canal, decided Nasser had to be removed from power. Israel also wanted to see Nasser deposed and on 23 October 1956, British, French and Israeli representatives met in Paris to devise a military plan (Shlaim, 2000).

On 29 October 1956 the Israeli Defence Forces (IDF) launched an attack on Egyptian forces in the Sinai peninsula. The next day Britain and France issued an ultimatum to Egypt and Israel to withdraw their forces to a distance of ten miles from the Suez Canal. Israel complied, Egypt refused, and the following day Britain and France began an aerial bombardment of the Egyptian airfields. Israel quickly secured an overwhelming military victory, capturing Gaza on 2 November and the whole Sinai peninsula three days later. On 7 November Ben-Gurion delivered a speech to the Knesset in which 'he hinted that Israel planned to annex the entire Sinai peninsula as well as the Straits of Tiran' (Shlaim, 2000: 179). However, under strong pressure from the US and the USSR and threats of United Nations sanctions,

Israel was eventually forced to withdraw from all of the Sinai after six months. Israel's motivations have been the subject of much controversy. One version maintains that Israel was driven to attack Egypt for three main reasons. Firstly, it is argued that the Egyptian leader Nasser was planning to lead a combined Arab force (Egypt, Jordan, Syria) in an attempt to destroy Israel, and the Suez conflict was necessary as a pre-emptive military strike to prevent this. Sachar (1977) points to belligerent speeches made by Arab leaders in the months preceding the war, which he argues were proof of imminent Arab plans to destroy Israel. He also suggests that Egypt's acquisition of large shipments of arms from Czechoslovakia in 1955 had shifted the balance of power against Israel. Sachar also claims that Israel wanted to break Egypt's blockade of the Suez Canal, and stop Palestinian guerrilla attacks on Israel. This perspective on Israeli motivations sees the attack on Egypt as defensive in orientation and concerned only with strengthening the country's security situation.

Other historians have pointed to other reasons for the attack. Shlaim (2000) argues that Israel's military establishment led by Ben-Gurion and Moshe Dayan was determined to goad Nasser into a war by carrying out provocative raids against Egyptian forces, despite Egyptian attempts to curb infiltration. The most serious of these raids occurred in February 1955 when an Israeli unit led by Ariel Sharon attacked the Egyptian army headquarters on the outskirts of Gaza killing 37 Egyptian soldiers. Hirst claims that Egypt had consistently tried to avoid military confrontation with Israel, and had only 'unleashed the *fedayeen* [Palestinian guerrillas] under pressure from his own public opinion in the wake of further provocations from Israel' (1977: 200). Both Hirst (1977) and Shlaim (2000) argue that there was no credible evidence that Nasser was planning a war with Israel, nor that the balance of power had shifted in Egypt's favour. They suggest that the war was undertaken to expand the borders of Israel and overthrow Nasser's regime. Shlaim maintains that Israel hoped to absorb the whole of the Sinai peninsula, the West Bank and part of the Lebanon. He argues that Ben-Gurion 'exposed an appetite for territorial expansion at the expense of the Arabs and expansion in every possible direction: north, east and south' as well as 'a cavalier attitude to toward the independence, sovereignty and territorial integrity of the neighbouring Arab states' (2000: 178).

1967: THE SIX DAY WAR

During the 1960s the Middle East became a site of Cold War rivalry between America and the Soviet Union, both of whom were supplying the region's states with weapons. In spring 1967 the Soviet Union informed the Syrian government that Israel was amassing troops on its northern border in preparation for an attack on Syria. Whether such troop movements had actually taken place is a matter of dispute amongst historians (see Shlaim, 2000 and Hirst, 1977 for conflicting views). The previous year had also seen a number of border clashes between the two nations and tensions had been running high. Israel had threatened publicly to overthrow the Syrian regime unless it stopped Palestinian guerrilla attacks launched from Syrian territory. Syria, alarmed by the Soviet reports, turned to Egypt with whom it had a mutual defence pact. Egypt then sent a number of troops into the Sinai, bordering Israel, and asked the United Nations troops, who formed a buffer between the two countries, to evacuate their positions. The Egyptian troops then moved into Sharm al-Shaykh and proclaimed a blockade of the Israeli port of Eilat, which was accessible only through Egyptian waters. Two weeks later, at 7.45 a.m. on 5 June 1967, Israel launched an aerial attack on Egyptian airfields destroying 298 warplanes, the bulk of the Egyptian air force, in a single day. Israeli ground forces also launched an almost simultaneous land invasion of Egyptian territory, forcing their way to the Suez Canal and capturing the Sinai peninsula in two days. At noon on 5 June, as part of a defence pact with Egypt, Syrian, Jordanian and Iraqi forces attacked targets inside Israel. Within two hours the air forces of all three were destroyed by the Israeli air force, as well as an Iraqi military base near the Jordanian border. Jordanian land forces also intervened in support of Egypt. Jordanian artillery shelled Israeli towns and its troops entered Arab East Jerusalem and occupied Government House. Israel then drove the Jordanian army out of the West Bank and East Jerusalem, occupying them both by 7 June. The following day Israeli warplanes attacked the American spy ship, the USS *Liberty*, with cannon, missiles and napalm, killing 34 US service personnel and injuring 171.[12] On 9 June Israel attacked Syria, despite strong UN pressure, and occupied the Golan Heights. There have been allegations in the Israeli press that about 1,000 unresisting Egyptian soldiers, as well as many Palestinian refugees, were killed by the Israeli army. The war was an overwhelming military success for Israel. In six days it destroyed three Arab armies and made large territorial gains, capturing the Sinai peninsula, the Golan Heights, the West Bank, the Gaza Strip and Arab East Jerusalem.

The reasons behind Israel's decision to launch the Six Day War are disputed. The official Israeli cabinet documents stated that the 'Government [of Israel] ascertained that the armies of Egypt, Syria and Jordan are deployed for immediate multi-front aggression, threatening the very existence of the state' (cited in Finkelstein, 2001: 130). Three years previously Arab leaders had declared in an official document their intention to achieve 'collective military preparations' for the 'final liquidation of Israel' (Shlaim, 2000: 230). Sachar points to Nasser's decision to replace United Nations peacekeeping troops in the Sinai with Egyptian troops, and military preparations by other Arab nations, as evidence that 'the garrote ... was rapidly tightening around Israel' (1977: 632). He also points to Israeli motivations to stop Syrian shelling of Israeli settlements in the demilitarised zone (DMZ) between Israel and Syria, and guerrilla raids into Israeli territory. Another justification given for Israel's attack was that Egypt's decision to blockade of the Straits of Tiran which prevented access to the Israeli port of Eilat, was, according to the Israeli Foreign Minister Abba Eban, an 'attempt at strangulation' which constituted an 'act of war' (Eban, 1992: 334, cited in Finkelstein, 2001: 137).

Some other historians have questioned these explanations and pointed to an alternative set of motivations. The twin assertions that the Arab states were planning an imminent attack and that they had the military strength to threaten Israel's existence are disputed. Finkelstein claims that 'exhaustive US intelligence at the end of the month [May 1967] could find no evidence that Egypt was planning to attack' (2001: 134). Menachem Begin and Yitzak Rabin later argued that the Arab states had not been planning an attack and that the Israeli government had been aware of this at the time.[13] The claim that the combined Arab armies posed a mortal threat to the state of Israel is also disputed. The CIA produced a report in May 1967 predicting (British intelligence had reached the identical conclusion), that Israel would win a war against one or all of the Arab states combined, whoever attacked first, in about a week (Finkelstein, 2001). Menachem Begin and Ezer Weizman have also argued that Israel's existence was never threatened.[14] Five years after the war, in an Israeli newspaper article, one of the chief military planners of the campaign General Mattityahu Peled, was dismissive of the Arab threat in 1967:

There is no reason to hide the fact that since 1949 no one dared, or more precisely, no one was able to threaten the very existence of Israel. In spite of that, we have continued to foster a sense of our own inferiority, as if we were a weak and insignificant people, which, in the midst of an anguished struggle for its existence, could be exterminated at any moment ... it is notorious that the Arab leaders themselves, thoroughly aware of their own impotence, did not believe in their own threats ... I am sure that our General Staff never told the government that the Egyptian military threat represented any threat to Israel or that we were unable to crush Nasser's army, which with unheard of foolishness, had exposed itself to the devastating might of our army ... To claim that the Egyptian forces concentrated on our borders were capable of threatening Israel's existence not only insults the intelligence of anyone capable of analysing this kind of situation, but is an insult to the Zahal [the Israeli army]. (*Ma'ariv*, 24 March 1972, cited in Hirst, 1977: 211)

Other posited explanations for Israel's decision to attack its Arab neighbours include a desire to safeguard the deterrent image of the IDF. Shlaim (2000) suggests that the Egyptian blockade represented a threat to Israel's 'iron wall' of militarised strength. Others suggest different motivations. Neff claims that on the eve of the 1967 war the CIA had identified three Israeli objectives: 'the destruction of the centre of power of the radical Arab socialist movements' [that is, Nasser's regime], 'the destruction of the arms of the radical Arabs' and the 'destruction of both Jordan and Syria as modern States' (Neff, 1985: 230, cited in Finkelstein, 2001: 143). Hirst (1977) argues that Israeli military planners had been preparing the attack since they were forced to leave the Sinai in 1956, and cites comments from General Burns, the chief of staff of the United Nations Truce Supervision Organisation (UNTSO) in the early 1960s that Israel would probably seek to go to war again soon to break the Arab economic blockade and overcome its economic difficulties. Another explanation that has been cited as a motivation for Israel's decision to go to war involved a desire to expand the boundaries of Israel. Proponents of this view, point to comments made by the Israeli commander Yigal Allon shortly before the 1967 war that 'in the case of a new war' Israel must seek as a central aim 'the territorial fulfilment of the land of Israel' (cited in Finkelstein, 2001: 143). There is evidence since the 1950s in the writings of David Ben-Gurion and other Israeli leaders that there had been a desire to expand Israel to incorporate all of Jerusalem and the West Bank. The Israeli historian Benny Morris notes:

A strong expansionist current ran through both Zionist ideology and Israeli society. There was a general feeling shared by prominent figures as Dayan and Ben-Gurion, that the territorial gains of the 1948 war had fallen short of the envisioned promised land. *Bechiya Le Dorot* – literally a cause for lamentation for future generations – was how Ben-Gurion described the failure to conquer Arab East Jerusalem; leading groups in Israeli society regarded the Jordanian controlled West Bank with the same feeling. (Morris, 1989: 410–11, cited in Finkelstein, 2001: 221)

The conflict triggered a second mass exodus of Palestinians, many of whom became refugees for a second time, as they had sought refuge in the West Bank and Gaza after having to abandon their homes in 1948–49. Nur Masalha, senior lecturer at the Holy Land Research Project at the University of Surrey, argues that 'there is no evidence to suggest that there were wholesale or blanket expulsion orders adopted or carried out by the Israeli army in June 1967, although the policy of selective eviction, demolition and encouragement of "transfer" continued for several weeks after the Israeli army occupied the West Bank and Gaza Strip' (Masalha, 1999: 100). Masalha maintains that in 1967 'evictions and demolitions were evident in numerous geographical locations in the West Bank' and that 'young men from several cities and refugee camps were also targeted for deportation' (1999: 101). Peter Dodd and Halim Barakat, in their study of the 1967 exodus, *River without Bridges*, provide similar explanations for the exodus:

The exodus was a response to the severe situational pressures existing at the time. The situational pressures were generated by the aerial attacks upon a defenceless country, including the extensive use of napalm, the occupation of the West Bank villages by the Israeli army, and the actions of the occupying forces. Certainly the most dramatic of these was the eviction of civilians, and the deliberate destruction of a number of villages [Imwas, Yalu, Bayt Nuba, Bayt Marsam, Bayt Awa, Habla, al-Burj and Jiftlik]. Other action, such as threats and the mass detention of male civilians, also created situational pressures. (Dodd and Barakat, 1968: 54, cited in Masalha, 1999: 96)

William Wilson Harris (1980), who reached similar conclusions himself in his analysis of the exodus, estimates that 430,000 residents of the newly occupied territories were forced to flee their homes during 1967. The displaced residents of the West Bank were prevented from returning to the area by harsh measures. Testimony in the Israeli press, from an unnamed soldier serving in the 5th Reserve Division on the Jordan river, details the fate of displaced Palestinians attempting to return to their homes:

We fired such shots every night on men, women and children. Even during moonlit nights when we could identify the people, that is distinguish between men, women and children. In the mornings we searched the area and, by explicit order from the officer on the spot, shot the living, including those who hid or were wounded, again including the women and children. (*Haolam Haze*, 10 October 1967, cited in Masalha, 1999: 99)

There were reports that after the war Israel began destroying Palestinian homes in the newly occupied territories. The American historian Alfred Lilienthal claims that:

according to UN figures, the Israelis destroyed during the period between 11 June 1967 and 15 November 1969 some 7,554 Palestinian Arab homes in the territories seized during that war; this figure excluded 35 villages in the occupied Golan Heights that were razed to the ground. In the two years between September 1969 and 1971 the figure was estimated to have reached 16,312 homes. (Lilienthal, 1978: 160)

On 19 June 1967 Israeli leaders formulated an offer to hand back the Golan Heights, the Sinai and the Gaza Strip in return for demilitarisation agreements, peace treaties and assurance of navigation rights from Egypt, Syria and Jordan. Bregman (2003) suggests that the decision, taken two months later, by Arab leaders meeting in Khartoum to issue the famous 'three noes' to peace, recognition and negotiations with Israel led to the Israeli decision taken on 30 October to officially withdraw the offer, and harden its attitude. Shlaim disagrees, arguing that there was no evidence that the conditional offer of withdrawal was ever presented to the Arab states, and that the offer was almost immediately killed by political and military leaders who wanted to retain a large part of the captured territories, and began in mid July to approve plans for constructing settlements on the occupied Golan Heights. He maintains that the 'three noes' at Khartoum referred to 'no formal peace *treaty*, but not a rejection of a state of peace; no *direct* negotiations, but not a refusal to talk through third parties; and no *de jure* recognition of Israel, but acceptance of its existence as a state' (Shlaim, 2000: 258). He argues the conference was 'a victory for Arab moderates who argued for trying to obtain the withdrawal of Israeli forces by political rather than military means' (2000: 258). There have also been claims that Israel turned down a peace treaty with Egypt and Jordan at the conference.[15]

Shlaim claims that there was no Israeli debate about handing back East Jerusalem, but that Israeli leaders were split on how much of the West Bank they wanted to retain. He suggests outright annexation was favoured by only a few, because it would mean absorbing large numbers of Arabs into the Jewish state. Most favoured one of two options. The Allon Plan proposed limited autonomy for Palestinians in part of the West Bank (Israel would still own the land and control security in the autonomy area), with Israel taking control of a large strip of the Jordan valley, much of the area around Jerusalem and the Judean desert. These parts of the West Bank would then be colonised with Jewish settlements and army bases.

The second option involved handing back to Jordan part of the West Bank with Israel keeping approximately a third of the area. Neither proposal was acceptable to King Hussein or the Palestinians.

RESOLUTION 242 AND THE WAR OF ATTRITION

The 1967 war was followed by the UN Security Council unanimously adopting Resolution 242, which has become the framework document for successive attempts to resolve the conflict. The resolution called for the 'withdrawal of Israeli armed forces from territories occupied in the recent conflict' in line with the principle 'emphasise[d]' in the preambular paragraph of the 'inadmissibility of the acquisition of territory by war'. It also 'emphasised' the 'need to work for a just and lasting peace in which every State in the area can live in security' as well as a 'just settlement of the refugee problem' and the establishment of navigation rights. Egypt and Jordan agreed to Resolution 242 whilst Syria rejected it. The Palestinians also rejected it on the grounds that it spoke only of their plight as a refugee problem, making no mention of their rights to self-determination and national sovereignty. Israel accepted the resolution in 1970. The meaning of the withdrawal clause has been contested. Israel has argued that because the definite article 'the' was not included in the English version of the resolution ('from territories occupied' rather than 'from the territories occupied') it means that the scope of withdrawal was left vague and that Israel did not have to withdraw from all the territories it occupied in the conflict. Israel has also argued that many of the nations who endorsed the resolution, including the US, the UK, the USSR and Brazil, agreed that Israel did not have to withdraw from all the territories (Israeli Ministry of Foreign Affairs, 1999). Finkelstein (2001) disputes this. He points to statements made by the president of the UN General Assembly that 'there is virtual unanimity in upholding the principle that conquest of territory by war is inadmissible in our time under the Charter' (UN General Assembly, 1967, cited in Finkelstein, 2001: 145). This affirmation, the president continued, was 'made in virtually all statements' and 'virtually all speakers laid down the corollary that withdrawal of forces to their original position is expected' (UN General Assembly, 1967a, cited in Finkelstein, 2001: 145). The debates at the UN Security Council, Finkelstein argues, were similarly unambiguous with virtually all representatives stressing both the inadmissibility clause and the need for a complete Israeli withdrawal.[16] He also argues that the American position was for a full Israeli withdrawal.[17]

Having failed to secure an Israeli withdrawal from the occupied territories, Egypt fought the 'War of Attrition' against Israel between 1967 and 1970. Shlaim argues President Nasser's immediate purpose was to 'prevent the conversion of the Suez Canal into a de facto border, while his ultimate goal was to force Israel to withdraw to the pre war border' (2000: 289). Egypt bombed Israeli troop concentrations in the occupied Sinai and Palestinian guerrillas launched cross-border attacks against Israel. Israel then attacked military and civilian targets within Egypt and Jordan. Numerous Egyptian coastal towns and cities were heavily damaged by Israeli air attacks. The Israeli commander Ezer Weizman recalled the fate of an Egyptian border city Ismailia which the Israeli army bombarded 'incessantly, devastating it from the air as well as with land-based artillery' so that aerial photographs 'showed its western portions resembling the cities at the end of World War II' (Weizman, cited in Gilbert, 1999: 410). The former Israeli chief of staff, Mordechai Gur, was later to claim that Israeli attacks during the War of Attrition had created 1.5 million Egyptian refugees as well as emptying the entire Jordan valley of its inhabitants (*Al Hamishar*,

10 May 1978). The war was finally brought to a halt in August 1970 when both sides agreed to a US-sponsored ceasefire. Morris (1992) estimates that in the three years of conflict, 367 Israeli soldiers and more than 10,000 Egyptian soldiers and civilians were killed.

SETTLEMENT BUILDING AND ECONOMIC INTEGRATION

In the aftermath of the 1967 war Israel established settlements on the newly captured territories and placed the Palestinian residents under military rule. Two major reasons were given for the creation of settlements. One stressed their security value:

> There was also a strategic justification for not wanting to give up the occupied West Bank and that was that it turned Israel's 'narrow waist' into something wider. Before seizing the West Bank Israel's width at some parts measured scarcely nine miles from the Jordan bulge to the Mediterranean, and by clinging to the occupied territories west of the Jordan river Israel made it more difficult for a potential Arab invasion force coming from the east to cut in two. (Bregman, 2003: 126–7)

Some Israelis were dismissive of the security argument alleging it was a pretext to satisfy international public opinion. One official writing in the Israeli press claimed that 'we have to use the pretext of security needs and the authority of the military governor as there is no way of driving out the Arabs from their land so long as they refuse to go and accept our compensation' (Ha'aretz, 23 November 1969, cited in Hirst, 1977: 241). A second strand of thought justified settlement building and retention of the occupied territories, on the basis of divine rights. Victory in the Six Day War was seen by many religious Jews as a sign of support from God and evidence that the messianic era was at hand, leading to a surge in support for religious nationalism. A number of new parties and organisations were formed who advocated permanent control and settlement of the West Bank and Gaza Strip, because, it was argued, these areas were a central component of the biblical land of Israel. Harold Fisch, the former rector of Israel's Bar-Ilan University, argues that God promised Abraham the land of Israel as an eternal possession, and this provides justification for sovereignty over the West Bank and Gaza Strip:

The covenant between the people of Israel and its God, which includes the promised land as an integral part, is an important objective within the entire scheme of creation. It is from this fact that the linkage between the people of Israel and its land is rooted in the transcendental will of God who created all in his honor. (Fisch, 1982: 189)

These arguments are echoed in more contemporary comments. In a recent interview in the *Observer*, Ariel Sharon, the Israeli prime minister, was quoted as saying 'Israel is the promised land – promised to Jews and no-one else' (13 July 2003). The viewpoint has also gained ground in the US via the Christian fundamentalist movement, who are key supporters of George W. Bush and the Republicans. A BBC programme interviewed the pastor of a major church in Texas who explained his view:

Well you understand that the Jewish state was something that's born in the mind of God and we are a people who believe the scripture and the scripture says very clearly that God created Israel, that God is the protector and defender of Israel. If God created Israel, if God defends Israel, is it not logical to say that those who fight with Israel are fighting with God? (BBC Radio 4, *A Lobby to be Reckoned With*, 7 May 2002)

Other arguments for Israel's rights to keep and settle the lands captured in 1967 included the position that since the land has changed sovereignty many times over the last 2,000 years, the Jews have as much claim as any others who had controlled it since they were exiled.[18] Some Israelis have argued that since the Arabs rejected partition in 1947 they have given up their rights to a share of mandatory Palestine. Others point to the legal status of the Balfour Declaration or argue that since Israel won the territories in a 'war of self-defence' they have a right to keep them. Binyamin Netanyahu argues that to prevent Jews from building settlements in the occupied territories is a form of apartheid:

Careful manipulation of the media by the Arabs has left many Westerners with the indelible impression that Arab paupers are being kicked off their hovels in droves to make way for Jewish suburbs in the 'densely populated West Bank' ... For what is manifestly occurring is that the West, which so sharply condemned anti-black apartheid in South Africa, is being used by the Arabs as an enforcer of anti-Jewish apartheid that pertains in the Arabs' own countries. (Netanyahu, 2000: 189–92)

In a review of Israel's settlement-building programmes, Israel Shahak and Norton Mezvinsky (1999) note that until 1974, Moshe Dayan oversaw settlement activity. His policy was to limit settlements primarily to Hebron, northern Sinai and the Jordan valley, as part of a bargain he made with the Palestinian feudal notables who controlled the villages. Shahak and Mezvinsky argue that, after 1974, religious settler groups, primarily Gush Emunim and their political allies in the Knesset, came to the fore in determining settlement policy, with the support of both Labour and particularly the Likud Party. In 1973 Israel introduced the Galili Plan which Shafir suggests transformed the Allon Plan's *'military frontier* to a combination of a *messianic frontier* and a *suburban frontier'* (1999: 92). Some commentators have pointed to the extreme ideological views of many religious settlers which justify attacks on Palestinians and attempts to expel them from the occupied territories in what is seen as a process of 'purification' or 'sanctification' of the land.[19] Hirst has suggested that even prior to 1974, the creation of settlements was at the expense of Palestinians:

Sometimes it was necessary to uproot an entire village – though not necessarily all at once. For years the impoverished inhabitants of Beit Askariyah watched in impotent dismay as the great cantonments of the Kfar Etzion settlement went up around them, relentlessly encroaching on their agricultural and grazing land before swallowing up their homes too. In January 1972, the army expelled 6,000 bedouins from Rafah in north-east Sinai. It demolished their houses, poisoned their wells, and kept them at bay with a barbed wire fence. The Bedouins were eventually employed as night watchmen or labourers – on their own property and in the service of those who had taken it from them. (Hirst, 1977: 242)

In 1981 the Likud administration introduced the Drobless Plan. Shafir suggests that its purpose was to 'scatter Jewish settlements among Arab towns and villages in order to ensure that no homogenous Palestinian inhabited area, the potential core of a Palestinian state would remain' (1999: 92). In a more recent study

Amnesty International (1999c) examined how settlement building and Palestinian house demolitions are 'inextricably linked with Israeli policy to control and colonize areas of the West Bank', a policy that has been 'energetically followed for over 30 years by all administrations from 1967 until the present time'. The process of colonisation, the report continues, depends 'not just on finding land that is physically "suitable", but on alienating it from the Palestinians, defending it against Palestinian use, and ensuring through such processes as registration and leasing that Palestinians are disqualified from having any future benefit from that land'. Amnesty International argue that the damage to the 'tight knit pattern of Palestinian villages' has been pervasive. Settlement building is prohibited by the Fourth Geneva Convention, Article 49 of which stipulates that 'the occupying power shall not deport or transfer parts of its own population into the territory it occupies'. The Israeli government has disputed this, arguing that the area is 'administered' rather than 'occupied' and that Article 49 has 'no bearing' on the Israeli settlements because the convention was intended to cover forced transfers during the Second World War, whilst 'the movement of individuals to these areas is entirely voluntary, while the settlements themselves are not intended to displace Arab inhabitants, nor do they do so in practice' (Israeli Ministry of Foreign Affairs, 1996). The practice has, however, been repeatedly condemned by the European Union and the United Nations who have deemed the settlements illegal and in need of removal in multiple resolutions. The practice was recently condemned in UN Resolution 55/132 by 152 votes to four (Israel, the United States, Micronesia, and the Marshall Islands).

In Jerusalem, Israel initiated a policy of 'Judaisation' in an attempt to change the demographic, physical, cultural, legal and economic status of the city. It appropriated Arab land in the city and demolished Arab housing. In the Jewish Quarter prior to 1948, approximately 20 per cent of the property was Jewish owned. After 1967, Hirst suggests that Israelis 'relentlessly forced out the 5,500 [Arab] inhabitants who lived there' (1977: 235). The demolitions and evictions occurred all over the city, with the victims of land expropriations receiving either inadequate levels of compensation or sometimes none. Moves to change the legal and demographic structure of Jerusalem have drawn criticism from the international community. In 1999 the United Nations condemned such actions by 139 votes to 1 (Israel).[20] Hirst also notes that Arab culture was suppressed or denigrated especially in schools.[21] The Israeli state quickly moved to integrate the Arabs living in the occupied territories into the Israeli economy. Some historians such as Sachar suggest that for Palestinians this was a generally beneficial process creating 'unprecedented affluence' as part of a 'comparatively painless' occupation (1977: 688–9). Other Israelis were critical of this process, arguing that Israel was instituting colonial policies in which a powerful Israeli minority was exploiting a captive Arab population for the benefit of its cheap labour and its role as a market for Israeli products:

> Better men than I have enlarged on the grim paradox that threatens the Zionist vision, the social and moral failure of that vision, which are to be expected from the transformation of the Jews into employers, managers and supervisors of Arab hewers of wood and drawers of water, and all of it plus the slogan of 'Integration' ... There is an inescapable process in a population that is divided into two peoples, one dominant, the other dominated. No! The State of Israel will not be such a monstrosity. (Ya'akov Talmon, cited in Sachar, 1977: 713)

There has also been commentary in the Israeli press suggesting the conditions under which the Palestinians were obliged to work for Israelis were exploitative and humiliating. Palestinians with jobs in Israel were not legally allowed to spend the night there so that many had to be bussed in over long distances from the occupied territories, sometimes extending their working day to 17 hours. The Israeli magazine *Haolam Haze* reported on those that were permitted to sleep illegally on Israeli farms: 'Too far away for the eye to see, hidden in the orchards, there are the sheep pens for the servants, of a sort that even a state like South Africa would be ashamed of' (22 December 1982, cited in Chomsky, 1999: 141). In a *Jerusalem Post* interview, the Israeli journalist Aryeh Rubinstein asked Amos Hadar, Secretary-General of the Moshav (agricultural) movement whether he agreed with the use of Arab labour 'but only on condition that they will live in subhuman conditions, degraded, and not under human conditions, more or less?' 'Correct', replied Hadar, stressing that 'there is a difficult question here'. 'There is no choice but to employ Arabs' but they must be bussed in and out of Israel every day. 'It is hard, it is costly it is problematic from an economic standpoint but there is no other solution' (26 December 1982, cited in Chomsky, 1999: 141). There has also been criticism of Israeli use of Arab child labour.

Israel's Arabic-language communist newspaper *Al-Ittihad* described
a child labour market at Jaffa:

> In this market foremen get rich by exploiting the labour of children
> and young men from the occupied areas. Every morning at 4 a.m.
> cars from Gaza and the Strip start arriving there, bringing dozens
> of Arab workers who line up in the street in a long queue. A little
> later at 4:30 a.m. Arab boys who work in restaurants in the town
> begin to arrive. These boys work in restaurants for a month on
> end, including Saturdays ... Dozens, indeed hundreds of boys,
> who should be at school come from Gaza to work in Israel. The
> cars can be seen coming and going from earliest dawn. At about
> 6 a.m. Israeli labour brokers start arriving to choose 'working
> donkeys' as they call them. They take great care over their choice,
> actually feeling the 'donkeys' muscles. (30 April 1973, cited in
> Hirst, 1977: 246)

MILITARY OCCUPATION/ADMINISTRATION

Israel imposed a military administration on the occupied territories
which seriously restricted the social and political rights of its residents.
According to the United Nations and human rights groups, it also
involved extensive human rights violations. Israel argued that the
policies were necessary to protect the state from attacks by infiltrators
or Palestinians in the occupied territories, who they claimed were
susceptible to Palestine Liberation Organization (PLO) incitement.
Morris suggests that that severe repression coupled with 'massive use'
of informers and collaborators by the Israeli security service Shin Bet
meant that armed activity by the PLO in the occupied territories was
'virtually eradicated' by 1971 (1992: 279). Some commentators such
as Chomsky have suggested that the imposition of such policies had
another objective, that by making life difficult for the Palestinians
in the occupied territories, they would emigrate and allow Israel to
absorb the parts of the occupied territories that it wanted, without
having to worry about a large Arab population that would 'dilute' the
Jewish character of the Israeli state. Chomsky points to the official
government records of a meeting at the start of the Israeli occupation
in September 1967, when Moshe Dayan urged government ministers
to tell the Palestinian residents of the occupied territories that 'we
have no solution, that you shall continue to live like dogs, and
whoever wants to can leave – and we will see where this process

leads ... In five years we may have 200,000 less people – and that is a matter of enormous importance' (Beilin, 1985, cited in Chomsky, 1992: 434). Professor Ian Lustick suggests that Israel also wanted to break up the territorial continuity of Israeli Arab villages in Galilee and points to the 1976 Koenig memorandum in which the Israeli Minister of the Interior recommended the 'coordination of a smear campaign against Rakah activists ... the harassment of "all negative personalities at all levels and at all institutions" and the employment of techniques for encouraging the emigration of Arab intellectuals, and for downgrading the effectiveness of Arab university student organizations' (Lustick, 1980: 256). It is widely argued that the policies Israel instituted breached international law. They also led to it being frequently condemned at the United Nations General Assembly and Security Council by near unanimous votes.[22] These policies included the systematic torture of prisoners,[23] imprisonment without trial,[24] collective punishments,[25] theft of natural resources, curfews and searches,[26] house demolitions and deportations. The practices have also attracted criticism from human rights groups:

> Amnesty International has for many years documented and condemned violations of international human rights and humanitarian law by Israel directed against the Palestinian population of the Occupied Territories. They include unlawful killings; torture and ill-treatment; arbitrary detention; unfair trials; collective punishments such as punitive closures of areas and destruction of homes; extensive and wanton destruction of property; deportations; and discriminatory treatment as compared to Israeli settlers. Most of these violations are grave breaches of the Fourth Geneva Convention and are therefore war crimes. Many have also been committed in a widespread and systematic manner, and in pursuit of government policy; such violations meet the definition of crimes against humanity under international law. (Amnesty International, 2002)

NATIONALISM AND THE RISE
OF THE OPPOSITION MOVEMENTS

In the aftermath of 1948 the refugees who were displaced had begun to formulate a vision of 'the return'. Initially it was hoped that the United Nations or the Arab states themselves would help the refugees achieve this objective. However, as the years passed the lack of concrete progress began to frustrate the refugees and they became increasingly disillusioned by the leaders of the Arab states. By 1964 Yasser Arafat had established a small guerrilla organisation, Fatah, which was granted a secure base by Syria's radical Baathist regime. Fatah's philosophy from the outset was to mobilise popular Arab support behind guerrilla operations of increasing scale and intensity conducted against Israel. Prior to the 1967 war, Hirst (1977) alleges that Egypt, Jordan and Lebanon had all tried to prevent guerrilla incursions into Israel, but that after the war this became more difficult as popular support for guerrilla operations increased. By February 1968, Fatah members had taken control of the National Council of the PLO and Arafat became chairman. The aftermath of the war also saw the formation of Dr George Habash's Popular Front for the Liberation of Palestine (PFLP), which began to build a strong base of support in the refugee camps of the Gaza Strip.

In March 1968 Israeli forces launched an attack on the Karameh refugee camp in Jordan. Israel claimed the attack was in retaliation for attacks which had killed six people and wounded 44. Fifteen thousand troops backed by tanks attacked the camp. Rather than retreat to the hills the guerrilla forces stayed and fought and suffered huge losses. Half the Palestinian guerrillas, 150 in all, were killed, together with 128 members of the Jordanian army and 29 Israeli soldiers (Hirst, 1977). Although the guerrillas had lost many fighters it was considered a significant victory because the Israelis had suffered unusually high casualties and met fierce resistance. The battle of Karameh led to an influx of volunteers from across the Arab world to join the guerrilla movements. In the years after 1967, as well as engaging in a guerrilla war, the Palestinians began to formulate a vision of what a future Palestinian entity would look like. The result of this was the vision of the 'Democratic State of Palestine'. The brainchild of the PLO planner and negotiator Nabil Shaath, the Democratic State of Palestine would involve the dismantling of the Israeli state and its replacement with a non-sectarian bi-national Palestine in which Christian, Muslim and Jew would live together in equality (Hirst, 1977). The new entity would, it was claimed, include the Jews already residing there and the Palestinians who had been displaced in 1948 and 1967. These proposals were not immediately or universally accepted by Palestinians. Hirst (1977) suggests that some saw them as capitulation to the enemy or at best premature considering that Israel was still militarily dominant. Others feared that the more technologically advanced Jews would dominate them, whilst some considered it a tactical propaganda move aimed at international opinion. The concept was a complete non-starter for almost all Israelis. Israel had been constructed out of Palestine with huge military and diplomatic effort as a state for the Jewish people and there was no desire to dilute its Jewish character. Furthermore, Israelis were fearful of the extreme anti-Jewish rhetoric emanating from their Arab neighbours and worried that any returning refugees might want to take revenge for being displaced from their lands.

In the two years after the 1967 war the forces of Fatah and the other guerrilla movements had increased from 300 to more than 30,000 and substantial funding was coming in from the Arab world. The number of operations also increased dramatically. Fatah records claim that 98 per cent of these occurred outside the State of Israel with two-thirds of them occurring in the West Bank. Fatah regularly insisted that the army and 'Zionist institutions' were its real targets and not civilians, especially women and children, and if these were attacked it was in response to attacks on Palestinian civilians, and was selectively done. However, Hirst (1977) points out that although the 'great bulk' of attacks were aimed at military targets, civilians were unquestionably targeted. Bombs were planted in supermarkets in Jerusalem and bus stops in Tel Aviv and rockets were fired on settlements in Kiryat Shmoneh and Eilat. Whilst Fatah confined its actions to historic Palestine, the PFLP did not. It attacked targets all over the world. It hijacked foreign airliners. It firebombed branches of Marks and Spencer because of their fundraising for Israel. It blew up an Arab oil pipeline because the extraction was by an American oil company on behalf of a 'feudal' Arab monarchy. The main purpose of these actions, George Habash maintained, was publicity:

> When we hijack a plane it had more effect than if we killed a hundred Israelis in battle. For decades world public opinion has been neither for nor against the Palestinians. It simply ignored us. At least the world is talking about us now. (*Der Stern*, 19 September 1970, cited in Hirst, 1977: 304)

However, the opposition movements were to suffer a major blow in 1970. The PLO had formed a state-within-a-state in Jordan, openly threatening the rule of the Hashemite monarchy. Following an assassination attempt on King Hussein and a series of hijackings carried out by the PFLP, the king set his army upon the guerrillas. In ten days of bloody struggle thousands of guerrillas were killed, and within a year most of the fighters and political elements of the Palestinian movement were expelled and ended up in Lebanon. 'Black September', as it became known amongst Palestinians, produced an organisation bearing the same name. Its most well known operation was the taking of Israeli athletes as hostages at the 1972 Munich Olympics. Eight Black September members took eleven Israeli athletes hostage at the Olympic village in Munich demanding the release of 200 Palestinians imprisoned in Israel. In the German rescue operation four of the Palestinian hijackers and all eleven Israeli hostages were killed. Three days later Israel launched attacks on Syria and Lebanon. There were reports that up to 500 people, mostly civilians, were killed in nine separate simultaneous Israeli air attacks (*Al-Nahar Arab Report*, 18 September 1972):

> The Phantoms and Skyhawks swooped on the suburban Damascus resort of al-Hama; the bombs fell indiscriminately on Palestinians in their hillside dwellings and on Syrians, in their cars or strolling by the river Barada on their weekend outing. Survivors recounted how they were machine-gunned as they ran for cover. (Hirst, 1977: 251)

In 1973 there were further hijackings by militant Arab groups. In that year Israel had also shot down a Libyan airliner which had strayed over the occupied Sinai peninsula, killing all 106 passengers. Later, Black September militants took over the Saudi Embassy in the Sudanese capital demanding the release of Palestinian militants held in Jordanian jails. The authorities refused and a Jordanian together with an American and a Belgian diplomat were killed. There followed, in quick succession, hijackings of Japanese, American and Dutch airliners. The worst loss of life occurred at Rome airport in December 1973 when Palestinian militants killed 34, mainly American, civilians. Eleven months later a British Airways VC10 was hijacked by the Martyr Abu Mahmud Group, who called on the British government to 'declare its responsibility for the greatest crime in history, which was the establishment of the Zionist entity, and foreswear the accursed Balfour Declaration, which brought tragedies and calamities to our region' (cited in Hirst, 1977: 321–2). In the wake of this hijacking Yasser Arafat very publicly attempted to rein in the militants by arresting a number and amending the PLO criminal code to make hijacking that resulted in loss of life a capital offence (Hirst, 1977).

1974 UN 3236

The early 1970s had also seen the PLO begin to make diplomatic headway at the United Nations in its quest for institutional legitimacy and support for Palestinian nationalism. In 1970 a General Assembly resolution was passed recognising the need for Palestinian self-determination. General Assembly Resolution 2649 'condemn[ed] those Governments that deny the right to self-determination of peoples recognised as being entitled to it, especially of the peoples of southern Africa and Palestine'. In 1974 UN Resolution 3246 was passed which again stressed the need for Palestinian self-determination but also added as a corollary that it was legitimate to 'struggle for liberation from colonial and foreign domination and alien subjugation by all available means, including armed struggle'. In November 1974 the UN adopted Resolution 3236 which established UN support for the creation of a Palestinian state: 'The General Assembly ... reaffirms the inalienable rights of the Palestinian people in Palestine, including (a) the right to self-determination without external interference (b) the right to national independence and sovereignty'.

Many Israelis especially on the right disputed the whole notion of Palestinian nationalism arguing that it was a post-1967 invention created by the Arab states in order to wage a surrogate war against Israel. In 1969 the Israeli prime minister Golda Meir stated that 'It was not as though there was a Palestinian people in Palestine considering itself as a Palestinian people and we came and threw them out and took their country away from them. They did not exist' (*Sunday Times*, 15 June 1969, cited in Shlaim, 2000: 311). Similarly, Netanyahu has argued that both Palestinian Nationalism and Palestinian refugees are post-1967 fabrications:

> Indeed, most Palestinian Arabs have homes. Many of them, in fact, live as full citizens in Eastern Palestine-today called the Hashemite Kingdom of Jordan. Similarly, most of the Arabs of Judea-Samaria are not homeless refugees; they live in the same homes they occupied before the establishment of Israel. The number of actual refugees is close to nil. (Netanyahu, 2000: 156–8)

This is disputed by multilateral bodies such as the United Nations, who have explicitly recognised in many resolutions the existence of a distinct Palestinian people, their rights to national self-determination, and the existence of over 3.5 million refugees.

1973: THE OCTOBER WAR

The War of Attrition had failed to secure the return of the occupied Sinai for Egypt but had instead left many of the Suez coastal cities devastated by Israeli raids. Shlaim (2000) claims that in the early 1970s Egypt made numerous attempts to regain the occupied Sinai through diplomacy but its peace overtures were rejected by Israel.[27] Shlaim suggests Israel's 'diplomacy of attrition' together with its openly annexationist plans for the Sinai left Sadat with no diplomatic option and made war inevitable.

On 6 October 1973 Egyptian and Syrian forces attacked Israeli troop concentrations in the occupied Sinai peninsula and Golan Heights. The Arab armies achieved early successes with the Egyptian army crossing the Suez Canal and advancing into the Sinai, and the Syrian army forcing back the Israelis on the Golan Heights. Eventually the Israeli army turned the tables and regained the territorial losses it initially sustained. The war cost the lives of 2,832 Jews and 8,528 Arabs (Shlaim, 2000). There have been suggestions that the conflict nearly precipitated both a nuclear exchange between the superpowers and an Israeli nuclear strike on Egypt.[28]

The nature of the attack and the motivations of Syria and Egypt are contested. Netanyahu argues that the Arab forces had 'enormous advantages' over the Israelis, and the Israeli army had fought a 'pulverizing battle to keep the front from collapsing in the face of overwhelming numbers' (2000: 282). He claims that 'Israel's army was able, albeit by a hair's breadth, to prevent defeat in the face of a surprise attack' and that having 'so little to show for an onslaught stacked so decisively in their favour' was what brought Sadat to the negotiating table to sign a peace treaty with Israel at Camp David in 1979 (2000: 282). In contrast, Shlaim suggests that the Egyptian/Syrian attack was a limited venture designed to bring Israel to the negotiating table and force a political settlement in which the lands captured in 1967 would be returned. In an exact reversal of Netanyahu's thesis, Finkelstein (2001) argues that it was Israel who finally agreed to come to the negotiating table at Camp David after Egypt and Syria demonstrated that they possessed a 'military option'.

Following the Yom Kippur War the Arab world led by Saudi Arabia instituted an oil embargo on the West leading to a sharp rise in oil prices, which it is argued precipitated a major global recession. This again had the effect of focusing international attention on the need to resolve the conflict, or at least to neutralise some of its more dangerous elements.

CONFLICT IN LEBANON

Having been forced out of Jordan in 1970, the PLO relocated to Lebanon from where it fought a guerrilla war against the Israeli state, attacking both military and civilian targets. Sachar (1977) lists numerous deadly attacks by Palestinian infiltrators on Israelis and argues that during the mid 1970s the 'violence continued almost without respite' (1977: 810). Netanyahu notes that the PLO were using Lebanon as a base from which to fire Katyusha missiles across the border into Israel, which he maintains had a very damaging effect on the lives of those in Israel's northern settlements:

> The PLO used the territory of its de facto state to shell Israeli cities and towns. For years, the entire population of the northern border towns and villages were regularly driven into underground bomb shelters by barrages of PLO launched Katyusha missiles, the little brothers of the Scud missiles that Iraq launched against Israel in 1991. By 1982, the population levels of Kiryat Shemona and Nahariya had fallen ominously; factories, schools and beaches were being closed repeatedly to avoid mass casualties during the shellings; and fear of economic ruin and depopulation had spread. (Netanyahu, 2000: 218–19)

During this period Israel bombed PLO positions, Lebanese villages and Palestinian refugee camps. The Israeli military analyst Ze'ev Schiff justified attacks on civilians on the basis that guerrillas used the villages and refugee camps for shelter:

> In south Lebanon we struck the civilian population consciously because they deserved it ... the importance of [Mordechai] Gur's [Israeli chief of staff] remarks is the admission that the Israeli army has always struck civilian populations, purposely and consciously ... the army, he said, has never distinguished civilian [from military] targets ... [but] purposely attacked civilian targets even when Israeli settlements had not been struck. (Ha'aretz, 15 May 1978, cited in Chomsky, 1999: 181)

The Israeli Foreign Minister Abba Eban argued that 'there was a rational prospect ultimately fulfilled that affected populations would exert pressure for the cessation of hostilities' (*Jerusalem Post*, 16 August 1981, cited in Chomsky, 1999: 182). The Lebanese villagers, however, were unarmed and could do little to stop the armed guerrillas, and the Lebanese army was too weak to remove the Palestinians, who had virtually formed a state within a state. Official government casualty statistics suggest that the scale of Israeli raids was disproportionate to the Palestinian attacks. The Israeli army estimated that 106 Israeli civilians were killed in attacks by Palestinian guerrillas on Israel's northern border in the period between 1967 and the 1982 Israeli invasion (*Ha'aretz*, 22 June 1982, cited in Chomsky, 1999: 74). The American journalist Judith Coburn reported that diplomats in Beirut and UN officials estimated 3,500 Lebanese, Syrian and Jordanian civilians were killed between 1967 and 1975 by Israeli attacks. There were no figures for Palestinian civilians killed but they were estimated to be twice as high as the Lebanese. Touring Southern Lebanon in the mid 1970s Coburn found many villages 'attacked almost daily in recent months ... by airplane, artillery, tanks and gunboats' with the Israelis employing 'shells, bombs, phosphorous, incendiary bombs, CBUs [cluster bombs] and napalm' as part of what Lebanese diplomats claimed was a 'scorched earth' policy to remove the population and create a demilitarised zone (*New Times*, 7 March 1975, cited in Chomsky, 1999: 190). By 1977 it was estimated that 300,000 Lebanese Muslims had fled Southern Lebanon (*New York Times*, 2 October 1977, cited in Chomsky, 1999: 191).

The PLO continued its diplomatic offensive at the United Nations. In November 1974 the United Nations officially granted the PLO observer status and later that month Yasser Arafat addressed the UN General Assembly for the first time, giving his 'gun and olive branch' address. The leadership of the PLO argued for the ending of the armed struggle in return for the creation of a mini Palestinian state in the West Bank and Gaza Strip and a settlement of the refugee issue. This move was not accepted by all factions within the organisation, the PFLP leading the rejectionist wing which was against the concept of the mini-state and recognising the legitimacy of Israel. These moves did not impress the Israelis. Israel's Foreign Minister claimed that 'the voice of Arafat was, and remains the voice of indiscriminate terror, the voice of the gun, with nothing in it of the olive branch of peace' (cited in Hirst, 1977: 335). The call for the creation of a Palestinian mini-state between Israel and Jordan was similarly dismissed as a platform from which the PLO would attempt to destroy Israel. The Israeli daily *Yediot Ahronot* argued that 'no reasonable person ... can ask us to hand over these regions to the PLO, unless it expects Israel to commit suicide' (14 November 1974, cited in Hirst, 1977: 336).

In the mid 1970s both sides as well as Syria became involved in the Lebanese civil war. The relative stability which had prevailed in the country after the 1943 power-sharing National Pact broke down in the mid 1970s, culminating in the all-out civil war of 1975–76. To simplify greatly, the conflict concerned two rival groupings, the right-wing Christian-Maronite-Phalangist alliance backed by Israel, which was economically dominant in the country, and the predominantly poor majority leftist Muslim-Lebanese-Palestinian grouping. In mid 1976, with the leftist Muslim coalition gaining the upper hand in the conflict, the Syrians intervened on the side of the Christians occupying most of Lebanon apart from a southern strip bordering Israel. The intervention of the Syrian army at the behest of the Christians (and with the tacit support of Israel) brought a truce and relative calm to all but Southern Lebanon. The 18 months of civil war had devastated Beirut, which became partitioned, and killed tens of thousands of Palestinians and Lebanese. In April 1976 Israel and Syria reached a secret agreement with American mediation, splitting the area into 'spheres of influence'. Syria agreed to keep its troops north of the Litani river and not to install surface-to-air missiles there, recognising Southern Lebanon as Israel's security buffer.

In the mid 1970s Israel began supplying the two major Christian Maronite militias, the Phalangists and Chamouns with weapons. Jonathan Randal (1983), the former senior foreign correspondent of the *Washington Post*, suggests it was strategically useful for Israel because it tied down two of Israel's enemies, the Syrians and Palestinians, both of whom had come into conflict with the Christians by 1977. Israel was also backing General Haddad's South Lebanon Army (SLA) which was acting as its proxy force in South Lebanon. Randal (1983) notes that this was controversial because Haddad's forces had been involved in serious abuses including many instances of large-scale killings of civilians and involvement in the unlawful deaths of UN personnel. In 1978 Israel mounted a large-scale invasion of Southern Lebanon claiming that it was in response to a Palestinian attack in Israel which had left 37 Israelis and nine Palestinians dead. The scale and effects of the invasion are disputed. Gilbert claims that 'several dozen PLO soldiers were killed or captured' and 'all PLO installations were systematically destroyed' (1999: 490). Randal claims it was civilians rather than guerrillas who bore the brunt of the attack:

> The destruction was on a scale well known in Vietnam. Aping the prodigal use of American firepower in Indochina, the Israelis sought to keep their own casualties to a minimum – and succeeded. But they failed to wipe out the Palestinian commandos, who had plenty of time to scamper to safety north of the Litani River. Piling mattresses, clothes and families in taxis and overloaded pickup trucks, more than two hundred thousand Lebanese also fled north out of harm's way. They became exiles in their own country, squatters seizing unoccupied apartments, the source of yet more tension in West Beirut. The Israelis did succeed in massive killing: almost all the victims were Lebanese civilians – some one thousand according to the International Committee of the Red Cross. More than six thousand homes were badly damaged or destroyed. Half a dozen villages were all but levelled in a frenzy of violence in which Israeli troops committed atrocities. (Randal, 1983: 209)

After three months, under pressure from the United Nations who condemned the attack, the IDF withdrew from Southern Lebanon to be replaced by a UN force. Most of the positions abandoned by the IDF were taken by the SLA. In January 1979 Ezer Weizman, the Israeli Defence Secretary, announced a controversial pre-emptive policy against Palestinian guerrillas in Southern Lebanon. He declared that Israel would not only strike in retaliation but 'at any time and any place that Israel deemed desirable' (cited in Randal, 1983: 220). In 1981 hostilities escalated in Lebanon. On 17 July Israel launched a major bombing raid on Southern Lebanon hitting refugee camps, ports, Lebanon's main oil refinery and all but one of the bridges over the Litani and Zahrani rivers (Randal, 1983). The Israelis claimed that the raids were necessary to deal with a PLO arms build-up in Southern Lebanon. The Palestinians held fire for three days and then began shelling and rocketing Northern Israel. On 17 July Israel bombed the Fakhani district in West Beirut, home to the PLO offices. More than 120 Palestinian and Lebanese civilians were killed, leading to international condemnation of the raid. The Palestinians then launched artillery attacks on 28 Israeli towns and settlements, damaging crops and orchards, whilst tens of thousands of Israelis were temporarily forced to flee their homes in northern

Israel (Randal, 1983). In the wake of this exchange both sides agreed to an American-brokered ceasefire.

DIPLOMACY AND THE CAMP DAVID ACCORDS

During this period a number of attempts were made by the Palestinians to push for a peace settlement. Palestinian representatives backed a United Nations Security Council resolution in January 1976 which called for a two-state solution on the 1967 borders 'with appropriate arrangements ... to guarantee ... the sovereignty, territorial integrity and political independence of all states in the area and their right to live in peace within secure and recognised boundaries' (UN Security Council Resolution S/11940). The resolution received nine votes in favour, including France and the Soviet Union, but was blocked by a single vote against from the United States. Chomsky (1999) points to PLO acceptance of the Soviet-American peace plan of October 1977, the Soviet peace plan of 1981 and the Saudi 1982 peace plan as well as a number of public statements by PLO representatives in the late 1970s to suggest that the Palestinians were proposing to end the armed struggle in exchange for the creation of a mini-state in Gaza and the West Bank.[29] He notes that all such overtures were rejected by Israel. Some Israelis such as Binyamin Netanyahu have dismissed all Palestinian peace overtures as part of an attempt to force Israel to accept a PLO 'Trojan horse' whose purpose is to destroy the Israeli state. He argues that after the 1973 war the Palestinians realised they couldn't destroy Israel with a 'frontal military assault' but were planning 'an interim phase in which Israel would be reduced to dimensions that made it more convenient for the coup de grace'. This would be achieved in two phases: 'first create a Palestinian state on any territory vacated by Israel' and 'second mobilize from that state a general Arab military assault to destroy a shrunken and indefensible Israel' (Netanyahu, 2000: 239). Netanyahu claims that the Arabs have been deceiving the Western nations with a moderate front:

> For the PLO is a Pan-Arab Trojan Horse, a gift that the Arabs have been trying to coax the Arabs into accepting for over twenty years, so that the West in turn can force Israel to let it in at the gates. The Arabs paint their gift up prettily with legitimacy with the pathos of its plight, with expressions for the cherished ideas of freedom, justice, and peace. Yet no matter how it is dressed up to conceal the fact, the ultimate aim of the gift remains: to be allowed within

Israel's defensive wall, to be parked on the hills overlooking Tel-Aviv, where it can perform its grisly task. Every inch of Western acceptance – the cover stories, the banquets, the observer status, the embassies, and any territory the PLO has been able to get its hands on – it uses to push ever closer to its goal. (Netanyahu, 2000: 256)

In March 1978, 350 Israeli reservists sent a letter to Menachem Begin which accused the government of preferring to build settlements and create a 'Greater Israel' rather than make peace with the Arab world. This was partly in response to Prime Minister Begin's decision to support the creation of a number of new Gush Emunim settlements deep in the occupied territories. The letter marked the creation of the Peace Now movement which in September 1978 organised a mass rally of 100,000 Israelis in Tel Aviv, the largest political demonstration in the state's history. The European Economic Community also pushed for a solution to the conflict during 1979. Leaders of the EEC meeting in Venice in June 1979 issued statements supportive of Palestinian statehood, and the president-elect of the European Commission, Gaston Thorn, travelled to the Middle East and met Yasser Arafat. The PLO was recognised by Ireland and Austria and Giscard d'Estaing recommended the group be accepted as a partner in peace negotiations. The Europeans also attempted to widen Resolution 242 to include Palestinian self-determination. Ovendale (1999) claims that the United States made it clear that it would veto any European resolution in the Security Council which supported Palestinian rights.

In March 1979 Israel signed a peace agreement with Egypt in Washington, on terms very similar to the ones rejected by Israel in 1972. The progress to the final settlement had been long and tortuous, involving diplomacy stretching over several continents and many years. Israel agreed to hand back the Sinai peninsula in exchange for a comprehensive peace treaty and demilitarisation of most of the Sinai. Both parties had compromised. Israel agreed to remove the settlements and airfields, Egypt dropped the issue of Jerusalem, and the two sides agreed on only a vague autonomy plan for the Palestinians that would be implemented in stages over a number of years. The two signatories took a great deal of criticism over the conclusion of the peace treaty. Begin was attacked by the right and religious parties for returning the Sinai, while Sadat was criticised for breaking with Arab unity by signing a peace treaty with Israel without having achieved a deal on Jerusalem, Palestinian statehood or a full Israeli withdrawal from Arab territory. Finkelstein (2001) suggests that the Israeli government agreed to peace with Egypt because it would neutralise the most powerful Arab military force threatening it, and subsequently allow it to break the nexus of the Palestinian national movement in Lebanon. On 30 July 1980 the Israeli government formally annexed all of Jerusalem, and the following year the Golan Heights were annexed in violation of the Israel–Egypt peace agreement and Resolution 242. Both annexations drew immediate condemnation from the UN Security Council (Resolutions 478 and 497) who declared the annexations illegal and demanded their rescission. The plans for Palestinian autonomy were not developed. Shlaim suggests that the Begin administration deliberately sabotaged the autonomy negotiations and expanded expropriations of Palestinian land and settlement building because it wanted to retain control over the West Bank and Gaza Strip:

> Begin managed the autonomy talks in such a way that nothing could possibly be achieved. The first sign was Begin's appointment of Dr. Yosef Burg, the minister of the interior, to head Israel's six-man negotiating team. Burg was the leader of the National Religious Party, which saw Israel's right to Judea and Samaria [the West Bank] as embedded in Scripture and supported the settlement activities of Gush Emunim. (Shlaim, 2000: 381–2)

1982: THE INVASION OF LEBANON

On 6 June 1982 Israel invaded Lebanon and attacked PLO forces. It also engaged the Syrian army in its drive towards Beirut. In the early days of the conflict the *Economist* correspondent G.H. Jansen reported that the Israeli policy was to surround towns and cities 'so swiftly that civilian inhabitants were trapped inside, and then to pound them from land, sea and air. After a couple of days there would be a timid probing attack: if there was resistance the pounding would resume' (*Middle East International*, 2 July 1982, cited in Chomsky, 1999: 219). By the time an American-sponsored ceasefire came into effect on 11 June the Israeli army had reached the southern outskirts of Beirut. Shlaim (2000) suggests that Israel was expecting its Christian allies in Lebanon, led by Bashir Gemayel, to attack the PLO forces who by this time were trapped in West Beirut. However, Gemayel was reluctant to take on the Palestinians and the Israelis did not want to get involved in potentially costly street-fighting. By 13 June the Israelis had surrounded Beirut and for the next two months they laid siege to the city and bombarded it with heavy weaponry. The Israeli commander Ariel Sharon, who led the Israeli attack, claimed that 'no army in the history of modern warfare ever took such pains to prevent civilian casualties as did the Israeli Defence Forces' and that the 'Jewish doctrine' of *tohar haneshek* (purity of arms) was adhered to 'scrupulously' with the Israeli army 'attacking only predetermined PLO positions and in bombing and shelling buildings only when they served as PLO strongholds' (*New York Times*, 29 August 1982, cited in Chomsky, 1999: 243–4). Gilbert (1999) also stresses that the Israelis concentrated their attacks on PLO strongholds, although he notes that on one occasion a hospital was seriously damaged. Other reports from journalists in Beirut suggested that the Israeli bombing was more indiscriminate. The *Independent* journalist Robert Fisk claimed the Israelis were employing 'time-on-target salvos' which 'laid 50 shells at a time' across residential areas 'slaughtering everyone within a 500 yard radius of the explosions' (2001: 284). He also claimed that the Israelis used cluster bombs, and phosphorus bombs, which were designed to create fires and cause untreatable burns. The Israeli daily *Ha'aretz* reported that vacuum bombs, which ignite aviation fuel in such a way as to create immense pressure and literally implode large buildings, were also used by the IDF (11 August 1982, cited in Chomsky, 1999: 214). Chris Giannou, a Canadian surgeon who had been working in a Palestinian hospital, testified before the US Congress that he had witnessed the 'total, utter devastation of residential areas, and the blind, savage, indiscriminate destruction of refugee camps by simultaneous shelling and carpet bombing from aircraft, gunboats, tanks and artillery'. He testified that cluster bombs and phosphorus bombs had been used widely in residential areas and that he had seen 'savage and indiscriminate beatings' of prisoners, which were sometimes fatal, as well as frequent use of torture.[30] The bombing intensified during July and August and Hirsh Goodman reported that it continued even after an agreement in principle for the PLO to leave had been reached (*Jerusalem Post*, 1 October 1982, cited in Chomsky, 1999: 241). In July supplies of food, water, medicines and fuel to the city were cut. By 4 August Elaine Carey reported that eight of the nine orphanages in Beirut had been destroyed by cluster and phosphorus bombs, despite clear markings and Israeli assurances that they would be spared (*Christian Science Monitor*, 4 August 1982, cited in Chomsky, 1999: 225). On 12 August the bombing reached a peak. The American journalist Charles Powers argued that:

> To many the siege of Beirut seemed gratuitous brutality ... The arsenal of weapons unleashed in a way that has not been seen since the Vietnam war, clearly horrified those who saw the results firsthand and through film and news reports at a distance. The use of cluster bombs and white phosphorus shells, a vicious weapon, was widespread ... In the last hours of the last air attack on Beirut, Israeli planes carpet bombed Borg el Brajne [a refugee camp]. There were no fighting men left there, only the damaged homes of Palestinian families, who once again would have to leave and find another place to live. (*Los Angeles Times*, 29 August 1982, cited in Chomsky, 1999: 242)

Eventually at the end of August the PLO forces were evacuated from Beirut to Tunis. Outside Beirut there were reports of widespread destruction of refugee camps and Lebanese villages. In Sidon, Fisk claims over 2,000 Lebanese civilians were killed in air attacks he describes as 'the most ferocious ever delivered upon a Lebanese city' (2001: 204). Olof Rydbeck, head of the UN refugee agency that administered the camps, said that 32 years of work had been 'wiped out' with 'practically all of the schools, clinics and installations of the agency in ruins' (*New York Times*, 19 August 1982, cited in Chomsky, 1999: 223). The scale of civilian and PLO casualties during the war are contested. Gilbert (1999) claims that 460 Lebanese civilians and 6,000 PLO fighters were killed. The Lebanese police estimated 19,085 killed through to August with 6,775 killed in Beirut, 84 per cent of them civilians (*Christian Science Monitor*, 21 December 1982, cited in Chomsky, 1999: 221). The United Nations estimated 13,500 houses severely damaged in West Beirut and thousands more in other parts of the country, not taking into account damage to the refugee camps which were towns themselves (*Christian Science Monitor*, 18 November 1982, cited in Chomsky, 1999: 223). There were also reports that all the teenage and adult Lebanese and Palestinian males were taken to camps where they were humiliated and tortured.[31] Chomsky cites testimony from IDF Lieutenant Colonel Dov Yirmiah which appeared in the Israeli press on the fate of Palestinian and Lebanese detainees:

He tells story after story of prisoners savagely and endlessly beaten in captivity, of torture and humiliation of prisoners, and of the many who died of beatings and thirst in Israeli prisons or concentration camps in Lebanon ... The long and repeated interrogations were accompanied by constant beatings, or attacks by dogs on leashes, or the use of air rifles that cause intense pain but do not kill ... New loads of clubs had to be brought into the camps to replace those broken under interrogation. The torturers were 'experts in their work,' the prisoners report, and knew how to make blows most painful, including blows to the genitals, until the prisoners confessed that they were 'terrorists'. (Chomsky 1999: 240)

Other reports in the Israeli press claimed that members of Israel's proxy militia the South Lebanon Army were allowed into the camps to torture prisoners and that some gang-raped women and attempted to force them to have sex with dogs (*Koteret Rashit*, 16 March 1983, cited in Chomsky, 1999: 236). After the PLO had agreed to leave Lebanon, one of the war's most notorious incidents occurred at the refugee camps at Shatila and Sabra. After the departure of the PLO from Lebanon, the Israeli forces sealed off the Sabra and Shatila refugee camps on 16 September and allowed between 100 and 130 Phalangist and Haddadist troops in. Ariel Sharon claimed that the camps contained 2,000 well armed Palestinian fighters and the Christian forces had been sent in to clear them out. However, Edward Walsh argues that 'no one has publicly explained how the Israelis expected 100 to 130 Phalangists to defeat such a force of Palestinians' (*Washington Post*, 26 December 1982, cited in Chomsky, 1999: 369), and in a visit to the camp a few days before the killings journalists reported finding no military presence (*Time*, 4 October 1982, cited in Chomsky, 1999: 369). Once in the camps the Phalangist forces raped and killed many of the camps inhabitants who were primarily women, children and the elderly. The death toll is disputed. The official Israeli Kahan Commission estimated 700–800 killed, the Lebanese authorities put the figure at approximately 2,000, whilst the Israeli journalist Amnon Kapeliouk (1984), citing evidence from the International Committee of the Red Cross, estimated 3,000–3,500. Responsibility for the killings has also been partly attributed to the United States who gave explicit assurances that the Muslim civilian population of West Beirut would be protected as part of the PLO deal to evacuate Beirut (Ovendale, 1999). The massacres were condemned by the United Nations by 147 votes to 2 (Israel and the

US), and lawyers in Belgium have since attempted to indict the Israel commanders Ariel Sharon and Amos Yaron for war crimes.

The Lebanon war appeared to split Israeli society. Some questioned whether the scale of death and destruction inflicted on Southern Lebanon was proportionate to the threat posed by Palestinian militants. In 1983 a debate on Zionism was held at Tel Aviv University where Aluf Hareven of the Van Leer Institute commented:

> According to the figures provided by the Ministry of the Interior Yosef Burg, in 1980, 10 Jews were killed by terrorists and in 1981 – 8. In contrast we have killed about a thousand terrorists in 1982, and caused the loss of life of thousands of inhabitants of an enemy country. If so, it results that for every 6–8 Jews sacrificed, we kill in return thousands of Gentiles. This is undoubtedly a spectacular situation, an uncommon success of Zionism. I might even dare to say – exaggerated. (*Migvan*, October/November 1982, cited in Chomsky 1999: 74)

The massacres at Sabra and Shatila also led to the largest protests in Israel's history. On 25 September 1982 more than 400,000 Israelis joined a Peace Now demonstration in Tel Aviv. Others suggested that a large part of the population was unconcerned if not approving of the events at the refugee camps:

> In the matter of Sabra and Shatila – a large part of the community, perhaps the majority, is not at all troubled by the massacre itself. Killing of Arabs in general, and Palestinians in particular, is quite popular, or at least 'doesn't bother anyone' in the words of youth these days. Ever since the massacre I have been surprised to hear from educated, enlightened people, 'the conscience of Tel Aviv', the view that the massacre itself, as a step towards removing the remaining Palestinians from Lebanon is not terrible. It is just too bad that we were in the neighbourhood. (*Ha'aretz*, 19 November 1982, cited in Chomsky, 1999: 395)

Israel's motives for launching the attack are contested. Mitchell Bard (2003), the director of the American-Israeli Cooperative Institute, points to three reasons for Israel's decision to attack Lebanon. Firstly, he claims that the PLO was repeatedly breaching the ceasefire negotiated by the Americans in July 1981 and attacking Israelis across the Lebanese border. Secondly, he alleges that 15,000–

18,000 PLO members were encamped in Southern Lebanon and were equipping themselves with a huge arsenal including rockets, surface-to-air missiles, mortars, tanks and enough weapons to arm five brigades. He suggests that Israeli strikes and commando raids could not prevent the emergence of this 'PLO army'. Finally, Bard points to the attempt on the life of the Israeli ambassador to London, Shlomo Argov, by the Abu Nidal group. All of these explanations have been disputed.[32] Shlaim suggests that Israel had two objectives: to create a new political order in Lebanon and to 'destroy the PLO's military infrastructure in Lebanon and to undermine it as a political organisation' (2000: 396). Former IDF education officer Mordechai Bar-on argued that 'there is no doubt that the [war's] central aim was to deal a crushing blow to the national aspirations of the Palestinians and to their very existence as a nation endeavouring to define itself and gain the right to self-determination' (*New Outlook*, October 1982, cited in Chomsky, 1999: 203). With the PLO infrastructure destroyed and the refugees dispersed, some commentators suggested that the organisation might revert to hijacking and therefore undermine its growing political status:

> If the PLO were now thrown out of Lebanon – or, better yet, reduced to mad dog terrorism that would destroy its growing political and diplomatic legitimacy – then Israel stood a better chance of annexing the West Bank and Gaza strip still thoroughly loyal to Arafat's leadership despite his many errors. (Randal, 1983: 250)

Shlaim (2000) suggests that another aspect of Sharon's 'big plan' was to install Israel's Christian ally Bashir Gemayel in power in Lebanon and force the Palestinian refugees out of Lebanon to Jordan, leading to the overthrow of the Hashemite monarchy and its conversion to a Palestinian state, thereby weakening international pressure on Israel to vacate the West Bank and allowing Israel to annex the territory. Neither of the larger geostrategic aims were achieved. Bashir Gemayel was assassinated shortly after the war whilst the Hashemite monarchy remained intact in Jordan.

In the aftermath of the Sabra and Shatila killings, American marines returned to Lebanon as part of a multinational force. However, they soon came into conflict with Shia and Druze forces opposed to Israel's occupation of Southern Lebanon. When US warships shelled Druze positions, it appeared that the US had entered the civil war in support of the Christian-Israeli alliance. On 23 October a suicide bomber killed 256 American and 58 French troops, leading to the withdrawal of American and European forces. A Shiite group with links to Iran later claimed responsibility for the attack. Ovendale (1999) claims that after the 1982 war Israel and the United States strengthened their political and military ties by embarking on joint weapons projects. In 1986 the Israeli nuclear technician Mordechai Vanunu revealed in a *Sunday Times* interview the existence of Israel's substantial nuclear arsenal, revelations which were to earn the Israeli an 18-year prison term. Recent newspaper reports suggest that the Israeli nuclear arsenal has increased to approximately 200 warheads, many of which are fitted to American-supplied Harpoon cruise missiles capable of hitting any of Israel's Arab neighbours (*Observer*, 12 October 2003).

In the mid 1980s further attempts were also made to find a negotiated solution to the conflict. In February 1985 Yasser Arafat and King Hussein of Jordan issued the Amman Declaration which proposed Palestinian self-determination within a Palestinian-Jordanian confederation. The composition of the negotiating team proved a problem, with Israel refusing to negotiate with any PLO members. Margaret Thatcher attempted to push the plan and proposed a peace conference to include PLO members. However, the plans were derailed by a series of events. Firstly, Abu Nidal, backed by Syria, threatened to assassinate any PLO members who accepted Thatcher's invitation. Then on 25 September 1985 three Israelis were killed on a boat in Larnaca. The Israeli government blamed the PLO. The PLO claimed the three were Mossad agents. Israel then dispatched a number of American-made F-16 fighters to bomb the PLO headquarters in Tunis. In the attack, 58 Palestinians and 15 Tunisians were killed. The attack was supported by the US but condemned by the European Community and the United Nations. Soon afterwards a small Palestinian group, the Palestine Liberation Front, hijacked the *Achille Lauro* and killed an elderly disabled Jewish passenger before surrendering. Following the hijacking the US pressurised Britain to cancel a scheduled meeting between the Foreign Secretary and PLO members. Britain then insisted that the PLO members sign a statement denouncing all forms of political violence. The PLO members refused, arguing that this would cover armed resistance to the Israeli occupation of the West Bank and Gaza Strip, and the meeting was cancelled. Soon afterwards King Hussein of Jordan announced the end of his collaboration with the PLO leadership, blaming Arafat's refusal to accept Resolutions 242 and 338. In the wake of this rupture between the PLO and Jordan, King Hussein and Shimon Peres kept close diplomatic links and considered ways of restarting peace talks whilst excluding any members of the PLO from negotiations (Shlaim, 2000). Israel's pursuance of the 'Jordanian option', Shlaim suggests, was blocked by the Israeli premier Yitzak Shamir who was opposed to any international conference which might involve pressure from outside mediators.

1987: THE FIRST INTIFADA

On 9 December 1987, following the death of four Gazans the previous day in a road traffic incident, Palestinians from the Jebalya refugee camp began throwing stones at an Israeli army compound. Within days unrest spread to the West Bank. Unarmed Palestinian men, women, and children attacked Israeli soldiers and armoured personnel carriers. Benny Morris claims that the intifada was 'not an armed rebellion but a massive, persistent campaign of civil resistance, with strikes and commercial shutdowns accompanied by violent (though unarmed) demonstrations against the occupying forces' (1992: 561). The factors behind the intifada, which was to last six years until it was called off by the Palestinian leadership in the wake of the Oslo agreements, are contested. Netanyahu has argued that the Israeli administration in the occupied territories had instituted a 'liberal policy aimed at radically improving the lives of the Palestinians' and that material and educational prosperity had gone hand in hand with political rights, including 'a press consisting of newspapers representing various factions (some openly sympathetic to the PLO) and the right to directly appeal all decisions to the democratic court system' (2000: 176). He argues that the impetus for the intifada was 'virulent PLO agitation' that led the population in the occupied territories to adopt 'ever more extreme and implacable positions' (2000: 177). He also claims that the PLO had forced children out of their schools to take part in confrontations with Israeli forces. Gilbert blames Jordan for not integrating the Palestinians living in the West Bank into Jordanian society before 1967, and argues that the impetus for the intifada came from a 'bitter hard core of extremists who were prepared to face Israeli bullets in order to defy the occupiers and assert their national identity' (1999: 525). Some Israelis blamed outside agitation for the intifada. Yitzak Rabin accused Iran and Syria of fermenting unrest. Others have questioned whether Israeli policy in the occupied territories was really liberal and suggest that the intifada was the result of severe and persistent human rights abuses.

A report by the Israeli Committee for Solidarity with Bir Zeit (the West Bank University periodically closed by the Israeli authorities) described the Israeli administration in the occupied territories as an 'attempt to revive an old well-known colonial method in a new "original" Israeli form' in order to create 'an Israeli Bantustan, which imposes on the Palestinians the role of hewers of wood and drawers of water for Israeli society'. To achieve this the report claimed that there was widespread and violent suppression of all forms of political activity, and that 'quislings from the Village Leagues' together with settler groups inflicted 'humiliation, harassment and terror' on the Palestinian population.[33] The United Nations also produced a number of reports in the mid 1980s which were critical of Israeli human rights abuses in the occupied territories and pointed to widespread acts of violence committed against Palestinians by armed settlers.[34] Israel Shahak argues that such abuses were the main factor behind the intifada and cites examples from the Israeli press:

> In fact, before the intifada, the daily oppression, humiliations, land confiscations and arbitrariness of the Israeli regime were steadily increasing. This increase, duly recorded by the Hebrew press, was the chief reason for the outbreak of the intifada. Readers of Israel's Hebrew-language press are aware of how outrageously the Israeli armed forces were behaving before the intifada. On June 19, 1987, Eyal Ehrlich reported in an article in *Ha'aretz* headlined, 'An occupier against his will,' the testimony of a young Israeli soldier assigned to serve in the border guards. Whenever a Palestinian is accosted to show his I.D., the soldier wrote, its checking is always accompanied by 'a slap, a punch, a kick.' 'The border guards usually enjoy beating the Arabs,' the account continues. 'They derive pleasure from it ... Sometimes I feel like a Nazi when I watch my friends in action. I try hard to stay away from one of my commanders ... He always behaves very badly toward the locals: with violence, beatings, and the like ... The soldiers spit in the faces of the Arabs, or they kick them in the testicles. And there is always that slap in the face.' An article in *Hadashot* of July 7, 1987 by Menahem Shizaf was headlined, 'Border guards order the Arabs to masturbate and to lick the floor.' It described the treatment meted out to Palestinian workers from the occupied territories who were found spending the night in shacks in Israel rather than returning to their homes. (*Washington Report on Middle East Affairs*, March 1991)

The Israeli Minister of Defence Yitzak Rabin explained that the Israeli response to the intifada would consist of 'force, might, beatings' (*New York Times*, 23 January 1988, cited in the *New York Review of Books*, 17 March 1988), whilst Prime Minister Shamir was reported in the Israeli publication *Hadashot* as warning those protesting against the occupation that they would be crushed 'like grasshoppers' with their heads 'smashed against the boulders and walls' and that 'we say to them from the heights of this mountain and from the perspective of thousands of years of history that they are like grasshoppers compared to us' (6 January 1988, cited in Chomsky, 1999: 482). By February 1988 the intifada became formalised with the establishment of the United National Leadership of the Uprising. The organisation encouraged strikes amongst those who worked in Israel and attacks on the Israeli administrative structure. Taxes were withheld, those who worked as administrators and tax collectors resigned and Israeli goods were boycotted (Ovendale, 1999). Roadblocks were set up to keep out the Israeli army and Palestinians tried to create an alternative system of local self-government independent of the military authority.

In February 1988 the United States attempted to put forward a peace plan based on Palestinian autonomy in the occupied territories. The plan was rejected by Israel, and the PLO who noted it made no mention of statehood. In April Abu Jihad, the PLO second in command, was assassinated by Israel in Tunis. The Tunisian government complained to the United Nations Security Council. The Israeli daily *Ma'ariv* later reported that the future prime minister, Ehud Barak, had directed the assassination from a navy ship off Tunis (4 July 1988). In July King Hussein of Jordan announced that his country was severing its links with the West Bank, effectively killing the 'Jordanian option' that had long been favoured by the US and some Israeli leaders. In September Yasser Arafat told the European Parliament in Strasbourg that the PLO would accept Israel's right to security if Israel recognised a Palestinian mini-state. In November the Palestinian National Council meeting in Algiers agreed to recognise Israel, as well as all UN resolutions dating back to 1947 and to forswear its claim to all of mandatory Palestine. It also proclaimed the establishment of the state of Palestine with East Jerusalem as its capital. The Israeli prime minister, Shamir, dismissed the resolutions as a 'deceptive propaganda exercise, intended to create the impression of moderation and of achievements for those carrying out violent acts in the territories of Judea and Samaria' (cited in Shlaim, 2000: 466). Yasser Arafat wanted to appeal to the UN General Assembly, but despite being recognised by more than 60 nations the United States refused him an entry visa (Ovendale, 1999). The General Assembly then voted to hold its plenary session in Geneva, and Arafat, under strong pressure from US Secretary of State George Shultz, announced that the PLO accepted Resolutions 242 and 338, as well as Israel's right to exist, and renounced 'terrorism'.

Meanwhile, Israel's response to the intifada was attracting widespread international criticism. By January 1989 the US State Department reported that the unrest had claimed the lives of eleven Israelis and 366 Palestinians. Some on the Israeli right argued that the criticism of Israel and media coverage of the intifada was biased and unfair, and that the Israeli response was restrained and proportionate:

> Ignoring the Arab reign of terror in the Palestinian streets, the media created for themselves nightly instalments of a popular romance drama: heroic underdog in search of self-determination taking on a terrifying Israeli tyrant ... Since viewers were being told this was an 'army of occupation' – that is, it had no right to be there in the first place – the media managed to transform even the most necessary aspects of maintaining law and order into unforgivable crimes. Utterly lost from the images on the screen was the organised nature of the rioting, the internecine violence, and the terrorised lives of the innocent Arabs (and Jews) who were ground under the intifada's heel. Similarly lost were the restrictive firing orders that stayed the hand of every Israeli soldier, and the swift trial of the 208 Israelis who in any way disobeyed these orders – as against the tens of thousands of Israeli soldiers and reservists who followed the regulations with impeccable restraint. (Netanyahu, 2000: 181–2)

The United Nations, NGOs, human rights groups and some Israeli soldiers disputed this. In December 1988 the United Nations General Assembly passed a resolution by 106 to 2 (Israel and the US) which condemned the conduct of the IDF and settlers during the intifada. The resolution 'Declare[d] once more that Israel's grave breaches of that Convention are war crimes and an affront to humanity'. Amongst many criticisms the resolution 'strongly condemned' the

> implementation of an 'iron-fist' policy against the Palestinian people ... the escalation of Israeli brutality since the beginning

of the uprising ... the ill-treatment and torture of children and minors under detention and/or imprisonment ... the killing and wounding of defenceless demonstrators ... the breaking of bones and limbs of thousands of civilians ... the usage of toxic gas, which resulted, inter alia, in the killing of many Palestinians. (United Nations, 1988)

Israel was particularly criticised for its treatment of children during the intifada. A 1,000-page Save the Children study documented the 'indiscriminate beating, tear-gassing, and shooting of children'. The report found that the average age of the victims was ten years old and that the majority of those who were shot were not participating in stone-throwing. The report also alleged that in 80 per cent of cases where children were shot the Israeli army prevented the victims from receiving medical attention. The report concluded that more than 50,000 children required medical attention for injuries including gun-shot wounds, tear-gas inhalation and multiple fractures (report cited in Finkelstein, 1996: 47). The August 1989 bulletin from the Israeli League for Human and Civil Rights was entitled 'Deliberate Murder' and reported on the targeting of Palestinian children in leadership roles. It found that the Israeli army and snipers from 'special units' had 'carefully chosen' the children who were shot in the head or heart and died instantaneously (report cited in Finkelstein, 1996: 47). Other reports from Israeli human rights groups and articles in the Israeli press also allege that torture, including severe beatings and electric shocks, were used extensively against detainees, including children.[35]

The intifada also saw the birth of Hamas, the Islamic opposition movement formed by Sheikh Yassin in February 1988. The organisation, which emerged out of the Muslim Brotherhood, stressed a return to conservative Islamic values and provided a network of health and social services for Palestinians in the occupied territories. For many years the organisation received extensive funding from Israel (Chomsky, 1999; Shlaim, 2000; Mishal and Sela, 2000). Shlaim claims that this was done 'in the hope of weakening the secular nationalism of the PLO' (2000: 459). Chomsky (1999) suggests such a weakening would be beneficial to Israel because it would allow them to evade a political solution to the conflict which might involve returning the occupied territories. The Hamas charter issued in August 1988 argued that all of Palestine belonged to the Muslim nation as a religious endowment and that it was each Muslim's duty to engage in jihad (religious war) to 'liberate' Palestine. The degree to which its intentions match its rhetoric is disputed. Most Israelis regard the organisation as fundamentalist and uncompromising, dedicated to killing Jews and destroying the Israeli state. Two Israeli academics, Shaul Mishal and Avraham Sela, suggest that the organisation is more complex and pragmatic than this. They suggest that Hamas utilises 'controlled violence' as a 'means rather than an end' to mobilise political support and is 'cognizant of power relations and political feasibility' (2000: vii). They argue that its main purpose has been to establish itself as a major force in Palestinian political life and that in the future it 'may find that it can accept a workable formula of co-existence with Israel in place of armed struggle' (2000: ix). In 1989 the group's founder, Sheikh Yassin, was arrested by Israel, and in the occupied territories the Israelis increased their use of deportations and curfews in an attempt to suppress the intifada. They also outlawed the committees administering the uprising. This was a problem for Palestinians as they saw the committees as the nucleus of the self-governing institutions they hoped to build once the occupation ended.

In 1989 Yitzak Shamir put forward an initiative which proposed elections and expanded Palestinian autonomy in exchange for the ending of the intifada. Shamir set down certain preconditions: there would be no Palestinian state, no PLO involvement (even if its representatives triumphed in the elections) and no participation in the elections for the inhabitants of East Jerusalem. The plans were eventually derailed by members of Shamir's own cabinet, principally Ariel Sharon, David Levy and Yitzhak Moda'i, who argued that Israel was giving too much away and was adopting too liberal an attitude to the intifada (Shlaim, 2000). Egypt and the United States then put forward their own peace initiatives. These precipitated a split in what was then a National Unity government in Israel, which led to its downfall. One part of the government, the Labour Alignment, unsuccessfully urged Shamir to accept the American initiative, whilst some members of the right-wing Likud Party felt Israel was making too many concessions and not cracking down sufficiently hard on the intifada. For six weeks the Labour Party's Shimon Peres tried unsuccessfully to form a new coalition, and eventually Yitzak Shamir formed one in which his Likud Party linked up with ultra-nationalist and religious parties. This new coalition which Shlaim (2000) claims was the most right-wing and hard-line (in its attitudes to the Arabs) in Israel's history, immediately announced that it would end the intifada, create new settlements and expand existing ones. It also insisted there would be no Palestinian state, no negotiation with the PLO and no sharing of Jerusalem.

The intifada, which continued to smoulder during this period, was reignited in October 1990 when Israeli troops killed 21 Palestinians on the Temple Mount in Jerusalem. The Israelis claimed they had responded to acts of stone-throwing directed at Israeli worshippers. The Palestinians claimed that the stone-throwing only began after the Israelis started shooting. The United Nations Security Council condemned the killings, but Israel managed to prevent the United Nations from acting on Palestinian demands to replace the Israeli military government in the occupied territories with a UN force (Ovendale, 1999).

In August 1990 the Iraq war intervened when Saddam Hussein invaded Kuwait and occupied the country. Five months later an American-led coalition attacked Iraq, forcing its withdrawal from Kuwait. Both the Palestinians in the occupied territories and the PLO leadership allied themselves with Saddam Hussein because of the Iraqi dictator's attempt to make a 'linkage' between Iraqi withdrawal from Kuwait and Israeli withdrawal from the occupied territories, and because he struck at the Israeli state with scud missiles. In doing so the Palestinian leadership effectively lost much of the political capital it had built up over many years, whilst Israel benefited internationally by not responding to the Iraqi attacks. In the aftermath of the war the US moved to bring Israel and its Arab adversaries together in an international peace conference.

THE BEGINNING OF THE OSLO PROCESS

In Madrid at the end of October 1991 an Israeli delegation met Palestinian and other representatives from Israel's 'confrontation states' (Syria, Jordan and Lebanon). Although the Palestinian representatives were pro-PLO, they were not publicly stated as being members of the organisation, as this would have landed them in jail under Israeli law. The Americans who set up the conference insisted that it be based around UN Resolutions 242 and 338 and the principle of 'land for peace'. This premise was accepted by the Palestinians but rejected by the Israelis (Shlaim, 2000). In the run-up to the conference the Likud administration announced a new wave of settlement building designed to double the settler population in the occupied territories in four years. Little progress was made in negotiations either at Madrid or in the five rounds of bilateral talks which took place in Washington. Shlaim argues that an 'immense gap' separated the parties:

> The Palestinians started with the assumption that they were a people with national rights and that the interim arrangements under discussion were the precursor to independence and should be shaped accordingly. The Israeli government started with the assumption that the Palestinians were the inhabitants of the territories with no national rights of any kind and certainly no rights to independence, not even after the end of the transitional period. (Shlaim, 2000: 493)

In June 1992 the Israeli population went to the polls to elect a new administration. The Likud Party pledged to continue the peace process whilst retaining all the occupied territories and expanding settlement building. The Labour Party vowed to conclude a deal on Palestinian autonomy, to allow residents of East Jerusalem to take part in negotiations and to freeze the construction of the 'political settlements' deep in the occupied territory. Labour won the election under Yitzak Rabin in a major political swing which ended 15 years of Likud rule. In an Israeli newspaper interview just after his election defeat Shamir declared that 'I would have carried on autonomy talks for ten years, and meanwhile we would have reached half a million people in Judea and Samaria' (Ma'ariv, 26 June 1992).

Over the next 20 months Israelis and Palestinians sympathetic to but not members of the PLO engaged in ten rounds of negotiations in Washington that produced no tangible results. In the middle of those negotiations Rabin deported 416 Hamas activists to Lebanon following the killing of an Israeli border policeman. This move, which was condemned by the UN as a breach of international law, was intended to curb Hamas' influence but actually had the opposite effect. Mishal and Sela argue that the deportations were a 'milestone in Hamas' decision to use car bombs and suicide attacks as a major modus operandi against Israel', because they came into contact with Hezbullah guerrillas who provided training in such techniques (2000: 65–6). They note that Hamas first used suicide attacks shortly after the return of the deportees to the occupied territories.[36]

THE DECLARATION OF PRINCIPLES

While the official negotiations continued the Israelis decided to open up a second and secret channel of diplomacy in Oslo. For the first time they agreed to negotiate with a section of the PLO. These talks bypassed the bulk of the PLO and Fatah, with negotiations directed only towards Yasser Arafat and a few close associates. In September 1993 the Declaration of Principles between the Palestinians and Israel was finally brought into the open and signed by both parties on the White House lawn. The declaration was an agenda for negotiations which stipulated that within four months of signing the agreement Israel had to withdraw completely from Gaza and Jericho, with a Palestinian police force taking over internal security in those areas, though Israel would still maintain overall responsibility for external security and foreign affairs. Elsewhere in the West Bank Palestinians were to take control of five spheres: education, health, social welfare, direct taxation and tourism. Within nine months elections were to be held for a Palestinian Authority which was to assume responsibilities for those municipal affairs. Final status negotiations were scheduled to start within two years and were due to be completed within five years. All of the most serious issues affecting the two parties, including possible Palestinian statehood, borders, refugees, settlements and Jerusalem, were postponed to the final settlement talks. The PLO agreed to accept UN Resolutions 242 and 338, end the armed struggle against Israel and amend the parts of the Palestinian National Charter which called for the destruction of the Israeli state. Israel agreed to recognise the PLO as the representative of the Palestinian people. The Declaration of Principles brought to an end the first intifada which, according to the Israeli human rights group B"Tselem, had seen 160 Israelis and 1,162 Palestinians killed (B'Tselem, 2003a).

The treaty met with opposition on both Israeli and Palestinian sides. Likud and the right-wing nationalist and religious parties denounced the agreement as a betrayal of the settlers in the occupied territories, an end to biblical Greater Israel, and a mortal threat to the security of the state. They argued that the occupied territories could not be ceded by politicians as they had been eternally promised to the Jews by God. Binyamin Netanyahu, the Likud leader, completely rejected the accord and pledged to cancel it if he became prime minister. He compared the agreement to the appeasement of Hitler, and told Peres: 'You are even worse than Chamberlain. He imperilled the safety of another people, but you are doing it to your own people' (cited in Shlaim, 2000: 521). The Accord was eventually approved by the Knesset by a margin of 61 votes to 50. Israeli public opinion on the Accords was generally favourable with 65 per cent saying they approved of the agreement and only 13 per cent declaring themselves 'very much against' it (Shlaim, 2000). In an analysis of Palestinian reaction to the Oslo Accords, Mouin Rabbani identified four distinct positions and argued that 'contrary to most press reports the fault line ... within the Palestinian body politic is not an ideological one separating peace-loving moderates from violent extremists' but rather one which revolves 'primarily around issues of substance and procedure' (*Middle East International*, 24 September 1993). He claimed that only a few Palestinians were 'enthusiastic supporters', and the majority, whom he characterised as 'optimistic and desperate in equal measure', had serious doubts but were prepared to give the agreement a chance. He suggested that this large group could quickly turn against the agreement if the human rights situation did not improve and the settlement activity and occupation continued. The third group he identified comprised senior political and cultural figures[37] such as Edward Said, who, although supporting a peaceful resolution of the conflict, nevertheless regarded the Accords as 'deeply flawed' and 'potentially fatal to Palestinian national aspirations'. They objected to Arafat signing the document without public debate or consultations and believed it was a bad deal. They pointed out that the Palestinians were agreeing to end the intifada and renounce their rights to 78 per cent of historic Palestine without any guarantee of statehood, agreement to remove settlements (or even stop settlement building), or any commitments to improve the human rights situation, or to resolve the refugee issue and status of Jerusalem. For this group the agreement undermined the internationally recognised rights of Palestinians and 'foreshadows permanent dispossession of the majority of Palestinians' as well as creating the potential conditions for civil war. The fourth position that Rabbani identifies is that of the rejectionists who comprise both the radical Islamic and secular movements such as Hamas and the PFLP, and their supporters in the occupied territories. These groups, argues Rabbani, regarded the agreement as a 'textbook case of Bantustanisation' in which the principal Palestinian weapon, the intifada, was being liquidated so that Palestinians could become the joint administrators of the occupation, in a weak subservient statelet or series of statelets. Rabbani suggests that had the agreement involved moves towards real statehood and been reached in 'conformity with the Palestinian national consensus and properly ratified' then much of the rejectionist camp with the exception of Islamic Jihad and sections of Hamas and the PFLP would at least have tacitly accepted the deal.

The 1993 Declaration of Principles was followed in February 1994 by the signing of the new set of documents in Cairo. The IDF agreed to redeploy its forces from urban centres to rural areas allowing it to maintain control of overall security and land crossings. On 25 February Dr Baruch Goldstein, an American-born settler and member of the Kach Party, opened fire with an IDF-issued Galil assault rifle on Muslim worshippers at the Tomb of the Patriarchs in Hebron, killing 29 people before he himself was killed. Rachelle Marshall, a journalist and member of the Jewish Peace Union, writes that the killings were followed by a five-week round-the-clock curfew imposed on more than a million Palestinians, during which the IDF killed a further 76 Palestinians, mostly stone-throwing youths (*Washington Report on Middle East Affairs*, June 1994). The Israeli journalist Danny Rubinstein was later to argue that the Hebron killings 'directly and immediately created the chain of suicide bombings and the appalling upward spiral composed of Israeli responses and Palestinian counter-responses' (*Ha'aretz*, 28 September 1998). In the wake of these events the Israeli government, under pressure from the Palestinians and sections of Israeli public opinion, moved to outlaw the overtly racist Kach Party, but refused Palestinian demands to remove the few hundred heavily armed and guarded settlers who lived among more than 100,000 Palestinian Hebronites. The Israeli government also refused PLO requests to put the issue of settlements on the negotiating table, arguing that under the Declaration of Principles it was not obliged to do so until the third year of the interim period. Hamas vowed revenge for the Hebron killings, and shortly before the signing of the next stage of the interim agreements in Cairo in May 1994 it carried out a car bombing in Afula which killed eight, and the first ever suicide bombing in Israel which killed five people. Suicide bombings involve individuals strapping explosives, nails and ball bearings to their bodies which are then detonated in densely packed areas such as markets or buses. This new and indiscriminate weapon left those who survived permanently scarred or disabled, and significantly intensified security fears amongst Israelis. A report from a BBC1 news bulletin describes the aftermath of a suicide attack on a crowded Israeli market:

The two explosions came within seconds of each other cutting down scores of people in the heart of the crowded market. It was just after one o'clock and the market was full of shoppers. Streams of ambulances came to carry away the dead and the injured. It was a place of appalling suffering ... Those who escaped injury were led away from the devastation and others arrived desperate to see if their friends and relatives had escaped the carnage. (BBC1 evening news, 30 July 1997)

Some Palestinians have tried to justify such attacks by arguing that they are in response to the killing of Palestinian civilians by Israelis. Others have argued that they are resisting an illegal occupation, or that it is the only effective weapon against a much more powerful adversary. Dr Eyad El-Sarraj, a psychiatrist and winner of the 1998 Martin Ennals human rights award, has noted that most suicide bombers had suffered a severe trauma when young, 'often the torture of a close relative' and that 'children grow up wanting to take revenge for their trauma. Torture is an integral part of that cycle of violence' (*Guardian*, 24 January 2003). Whatever the motivations or factors behind suicide bombings, human rights groups have unequivocally condemned such attacks and demanded that those involved in planning attacks be brought to justice. In a report entitled 'Without Distinction: Attacks on Civilians by Palestinian Armed Groups', Amnesty International argues that indiscriminate attacks on civilians cannot be justified whatever the circumstances or provocations:

The obligation to protect civilians is absolute and cannot be set aside because Israel has failed to respect its obligations. The attacks against civilians by Palestinian armed groups are widespread, systematic and in pursuit of an explicit policy to attack civilians. They therefore constitute crimes against humanity under international law. They may also constitute war crimes, depending on the legal characterisation of the hostilities and interpretation of the status of Palestinian armed groups and fighters under international humanitarian law. (Amnesty International, 2002)

THE CAIRO AGREEMENT AND OSLO II

The agreement signed in Cairo on 4 May 1994 concluded the Gaza and Jericho phase of the redeployment and set the terms for expanding Palestinian autonomy in the West Bank. These had three stages. Firstly, the Palestinian National Authority was to take charge of a number of municipal functions; secondly, the IDF would withdraw from population centres, and finally, there would be Palestinian elections for a new Authority. However, Palestinian negotiators were disappointed with the new agreement. They had hoped that Israel would replace the complex system of military ordinances and occupation laws, with the Fourth Geneva Convention and international law within the occupied territories, but this was not forthcoming (Shlaim, 2000). The United Nations Commission on Human Rights continued to be critical of Israeli human rights abuses in the occupied territories. In 1994 it issued a resolution 'condemning' settler and IDF killings, torture, imprisonment without trial, house demolitions and land expropriations, curfews, collective punishments, restrictions on movement and settlement building (United Nations, 1994).

The construction of illegal Jewish settlements had accelerated following the election of the Rabin administration in 1992. Between 1992 and 1995 the settler population in the occupied territories (excluding East Jerusalem) rose from 74,800 to 136,000 (Foundation for Middle East Peace, 1997). Palestinians believed that increased settlement building and expropriations of Palestinian land was a violation of the spirit if not the letter of the Oslo Accords, and would ultimately prejudice the possibility of a viable Palestinian state. The American historian and Middle East commentator Geoffrey Aronson argued that 'there is no missing the fact that Rabin's settlement drive is aimed at putting the future of the city [Jerusalem] and its West Bank environs beyond the reach of diplomacy' (*Report on Israeli Settlement in the Occupied Territory*, May 1995). He also cited statements from the Israeli commentator Ze'ev Schiff that 'when we come to the final stage [of negotiations] nothing will be left [in Jerusalem] for the Palestinians to negotiate, apart from the Islamic holy places'. Rabin's administration also embarked on a process of building bypass roads linking settlements which could only be used by Jewish settlers and the IDF. This plan, Israel Shahak (1995) claimed, was originally conceived by Ariel Sharon in 1977 but was finally implemented by Rabin directly after the Declaration of Principles. He argued that its purpose was to create a matrix of control whereby all the Arab population centres were split into enclaves criss-crossed by the roads and settlement blocks so that the Israeli army will be able to control the discontinuous cantons 'from outside'. Tel Aviv University professor Tanya Reinhart argued that Rabin's policies 'resemble[d] the beginning of Apartheid rather than its end' and were 'almost identical' to the South African Bantustan model (*Ha'aretz*, 27 May 1994). The construction of the bypass road network also allowed the Israeli government to enforce closures on the Palestinian areas which restricted Palestinian movement and access to employment. Israel justified such measures by arguing that it was necessary to prevent attacks by Palestinian militants against Israelis. It did, however, have a very serious effect on the Palestinian economy. The Israeli journalist Nadav Ha'etzni reported that, by May 1995, curfews and closures had 'devastated the Palestinian economy and destroyed 100,000 families in Gaza alone' (*Ma'ariv*, 5 May 1995, cited in Chomsky, 1999: 548). The deteriorating economic situation for Palestinians was compounded by Israeli moves to achieve 'separation' by replacing Palestinian workers with migrant labour from Thailand, the Philippines, Romania and other parts of Eastern Europe. Such factors, Shlaim suggests, 'actually worsened the situation in the occupied territories and confounded Palestinian aspirations for a state of their own' (2000: 530). Furthermore, there was no halt to the bloodshed on both sides. Between the signing of the Declaration of Principles in September 1993 and the end of 1994, 93 Israelis and 194 Palestinians were killed in violent incidents (B'Tselem, 2003a).

In late September 1995 Yasser Arafat and Yitzak Rabin concluded the next stage of the interim agreement under which the West Bank was divided into three areas. Area A (3 per cent of the West Bank incorporating Nablus, Jenin, Tulkarem, Kalkilya, Ramallah, Bethlehem and subsequently, in January 1997, 80 per cent of Hebron) would have its civilian administration and internal security controlled by the Palestinian Authority. Area B (23 per cent of the West Bank comprising 440 villages and surrounding lands) was to have certain municipal functions administered by the Palestinian Authority whilst security would be dealt with by joint Palestinian-Israeli patrols. Area C (comprising 74 per cent of the West Bank, including all of the 145 settlements including those around East Jerusalem) would remain under complete Israeli control.

On 4 November 1995 Yitzak Rabin was assassinated by a 25-year-old settler, Yigal Amir. After the killing the unrepentant Amir accused Rabin of selling out the settlers and preparing to give away the occupied territories to the Palestinians. Rabin was succeeded as prime minister by Shimon Peres who pledged to maintain the momentum of the peace process. No Israelis had been killed in suicide attacks since the 21 August bombing in Jerusalem which had killed three Israelis and an American. Mishal and Sela (2000) suggest that both Hamas and Islamic Jihad were under pressure from both the Palestinian Authority and Israel, and did not want to antagonise Palestinian public opinion by precipitating a halt to the scheduled Israeli redeployments. Mishal and Sela also note that militant groups had been pushing for 'a conditional cease-fire with Israel to stop the bloodshed of innocents on both sides' (2000: 71). In early 1996 Peres ordered the killing of Yahya Ayyash, a Hamas leader who had previously masterminded several suicide attacks which had killed approximately 60 Israelis. Shlaim claims that the Israeli media had exaggerated his status presenting him as 'public enemy number one' whilst 'omitting to mention that the attacks he organized came as a response to the [Hebron] massacre' (2000: 556). The assassination of Ayyash using a booby-trapped phone led to Hamas vowing revenge, and there followed six suicide bombings in February and March 1996 which left 62 Israelis dead (Israeli Ministry of Foreign Affairs, 1999). Peres' popularity declined under attacks from the right, and he moved to suspend talks with the newly elected Palestinian Authority and closed the borders to all workers from the occupied territories.

Shortly afterwards Peres launched a major offensive against Hezbullah guerrillas in Southern Lebanon. Israel had been fighting a long guerrilla war against Hezbullah militants. Hezbullah claimed they were trying to end the illegal Israeli occupation of Southern Lebanon, which had been ongoing since 1978, in violation of United Security Council Resolution 425.[38] Israel claimed that Hezbullah were intent on the destruction of the Israeli state. Casualty statistics suggest that Palestinian and Lebanese civilians had suffered disproportionately in the conflict. In the period between 1985 and 1996 the Israeli army estimate that Hezbullah guerrilla and rocket attacks had killed six Israeli civilians (IDF, 2003). In a single operation in 1993 Amnesty International (1996a) reported that Israel killed 118 Lebanese civilians and displaced a further 300,000. The journalist and former chief inspector of the US Information Agency, Richard Curtiss, argues that after this operation, unwritten rules of engagement were crafted by the US State Department's Warren Christopher with both sides agreeing to confine attacks to combatants in South Lebanon (*Washington Report on Middle East Affairs*, May/June 1996). On 11 April 1996 Peres launched Operation 'Grapes of Wrath'. This was claimed to be in retaliation for rocket strikes on Israeli settlements which had injured 34 civilians, and other attacks which had killed eight members of the IDF in Southern Lebanon. Hezbullah's view was that they had a right to resist the Israeli troops illegally occupying Southern Lebanon, and that the rockets fired on Israeli settlements were retaliation for the killing by Israel of three Lebanese civilians. The attack involved more than 1,000 air sorties and 16,000 shells against less than 500 Hezbullah fighters (*Ha'aretz*, 21 May 1996). Curtiss claims that many of attacks were 'targeted at electric power plants and relay stations, bridges, and other parts of Lebanon's war-battered basic infrastructure' (*Washington Report on Middle East Affairs*, May/June 1996). The Israeli journalist Ari Shavit alleges that 400,000 civilians were forced to flee their homes in eight hours, after which the Israeli air force treated the abandoned properties as military targets and shelled them (*Liberation*, 21 May 1996). On 18 April Israel bombed the United Nations compound at Qana, killing 106 refugees who had sought sanctuary there. Israel stated that the bombing which involved anti-personnel munitions was a mistake and that the real target was an area nearby where Hezbullah militants had been operating. Both a UN (1996) report and an Amnesty International (1996b) report found that the attack on the UN compound was unlikely to have been accidental, and also condemned Israeli missile attacks on ambulances and residential areas which killed many civilians. Shlaim suggests that the operation was an attempt by Shimon Peres to revive his flagging political fortunes and recast himself 'as the hard man of Israeli politics ahead of the crucial general elections' (2000: 560). However, it did nothing to revive his political fortunes and the following month he was beaten in the general election by the Likud candidate Binyamin Netanyahu.

THE NETANYAHU ADMINISTRATION

Netanyahu's attitude towards the peace process before his election had been one of undisguised antipathy. He had campaigned publicly against its implementation in speeches and in print, and had been accused by Rabin's widow of inciting his assassination by making inflammatory public speeches which likened Rabin to an SS officer. His coalition included the far right and settler groups who called for the forced deportation of all Palestinians from the occupied territories. Netanyahu's central argument was that the peace process had illustrated Israel's weakness, reduced the deterrent power of the IDF and damaged the nation's security. He argued that Israel had adhered to the Oslo formula whilst the Palestinians had failed to keep their side of the bargain, by failing to dismantle militant organisations, collect their weapons or extradite their members to Israel. Netanyahu's alternative was to renegotiate the redeployments that had been agreed in principle. He argued that these threatened Israel's security and that 'whatever the officials of the previous Labor administration had whispered in Palestinian ears was irrelevant' (Netanyahu, 2000: 343). He was also against full statehood for the Palestinians, arguing that Israel had to control the exit and entry points to the Palestinian entity as well as its airspace, much of the Jordan valley and the West Bank water supply. He also argued that Arab nations should resettle the Palestinian refugees. Shlaim claims that as soon as he took power Netanyahu began to renege on Israel's Oslo obligations:

> Serious deterioration occurred in Israel's relations with the Palestinians as a result of Netanyahu's backtracking. He adopted a 'work-to-rule' approach designed to undermine the Oslo process. There was no Israeli pullout from Hebron, no 'opening of the safe passage' route from Gaza to the West Bank, and no discussion of the further West bank redeployment that Israel had pledged to carry out in early September. Instead Palestinian homes without an Israeli permit were demolished in east Jerusalem, and plans were approved for the construction of new Israeli settlements. The quality of life for the Palestinians deteriorated progressively, and hopes for a better future were all but extinguished. (Shlaim, 2000: 576)

In October 1996 serious violence erupted in Jerusalem when Netanyahu ordered the blasting open of an archaeological tunnel close to the Al-Aqsa mosque. This was taken by Palestinians as a statement of sovereignty over Islamic holy sites and triggered disturbances in which 15 Israeli soldiers and 80 Palestinians were killed, and a further 1,500 Palestinians wounded. Under pressure from the Americans Netanyahu agreed to the delayed redeployment of Israeli troops from Hebron in January 1997 by signing the Hebron protocol, which also committed Israel to three further redeployments in the West Bank over the next 18 months. Under the agreement Hebron was split into Jewish and Arab zones. The Jewish zone reserved for the 450 settlers constituted 20 per cent of the city, including its best commercial areas. The remaining 80 per cent of the city was reserved for the 130,000 Palestinian Hebronites who were subject to frequent curfews and restrictions on movement.

After the signing of the Hebron protocol Netanyahu approved a number of new settlements. In February 1997 he announced plans for 6,500 new dwellings for 30,000 settlers at Jabal Ghneim (Har Homa) on the outskirts of annexed East Jerusalem. Har Homa would complete the chain of concentric settlements around Jerusalem and cut off Arab East Jerusalem from the rest of the West Bank. The move was met with anger from Palestinians and condemned by the United Nations (1997) General Assembly by 130 votes to 2 (Israel and the US). Palestinians were unhappy with more expropriation of their land and called a general strike in protest. The US twice vetoed Security Council resolutions condemning the project, whilst the General Assembly passed further resolutions calling for a halt to the Har Homa project, the removal of settlements in the occupied territories, and the application of the Fourth Geneva Convention within the territories. None of these moves stopped the construction of the new settlements. In June 1997 the Israeli journalist Jay Bushinsky reported that Netanyahu had outlined his 'Allon Plus' plan for a possible settlement with the Palestinians. The plan involved Israel annexing approximately 60 per cent of the West Bank that would include Greater Jerusalem, the hills east of Jerusalem, the Jordan valley, the settlements and all the bypass roads connecting them, plus permanent Israeli control of the West Bank water supply (*Jerusalem Post*, 5 June 1997). The proposals were met with dismay by Palestinian leaders who accused Israel of violating the Oslo Accords and trying to destroy the peace process.

Although the conflict between Palestinian militants and the IDF and settlers in the occupied territories continued to claim more lives, there were no suicide attacks in Israel between March 1996 and March 1997. Between 21 March 1997 and 4 September 1997 militants carried out three suicide attacks killing 24 Israelis. Hamas representatives argued that the attacks were the only way to stop the expropriation of more Palestinian land for settlement building and the 'Judaisation' of the holy places. On 23 September 1997 the Hamas leadership sent a letter to Netanyahu, delivered by King Hussein of Jordan, in which Hamas suggested setting up an indirect dialogue with the Israeli government that would be mediated by King Hussein. The purpose of the dialogue would be to achieve a cessation of violence as well as a 'discussion of all matters' (*Ha'aretz*, 9 October 1997, cited in Mishal and Sela, 2000: 72). Two days later Netanyahu ordered the killing of the head of Hamas' Political Bureau, Khalid Mash'al, in Jordan. The attempted assassination by two Mossad agents was botched and

Mash'al's bodyguard captured the two assassins who were later traded for the imprisoned Hamas spiritual leader Sheikh Ahmed Yassin. The attempted killing soured relations with King Hussein, Israel's closest ally in the Arab world, and ended any opportunity for a ceasefire. The release of Yassin followed by his return to Gaza strengthened Hamas' support.

In March 1998, 1,500 reservists, including twelve retired major-generals, called on Netanyahu to stop settlement building and try to end the conflict and normalise relations. (Shlaim, 2000). However, Netanyahu cancelled the scheduled Israeli redeployments, citing security concerns. Despite efforts by both Britain and the US to revive the process, it ground to a halt. Both sides in the conflict accused the other of bad faith in reneging on their Oslo obligations. Netanyahu reiterated his claims that the PLO had failed to disarm or arrest militant groups, prevent attacks against Israelis, and amend the PLO charter. Others contested this. Tanya Reinhart, writing in the Jewish American publication *Tikkun*, claimed that Arafat had taken strong action against Hamas and that this was recognised by Israel's security services:

> Arafat's security services carried out this job [maintaining Israeli security] faithfully, by assassinating Hamas terrorists (disguised as 'accidents'), and arresting Hamas political leaders ... Ample information was published in the Israeli media regarding these activities, and 'security sources' were full of praises for Arafat's achievements. For example, Ami Ayalon, then head of the Israeli secret service (Shabak), announced, in a government meeting on April 5, 1998 that 'Arafat is doing his job – he is fighting terror and puts all his weight against the Hamas' (*Ha'aretz*, April 6 1998). The rate of success of the Israeli security services in containing terror was never higher than that of Arafat; in fact, it was probably much lower. (*Tikkun*, March/April 2002)

In a 1998 report, the Israeli peace group Gush Shalom (1998) blamed the Netanyahu administration for the breakdown in the peace process and accused the government of 19 separate violations of the Oslo Accords including settlement and bypass road building, use of closures, failure to release Palestinian prisoners, torture and other human rights abuses, and failure to undertake scheduled military withdrawals and move towards final status negotiations. During this period support for militant organisations such as Islamic

Jihad and Hamas grew whilst the PLO and particularly Yasser Arafat lost popularity. This was partly because of corruption scandals that engulfed the PLO leadership which was accused of nepotism and siphoning off funds meant for the Palestinian Authority. It was also because of Arafat's autocratic style and the serious human rights abuses committed by the Palestinian security forces who were using torture and engaging in extrajudicial killings against suspected militants. There was also widespread anger that Arafat had failed to stop settlement building. Geoffrey Aronson claimed that Arafat and the other PLO 'outsiders' (those from outside the occupied territories) failed to appreciate the significance of the settlements:

> PA chairman Yasser Arafat is briefed infrequently on Israel's settlement policy, and his response is generally stunned silence as he looks at the maps depicting the dimensions of the enterprise. Palestinian Authority negotiators Mahmoud Abbas (Abu Mazen) and Ahmad Quray (Abu Ala) have never been on a 'settlement tour.' If one is to judge by their negotiating priorities, they have no concept of the role of settlements in the history of Israel's policies in the occupied territories, nor do they believe that such an understanding is required. (Aronson 1998)

In October 1998 Israel and Palestinian negotiators concluded the next phase of the peace process signing the Wye Accords in Maryland. Israel undertook to redeploy its troops from a further 13 per cent of the West Bank in three stages.

The Palestinians agreed to amend the parts of the Palestinian National Charter calling for Israel's destruction and to work with Israeli security services and the CIA to improve Israel's security. The security component of the agreement was heavily criticised by human rights groups both before and after the signing, who argued it was likely to increase human rights abuses.[39] The Wye Accords passed in the Knesset by a large majority, though Netanyahu received virtually no support for the agreement amongst his right-wing/religious coalition. Although both parties to the agreement had agreed not to undertake 'unilateral actions' to change the status of the occupied territories, members of Netanyahu's coalition publicly called on settler groups to take as much land as possible to keep it out of Palestinian hands. Ariel Sharon, the infrastructure minister, told a Tsomet Party gathering on 15 November that 'Everyone should take action, should run, should grab more hills ... We'll expand the area. Whatever is seized will be ours. Whatever isn't seized will end up in their hands' (BBC News Online, 16 November 1998). Netanyahu promoted the same policies, though less overtly: 'There is no such thing as a freeze [on construction] ... Our policy is to grow and expand ... This issue must be coordinated behind closed doors with the army and not in front of the media' (Ha'aretz, 24 November 1998). On 20 December 1998 the Israeli government suspended the second redeployment stipulated in the Wye Agreement unless the Palestinian Authority met five conditions, most of which were new. Netanyahu claimed that it was necessary to suspend the redeployments to safeguard Israel's security. Shlaim suggests the move was intended to 'torpedo the peace process and put the blame on the Palestinians' (2000: 605). Three days later the Knesset voted to dissolve itself and schedule new elections for May 1999.

THE BARAK ADMINISTRATION

The May elections brought Labour's Ehud Barak to power. Three months into Barak's tenure the American journalist Deborah Sontag reported that his administration had 'authorized new construction in the West Bank's Jewish settlements at a pace exceeding that of the right-wing administration of Benjamin Netanyahu' (New York Times, 28 September 1999). Barak also moved to initiate negotiations with Syria rather than with the Palestinians, which the Palestinians took as a snub and an attempt to pressurise them. Barak argued that he pursued the Syrian track first because the problem was considered less intractable, and secondly because Syria with its large army and non-conventional weapons was considered an 'existential threat' (New York Review of Books, 9 August 2001). After four months of negotiations the peace talks between Israel and Syria collapsed without a settlement. Both parties blamed the other.[40] In May 2000 Barak took the decision to withdraw the Israeli army and its proxy forces from South Lebanon. The occupying Israeli army had been taking increasing heavy casualties from Hezbullah guerrilla raids and the casualties were politically unpopular. Rachelle Marshall suggests that the withdrawal allowed hundreds of thousands of Lebanese refugees to return to their devastated villages, and Hezbullah to set up medical facilities and begin rebuilding the civilian infrastructure (Washington Report on Middle East Affairs, July 2000).

Following the failure of the Syrian track Barak turned his attention to the Palestinians. Barak's tenure (up until the outbreak of the second intifada) had seen a decline in attacks by Palestinian militants and no suicide attacks (B'Tselem, 2003a). Marshall claims in early 2000 that Barak suspended a number of Israel's Oslo commitments. These included the scheduled release of 1,650 Palestinian prisoners arrested before the Oslo process began, and the scheduled handover to Palestinian control of three small villages bordering Jerusalem: Abu Dis, Al Ezzariyye and Swarah (*Washington Report on Middle East Affairs*, July 2000). Marshall claims that instead, Barak authorised the seizure of 162 acres from these villages for the construction of a new bypass road linking settlement blocks to Jerusalem, and the construction of 200 Jewish housing units in Abu Dis. Barak also decided to renegotiate the agreements that the PLO had signed with Netanyahu, and cancelled the third partial redeployment of Israeli troops. The Oslo Accords had specified that by the time that final-status talks began Israel should have withdrawn from approximately 90 per cent of the occupied territories, but by the end of May 2000 the figure was only 18 per cent. In March 2000, as preparatory talks between Israeli and Palestinian delegations on final status issues were beginning, 120 Palestinian intellectuals and cultural figures sent an open letter to the 'Israeli and Jewish Public' calling for a just solution to be based on either the 1967 borders or a binational state. It argued that 'one side believes the present balance of power to be in its favour, and that it can impose a humiliating agreement on the other side, forcing it to accept virtually anything it chooses to enforce' (*Ha'aretz*, 13 March 2000). The Israeli commentator Danny Rabinowitz argued that the letter revealed the deep chasm between Israeli and Palestinian evaluations of the peace process:

> One view, which is accepted by the majority of Israelis, considers Oslo a positive, symmetric process: an elected government in Israel is conducting peace negotiations with a Palestinian leadership that reflects the true interests of the Palestinian people. Pursuing this joint path will ultimately lead to a durable peace between the two peoples. The second view, which is asserted by the signatories to the letter, considers Oslo an inherently asymmetric process whose forgone conclusion is not only unfair, but also dangerous. The gist here is that Israel, which is strong, big, rich and backed by a superpower, is conducting negotiations of a coercive nature with a weak Palestinian leadership that has sold out. Arafat, his aides

and the few thousand families that are close to his government are mere puppets with no will of their own and without the ability to engage in true diplomatic manoeuvring. The corruption and despotism constantly being exposed in the economy, judicial system, human rights record and other areas of the Palestinian Authority demonstrate that the thrust of the leadership in the West Bank and Gaza is to preserve its own rule and to divvy up the financial and symbolic spoils flowing in from donor nations. This view of the process sees the true national interest of millions of Palestinians in the territories and the Diaspora ground into the dust. (*Ha'aretz*, 19 March 2000)

In the run-up to the final status talks in May 2000 Israel released maps of a projected final settlement indicating that Palestinian self-rule would be limited to three or four discontinuous pieces of territory.

THE CAMP DAVID FINAL STATUS TALKS

On 11 July 2000 Yasser Arafat and Ehud Barak met for final status negotiations at Camp David in the United States. After two weeks the talks broke down amid bitter recriminations. Israel argued that they had made a 'generous offer' to return 97 per cent of the occupied territories, which the other party spurned, turning to violence to force concessions it could not achieve at the negotiating table. The Palestinians argued that the offer was vague and unacceptable, 'less than a Bantustan' in Arafat's words (*New York Times*, 26 July 2001). Analysing the conference is difficult because all of Israel's offers were made orally, with no maps or written proposals presented.

In an interview with Israeli historian Benny Morris, Ehud Barak laid out the Israeli government's perspective on the failure of the talks (*New York Review of Books*, 9 August 2001). Barak claimed that he had offered Arafat 92 per cent of the West Bank and 100 per cent of the Gaza Strip, together with some territorial compensation from pre-1976 Israel. He denied that the state would consist of Bantustans, claiming that although the West Bank would be sliced in two by a 'razor thin Israeli wedge' running from the settlement of Ma'ale Adumim to the Jordan river, 'Palestinian territorial continuity would have been assured by a tunnel or bridge'. He also claimed to have offered to dismantle most of the settlements and concentrate the bulk of the settlers in the 8 per cent of the West Bank that was to be annexed to Israel. A Palestinian capital would be set up in East

Jerusalem, with some neighbourhoods to become Palestinian territory and others to enjoy 'functional autonomy'. The Palestinians, it is claimed, were offered custodianship, though not sovereignty over the Temple Mount. Barak also alleged that Israel offered a right of return for Palestinian refugees to the prospective Palestinian state, though no admission of Israeli responsibility for the creation of the refugee problem, and no return of any refugees to Israel. Barak accused Arafat of saying no to every proposal and offering no counter-proposals. Barak also claimed that Arafat believes that Israel 'has no right to exist and he seeks its demise'. This, argued Barak, would be achieved by using the Palestinian refugees as a demographic tool to subvert the Israeli state. Barak also accused Arabs in general, and Arafat in particular, of being 'a product of a culture in which to tell a lie ... creates no dissonance' because Arabs 'don't suffer from the problem of telling lies that exists in Judeo-Christian culture'. In Arab societies, he stated, 'there is no such thing as "the truth"'. In making this charge, Barak had perhaps overlooked the comments of Yitzak Shamir when responding to a charge of dishonesty. He was quoted in *Ha'aretz* as saying that 'for the sake of the land of Israel, it is permissible to lie' (14 February 1992, cited in Shlaim, 2000: 496). Barak also suggested that it would probably take 80 years from 1948 before the Palestinians were ready to make the necessary compromises for peace, because of what Barak described as a 'salmon syndrome' amongst Palestinians. Eighty years after 1948, the Palestinians who experienced displacement first-hand will have largely died, so there will be 'very few "salmons" around who will still want to return to their birthplaces to die'.

Robert Malley, a special advisor to President Clinton, and Hussein Agha, the Oxford historian, have criticised Barak's analysis as 'remarkably shallow' and suggested all the protagonists share some responsibility for the failure of the talks. Malley and Agha (in the *New York Review of Books*, 9 August 2001) argue that Barak's decision to renege on Israel's interim commitments such as troop withdrawals and prisoner releases whilst expanding settlements was designed to reduce political friction from the Israeli right in the run-up to the talks and husband his political capital. He could then present 'all concessions and all rewards in one comprehensive package that the Israeli public would be asked to accept in a national referendum'. This 'all or nothing' approach, Malley and Agha allege, put Arafat under tremendous pressure from powerful Palestinian constituencies such as the security establishment, intellectuals, civil servants and the business community who had lost faith in Barak. They also suggest that Barak's refusal to withdraw from territory scheduled in the interim agreements directly affected the perceived balance of power because the Palestinians believed that they would also have to negotiate over that land in the final status talks. Malley and Agha maintain that all of these factors left Arafat with the impression that the Israelis and Americans were trying to 'dupe' him into accepting a humiliating deal, which led him to adopt a siege mentality, unamenable to fluid negotiations and the presentation of counter-proposals. They also suggest that not enough time had gone into laying the groundwork with preparatory negotiations prior to the summit, and that a month prior to the talks Arafat had warned US Secretary of State Madeleine Albright that because of all these factors the talks were very likely to fail.

Other commentators, such as the Israeli human rights group Gush Shalom (2003), have questioned whether a 'generous deal' was offered to Palestinians. They argue that Palestinians made their historic compromise at Oslo in agreeing to cede to Israel 78 per cent of mandatory Palestine, and that they were never offered 95 per cent of the occupied territories at Camp David in July 2000. Gush Shalom allege that Barak insisted on annexing 10 per cent of the West Bank comprised of settlement blocks which, they argued, would 'create impossible borders which severely disrupt Palestinian life in the West bank'. They also claim that Barak wanted 'temporary Israeli control' of another 10 per cent of the West Bank for an unspecified duration. They argue that 'what appears to be territorial continuity is actually split up by settlement blocs, bypass roads and roadblocks', and that 'the Palestinians have to relinquish land reserves essential for their development and absorption of refugees' as well as accepting 'Israeli supervision of borders crossings together with many other restrictions'. They suggest that nobody would accept foreign control of domestic border crossings or traveling 50 miles between areas when the real distance was only five miles. Jeff Halper, an anthropology professor at Ben-Gurion University and coordinator of the Israeli Committee against House Demolitions, argues that the focus on whether the Palestinians were offered 81 per cent or 91 per cent or 95 per cent or 96 per cent is misplaced because even if Israel agreed to hand back 96 per cent of the occupied territories it would still possess a 'matrix of control' which would completely undermine Palestinian sovereignty and independent development:

What is the matrix of control? It is an interlocking series of mechanisms, only a few of which require physical occupation of territory, that allow Israel to control every aspect of Palestinian life in the Occupied Territories. The matrix works like the Japanese game of Go. Instead of defeating your opponent as in chess, in Go you win by immobilizing your opponent, by gaining control of key points of a matrix so that every time s/he moves s/he encounters an obstacle of some kind ... The matrix imposed by Israel in the West Bank, Gaza and East Jerusalem, similar in appearance to a Go board, has virtually paralysed the Palestinian population without 'defeating' it or even conquering much territory. (*Middle East Report*, Fall 2000)

Part of this matrix, argues Halper, involves the expansion of 'Metropolitan' Jerusalem, which he claims, stretches almost all the way to the Jordan river and incorporates 40 per cent of the West Bank, including Ramallah and Bethlehem. Halper suggests that Israeli control of this area, which cuts off Palestinians in East Jerusalem from the rest of the West Bank, 'renders the sovereignty of a future Palestinian state meaningless'. Halper also points to the grid of bypass roads criss-crossing the West Bank, linking settlements, which would also require a substantial permanent Israeli military presence across the Palestinian state. All of these factors, suggests Halper, meant that even if Yasser Arafat had agreed to Barak's proposals at Camp David, the agreement would not have held:

The issue in the Israeli-Palestinian negotiations, then, is not simply territory – it revolves around questions of control, viability and justice. A Palestinian state carved into small, disconnected enclaves, surrounded and indeed truncated by massive Israeli settlement blocs, subject to Israeli military and economic closures, unable to offer justice to its dispersed people and without its most sacred symbols of religion and identity, can hardly be called a viable state. 'Peace' may be imposed, but unless it is just it will not be lasting. (*Middle East Report*, Fall 2000)

The breakdown of the Camp David talks was followed by months of secret negotiations between Palestinian and Israeli officials. On 28 September 2000 Ariel Sharon and 1,000 armed police visited Islam's third holiest site, the Al-Haram al-Sharif. Palestinians considered this visit to be a statement of sovereignty over one of the

Muslim world's holiest sites, and a provocative gesture. It was followed by riots and fighting, from which developed the second intifada. On 7 October the UN Security Council passed Resolution 1322 condemning both Ariel Sharon's visit to the Al-Haram al-Sharif and Israel's 'excessive use of force against Palestinians'. Throughout the remainder of 2000, Palestinian residents of the occupied territories clashed with the IDF. By the end of the year 279 Palestinians, including 82 minors and 41 Israelis (no minors), had been killed in the unrest (B'Tselem, 2003b).

On 21 January 2001 Palestinian and Israeli delegates met with President Clinton at Taba for further peace talks. Israel put forward an improved offer, but after a week Ehud Barak broke off the talks without an agreement, citing the nearness of the Israeli general election. Arafat condemned the decision to call off the talks and accused Israel of waging 'a savage and barbaric war against the Palestinians'. Nevertheless, both sides issued a statement stating that they had made progress and were closer to a deal than ever (*Guardian*, 29 January 2001). In an analysis of the talks, Aronson claims that both sides moved closer on the territorial dimensions of a settlement. Israel dropped its demand for indefinite control of the Jordan valley, southern West Bank perimeter and area around Kiryat Arba, which comprised about 10 per cent of the West Bank (Aronson, 2001). Instead, their security concerns would have been met by 'the creation of discreet, limited security points in the Jordan Valley, arrangements which would have no territorial or settlement dimension and which would not be conditioned on Israeli control of principal transport routes' (Aronson, 2001: 4). There was also a reduction in Israeli demands for the annexation of the settlement corridors which protrude deeply into the prospective Palestinian state, breaking up territorial continuity, controlling roads and cantonising the territory. Aronson claimed that there still remained 'defects impacting upon both territorial continuity and transport corridors in crucial locations near Jerusalem, Ramallah, Bethlehem, Kalkilya and Nablus' (2001: 7). The Palestinian negotiator Abu Ala put forward a map designed to overcome these. The map fulfilled three Palestinian territorial objectives:

> reducing the area to be annexed by Israel to twice the settlements' current built-up areas; minimizing the number of West Bank Palestinians to be annexed by Israel from more than 20,000

projected by Israel's Taba map to practically zero; rejecting the annexation of any part of the Jerusalem area settlements of Ma'ale Adumim or Givat Ze'ev. (Aronson, 2001: 7)

Aronson noted that the plan represented a 'historical and diplomatic landmark' in that it was the first official Palestinian proposal to accept Israeli annexation of part of the occupied territories. Dr Ron Pundak, director of the Peres Centre for Peace in Tel Aviv and a central figure in the Oslo process, claims that 'on the delicate issue of the Palestinian refugees and the right of return, the negotiators reached a draft determining the parameters and procedures for a solution, along with a clear emphasis that its implementation would not threaten the Jewish character of the State of Israel' (2001: 44). Pundak maintains that the talks had seen 'dramatic progress on all the most important issues' (2001: 44).

THE SHARON ADMINISTRATION

On 6 February 2001 Ariel Sharon won the Israeli election, pledging no negotiations with the Palestinians until the intifada ended. The following week Massoud Ayad, a member of Arafat's Force 17 bodyguards was assassinated by an Israeli helicopter gunship, the first official killed since the assassination of the Fatah leader Thabet Thabet on New Year's Eve. This killing had led to international condemnation because of Thabet's close association with Israeli peace activists (*Guardian*, 14 February 2001). Six days later, Mahmud al-Madani, a Hamas leader, was assassinated in Nablus. On 27 March the Non-Aligned States put forward a resolution (SC/7040) at the Security Council calling for a UN observer force to be dispatched to the occupied territories to protect Palestinian civilians. The resolution was vetoed by the United States which cast the sole negative vote. In April and May 2000 Israel launched attacks on refugee camps and temporarily reoccupied areas under Palestinian Authority control. The unrest continued throughout the summer with increasing casualties on both sides. By the end of August 2001, 154 Israelis (28 minors) and 495 Palestinians (123 minors) had been killed in the intifada (B'Tselem, 2003b).

After the 11 September 2001 attacks on America, Yasser Arafat met with Shimon Peres on 26 September to reach a truce, but it failed to halt the bloodshed. There were extensive incursions by the Israeli army plus widespread attacks and a number of suicide bombings. In Operation 'Dull Blade' in October 2001 Israel sent tanks into Ramallah and Tulkarem. Between the 11 September attack and the end of 2001, a further 75 Israelis (8 minors) and 252 Palestinians (42 minors) were killed.

In March and April 2002 Ariel Sharon launched Operation 'Defensive Wall', which involved incursions into most of the West Bank cities and extensive destruction, notably in Jenin, Nablus and Bethlehem. Many of the events in the second intifada and media coverage of them are discussed in more detail in the content analysis which follows. In June 2002 Israel began construction of a wall separating Israel from the occupied territories.

Israel has argued that the fence is necessary to stop the entry of suicide bombers into Israel, who have killed hundreds of civilians during the second intifada. Aronson suggests that the purpose of the wall is to create de facto borders in which Israel will absorb approximately 50 per cent of the West Bank, whilst Palestinians will be 'separated from each other and from Palestinian citizens of Israel by borders based upon settlement blocs' (Aronson, 2003). The Israeli human rights organisation B'Tselem (2003c) have condemned the wall which they project will cause 'direct harm' to 210,000 Palestinians, turning some villages into 'isolated enclaves' and separating Palestinians from their farm lands, villages and livelihoods. They also argue that the wall breaches international law and will have a severe impact on education and health services.

There was one further attempt at a peace plan which followed the Iraq war of 2003. The 'Road Map' drawn up by the US, the EU, the UN and Russia called for the setting up of a Palestinian state in the West Bank and Gaza Strip by 2005. The plan had three stages. In the first stage, all Palestinian violence must stop, Palestinian political structures must be reformed, Israel must dismantle the settlement outposts built since March 2001, and there must be a phased Israeli withdrawal from parts of the occupied territories. In the second stage an international peace conference would take place and a provisional Palestinian state would come into being. The final stage would involve a solution to the most intractable issues, such as borders, refugees and the status of Jerusalem. Arab states would also sign peace deals with Israel. The plan had encountered difficulties by September 2003 in the face of continued killings by Israel of Hamas leaders, and suicide bombings. In September 2003 the intifada reached the end of its third year. The death toll stood at 795 Israelis (100 minors) and 2,235 Palestinians (409 minors).

Our intention in giving these histories was to illustrate the range of contested positions which exist over this conflict. In the chapters which follow we will show how the arguments of the different sides appeared on television news and how they were received and understood by audiences.

2
Content Studies

INTRODUCTION: THE DISPUTED ORIGINS OF THE CONFLICT

Our content studies focus on TV news coverage of the second Palestinian intifada or uprising, following its outbreak in September 2000. We have already indicated in the histories above that the events leading up to this are complex and contested by different parties. We can see this if we look at key issues such as the origins and history of the Palestinian refugees. These people were displaced from their land when the Israeli state was formed in 1948. The account of how they were displaced varies and for many years Israel claimed that they had simply fled the fighting in 1948 (when the nascent state of Israel fought with its Arab neighbours) or they had been told to leave by their leaders. More recently, the Israeli historian Avi Shlaim has given a carefully documented account which suggests that many were forced to leave and the military offensive on civilian areas began in the period before the official outbreak of hostilities on 15 May 1948. He shows that the military forces of what was to become Israel had embarked on a new offensive strategy which involved destroying Arab villages and the forced removal of civilians. The intention was to clear the interior of the future Israeli state of what were seen as potentially hostile 'Arab elements'. As he writes:

> The novelty and audacity of the plan lay in the orders to capture Arab villages and cities, something [they] had never attempted before ... Palestinian society disintegrated under the impact of the Jewish military offensive that got underway in April, and the exodus of the Palestinians was set in motion ... by ordering the capture of Arab cities and the destruction of villages, it both permitted and justified the forcible expulsion of Arab civilians. (Shlaim, 2000: 30)

He also notes how the displacement of the Palestinians and its consequences were clearly acknowledged by Moshe Dayan, one of the most prominent of Israel's military leaders and politicians.

Speaking in 1955 at the funeral of an Israeli killed by Arab insurgents, Dayan commented:

> What cause have we to complain about their fierce hatred for us? For eight years now they sit in their refugee camps in Gaza, and before their eyes we turn into our homestead the land and villages in which they and their forefathers have lived. (quoted in Shlaim, 2000: 101)

The Palestinian view was indeed that they had been forced from their land and homes in 1948. They had then to live as refugees in countries such as Lebanon, Syria, Jordan and on the West Bank (of the Jordan river) and the Gaza Strip. There followed a series of conflicts and at times outright war between Israel and its Arab neighbours. The most significant of these conflicts was perhaps the 1967 Six Day War. In this, Israel occupied the West Bank and East Jerusalem (which had been under the control of Jordan), the Gaza Strip (which had been under the control of Egypt) and the Golan Heights (which were Syrian). This occupation brought many Palestinian refugees under Israeli military control and was bitterly contested. Jerusalem as a religious centre for both Muslims and Jews became a major point of conflict. The Israelis also built settlements in the newly occupied areas of Gaza and the West Bank and they exploited natural resources, in particular taking control of the vital resource of water. To occupy and exploit land in this fashion is widely seen as a violation of international law and for this reason newspapers in Britain such as the *Guardian* routinely refer to the Israeli settlements as 'illegal'. This has also been the view of the British government. In 1997 the Conservative Foreign Secretary Malcolm Rifkind referred to the building of a large settlement in occupied East Jerusalem as follows: 'The start of construction can do nothing but harm the peace process … like all settlements this one will be illegal' (quoted in Shlaim, 2000: 582). As Avi Shlaim suggests, these settlements were about much more than simply building houses and farms. They were part of a systematic policy of exerting strategic and military control, which in this case involved 'surrounding the huge Greater Jerusalem area with two concentric circles of settlements with access roads and military positions' (2000: 582).

Within Israel there were divisions over the occupation and the settlement policies. Some argued that occupied land should be returned to the Palestinians in exchange for a final peace agreement.

But many Israelis defended the occupation arguing that they had religious claims (from the time of the Bible) on the land and Jerusalem. It was also argued that Israel's security needs could only be met by extending its borders as, for example, when Israel expropriated a part of Southern Lebanon in 1982/83 as a 'security zone'. This action had led to an extended conflict with Hezbullah guerrillas from Lebanon, and Israel eventually withdrew in 1999 after suffering serious losses. The conflict with the Palestinians in the occupied territories resulted in two major intifadas (or uprisings) in 1987 and 2000. In the period between these there was a series of American-led peace efforts, notably the Oslo agreements of 1993 and 1995, and the Wye Accords of 1998. These in practice gave the Palestinians some self-rule in parts of the West Bank and Gaza. But the Israeli army still controlled roads and access and could effectively seal off the Palestinian areas, thus exerting a stranglehold on economic movement. They also continued to control and exploit water supplies as well as keeping a large army and undercover police presence.

Despite the hostility which was generated by the occupation there is some evidence that by the time of the Wye Accords of 1998, most Palestinians still supported the peace process and many Israelis also accepted the principle of returning land in exchange for peace. But this was opposed by right-wing politicians in Israel who urged settlers to take more land even as Israeli troops were withdrawing from Palestinian areas under the Wye agreements. As Avi Shlaim writes:

Some hard-line ministers publicly urged the Jewish settlers to grab more West Bank land to keep it out of Palestinian hands. The first stage of the Israeli troop withdrawal was matched by a renewed spurt of land confiscations for the purpose of building Jewish settlements and a network of roads between them ... In sharp contrast to Israeli backsliding, the Palestinians scrupulously adhered to the course charted at Wye. (Shlaim, 2000: 605)

In May 1999 Ehud Barak was elected as prime minister of Israel with a commitment to establishing peace. However, his election stimulated further occupations by Israel settlers. Under the headline 'Settlers Race for Land', the *Guardian* described the situation on the ground. It quoted the mayor of a Palestinian village as follows:

When the settlers brought their bulldozers we went down with our papers to prove it was our land. Then the Israeli soldiers arrived and just went mad. It was like a war here, they were throwing tear gas grenades and firing CS gas canisters and live ammunition into our houses. (*Guardian*, 25 May 1999)

The control of water was also crucial and another *Guardian* report (2 November 1998) showed that the pattern of settlement construction since the 1970s was along the ridges and edges of aquifers and that 'this strategic consideration was part of the Jewish pattern in populating the area'. This was a central issue for Palestinians since a third of their economy was agricultural and could not be sustained without water. The report also noted that 26 per cent of Palestinian houses had no water and each Israeli was consuming over three times as much water as a Palestinian.

Under Barak's leadership in Israel, the peace process continued through 2000 and he met with Yassar Arafat and President Clinton at Camp David in the US. But no agreement was reached and there was a growing frustration with the peace process. This reached a climax in September 2000 when the right-wing Israeli politician Ariel Sharon walked through the most holy Muslim places in Jerusalem. Sharon was a notorious figure for Palestinians and was blamed by many for the killing of refugees in Lebanon in 1982. His action in Jerusalem was seen as a statement of Israeli control and sovereignty, and it was followed by riots which grew into the second intifada.[1] Our study focuses initially on media coverage of these events (particularly television news) and the potential influence which this has had on public understanding of the Israeli-Palestinian conflict.

This study has two main dimensions. The first is the content analysis of BBC and ITV news and is the focus of this chapter. The purpose of this work is to analyse how the news presented the conflict and the different ways in which it was explained. The second is a substantial audience study using both focus groups and question-naires, and is discussed in Chapter 3. In this we examine what TV audiences understood from what they had seen and their use of other sources of information such as formal education or direct experience of the conflict.

CONTENT ANALYSIS: METHODS

The media are central to the exercise of power in society. They can set agendas in the sense of highlighting some news stories and topics, but they can also severely limit the information with which we understand events in the world. The analysis of media content remains a prime concern. The method that the Glasgow University Media Group has developed to analyse the content of media texts is called *Thematic Analysis*. It is based on the assumption that in any contentious area there will be competing ways of describing events and their history. Ideas are linked to interests and these competing interests will seek to explain the world in ways which justify their own position. So ideology (by which we mean an interest-linked perspective) and the struggle for legitimacy go hand in hand. Part of our work has focused on the role of the media in these ideological struggles, and how the reporting of events can embody different ways of understanding which are linked to perspectives and interests. In our early work on television news content we analysed the public debate which existed at that time about the failings of the British economy. In the 1970s and 1980s, this was a matter of great concern as Britain was perceived to be falling behind the rest of the world's economies. In this public controversy the trade unions pointed to management mistakes in the organisation of industry and low levels of investment which meant that machines often broke down and production was much less efficient than that of competitors in other countries. In contrast, right-wing commentators (including the Conservative Party) preferred to point to the actions of the workforce and blamed strikes for the failings of the economy. This became a favourite theme of the Conservatives in the 1980s, in the early years of Margaret Thatcher's government (see Philo et al., 1995). We were interested in how the TV news reported such debates and the potential influence on public belief. The essence of our method was first to note each of the explanations and ways of understanding which were being put forward in public debate and the range of available evidence which could underpin different positions. We identified these from published materials such as books, reports, the press and TV and any other relevant sources. We then analysed the content of TV news programmes and showed how all of these different explanations were featured (or not). In practice we found that some explanations were given prominence in news headlines or interview programmes while others were downgraded or excluded. So for example, there were many headlines in the news about strikes and the problems these were allegedly causing, but none blaming management mistakes. If some explanations were present on the news and others were absent, then it seemed likely to us that this would affect what TV audiences understood and believed. Of course people might have access to other sources of information, for example if they had direct experience of working in a factory or if they read 'alternative' accounts which gave information which was not on the news. This might include the financial pages of newspapers, from which we derived much of our information.[2]

Using this method, we showed that the view that 'strikes were to blame' was clearly endorsed on the news while other explanations were downgraded or excluded. Sometimes the explanation would appear as a direct statement from a journalist, such as: 'It's the kind of strike which has done so much to contribute to the dire economic problems' (quoted in Philo et al., 1995: 10). But we also developed at this time the concept of the explanatory theme, by which we meant that an assumed explanation gave a pattern or structure to an area of coverage. For example, the explanatory theme that strikes were to blame underpinned the whole process of news reporting including going to a factory, interviewing workers, asking them about strikes and crucially *not* asking the management about investment policies or their own mistakes, and then perhaps listing in the bulletin other strikes or disputes which had occurred that week. The crucial point is that the pattern of the coverage and the subjects that it highlights can assume the explanation even without it being directly stated.

In analysing news coverage of the Israeli-Palestinian conflict we identified a number of areas where there were competing perspectives over how it was to be explained and understood. We have already indicated the disputes that exist over the history and origins of the conflict. Another area of controversy would be the motives of those involved – for example, are there deeply rooted causes for the intifada or are the Palestinians merely responding to incitement by mendacious leaders? We have examined other potentially contested areas such as who is portrayed as initiating violence and the reporting of casualties. Such accounts carry with them assumptions about cause, responsibility and consequences that connect directly to wider social values. For example, a story about children dying in conflict is not merely a disinterested account of the day's events. Such a story is implicitly linked to strongly held social values that children should not be killed by tanks or blown up by bombs and it is therefore likely to affect audience responses and judgements about the conflict. It is important to study how the inclusion or exclusion of certain types of descriptions or explanations and the use of emotive language (words such as 'murder' or 'atrocity') may influence public understanding. Journalists should strive to meet the crucial criteria of accuracy and balance, but it is always the case that the reporting of such events is infused by social values.

There are other social values that affect the structuring of news. These would include assumptions about hierarchy and status that affect how stories are chosen and told. For example, a news topic such as 'peace negotiations between world leaders' is chosen partly because peace is assumed to be important but also because 'world leaders' are given a special status and can command access to the media. So beyond the specific meanings and perspectives of a particular story, the construction of news is influenced by other value assumptions about who is seen as a legitimate authority and what status and deference is given to different speakers. This might affect how interviews are conducted – there is a difference between asking someone for a brief opinion in the street and the legitimacy and status which is implied by interviewing an 'expert' in a studio. It is also important to identify the manner in which journalists report the views of the different sides. Sometimes journalists go beyond simply reporting a view and directly endorse it. There is an important difference between stating that one side in the conflict '*claims* that there was a massacre' and saying directly 'this was a massacre'. We will discuss such issues later in conjunction with our main focus on how different perspectives and explanations are included or excluded and how some are highlighted and endorsed in news reports.

It is quite possible for the news to feature a range of perspectives and indeed it should do so if it is to meet the requirement of balance. We have often found, however, that some perspectives dominate in news stories. We have also found that sometimes a perspective that is highlighted in one bulletin can be undermined or contradicted by information that is given in another. To obtain some measure of the relative dominance of different accounts and perspectives we count their frequency and the manner in which they appear (for example, the number of appearances in headlines and the number of 'direct' and 'reported' statements from the different sides). We can illustrate this in relation to an actual case that we discuss in detail later in our results. This case is a news report that Hezbullah guerrillas from Lebanon had kidnapped three Israeli soldiers. ITV News had the headline: 'Trouble continues as Hezbullah take three Israeli soldiers prisoner' (7 October 2000). One side can therefore be seen as initiating the 'trouble'. This was commonly reported, but a small number of news programmes also reported that the Israelis had been holding Lebanese hostages for many years and that the kidnap was linked to this. If the audience has this information then it may alter how they understand the events and the judgements that they make. There are in effect two competing explanatory themes. The first implies that one side is a victim and the second shows that both sides have taken hostages.[3] The first of these themes actually dominated the news and this can be seen from its position in headlines and also the frequency of references to this way of seeing the events.

There is a further point to be made about our methods for analysing language. When we make numerical assessments of the presence of some explanations or the dominance of some types of description, we always attempt to keep as close as possible to the actual language used in the text. In other words, we count phrases, words or sentences that are actually used. We avoid employing a priori categories such as 'statements for' one side or 'statements against' and we do not attempt to group language within such categories. We are concerned that such methods can lead to the bundling together of a wide range of textual meanings into rather crude 'boxes'. We try to account for the range of subtlety of language, as it is used to convey a complex variety of meanings, and then to trace how these exact messages are received and understood by audiences.

In practice for this content analysis, we began by calculating the amount of coverage given to different subject areas, such as the depiction of violence or peace negotiations. We did this by counting lines of text from transcribed news programmes. We then engaged in a detailed examination of how the causes and origins of the conflict were represented. We followed this with a further analysis of how different perspectives were highlighted in headlines, interviews and in the routine reporting of events such as attacks, deaths and casualties. Much of our analysis deals with verbal text, but we have also looked at visual images and at how these were given meaning and context by the words that accompanied them. We may, for example, see a dramatic picture of riots and gunfire in streets, but not know much about why this is happening. The judgements that we form about it may depend upon the spoken description that accompanies the image.

This work was undertaken in conjunction with an analysis of audience understanding and reception of news, which we discuss below. It is important to combine such studies because research which rests on content analysis alone leaves the researchers in the position of having to assert what the audience would be likely to understand from the news. There are in fact wide variations between people in terms of how well they understand news items. We have argued elsewhere that when journalists construct news reports they assume levels of knowledge in viewers. But these levels of knowledge do not exist in all cases and many in the audience do not understand the causes of the events which are being shown (Glasgow University Media Group, 2002). In our present study it was apparent that the news sometimes offered explanations of the conflict which were brief and enigmatic. For example, a description of fighting in Jerusalem notes that 'The city's most holy place for Arabs and Jews became a battlefield … on this the eve of the Jewish New Year it's the age-old problem that is setting the agenda' (ITV late News, 29 September 2000). Those who know something of Middle East politics could understand this reference to the 'age-old problem' as being the struggle between Israelis and Palestinians over the ownership of Jerusalem, where the Israeli occupation is opposed by the Palestinians. But those who do not have this knowledge may simply be mystified as to why the two sides were fighting. The difficulty is that what may seem obvious to the researcher or the journalist may not be so to all members of the audience. As we will show, in order to establish how the text is understood by different audiences, it is necessary to work directly with them.

As part of this study, we also contacted and interviewed journalists and news editors who had a close working knowledge of the conflict. It was not our intention to write a full production analysis but we used these contacts to check information, to give us background on specific stories and to explain where necessary how processes of news gathering actually operated in Israel and the occupied territories. As a further dimension to the study, some of these journalists also took part in the audience reception work and sat in on focus groups, contributing to discussions (see Chapter 3).

SAMPLES AND RESULTS

SAMPLE ONE: 28 SEPTEMBER TO 16 OCTOBER 2000

Our first major sample of news content focused on news coverage of the outbreak of the intifada in September 2000. For this we examined the lunchtime, early evening and late news bulletins for BBC1 and ITV (Channel Three). The focus was on these because they are on the most popular channels and attract a very substantial audience. We have analysed bulletins which featured the conflict between 28 September 2000, the first day of the intifada, and 16 October 2000, the date of an attempted peace summit in Egypt (a total of 91 bulletins[4]). We used the national press and other programmes such as Channel 4 News and BBC *Newsnight* for purposes of comparison. We also examined news items from outside this period to see whether trends in coverage that we had identified were sustained in subsequent news reporting. These were drawn from three other sample periods: 17 October 2001 to 13 December 2001, 2–9 March 2002 and 9–16 April 2002 (a total of 98 bulletins).

There were four main elements to our first content analysis, 28 September to 16th October 2000:

1. We examined the main areas of coverage in news programmes and produced a quantitative assessment of their relative prominence. As part of this we identified the explanations which were given of the causes of the conflict.
2. We examined interviews and made an assessment of who got on to speak and the circumstances in which they did so.
3. We analysed news headlines and how they might shape ways of understanding the conflict.
4. We analysed coverage of a series of events in which Israelis and Palestinians were injured or killed to illustrate how the actions and motives of different parties in the conflict were presented, and the language used to describe the two sides.

Areas of coverage

There were five broad areas of coverage which we identified. The first was images and descriptions of conflict and violence. The second area was the coverage of funerals of people who had died in the conflict. In practice these offered scenes of agitation and rage and were frequently linked to further violence or to the possibility of it. The third area was discussions of peace negotiations and the prospects for peace. The fourth area was the discussion of the tactics being employed by different parties in the conflict in response to changing events. These included political or military manoeuvres and also the every-day responses of ordinary citizens. Finally we identified reasons for the conflict and references to its history.

Violence

The coverage as a whole was permeated with images, descriptions and references to conflict and violence including riots, mobs, stone-throwing, stabbings, shootings, kidnapping, protests and military attacks. In our audience groups these were the images which overwhelmingly dominated memories of what they had seen on television. In our analysis, such coverage constituted 28 per cent of this sample (measured in lines of text). Reporting of violence and conflict normally contained very little explanation of the history and origins of the conflict. As in the following example which is simply a list of the day's conflicts:

> Well you join me on the Mount of Olives overlooking the old city of Jerusalem and it was down there on Haram al-Sharif, as the Muslims call it, the Temple Mount as known to the Jews, where the clashes broke out again this morning. If the cameraman could just move a little to my left you'll see that down there on the edge of the wall of the Old City there's a fire burning, that's an Israeli police station that was set alight by Palestinian demonstrators about an hour ago and the fire still seems to be raging. A little bit before that I was down in exactly that area when the most ferocious battle broke out as young Palestinian worshippers came off the Haram al-Sharif after the Friday prayers [*images of crowd rioting*]. They had rocks in their hands, they started throwing these rocks at Israeli policemen and soldiers who fired back and for the rest of us trapped in the middle it was just a question of finding a rock to hide behind because there was a lot of ammunition being fired. There were rubber bullets, rubber-coated bullets and we think also some live ammunition, and we understand that there are quite a number of injured, and according to Palestinians who were on the Temple Mount at the time, we believe that at least one person was killed. Inevitably this has led to further trouble elsewhere on the West Bank today. We're getting reports already of disturbances in Ramallah, in other parts of the West Bank some injuries. We all thought that perhaps today the situation was going to calm down after the efforts at a diplomatic level to restore calm after this crisis that has lasted a week now. But it seems as though this morning's episode in the Old City of Jerusalem has triggered yet another round of confrontation. (BBC1 lunchtime News, 6 October 2000)

The emphasis here is on 'hot' live action and the immediacy of the report rather than any explanation of the underlying causes of the events. One BBC journalist who had reported on this conflict told us that his own editor had said to him that they did not want 'explainers' – as he put it: 'It's all bang bang stuff.' The driving force behind such news is to hold the attention of as many viewers as possible, but in practice, as we will see, it simply leaves very many people confused. Here is another example from BBC1:

> The Palestinians have been warned to call off their uprising by tonight but this was their answer to the Israelis, a hail of rocks, in Ramallah in the West Bank [*images of Palestinian crowd, noise of gunfire*]. Young boys join in what is called the new intifada and sometimes women too. On this occasion the rioters are forced to retreat. They say they won't be threatened by Israel's ultimatums and deadlines. They feel they have little to lose by fighting and little to gain from the peace process now on the brink of collapse. They flaunt pictures of the Iraqi leader, Saddam Hussein; some call on him to attack Israel. In the meantime the Palestinians use their catapults and their slingshots. Bucketloads of ammunition are brought up to the front line, but many told me what they really want are guns, so they can turn this crisis into a war. (BBC1 late News, 9 October 2000)

There is a hint of an explanation here in the reference to the Palestinians belief that they have 'little to gain from the peace process', but then the moment passes and the commentary is back to 'catapults and slingshots', 'Bucketloads of ammunition', and the desire for guns. The escalation of the conflict is clearly important but viewers might also want to know why. There are sometimes brief references to causes in such coverage, but the bulk of it is taken up with dramatic pictures and commentary on the latest 'clashes', as in this account from ITV:

> Minutes after the praying finished the fighting resumed and today saw violence in Jerusalem itself. Hundreds of Palestinian youths attacking Israeli security forces [*shouting, gunshots*]. Running battles were fought in the alleyways that make up this historic place. There were calls for calm, there were calls for restraint, but yet again all have been ignored. This is an Israeli police station inside the Old City of Jerusalem, a part of the City of Peace, is on fire [*shouting*].

Israeli soldiers have been trapped in the burning building, firing outside to keep rioters at bay [*gunfire*]. Colleagues had to come to the rescue [*gunshots*]. Using his M16 rifle, one conscript blew open the front door. It took a few minutes but they got their people out. Several had been injured [*shouting*]. Jerusalem, and who controls it, is at the centre of the conflict, for a time today the Palestinian flag flew, a direct challenge to Israeli sovereignty. There has been trouble elsewhere, but it is the fighting in the Holy City that is of most significance. Today this was the Via Dolorosa [*gunshots*], the path that's said Christ walked to his crucifixion. It is also called 'The Way of Sorrows'. (ITV late News, 6 October 2000)

The reference to Jerusalem and to who controls it is typical, in that it is so brief that it will only make sense to those who already understand Middle Eastern politics. To those who have a more limited grasp it does sound as if it is simply two groups of people fighting for control of a holy city and who can put their flag up over it. Some in our audience groups did indeed see the conflict in these terms, as if it was just two groups of neighbours who somehow could not get on.

Funerals

Funerals were often linked to the fighting and the coverage of them frequently included powerful and emotionally charged images.[5] In this example there is the suggestion that the grief and passion lead to more violence and the 'holy war' over Jerusalem is again mentioned, but there is no discussion of how the conflict originated:

There is a huge turnout for each and every Palestinian funeral. These people regard their dead as martyrs killed in a religious war over Jerusalem and therefore worthy of being honoured. How long the fighting and killing goes on will be determined by them and appearing at each funeral are many more men prepared to die. This is one of several funerals taking place on the West Bank today and it is not only an outpouring of grief, it is a call to arms, a call for retaliation. (ITV early evening News, 2 October 2000)

The screen is filled with images of passion and rage but with little opportunity to understand how this situation has come about. Here are three examples from BBC News:

When they are not fighting, Palestinians are busy burying their dead ... funerals like this are focal points not only for grief, but also for Palestinian rage and resentment and the dead man's cousin greets the idea of a ceasefire with derision. (BBC1 late evening News, 3 October 2000)

In Nablus a 22-year-old was buried this morning his funeral like so many others attracted a large embittered crowd ... there's a funeral going on, the streets are full of heavily armed angry men and up on the mountains above us, Israeli snipers are watching. With emotions still raw it will take more than words to end this crisis. (BBC1 lunchtime News, 4 October 2000)

Last night Israeli soldiers and Palestinian gunmen exchanged fire in a part of Hebron. Such night-time gun battles are becoming commonplace [images of Palestinian crowd chanting] in Ramallah, another funeral and another focus for Palestinian anger. (BBC1 lunchtime News, 9 October 2000)

Such images are prominent in the memories of television viewers but, as we will see from our work with audiences, the relationships which underpin the conflict and its history are much less well understood.

Prospects for peace and negotiations

Discussions on the prospects for peace and meetings between key figures in the conflict were another major category of news content (the largest category, accounting for 33 per cent of this sample). There were a series of meetings of political leaders in this period, the first in Paris on 4 October 2000 when the Israelis and Palestinians met with the US Secretary of State. The UN Secretary-General, Kofi Annan, flew to Israel on 9 October, and there was a summit of world leaders including the US president in Egypt on 16 October 2000. The coverage of these was taken up mainly with the comings and goings of the key figures and reports on the lack of progress in negotiations for a peaceful resolution of the crisis:

There are few smiles on display at this summit and for good reason, for while the Israeli and Palestinian leaders talk amid the grandeur of Paris, they have left behind them on the West Bank and in Gaza mounting chaos and bitterness. The best hope is American mediation led by the US Secretary of State Madeleine Albright, who is seeking a ceasefire on the ground and then an accelerated timetable for peace negotiations. For now, all of that seems out of her grasp. (ITV early evening News, 4 October 2000)

And on the BBC the summit in Egypt was headlined as follows:

Middle East peace summit gets underway, but no sign of a breakthrough. While they try to end the bloodshed, the killing continues on the streets. (BBC1 early evening News, 16 October 2000)

A significant point to emerge from this coverage is the manner in which the United States is presented and how this presentation influences the understanding of audiences. At this time the US was featured as being extensively involved in peace moves. Thus on ITV we hear that the 'Americans are desperately trying to broker a meaningful and lasting ceasefire' (ITV early evening News, 3 October 2000) and a later headline tells us that there are 'More Middle East clashes as Clinton vows to step in' (ITV lunchtime News, 9 October 2000). On the BBC, President Clinton is referred to as having a long history of 'trying to bring permanent peace':

Never before has President Clinton flown into a summit where the stakes are so high and the outcome so uncertain. Today and tonight the man who has spent eight years trying to bring permanent peace to the Middle East has to salvage something from the past 18 days of violence. (BBC1 lunchtime News, 16 October 2000)

On ITV, in a discussion between two journalists, one explicitly refers to 'the even-handedness which has characterised American diplomacy in the Middle East'. The second takes up the point and comments:

Well, the administration had been under a great pressure, as indeed have both the presidential candidates, to take a more pro-Israeli line, both from the Israeli lobby here and the Jewish lobby here and also from certain sections of the media. I don't expect that that pressure will affect this administration's policy or even the next one, because the Americans have long maintained that the only way they have any influence in the Middle East is to be a relatively neutral, honest broker. (ITV early evening News, 12 October 2000)

Yet there were other comments on the news which apparently contradict this view. For example, this BBC1 report mentions the distrust which young Palestinians have of the US:

> [visuals of fighting, stone throwing] ... a lethal game of cat and mouse in the narrow streets of Hebron. This is what the leaders in Paris are up against. The idea that Washington might act as honest broker depressed these young Palestinians. It was a similar picture all over the West Bank again today but the level of violence was significantly lower. After six days of this, people are getting tired, but in Gaza, Israel still wielded a big stick. Helicopters fired rockets killing at least one Palestinian. (BBC1 early evening News, 4 October 2000)

On ITV news we also hear that 'many [Palestinians] do not trust the Americans to be honest brokers when it comes to mediation' (late News, 4 October 2000). But that is all that we hear; there is no explanation given as to why this might be so. It would be difficult for viewers without specialist knowledge to make sense of this contradiction. One reason for the Palestinian response is that the US supplies $3 billion each year to Israel, a large part of which is spent on military equipment. In other words, the US arms one side in the conflict. Yet this is very rarely spoken of in news coverage. Other news in our sample showed pictures of Palestinians burning an American flag but again did not say why or give the information that the US was supplying weapons which were being used in the Israeli attacks. It was possible to find such information in news reports but it was very rare and was on the 'periphery' of television news, that is, late night on BBC2 or Channel 4 rather than on the mass audience programmes of BBC1 and ITV. This example is from Channel 4 News:

> With two billion pounds of US money every year, much of it spent on arms, Israel has never been such a supreme regional power ... Palestinians look up and see American-supplied Apache helicopters, just as Hezbullah in Lebanon look south and see American-supplied missiles, tanks and artillery. (Channel 4 evening News, 13 October 2000)

Without such information it is difficult to understand the actions or rationale of some of those who are portrayed in television news stories. In our audience sample of young people we asked why Palestinians might be critical of the US and burn the American flag. Most did not know that the US supplied money and arms to Israel. Reporting on such issues is complicated for journalists by the closeness of Britain's relationship with the US. In the TV news bulletins we found very little criticism of US policy, and this became perhaps more of a taboo area after the attacks on the US on 11 September 2001, often referred to as '9/11'. The BBC Director-General famously apologised for the content of a *Question Time* programme broadcast live shortly after 9/11, where such criticism had been made. To explain in detail the rationale of those who oppose US policy is to court controversy. It is simpler to avoid explanations or to leave them to the margins of television and radio. The difficulty with this is that it leaves many viewers ill informed.

Tactics

This is a substantial area of news coverage in which journalists discuss the actions and responses of the different parties in the conflict to the latest events and likely future developments. This may include consideration of political or military tactics or the everyday responses of local populations to events, which accounted for 14 per cent of this sample. In this example, the BBC describes military tactics:

> Later, we saw the Israelis bringing in extra tanks on low-loaders to reinforce their positions here on the West Bank. So another display of extremely tough tactics by Israeli security forces here in Ramallah. They are on the highest state of alert, extra troops have been drafted in and leave has been cancelled in Jerusalem. Israeli security forces prevented all male Palestinians under the age of 45 from getting into the old city. (BBC1 early evening News, 13 October 2000)

Political moves are also reported such as a statement by Ehud Barak, the Israeli prime minister, that he intended to form a government of national emergency (BBC1 late News, 12 October 2000). On the same day Yasser Arafat was reported as ordering a general mobilisation of his people. There is also some discussion of how the Israelis intend to cope with the revolt in the long term and to 'restore' order. On ITV two journalists take up these issues:

Journalist 1: So John, if there is no magic formula what might Israel do?

Journalist 2: Well the Israeli prime minister, Mr Barak, has pledged to use all means to restore order. Over the weekend we saw him move more heavy armour, more tanks onto the West Bank. They are now positioned around the Palestinian towns and villages where we have seen clashes over the past eleven days. It may be that the Israelis plan to surround these Palestinian areas to choke the life out of the revolt. (ITV late News, 9 October 2000)

The journalist concludes that the Palestinians would be likely to react violently to such a move. The theme is taken up again on the following day when the same journalist is asked again: 'What are the tactics of the Israeli government?'

Their intention appears to be to stifle this revolt economically. The Palestinian Authority is effectively a scattering of Arab communities on the West Bank and the Israelis appear to be trying to cut off those communities from each other and from Israel proper. (ITV lunchtime News, 10 October 2000)

It is perfectly proper to discuss the tactics of the Israeli government. However, there is no critical consideration here of the nature of the 'order' which they wish to restore. From the point of view of the Palestinians it would consist of military control, which has involved large-scale arrest, imprisonment without trial, torture and extrajudicial killing. There is no extensive discussion by journalists on what 'tactics' the Palestinians might employ to end this.

Explanations of the conflict[6]

This is a key area for the analysis of public understanding of events and their causes. Our audience research showed that many people had little knowledge of the reasons of the conflict and its origins. To understand the origins of the crisis there are at least two sequences of historical events of which the audience would need to be aware. The first is that when Israel was created in 1948, a large number of Palestinians were displaced from their homes and became refugees. The second is that many of these people then went to live on the West Bank of the Jordan, in East Jerusalem and in Gaza, all of which were occupied by Israel in the war of 1967. The Palestinians subsequently lived under Israeli military control which they bitterly contested.

There are of course many qualifications which each side would wish to make to these statements to explain and legitimise their own actions. But without a knowledge of these events, it is extremely difficult to understand the rationale of the different participants in the conflict or even where it was happening. This knowledge was not available on much of the news – indeed some bulletins would be likely to add to viewers' confusion.

When the intifada began in September 2000, some news reports seemed unclear that it was taking place in the occupied areas which were subject to military control. Instead it was sometimes described as taking place in 'Israel'. For example, some news programmes contained large visual backdrops saying 'Israel violence' when the events described took place in occupied East Jerusalem (ITV early evening News, 29 September 2000, and lunchtime News, 6 October 2000). A newscaster summarises the events by saying: 'Fighting over a sacred site in Israel' (ITV early evening News, 29 September 2000). The BBC also described the occupied Palestinian areas as 'Israel's West Bank' (early evening News, 2 October 2000). Later events in the Palestinian town of Ramallah were headlined on a BBC lunchtime news as 'Mob violence in Israel' (12 October 2000). ITV seemed unclear at times over whether Israel had sovereignty in East Jerusalem. It doesn't, and as a BBC Radio 4 journalist succinctly put it: 'just about every country apart from this one [Israel] believes that the occupation is illegal' (Today, 7 February 2002). A correspondent in the Guardian also noted that:

> Under international law East Jerusalem has been occupied by Israel since 1967, which is why only two states – Costa Rica and El Salvador – recognise Jerusalem as the capital of Israel and maintain embassies there. (Guardian, 26 January 2001)

ITV, however, reported that at one point in the conflict Palestinians had raised their own flag, challenging 'Israeli sovereignty': 'Jerusalem and who controls it is at the centre of the conflict. For a time today the Palestinian flag flew, a direct challenge to Israeli sovereignty' (ITV late News, 6 October 2000). In a later bulletin, the significance of the Temple Mount in Jerusalem is described: 'For Muslims it is the third holiest place in the world. It is, however, also sacred to the Israelis and they have sovereignty over it and are not prepared to give that up' (ITV late News, 12 October 2000).

There are other ways in which the areas of the conflict were described, sometimes by giving the name of towns or by references, such as the 'Palestinian-ruled Gaza Strip' (BBC1 early evening News, 2 October 2000) or the 'Palestinian-controlled West Bank' (ITV early evening News, 2 October 2000).

The key point is that if journalists are unclear over which territories are occupied and how they are controlled and what this signifies to those involved, then it is not surprising if viewers are confused. Another key reason for confusion and the lack of understanding in the television audience was that explanations were rarely given on the news and when they were, journalists often spoke obliquely, almost in the form of shorthand. For the audience to understand the significance of what they were saying would require a level of background knowledge which was simply not present in most people. For example, in the news bulletin which featured the progress of peace talks a journalist made a series of very brief comments on the issues which under-pinned the conflict:

The basic raw disagreements remain – *the future, for example of this city Jerusalem, the future of Jewish settlements and the returning refugees*. For all that, together with the anger and bitterness felt out in the West Bank then I think it's clear this crisis is not about to abate. (ITV early evening News, 16 October 2001 – our italics)

On the BBC, a journalist notes of the Palestinians that:

Their anger is fuelled by a lethal combination of economic discontent, frustration with the peace process, religious passion and the desire to avenge the deaths of friends and loved ones. (BBC1 late News, 3 October 2000)

The above news reports raise some of the key issues which underpin the continuing conflict. Each requires to be sufficiently explained such that an audience may understand their significance. We can now look in detail at these and other 'explanatory' areas as they appear on the news to see what was actually available to viewers.

History and origins of the conflict on TV news.   In the bulletins which we transcribed from 28 September until 16 October 2000, there were over 3,500 lines of text in total. Just 17 lines referred to the history of the conflict. The BBC offered this account which appeared in just one bulletin on 10 October:

> So where is the past 50 years of Arab-Israeli conflict now leading? From the moment of birth the Jewish state of Israel has been fighting for land against Palestinians forced into exile. In 1967 Israel doubled its territory in the Six Day War. For Arabs this was the great setback. Ever since, Israel has been trading land for guarantees of peace from its neighbours. The last great effort to secure total peace was launched in 1993. Seven years on it brought Bill Clinton and today's leaders to the brink of success at Camp David. But the division of land could not be agreed and today Israel's prime minister speaks of the peace process in the past tense. (BBC1 late News, 10 October 2000)

The journalist noted that: 'Ever since, Israel has been trading land for guarantees of peace.' This description of Israeli actions might be questioned. There were many press reports prior to this which showed how peace moves were actually accompanied by the expansion of Israeli settlements (see, for example, 'Land grab gathers pace in West Bank', *Guardian*, 8 January 1999). The BBC journalist does note that the Palestinians were 'forced into exile'. This is the only such reference in the whole period of this sample. We found a small number of references in other time periods, but they are apparently rare. In February 2002, for example, a BBC2 *Newsnight* presenter asked a Palestinian negotiator: 'Are you prepared to negotiate over the return of the Palestinians who were driven out of their homes in 1948?' (27 February 2002). In March 2002 a journalist on BBC1 mentioned in passing the 'Palestinians who were driven out or who fled when Israel was created in 1948' (BBC1 late News 26 March 2002). It is not surprising then that the great bulk of people in our audience sample did not know where the Palestinian refugees had come from and how they had become refugees. This has a crucial effect on how audiences can understand reports on issues such as the peace process. In the following example two journalists are discussing the prospects for negotiations and mention the issue of refugees without any further explanation. The first journalist asks what chance there is of a successful outcome, and the second replies:

> If both sides can now somehow come out of this, with some sort of ceasefire, some sort of end to the violence, then perhaps they

can move on to final status talks, perhaps after that concerning Jerusalem, and perhaps the return of Palestinian refugees. It is a very big day indeed for the Middle East tomorrow. (BBC1 early evening News, 15 October 2000)

The references which journalists made to the history of peace negotiations were similarly brief. On ITV, a news presenter puts this question to a correspondent: 'You've been following this process now for about nine years since it began, is this in your view one of the bleaker moments?' His colleague replies:

Well it's been a roller-coaster ride hasn't it, since the euphoria of the Madrid peace conference in '91, at the Oslo Accords and through to the shock of the Yitzak Rabin assassination, but what strikes me is how quickly it's all regressed. We are now hearing the same old tired debates ... (ITV early evening News, 16 October 2000)

The problem is once again that such a sequence of references to past events implies a level of knowledge which is simply not present in many viewers.

The cycle of violence.   As the intifada developed journalists began to speak of it as having taken on a life of its own. The assumption here was that violence produced more violence in a self-perpetuating cycle:

Five days of mayhem, the cycle of death and confrontation has acquired its own momentum. (BBC1 early evening News, 2 October 2000)

The funeral of a murdered Jewish settler called Rabbi Hilal Leibermen. He'd been shot dead. But in this crisis violence begets more violence and today was no exception. Mourners from the settlement ... were heavily armed including the women. After the funeral service the Jewish settlers attacked Arab homes nearby. They were fired up with grief and bent on revenge. (BBC1 main (late evening) News, 11 October 2000)

ITV also pursued the themes of a constant cycle and a 'self-perpetuating tragedy':

The cycle of violence is unbroken, the trouble spots are the same each day. (ITV early evening News, 4 October 2000)

It has become a self-perpetuating tragedy. Each day starts with the funerals, but afterwards many Palestinian men make their way to the usual flashpoint to confront their enemy. Then there is the familiar exchange. Stones for rubber-coated bullets, stun grenades and tear-gas canisters. (ITV early evening News, 9 October 2000)

Israelis and Palestinians are on the brink of war tonight after a day of tit-for-tat violence in the Middle East. (ITV main (late evening) News, 12 October 2000)

There were over 50 lines of text where such explanations were directly given (approximately similar numbers for each channel) and many other references to 'response' and 'revenge'. Of course it is the case that violence can beget further violence and an escalation of the tactics which are used. But it is not possible to explain the genesis of major conflicts with such an analysis. The 'reasons' for the Second World War, for example, were not that Britain and Germany kept bombing each other. The origins of a conflict and the implications that these have for how it may be resolved cannot be understood simply by reporting day-to-day events and responses. As the BBC journalist Paul Adams commented to us: 'It's a constant procession of grief – it's covered as if it's a very large blood feud, and unless there's a large amount of blood, it's not covered' (Interview, 22 August 2003). Such an approach is unlikely to leave much room for the analysis of underlying causes.

Land, water and economic discontent.   The economic consequences of the Israeli occupation have been cited as a key factor in the Palestinian uprising. These were well known from very early in the intifada and indeed before it began. In October 2000 the *Guardian* reported that resources and land disparity were behind the unrest ('Poverty and Resentment Fuel Palestinian Fury', 14 October 2000). It quoted a report from the UN Development Programme that noted that: 'The Palestinians are still suffering from the legacy of the prolonged occupation, which has a striking impact on their deteriorating social and economic conditions.' The UN report also noted the impact of the 'expansion of the Israeli settlements and military infrastructure'. Other reports had described what this process looked like on the ground. In January 1999 the *Guardian* had cited a critical account from the Israeli group Peace Now on the development of settlements. The newspaper also reported a process by which Palestinian villages were razed, their land was then declared to be a 'nature reserve', and subsequently became housing for Israeli settlers (8 January 1999). This was a very extensive programme of settlement and military expansion which could hardly be missed by journalists. In May 2002 the Israeli human rights group B'Tselem reported that Israel had seized 42 per cent of the West Bank. The report noted that the mechanisms for this included seizure for 'military needs', declaration of land as 'abandoned assets' and the expropriation of land for 'public needs'. These mechanisms according to the report were generally supported by the Israeli high court, thus giving them a 'mask of legality'. As a result of this, the report concluded, Israel was operating a regime with two separate legal systems in the West Bank based on racial discrimination (*Guardian* 15 May 2002).

An obvious question arises: if these issues are so crucial then why is there so little about them on television news? In the period of our sample there were a tiny number of scattered references to the issue of land. The peace process was referred to, as we have seen, as failing because of a lack of agreement on 'the division of land' (BBC1 main News, 10 October 2000). Clashes in Jerusalem are referred to as being over 'hotly disputed territory' (ITV early evening News, 29 September 2000). The Gaza Strip was described as being 'a 30-mile-long finger of land that is home to a million Palestinians and a few thousand Jews'. This report does not discuss the implications of the military occupation for the Palestinians, but instead goes on to say 'in one place, Nezarim, Israeli soldiers protect around 400 of those settlers' (ITV early evening News, 3 October 2000). The Palestinian perspective on these issues is simply not explained in these news programmes. We are told, for example, that they are 'frustrated by the peace process' (BBC1 main News, 6 October 2000), and that the 'peace process has simply not delivered' (BBC1 late News, 2 October 2000). But to understand the significance of such statements requires some knowledge of the control of resources and what has actually happened under the military occupation.

As we have indicated, the control of water supplies by Israel is another crucial issue in the conflict. It is an interesting area for media analysis since it clearly has an extraordinary visual impact on the areas in which Palestinians and Israelis live. This is described in a report by Suzanne Goldenberg in the *Guardian*. She notes of the

Gaza Strip that it is the most densely populated place on earth. As she writes:

> 1.1 million Palestinians live in a mere two-thirds of Gaza's 360 square kilometres, penned into wretched refugee camps or blocks of flats ... all are hemmed into the claustrophobic Strip by an electric fence on one side and the settlements on the other. Meanwhile 6,000 Jewish settlers and army installations occupy the rest – a full one-third of Gaza. That includes a fair chunk of the coastline and the underground aquifers in an area that is mostly sand dune and hard scrabble. (*Guardian*, 16 June 2001)

She then describes the visual difference that control of the water brings:

> The contrast between the communities could not be crueller. Inside the Jewish settlements, residents live in red-roofed bungalows, surrounded by well watered land. There are community centres, swimming pools and hot houses producing cherry tomatoes and lettuce. The Palestinian world outside is bone dry and dusty, narrow lanes crammed with donkey carts, children and push carts. (*Guardian*, 16 June 2001)

If a print journalist can describe a scene so vividly, then how did the ultimate visual medium of television portray it? In practice we found it was virtually absent from the coverage. Although TV journalists often went to settlements there were no comparisons made as above, linking the disparity of resources to the Israeli occupation. The issue of water was in fact barely mentioned. On ITV, there was a brief reference to it in this account of the issues that were frustrating a peace settlement:

> There is also the question of millions of Palestinian refugees that live in neighbouring countries or in impoverished camps. Will they ever be allowed to return home? And what will be the fate of Jewish settlers, the Israelis who now live on the West Bank, land the Palestinians say must be part of their future country? And there are other seemingly mundane issues like *access to water* which are so important in the Middle East and that are still eluding negotiators. (ITV early evening News, 2 October 2000 – our italics)

Such an account names a series of key issues but without explaining them. The audience could not understand from this, how the Palestinians became refugees or why they are impoverished. Water is said to be an important issue, but viewers would be unlikely to understand why. In the focus group interviews which we undertook for this study, less than 10 per cent knew that water was a key issue. In the period of this sample, the issue was not mentioned at all on BBC1. On BBC2 a journalist listed major issues for peace negotiations and commented that: 'last but not least [there would need to be] an agreement on water rights' (BBC2 *Newsnight*, 3 October 2000).

The occupation clearly had important effects on the economy and allocation of resources that were not explored on the news. There were a series of other consequences on social life, which were important factors in explaining the conflict.

The occupation: social consequences for Israelis and Palestinians.   From the Israeli perspective security is a major concern, and their continued presence in the West Bank and Gaza has been justified on these grounds. From the Palestinian perspective a central issue is that they are living under Israeli military control. The effects of the occupation on the everyday life of the Palestinians is substantially absent from media coverage. Phrases such as 'military occupation' or 'military rule' are not normally used. Yet the conditions which the military presence has imposed on the Palestinians are a major factor in the unrest. In December 1998, the *Observer* reported a survey that had been published by B'Tselem, the Israeli human rights group. The survey was to mark the fiftieth anniversary of the Universal Declaration of Human Rights and B'Tselem observed: 'Apart perhaps, from the article prohibiting slavery, the State of Israel violates each and every one of the Declaration's provisions in its behaviour towards the Palestinians in the territories' (*Observer*, 13 December 1998).

B'Tselem found that the killing of Palestinians by Israeli settlers was rarely punished. It also reported that of the 1,000–1,500 Palestinian prisoners interrogated by the Israeli Shin Bet security services each year, 85 per cent were tortured.[7] This was in the period before the intifada and at this time Palestinian security forces were working extensively with Israel to arrest and detain dissidents and militants who were opposed to the agreements which had been reached between the Israelis and Arafat's administration. The *Observer* reported that the 13 different Palestinian security forces had modelled themselves on Shin Bet and that three-quarters of their detainees had been tortured (13 December 1998). At the same time there were reports that thousands of Palestinians remained in Israeli jails, some from the time of the previous intifada 1987 (*Guardian*, 7 November 1998).

To live under such rule had profound effects on the everyday lives of Palestinians. From their perspective, the Israelis had used the peace to extend their military and economic dominance. It became more difficult for Palestinians to travel as more settlements and roads between them were built for the use of Israelis. These involved the bulldozing of large areas of land and the development of extensive systems of checkpoints and military security. One of the journalists we interviewed for this study had been the head of a news agency in Jerusalem in the period before the 2000 intifada. He commented to us:

My Palestinian neighbours could not go to the beach which you could practically see. They carry identity cards which tell everything about them. If an American viewer ever saw the extent to which the apartheid system is applied in the occupied territories – the pass laws make the South African system look benign. The Israelis say that [most] of the Palestinians are now under Palestinian Authority control. What they don't say is that they often can't even leave the town they are in.

He also commented that members of his Arab staff had been arrested and tortured by the Israelis. He made this criticism of TV news coverage of the conflict: 'They cover the day-to-day action but not the human inequities, the essential imbalances of the occupation, the day-to-day humiliations of the Palestinians' (interview, 10 June 2002).

Our own analysis of news content showed that the consequences to the Palestinians of living under military occupation were very rarely explored. There were occasional comments in the news that obliquely raised the issue. The BBC, for example, mentioned in a report that the Palestinians were 'tearing down security cameras', referring to these as 'hated symbols of Israeli authority' (BBC1 main News, 6 October 2000). Another report describes undercover police grabbing a demonstrator noting that 'these officers who never want to be identified, pretend to be Palestinians during a riot but when they spot a suspect they treat him with little mercy' (BBC1 early evening News, 13 October 2000). There are also occasional references to the occupation and occupied territories – as, for example, when a BBC journalist says of young Palestinians that 'they don't trust the Americans and after all, they say it's the occupation to blame' (BBC1 lunchtime News, 2 October 2000). It was clear from our audience studies that many people would not understand such a reference. Because the Israeli presence is not described as a military occupation and the significance of this is not explained, it was not clear what the word 'occupation' actually meant. Some understood it to mean simply that people were on the land (as in a bathroom being 'occupied').

There were two other occasions when news events were reported which could have been used to explain the nature of the occupation. On 13 October 2000, the Israelis were reported on BBC and ITV as stopping young Muslims from entering the Old City to pray. Also, as we have seen, on 9 and 10 October, ITV discussed how the Israelis had surrounded Palestinian areas to 'choke the life out of the revolt'. Both of these examples illustrate that the movement of Palestinians is subject to the wishes of the Israelis, but there was no commentary to indicate that movement could be routinely controlled, or discussion of this as a feature of the military occupation. The clearest statement on this issue came in a brief statement from a Palestinian who said that people are 'penned like chickens, they can't move freely' (BBC1 main News, 10 October 2000), but this comment is not taken up or developed by journalists.

There are two problems with coverage that does not explain the 'military' nature of the occupation and the consequences of this for the Palestinians. The first is that it is difficult for viewers to understand why the conflict is so intractable. It can appear simply as two communities who 'can't get on' and who are squabbling over the same areas of land. The second is that such coverage disadvantages the Palestinian perspective, as a key reason for their unrest and anger is left unexplained. Some observers have commented on their own surprise when viewing the conflict at first-hand. They noted how this revealed the limits of their previous understanding of the accounts that were prevalent in the media. For example, a businessman wrote as follows in the *Guardian*:

> I have had business interests in the Middle East for many years, I often travel to Israel and the West Bank and I'm in contact with journalists, aid workers and UN officials there. I can state categorically that all those whom I have met, who have come to work on the West Bank with an open mind, or even, like me, with some prejudice in favour of Israel, leave with disgust and rage

at Israeli brutality, racism and hypocrisy. Some are Jewish. It is experience on the spot that leads them to this perception.

He also commented how even a newspaper such as the *Guardian* 'seems never to address adequately the justice [or the tragedy] of the Palestinian position, or the frightening racism that seems to me to be at the core of Israeli arguments and actions' (letter, *Guardian*, 29 March 2001). Another correspondent discusses the role of the Israeli settlements in this system of control and also notes the absence of such analysis in media coverage:

A few days ago the BBC showed aerial film of a settlement. I was surprised by how unfamiliar it was to see one. I realised that few if any pictures are normally shown of settlements – their sheer scale, their facilities and their monopoly of the water supply. Nor is there any detailed map of their distribution ... nothing prepared me for the shock of the prevalence and scale of the settlements when I visited the occupied territories. It is as though every other hilltop in Devon and Cornwall was taken over by a Milton Keynes-like town and occupied ... looking down triumphantly over the indigenous locals corralled in the valleys below. (Letter, *Guardian*, 26 May 2001)

The issue that this raises is that the settlements have a key military and strategic function in the occupation. The point of being situated on the top of hills is that this offers a commanding position. At the time of the signing of the Wye Accords (supposedly a land for security agreement), Ariel Sharon, who was then the Israeli Foreign Minister, urged settlers in the West Bank to 'grab the hilltops' (*Guardian*, 8 January 1999). Yet when the BBC visits a settlement at the beginning of the intifada, the journalist stresses that it is 'intensely vulnerable, high on a hill'. There are no comments on how it functions in the occupation:

One regular target for Palestinian gunmen is the Jewish settlement of Passagot. It's *intensely vulnerable, high on a hill*, surrounded on all sides by Palestinian territory. Even a children's nursery had a bullet fired through the window. The settlers know they are in mortal danger. A dozen babies have been evacuated just a few minutes earlier to the settlement's bomb shelter. Settlers say Palestinians

are trying to force them out. (BBC1 late News, 5 October 2000
– our italics)

The settlers are then interviewed but there are no questions on what
the conflict is actually about:

> *Settler*: Well they want us out of here. They're shooting at us hoping
> that we'll pick up and leave.
> *Journalist*: Do you have any intention of leaving?
> *Settler*: No, no.
> *Journalist*: Some people would say you're crazy staying here with
> so many bullets flying.
> *Settler*: No, not crazy, we have our ideas and our ideals and we'll
> stick up for them and it's important to us. (BBC1 late News, 5
> October 2000)

The journalist then comments without explanation that 'This place
looks more like a fortress than a settlement' – which seems to miss
the key argument that this is indeed what many settlements are. It
is of course the case that some settlements are more exposed than
others, but as Avi Shlaim notes, their overall impact is to exert a
strategic and military control as well as to command land and water
resources. It is this analysis which is missing from news which
focuses on vulnerability and the 'threat' to settlers, and in reports
which present the Palestinians and Israelis as simply two warring
communities. The key issue that remains unexplained is the structural
division of society – one group is effectively controlling the lives of
the other (with some resistance). This point of view is not put to the
settlers and they are not asked if they think it is right that Palestinians
have lost their land so that settlements can be developed. In the
following example from ITV the initial emphasis is again on Israel
'defending' and 'protecting' the 'small Jewish enclaves', while the
Arabs are referred to as 'continuing their onslaught'. The reporter
does note that the Palestinians regard the settlements as a 'symbol
of the Israeli occupation'. But without an explanation of what this
occupation is and what it signifies for the Palestinians there is no
clear rationale for their action other than that they are 'driven by
hatred'. The report begins with a studio introduction that contrasts
the peace talks with the ongoing violence:

Newscaster: And even while those talks were on, the violence between Palestinians and Israeli security forces continued for the seventh day in a row. Among six Palestinians reported killed today was a boy of nine.

Journalist: The cycle of violence is unbroken, the trouble spots are the same each day. The Israeli army has again been defending the small Jewish enclaves on the West Bank and the Gaza Strip – pockets in the midst of Palestinian towns and villages ... here 400 people are protected by around a thousand soldiers. Some Israelis believe such little Alamos should be defended at all costs. The Arabs of course feel very differently and today *driven on by hatred* continued their onslaught and there's not much sign of conciliation here. These Palestinians regard the Jewish settlement here in Hebron as an affront, a symbol of the Israeli occupation that has not been brought to an end by the political process. (ITV main News, 4 October 2000 – our italics)

The official Israeli view is that the settlements are simply Jewish communities under threat from 'terrorists' and 'mobs', as in this report: 'Israeli soldiers are accused of using excessive force in response to the violence but insist they're only defending their communities from the stone-throwing mobs' (ITV lunchtime News, 4 October 2000).

This view of the settlements as essentially vulnerable and under 'threat' is clearly developed in other news accounts where journalists spend time following the lives and concerns of the settlers. The following report, which is from before the outbreak of the intifada, explored the worries which settlers have about the peace process. The initial focus is again on children's safety:

Machabi Lutz is worried about his children's safety. The Lutz family live in the settlement of Bet Al on land which Israel captured in the 1967 war because they feel this is the heartland of the Jewish people. Now they are disgusted that the prime minister they voted for is transferring more territory to the Palestinians. (BBC1 early evening News, 23 October 1998)

There is then an interview with the settler's wife:

Interviewee: This agreement endangers us more than we were endangered before. We're worried because we've seen friends of ours killed and the murderers run away – it takes them two minutes to flee into the autonomy areas and now there are going to be more of these areas and we are very scared and we are very disappointed.

The only reference to Palestinian views is a comment that 'the Palestinians here say Israeli settlers are trying to take their land'. There is no evidence given as to whether or not this claim is true. An Israeli peace activist is then interviewed who says that he does not want his grandchildren to die for nothing. The journalist then comments that these 'Israeli leftists believe their country will never have peace until the Palestinians have justice'. There is no explanation of what this justice would consist of or why the Palestinians need it. The report then returns to the settlers:

> Tonight in Jerusalem, the Jewish religion's most holy place, Mrs Chanie Lutz and other residents of the settlement of Bet Al went to pray for God's help. The settlers now plan a sustained campaign against the Washington agreement. (BBC1 early evening News, 23 October 1998)

There are no critical questions addressed to the settlers here on their role in the military occupation, on the control of land and water or indeed on accusations that settlers have killed Palestinians. In a later report in February 2002 a BBC Radio 4 journalist produces a 'diary' from Israel and the occupied areas. He also spent time with the settlers and travelled to work with them. This account was published on the BBC website:

> It did feel odd sitting in the front seat of their Mazda, flak-jacketed and helmeted with an M16 rifle jammed up against my leg, while Suzie [the settler's wife] looked after little Liam in his car seat behind me. It can't be much fun risking your life every time you drive to the office. This couple have paid heavily for their convictions. (*Tel Aviv Diary*, Radio 4 – BBC website, 7 February 2002)

A very different image of some settlers was given in a report by the Israeli human rights group, B'Tselem which discusses attacks by settlers against Palestinians:

> Among the settlers' actions against the Palestinians are setting up roadblocks to disrupt normal Palestinian life, shooting at rooftop

water heaters, burning cars, smashing windows, destroying crops and uprooting trees, and harassing merchants and owners of stalls in the market. (B'Tselem, 2003d)

They also state that the purpose of some of the settlers' violence is 'to force Palestinians to leave their homes or land, so that the perpetrators can take control over Palestinian land.' They describe the difficulties in gathering crops:

> During the olive-picking season, in which many Palestinians are at work in the olive groves, violent groups of settlers increase their attacks on Palestinians. In these attacks, settlers fire at olive pickers, killing and wounding them, steal their crop, and destroy their trees. (B'Tselem, 2003d)

A further report by Amnesty International on the deaths of children on both sides in the conflict notes the difference in response of the Israeli Army and describes the following attack:

> On 19 July 2001, Diya Marwan Tmeizi, a baby of almost four months from the village of Idna (near Hebron), was killed when the car he was travelling in with his family on their way home from the wedding of relatives, was shot at by Israeli settlers. Two other family members were also killed in the attack and five were wounded including, two year old Amira. The attack happened not far from the Tarqumiya roadblock, but the soldiers manning the roadblock did not stop the killer's car when it fled. (Amnesty International, 2002b)

As early as 1994, Israel Shahak reviewed a series of accounts in the Israeli press about the relations between settlers and Palestinians and the responses of the army. Quoting a report in *Ha'olam Ha'ze* he notes that 'Beating the Arabs, or humiliating them otherwise or vandalising their property before the very eyes of the army soldiers is not regarded as a 'sufficient reason' for arresting a settler'. He describes another report in *Kol Ha'ir* by a journalist who has travelled on a bus with religious settlers:

> 'On the way,' he reports, 'the religious youths from Kiryat Arba kept themselves busy slinging stones at Arab passersby, explaining their behaviour by saying, 'We are the settlers, aren't we?'' (Shahak, 1994)

The journalist describes graffiti at the entrance to Kiryat Arba reading, 'Only a sucker doesn't kill an Arab'. (Shahak, 1994)

These accounts contrast with the tv news images of settlers in our samples where there was a tendency to present them as worried members of small, vulnerable communities. It is a partial account which can disguise the very deep levels of racism which exist in some parts of Israeli society as well as the key role of the settlements in the occupation, i.e. that they are involved in the imposition of economic and military control and their own position is guaranteed by the Israeli army. To present settlers and Palestinians as simply two communities who can't get on, misses the point that one group is supported by an occupying military force, while the other is living under its control. Palestinians and settlers certainly do shoot at each other but the consequences for the two communities are very different. As B'Tselem has noted:

> The Israeli authorities employ an undeclared policy of leniency and compromise toward Israeli civilians who harm Palestinians.... This policy is in total contrast to the rigid policy of law enforcement and punishment where Palestinians harm Israelis. Towns and villages in the area of the incident are routinely placed under curfew...and intensive searches and arrests are made. (B'Tselem, 2003e)

The curfew system referred to is applied to Palestinians but not settlers, and can result in thousands of people being confined to their homes for 24 hours a day forbidden to leave even for medical help or schooling.

As we have indicated, what is missing from many news accounts is the structural imbalances of this society. Without such explanation it is difficult to understand the depth of hostility and the intractability of the violence. Conflicts can appear simply as a 'cycle' in which one death leads to more attacks or as unexplained friction between communities. In the following report settlers are described as attacking 'Arab homes' after the funeral of a Jewish settler:

> In this crisis violence begets more violence and today was no exception. Mourners ... were heavily armed, including the women. After the funeral service the Jewish settlers attacked Arab homes nearby. They were fired up with grief and bent on revenge. (BBC1 late News, 11 October 2000)

In the next example, we are told that the presence of pockets of Jewish settlements in Palestinian towns is a source of friction, but were not told why this is so:

> Violence in the West Bank too ... rioters attacked a Jewish religious outpost. The presence of small pockets of Jewish settlements in the midst of Palestinian towns is a constant source of friction. It was a similar story in Bethlehem. (BBC1 early evening News, 1 October 2000)

But the causes of 'friction' are not hard to find. In 1994, the Society of Saint Yves, the Catholic Legal Resource Centre for Human Rights, submitted a report to the high court in Israel. It noted that in East Jerusalem (which was occupied) 86 per cent of the land had been made 'unavailable for use by Arabs'. It also commented that the Arabs whose homes have been demolished for Jewish settlements often 'come from the lowest economic strata of their community' and now 'live in makeshift hovels, doubled and tripled up with other families, or even in tents and caves' (cited Chomsky, 1999: 547). But without such knowledge, Israelis and Palestinians can appear simply to be bad neighbours. As in this report:

> Violence spills over into Jerusalem itself. Here where Israeli and Palestinians live in close proximity, sometimes across the same street, the potential for friction is great. In Nablus [a 22-year-old] was buried this morning ... (BBC1 lunchtime News, 4 October 2000)

This news report on ITV comments on 'neighbours fighting' within Israel: 'Arabs and Jews took to the streets of Nazareth. The Israeli army were in the middle, preventing a huge street fight between neighbours' (ITV main News, 9 October 2000). There are qualifications which should be made to this analysis. As we will see, some reports did refer briefly to the intifada as a 'popular uprising', which does imply resistance, though what it was resistance to, and why, was less clear. There was also sympathetic coverage in this sample period of the deaths of Palestinian children. To this extent the consequences of the conflict for Palestinians were reported, but what remained unexplored was the nature of the military occupation and the distorted relationships it produced between the occupiers and the subject population.

Religion. There is a strong focus in news reporting on religious differences as a central explanation for the unrest. There are a large number of references to 'sacred' and 'holy' places from the first days of the intifada when Ariel Sharon is reported as 'visiting one of Islam's holiest sites in Jerusalem' and 'sparking off' the violence (BBC1 main News, 30 September 2000). The initial fighting was described as 'centred on a shrine sacred both to Muslims and Jews' (ITV early evening News, 29 September 2000). The BBC reported that:

> This was the holiest site in Jerusalem today. Palestinians tried to force the Israeli police out. The response came with live ammunition. At least four people died, over a hundred and fifty were injured – and many of these people had come here to pray. There was outrage amongst Palestinians that this could happen here, outside the third most sacred site in Islam of all places. (BBC1 late News, 29 October 2000)

On the following day we hear:

> Rioters attacked a Jewish religious outpost ... It was a similar story in Bethlehem. Behind the fortress is a place called Rachel's Tomb, religious Jews wanting to pray there today thought better of it. (BBC1 early evening News, 1 October 2000)

The references to religion and religious conflict run through the news accounts, particularly in the first days of the intifada. We are told that the Palestinians regard their dead as 'martyrs killed in a religious war over Jerusalem' (ITV early evening News, 2 October 2000), and on BBC that 'once again blood has been spilt in a place that is sacred to both Muslims and Jews' (BBC1 late News, 6 October 2000). There are also very explicit statements by journalists which explained the source of the violence as being religion. In this account from the BBC, the arguments over 'sacred ground' are presented as 'almost the last real barrier to peace':

> This magnificent vista is the source of the violence and almost the last real barrier to peace. It's a corner of the Old City of Jerusalem, sacred ground to Muslims and Jews alike and Israelis have sole control of this ground, but how is it to be shared? Jews call it the Temple Mount and it is flanked by the Western or Wailing Wall. The most sacred place of the Jewish religion, directly above it the

Al-Aqsa mosque which for Muslims ranks behind only Mecca and Medina in spiritual significance, and within it the Dome of the Rock. It's here according to the Koran that the Prophet Mohammed ascended to heaven. (BBC1 late News, 3 October 2000)

A report on ITV also highlights the key importance of religion and the holy sites. It also includes a rather optimistic view of how the Palestinians 'enjoy self-rule':

So the entire Middle East process has now come down to the most contentious issue of all, who controls Jerusalem's holy sites? Thanks to the peace process the Palestinians enjoy self rule in the Gaza Strip and over large swathes of the West Bank. But in the heart of Jerusalem no compromise seems possible. The Temple Mount is the site of the holy Al-Aqsa mosque crucial to Palestinian and Islamic identity, but the area is also bordered by the Western Wall which Jews all over the world see as the focus of their faith. (ITV early evening News, 2 October 2000)

The level of hostility and the explosion of anger might suggest that the Palestinians bitterly resent the military occupation, in spite of their having some local autonomy. The reasons for this, which we outlined above, were not explored on the news. This is important, because to reduce the conflict to 'religion' and to 'fighting over holy sites' can be misleading. To see it in these terms can lead to simplistic solutions such as advocating religious 'tolerance' between communities. Of course this is an admirable objective, but the problem is that such an explanation and solution miss out other key factors which are producing the conflict. As many commentators have noted, religious tensions are often underpinned by other social and economic problems (see, for example, 'Poverty and Resentment Fuel Palestinian Fury', *Guardian*, 14 October 2000). In times of great stress, populations often turn to religion or spiritual ideas which can become the focus of struggle. There are many historical examples of this and it is especially so when the conflict is unequal or particularly desperate. Religious ideas can of course be a motive in their own right, but violent and fearful struggles often intensify religious commitment. The crucial point in relation to the Israeli-Palestinian conflict is that by neglecting the social and economic factors, journalists sometimes presented it simply as a religious struggle. This apparently affected the belief of some audience members who were unaware of the deep

social and economic divisions and how they may have related to
the unrest.

Israeli perspectives on security needs, terrorism and incitement. These
areas relate primarily to Israeli rationales for their own actions and
the legitimacy or necessity of the occupation. While the Palestinians
see themselves as resisting an illegal military presence, the Israeli
perspective focuses on what they see as the vulnerability of their
own nation. As Nomi Chazan, a member of the Israeli Knesset,
has commented, 'we are trapped in two narratives which both
sides believe are incompatible: the Palestinian struggle for national
liberation against Israeli occupation, [and] Israel's continued struggle
to survive' (*Observer* 18 August 2002). This sense that the Israelis have
of being under threat is well expressed in the following report from
the BBC. It is from the early days of the intifada and mentions the
kidnapping of Israeli soldiers on the border with Lebanon as well as
the conflict with the Palestinians:

> [The Israelis] say from their point of view that they feel as if they
> are under threat, as if they are under attack from all sides. They
> say, and they truly believe, that it was a concerted effort on the
> side of the Islamic militants in Lebanon to attack Israel when they
> took the three soldiers hostage yesterday, and there were also some
> stone-throwing incidents up here on the border from where I'm
> speaking. And the Israelis also feel as if they are under attack from
> the Palestinians, they blame all the violence on them. (BBC1 early
> evening News, 8 October 2000)

Israeli security concerns and fears over terrorism are commonly
reported in news coverage and this appears to be a well established
historical pattern in TV reporting. A study of news coverage of peace
negotiations in the period before the intifada shows that these
security concerns were given a strong prominence, sometimes to
the exclusion of other issues such as the nature of the occupation
and its impact on Palestinian beliefs and action.[8] In the following
example, a journalist is asked about the main obstacles to peace, and
his reply focuses on the issues that concern the Israelis:

Newscaster: What are the main obstacles to peace?
Journalist: Well I *just mentioned security arrangements, and those are
the key issues* and in a sense the key obstacles. It's quite clear now

that the Israelis are committed to pulling back from a further 13 per cent of the West Bank but only if the Palestinians can convince them that they are able to offer new written cast-iron security commitments, better than anything they have offered in the past. *There are key issues like the Israelis wanting* the extradition of more than 30 Palestinian Islamic militants to Israel for trial. For example they want to make sure that illegal weapons held by Palestinians in the West Bank and Gaza are confiscated. Those are specific detailed issues the Israelis want the Palestinians to deliver and they want American intelligence to be involved to verify Palestinian compliance. (BBC1 early evening News, 18 October 1998 – our italics)

At the time of the intifada there were also references to Israeli fears: for example, the comment that 'what is increasingly worrying the Israelis is the prospect of some kind of terrorist attack' (ITV early evening News, 13 October 2000). And on the BBC the same day: 'But what the Israeli security forces really fear now is a new wave of terrorist bombings by Palestinian extremists' (BBC1 late News, 13 October 2000).

The Israelis are also described as feeling 'besieged', as in this report:

And in the meantime Israeli troops are still on high alert. We visited this space in Gaza where snipers are on the look out for Palestinian gunmen who frequently open fire on them. The troops here showed us a network of breeze block tunnels they use to protect themselves. *Many Israelis feel besieged at the moment* by a Palestinian uprising they didn't expect. (BBC1 main News, 10 October 2000 – our italics)

The above report is made without irony and there is no comment that the soldiers are actually imposing a military occupation upon the Palestinians. The paradox would also not be apparent to many viewers since the occupation and its routine effects on the lives of the Palestinians were not explored on the news. This raises a very significant point, that in the absence of such discussion new developments in Israeli tactics can be presented as 'security' requirements (from the point of view of Israel) rather than as an extension of military control or the occupation (which is how the Palestinians see it).[9] Thus when Palestinians were prevented from entering the Al-Aqsa mosque the reason was reported as being because 'security forces' were 'afraid of a riot' (BBC1 late News, 13 October 2000). The Palestinians were shown as being angry at this treatment, but key elements of the reason for this anger are missing from the coverage. This absence also made it easier for the Israelis to present their account of the cause of the unrest. Rather than it being seen as a popular uprising against a military occupation, they suggested that the main cause was 'incitement' by Arab leaders and particularly by Yasser Arafat. We will discuss this further below.

Yasser Arafat and Ariel Sharon: the instigation of violence. In the early days of the intifada both Yasser Arafat and Ariel Sharon were accused of having a role in causing or promoting the violence. The intifada was reported as having been 'sparked off' by the famous walk which Sharon made through Muslim holy places accompanied by hundreds of armed policemen. This was widely seen as a deliberate provocation and as an assertion of Israeli sovereignty. Sharon was already a notorious figure for the Palestinians. They blamed him for the killing of refugees at the Sabra and Shatila refugee camps in Lebanon in 1982. Before that in the 1950s he had commanded a unit that launched punitive raids against Jordan and Egypt. It was reported that 'in one of them at Qibya, scores of civilians were massacred'. In the early 1970s 'he was responsible for a brutal crackdown on Palestinian resistance activities in the Gaza Strip' (*Guardian,* 14 October 2000). This information on Sharon's history was not given on TV news. His walk was initially reported on the BBC as follows:

This man, Israel's right-winger Ariel Sharon, visited the religious compound yesterday and that started the trouble. He wants Israel alone to have sovereignty over the holy sites, an idea that's unthinkable to Palestinians. None of this will help the search for compromise. (BBC1 main News, 29 September 2000)

ITV did not report that day on the role of Sharon in its early evening or late bulletins, but noted that 'Israelis and Palestinians are blaming each other for the street violence that has followed today's events in Jerusalem, when the city's most holy places for both Arabs and Jews, became a battlefield' (ITV late News, 29 September 2000).

ITV news actually reports the role of Sharon rather less than the BBC. In this reference on 30 September, Sharon is not actually named: 'Arabs here are outraged at what happened on the disputed site, and they are blaming the disturbances on a visit to the holy compound on Thursday by a hard-line Israeli politician' (ITV early evening News, 30 September 2000). In the late News of that day the oblique reference to Sharon has gone altogether:

> Palestinian leaders had called a one-day general strike in memory of the people killed yesterday during rioting on Jerusalem's Temple Mount. However, the Israelis have accused the Palestinian security forces of not doing enough to quell the violence and they say Arab leaders have been guilty of incitement. (ITV late News, 30 September 2000)

The Israeli view is given here but there is nothing on the role of Sharon or his history. Without this it is not easy to understand why the Palestinians were so angry. Two days later ITV reported that 'The violence [was] sparked off by a provocative visit by right-wing Israeli politicians to a Muslim holy site' (ITV lunchtime News, 2 October 2000). And later that evening Sharon is actually named:

> It was the visit of Ariel Sharon, the hard-line Israeli politician, to Jerusalem's Temple Mount that appears to have triggered the wave of violence. It is a site holy to Jews and Muslims, and Palestinians judged it to be a deliberately provocative gesture. Sharon claimed it was the opposite.
> *Ariel Sharon*: 'I came here with the message of peace. I believe that we can live together with the Palestinians.'
> But his presence started days of rioting and armed clashes. (ITV early evening News, 2 October 2000)

Why his presence should so enrage the Palestinians is not clear from these accounts. The same problem occurs with the BBC coverage, though they are more forthright in naming Ariel Sharon and in pointing to the consequences of his actions:

> The violence was sparked off three days ago when the right-wing politician Ariel Sharon visited one of Islam's holiest sites in Jerusalem. (BBC1 late News, 30 September 2000)

> It all began with a gesture of calculated provocation by Israel's right-wing leader Ariel Sharon. Surrounded by hundreds of armed

policemen, Mr Sharon paraded in front of a Muslim holy site in Jerusalem.

Ariel Sharon: 'I came here with the message of peace.'

But it was no such thing. At a time when the future is at stake, Mr Sharon was appealing to Israeli hard-liners. The consequences were immediate and inevitable. (BBC1 early evening News, 2 October 2000)

The BBC makes clear its view on the intention of Sharon and he is termed a 'right-wing enemy of the peace process': 'Ariel Sharon, right-wing enemy of the peace process, knew exactly what he was doing when he very publicly walked the ground last week' (BBC1 late News, 3 October 2000). Later we hear:

It's just two weeks since the visit to Jerusalem's holy site by Israel's opposition leader Ariel Sharon touched off the wave of unrest which has ripped up the Middle East peace process. Mr Sharon has been a long-standing opponent of conceding territory to Palestinians and now he's being offered a place in a coalition cabinet. (BBC1 lunchtime News, 13 October 2000)

Sharon's role is clearly stated in these references. But as with the ITV news, it is not clear *why* what he did is of such significance to Palestinians. Without an account of the occupation and Sharon's history it is not likely to be.

There was also extensive reporting on the role of Arafat in the intifada. The Israeli view was that he was responsible for inciting street violence. This is a view that was frequently reported and persistently put forward by interviewees. But some journalists who were witnessing the events tended to discount the explanation. They suggested that the intifada was 'a popular uprising' over which Arafat had little control. Some commentators at the time had noted the difficulties that such an uprising created for Arafat. In the period before the intifada, he had co-operated extensively with the Israelis to suppress dissidents and those opposed to the agreements that he had reached. The Palestinian Authority was accused of repression, the use of torture and of corruption. At the same time, its co-operation with the Israelis was seen as resulting in their taking more land and water. As Edward Said wrote two years before the intifada:

Arafat and company have now completely delivered themselves
to the Israeli and US intelligence apparatus, thereby putting an
end to anything even resembling a democratic and independent
Palestinian national life. And this, by the way, has been sacrificed
to the survival of Arafat and his coterie of advisers, hangers-on, and
security chief, for whom the idea of Palestinian civil society with an
independent judiciary and legislative body is a silly inconvenience
to be disposed of like the land they have given up with scarcely a
look back. (*Guardian*, 7 November 1998)

When the intifada began, the Israeli journalist Amira Hass described
the difficulty of Arafat's position:

Seven years after the Oslo Accord all Palestinians feel betrayed,
because they are still living under occupation ... When six
Palestinians were killed by close-range bullets at the mosque by
Israeli police, the anger which swept everybody contained all other
angers, of seven years and longer. This time Arafat could not dream
of checking the spreading anger with his security forces. After
all, it was about al-Aqsa. All his credibility would have been lost.
(*Guardian*, 3 October 2000)

The important point made here is that the 'message' of the intifada
was meant 'not only for Israel but for Arafat too'. This suggests that
the problem for Arafat was that if he opposed a mass popular uprising,
he might be in danger of being swept away by it. Without such
background information it is difficult to understand the position
of Arafat or the anger of the Palestinians. ITV News did feature a
comment from a Palestinian referring to Arafat as 'useless', but it is
not made clear why he thought this:

This man was also shot during rioting yesterday, he has a bullet
lodged in his chest. I asked him about the peace efforts being
made today in Paris
Palestinian: 'Yasser Arafat the chairman is useless. Palestinian
Authority is useless. We do not need them any more.'
So who if anyone is in control? The Palestinian security forces did
manage to curb some of the trouble today, the death rate is down
but there were still plenty of battlegrounds. (ITV early evening
News, 4 October 2000)

None the less, both BBC and ITV News did question the view that Arafat could simply 'rein in' the protesters. Journalists on the ground who were witnessing the events were openly critical of the Israeli view:

Israel believes Yasser Arafat wants the violence to continue but it's doubtful whether the Palestinian leader could simply tell these young men to stop. (BBC1 lunchtime News, 2 October 2000)

Even if Mr Arafat agrees to stop the uprising, there are question marks over whether he can, whether it has spun beyond his control. (BBC1 late News, 9 October 2000)

ITV News also reports that 'this is not a campaign being waged by two armies, it is a popular people's uprising'. They also note that: 'The so-called ceasefire was never endorsed by ordinary Palestinians, for whom this remains a full-scale revolt. For the moment it seems, these people cannot be reined in' (ITV late News, 3 October 2000). There is a paradox here. Notwithstanding the clearly expressed comments that the intifada is a 'popular uprising', the view that Arafat is to blame actually takes precedence in the BBC's coverage (as measured by the amount of text which features it). This is because the Israelis used their superior media and public relations output, including the use of interviews to press the message. Their views on this were not challenged by the interviewers. This is particularly noticeable on the BBC where there was over twice as much coverage blaming Arafat as against that which criticised this view. On ITV News, which carried fewer interviews, the positions were more evenly expressed. There was also more coverage blaming Arafat than Sharon for instigating the violence. As we will see in this and later samples, the role of Sharon in instigating the conflict largely disappears, but there is a continued focus on Arafat. The Israeli view is given in reported statements such as the following from a BBC journalist:

I mean what we've been hearing for instance today from the Israeli prime minister Ehud Barak is all sorts of accusations and charges against Yasser Arafat the Palestinian leader. Mr Barak is saying that it is up to the Palestinians to end the violence, that they instigated it, that the Palestinian police have egged on and encouraged the crowds of stone-throwers and petrol-bombers by using ammunition themselves. Palestinian police brought the obvious response from the Israelis. Countering that, of course, Yasser Arafat condemned Israeli action of using gun-ships against civilians, the use of what he regards as excessive force. (BBC1 lunchtime News, 4 October 2000)

There is some sense of balance here in that 'both sides' are represented, but what is missing in the charges and counter-charges is any analysis of the nature of the conflict or its origins and history. The view that Arafat is to blame is highlighted in this BBC headline: 'Israel gives Arafat an ultimatum: stop the violence or no more peace talks' (BBC1 late News, 7 October 2000). The programme includes a direct statement from Barak:

> *Journalist*: Israel has accused Yasser Arafat's Palestinian Authority of failing to protect [a Jewish religious shrine]. In his toughest warning yet, the prime minister told Yasser Arafat to stop the violence.
> *Ehud Barak*: If we will not see an end to the violence within the next two days we will read it as a deliberate decision of Chairman Arafat to put an end to the peace process at this stage. (BBC1 main News, 7 October 2000)

In the following interview we can also see how Arafat is blamed for the violence without any challenge to this position from the interviewer:

> *Journalist*: The Palestinians want a wide-ranging international inquiry into what has happened over the last two weeks, the Israeli government is less keen on that, why?
> *Interviewee: (former Israeli government minister)*: The most important thing is to get calm restored. Unfortunately, we were in the best part of negotiations, very advanced, and Mr Arafat had not got wholly what he wanted, turned the tables, went to the streets, creating so much violence, deaths and injuries ... Why did he move to the street rather than go on negotiating with us?
> *Journalist*: Mr Barak when he came to power staked his whole prime ministership on finding peace ... it looks now as if he is on the brink of failure, doesn't it?
> *Interviewee*: Yes it does unfortunately ... I remember now the last days of Camp David, President Clinton desperate telling Arafat

'It is the last opportunity, take it, it is a wonderful offer', and he decided not to and he preferred violence. It is a pity.

Journalist: Now obviously the summit is still going on ... but if it were to fail ... what do you think are the consequences not just here but for the region?

Interviewee: Consequences are bad, and the future will be much more gloomy. I'm afraid we may see more violence. We will have to defend ourselves. We see the gathering of Saddam Hussein and Yasser Arafat telling everybody 'We have to exterminate Israel'. We see the Iranians helping with the kidnapping of people and using their language. We see the extremists in the street, the Muslim extremism and I think it is bad. We have to defend ourselves. I would rather have a positive conclusion than a bad one.

Journalist: We will have to leave it there. Thank you for joining us. (BBC1 lunchtime News, 16 October 2000)

There are a number of key points that emerge from this analysis. First, Ariel Sharon was presented on the news as having sparked the intifada through a deliberate provocation of the Palestinians, though there was little information given as to why they would see it as such. Second, there was actually more coverage of the Israeli view that Arafat was promoting the violence than of the role of Sharon. Third, this was in spite of the fact that journalists on the ground were reporting that the intifada was a popular uprising and were questioning whether Arafat *could* control it. Fourth, the reason for the prominence of the view that 'Arafat is to blame' was that the Israelis used their commanding position in TV interviews and in the supply of statements to the media. We will discuss the issues raised by interviews and headlines in the next section.

Interviews and headlines

These are key areas for understanding how some viewpoints are highlighted or developed in the flow of news coverage while others are downgraded or lost. In our analysis of interviews, we found important differences in the manner in which Israelis and Palestinians were presented. The Israelis had twice as much time to speak (as measured by lines of text).[10] Another major difference was in the way in which the two sides appeared. Israelis were more likely to be interviewed in calm and relaxed surroundings. We saw this for example in the above interview with the Israeli former cabinet minister. Shortly before this there is a brief comment included from a Palestinian. It is actually a couple of snatched sentences given while in the middle of the noise of a protest march: 'We want peace, every day we want peace but what we can do now, they shooting the kids and the people. We want peace. We need it more than them' (BBC1 lunchtime News, 16 October 2000). This is followed by a brief interview with an Israeli in a street and then the longer, more relaxed interview with the Israeli former cabinet minister. There are clear differences between these types of interview and it may be beneficial to express views at length in a calm atmosphere with all the implied status that it entails. These are all issues in the production of television programmes and involve decisions made by broadcasters about how the different sides will be presented. We asked a very experienced Middle East correspondent for the BBC to explain why these differences between Israelis and Palestinians occurred. He made two important points. The first is that the Israelis have a very well organised media and public relations operation; the second is that the Israelis limit what the Palestinians are able to do because of the impositions of their military occupation. As he commented:

> The way you sound is terribly important for credibility. If you are in an absolutely sound studio setting, you have more credibility. If you are on a scratchy telephone line you are at a disadvantage. The reason the Palestinians suffer is their limited facilities – the Israelis have more money to spend and spend it on a sophisticated Western style of media communications and links. The second point is that the occupation limits Palestinians' freedom of access to the media. Ninety-nine per cent of the media is based in Jerusalem. If you have a Palestinian minister and you want him to come to a studio in Jerusalem then he can't or it will take him hours because of the restrictions [on the movement] of the Palestinians on the roads. (Interview, 26 August 2002)

He also noted that the difficulties of movement applied to media teams trying to reach Palestinian areas could affect coverage. This cannot be an acceptable situation for a publicly accountable broadcasting corporation that is committed to impartiality. Broadcasters cannot absolve themselves from the requirement for balance by accepting a status quo in which one side can ensure that it receives more favourable treatment by imposing restrictions on the other. The broadcasters really have to devote the necessary resources to make sure that both sides are properly represented. It should also be clearly indicated to viewers where the difficulties that Palestinians have in making their case result from the actions of the Israelis. For example, if a Palestinian is speaking down a scratchy telephone because of the limitations of movement imposed by military rule, then viewers should be told that this is so. To avoid doing this is to legitimise a structural imbalance.

Headlines

The purpose of headlines is to attract viewers' attention and to focus on the key themes of a bulletin. For the purposes of this part of our study we analysed 67 headlines from bulletins on BBC1 and ITV News between 30 September 2000 and 16 October 2000. We found that some headlines offer a relatively neutral account of events such as the progress of negotiations or the arrival and departure of politicians or comments that the conflict is continuing, as in the following examples:

Chaos in the Middle East ahead of emergency peace talks tomorrow. (ITV early evening News, 3 October 2000)

A Middle East summit on Monday, but the fighting goes on. (ITV early evening News, 14 October 2000)

Clashes continue as leaders prepare for Middle East summit. (ITV late News, 15 October 2000)

Fighting rages on the West Bank as peace talks begin. (ITV early evening News, 16 October 2000)

The Middle East, more violence as the peace talks now reach a delicate stage. (BBC1 early evening News, 10 October 2000)

Tensions remain high as world leaders gather for Israeli and Palestinian peace talks. (BBC1 early evening News, 15 October 2000)

The Israeli and Palestinians leaders prepare for tomorrow's crucial peace talks. There is hope for the end of immediate violence but not of a lasting breakthrough. (BBC1 main News, 15 October 2000)

Urgent diplomacy tonight to try to bring Israel and the Palestinians together. America warns that if violence continues other nations could be sucked in. (BBC1 main News, 10 October 2000)

We say that these are relatively neutral in that they do not clearly endorse one side or the other in the conflict. None the less, they do contain value assumptions and judgements – for example, that peace may be found in the comings and goings of world leaders and that their priority is to urgently secure peace, rather than to pursue more narrowly defined concerns such as national interests or political support at home. We have already noted the military aid that Israel receives from the US and how the Palestinians perceive this. Some might see a contradiction in attempts to 'end bloodshed' while continuing to supply weapons to one side. But there is no hint of such thoughts in a headline such as this:

Middle East peace summit gets underway, but no sign of a breakthrough. While they try to end the bloodshed the killing continues on the streets. (BBC1 late News, 16 October 2000)

Other headlines can offer a relatively straightforward account of events, even though the event itself may be controversial. For example, statements that 'Israel has moved in tanks' or that 'Palestinians have been killed' or that 'A suicide bomber has killed Israelis' are relatively neutral as long as the actions of both sides are reported impartially. This impartiality is lost, however, if the actions of one side were reported differently from the other – for example, if killings by one side were under-reported while those of the other side were highlighted. We did actually find some differences in the reporting of Palestinian deaths between BBC and ITV News at the beginning of the intifada. In this period those who died were overwhelmingly Palestinian but this was not always made clear in news headlines. The BBC was more likely than ITV to indicate Palestinian deaths and to give specific numbers, as in the following examples:

At least twelve Palestinians have been shot dead in clashes with Israeli forces. Another 300 are injured in the worst fighting for four years. (BBC1 early evening News, 10 September 2000)

Fifteen Palestinians are killed in clashes with the Israeli army. At least 300 are injured in the worst fighting for four years. (BBC1 late News, 30 September 2000)

Israeli forces kill eleven more Palestinians on a fourth day of bloodshed. (BBC1 late News, 1 October 2000)

Two Palestinians are reported to have been killed and dozens injured after clashes with Israeli forces using anti-tank missiles and helicopter gunships. (BBC1 early evening News, 3 October 2000)

ITV was more likely to say simply that there had been 'more deaths' or 'more killings' or to give numbers without saying who had died:

Four die in violence at sacred shrine in Jerusalem. (ITV late News, 29 September 2000)

Four dead as Palestinian protests continue. (ITV early evening News, 30 September 2000)

At least a dozen dead as Palestinian protests continue. (ITV late News, 30 September 2000)

Four die in gunfights between Palestinians and Israelis. (ITV early evening News, 1 October 2000)

Nearly 30 are killed in Palestinian-Israeli gun battles. (ITV late News, 1 October 2000)

More die as Middle East violence spirals out of control. (ITV early evening News, 2 October 2000)

More die as Middle East erupts into all-out violence. (ITV late News, 2 October 2000)

More killings as ceasefire fails. (ITV late News, 3 October 2000)

More deaths in Mid-East clashes despite peace talks. (ITV early evening News, 4 October 2000)

Israelis kill ten during Palestinian day of rage. (ITV late News, 6
October 2000)

The ITV News made it clear in the text of the bulletins that the
deaths were Palestinian, but the lack of clarity in the headlines is
noteworthy. When two Israeli soldiers were killed, the ITV News gave
the headline 'Swift retaliation after Israeli soldiers are lynched' (ITV
early evening News, 12 October 2000).

There is a third category of headlines that are clearly prejudicial
in that they employ the assumptions and ways of understanding the
conflict of one side to the exclusion of the other. We can see this
in the reporting of what was termed an 'Israeli peace deadline' on 7
October 2000, in which Israel gave Yasser Arafat an ultimatum to 'stop
the violence'. As we have seen, from the perspective of the Israelis,
the main cause of the intifada was incitement by Arab leaders, but
for the Palestinians the cause was the continued military occupation
and the violence that this did to their lives. Thus when the Israelis
are reported as imposing 'peace deadlines' or demanding 'an end to
violence', such language is likely to be regarded as meaningless by
the Palestinians and they reject the assumptions that it contains.
From their perspective, the world would not be 'peaceful' just because
they stopped resisting the Israelis. They were also very critical of
assumptions that it is they who need to stop the violence. Between
29 September and 9 October, around 90 people were reported to have
been killed, nearly all of whom were Palestinians, while hundreds
more had been shot and wounded. The Palestinians and indeed other
commentators also believed that it was Israelis who had provoked the
trouble with the intention of ending the peace process. The important
point is that the Palestinians did not acknowledge or accept the
'normality' which the Israeli government was trying to impose. For
them, the 'peace deadline' was merely another threat from Israel. This
is clear from Palestinian comments in the text of some bulletins but
it is absent as a view from the headlines. Thus in a BBC bulletin on
8 October we hear that 'already senior Palestinian officials have said
that they are not going to respond to Israeli threats'. In the same
bulletin the journalist attempts to lay out the views of both sides:

... and the Israelis also feel as if they are under attack from the
Palestinians, they blame all the violence on them. Of course, there
are two sides to the story, and we've all seen the awful images over

the last ten days of how fierce the Israeli response has been. (BBC1 early evening News, 8 October 2000)

This may be contrasted with the following headlines that do not express both sides and report only the Israeli position:

Israel gives Arafat an ultimatum: *stop the violence* or no more peace talks. (BBC1 main News, 7 October 2000 – our italics)

Israel threatens to go in harder if Palestinian attacks don't stop. Palestinians are told they've seen nothing yet, but won't back down. (BBC1 early evening News, 8 October 2000)

Israel threatens to go in harder if Palestinian attacks don't stop. (BBC1 late News, 8 October 2000)

A peace process on a knife-edge as Israel's ultimatum to Arafat runs out. (BBC1 main News, 9 October 2000)

Israel crisis: Prime Minister delivers ultimatum to Arafat. (ITV early evening News, 8 October 2000)

Israel prepares for attack as *deadline to end violence* approaches. (ITV main News, 8 October 2000 – our italics)

Israeli peace deadline passes with no end to violence. (ITV main News, 9 October 2000)

It would have been quite possible for these headlines to be balanced by including the Palestinian view. For example, the news could have said: 'The Israelis say they are imposing a peace deadline to end violence, but Palestinians say it is the Israelis who have done most of the killing.'

We found other problems in headlines dealing with Israeli 'security operations'. On 13 October it was reported that 'in Jerusalem, Israeli security forces prevented all male Palestinians under the age of 45 from getting in to the Old City' (BBC1 lunchtime News). In this operation, the Palestinians were prevented from entering the Al-Aqsa mosque and had to pray in the street. They were reported to be 'seething with anger'. From the Israeli perspective, this was indeed a security operation designed to prevent riots and to ensure the safety of their own people. From the Palestinian perspective it is seen as an extension of Israeli military rule, but this perspective is absent from the headlines:

Israel mounts a massive security operation as Palestinians gather in Jerusalem. (BBC1 lunchtime News, 13 October 2000)

Israeli clamp down struggles to stop simmering Middle East violence. (ITV main News, 13 October 2000)

Here again we can see that the headlines could have included the Palestinian perspective. For example, the news might have said: 'Israel mounts a massive security operation, but Palestinians say it's more military rule.'

It is certainly the case that the Israeli authorities saw themselves as under attack. Some headlines followed this perspective, reporting, for example, on the kidnapping of three Israeli soldiers by Hezbullah guerrillas from Lebanon. On 7 October the BBC reported that

three Israeli soldiers have been kidnapped during fighting on the Lebanese border. The guerrilla group Hezbullah say they are responsible. Israeli warplanes have since attacked Hezbullah targets in Southern Lebanon. (BBC1 early evening News, 7 October 2000)

There is very little history given of the Lebanese conflict and consequently the kidnapping may have the appearance of being an unprovoked act. Two days later, however, the BBC did report that 'Hezbullah guerrillas are holding three soldiers and hope to swap them for Lebanese civilians being held as bargaining chips by Israel' (BBC lunchtime News, 9 October 2000). A report in the *Guardian* expands on this, noting that 'There are international efforts to get the three soldiers back safely probably by trading Lebanese who have been held hostage in Israeli jails for years' (9 October 2000). The information that the Israelis had been holding Lebanese hostages was given on two BBC1 bulletins (lunchtime and early evening News, 9 October 2000) but not on four other bulletins on BBC1 which reported the Hezbullah kidnap (early evening and late News, 7 October 2000; early evening News, 8 October 2000, and lunchtime News, 10 October 2000). ITV News reported the Hezbullah kidnap on five bulletins without saying that Israel had been holding hostages.

We can also see that the headlines for this story relate to the actions of Hezbullah rather than to those of Israel. It is Hezbullah who are apparently the source of the 'trouble':

> Trouble continues as Hezbullah take three Israeli soldiers prisoner. (ITV early evening News, 7 October 2000)

> Hezbullah kidnap three Israeli soldiers after the wave of violence spreads. (BBC1 early evening News, 7 October 2000)

There were very few headlines that could be said to express the Palestinian perspective. The following two highlight Palestinian losses and the desire to retaliate:

> As Palestinians bury their dead, there will be a Middle East summit. (BBC1 early evening News, 14 October 2000)

> Palestinians want their dead avenged but there will be a summit on Monday. (BBC1 late News, 14 October 2000)

Overall, there is a stronger tendency in the headlines to highlight Israeli statements, actions or perspectives. Palestinian views are featured but tend to be buried deep in the text of news bulletins. There is no obvious reason why they could not have been included in headlines and it is hard to avoid the conclusion that one view of the conflict is being prioritised.

Casualties and deaths: case studies

We will look here in detail at how violence, casualties and deaths on both sides of the conflict were reported.[11] As we have noted, in this sample period (28 September to 16 October 2000) the deaths and casualties were overwhelmingly Palestinian. The BBC reported four days after Ariel Sharon's walk through the Muslim holy places that 35 Palestinians had been killed and hundreds injured. By 16 October it was reported that 100 people had died, all but seven of whom were Palestinians/Arabs (ITV lunchtime News, 16 October 2000). It is clear that Palestinian/Arab deaths were far greater than those of Israeli armed forces or settlers, apparently by a ratio of around 13:1.[12] Yet when we analysed news content, we found that deaths and casualties of Israeli armed forces/settlers received about a third of the coverage allocated to this area.[13] While the Israelis received less in absolute terms at this point, these figures still represent a disproportionate emphasis upon them, relative to actual numbers of deaths and injuries. This imbalance continued in programmes from our later samples of news, to the point where there was actually more coverage of Israeli casualties, even though in real terms Palestinians were still experiencing much higher losses. As we will see, we also found differences in the language used to describe deaths on both sides, with certain words such as 'murder', 'atrocity', 'lynching', 'savage killing' and 'slaughter', being used by journalists to describe Israeli deaths rather than those of Palestinians.

However, some Palestinian deaths, particularly those of children, were treated with great sympathy. Reporting on the death of twelve-year-old Mohammed al-Durrah, a BBC journalist comments that 'there was a sickening gloom at his mother's house today' (BBC1 main News, 1 October 2000). Another BBC report focuses on the deaths of Palestinian children. The newscaster notes:

> The world has been shocked by the number of Palestinian children killed and injured in the last two weeks of fighting. At least 26 of the 100 or so people killed were children. The Palestinians claim that the Israeli army is deliberately shooting to kill. The Israelis say the Palestinians are using children to get the world's sympathy. (BBC1 main News, 13 October 2000)

The imbalance between the two sides is specifically referred to as a 'controversial and uneven pairing'. A journalist reports directly from a hospital and cites the comments of doctors that shots were deliberately aimed at the upper body 'and a quarter of those killed have been children. Doctors here believe these shots were carefully aimed at the upper body, in order to kill.' Later in the report there was a statement from an Israeli spokesperson:

> No one should be so naive to think this happens only because the children and something terrible happened on the way. It is a brutal and cynical way of using the image that the more casualties they have the more you are right.

The journalist then discounts this by reporting a mother's comments and noting that another Palestinian boy was shot with a satchel on his back:

But Mohammed wasn't sent to the protest by anyone. He has never been to a rally in his life, his mother told me, he wasn't the type. Another Palestinian boy was shot this week with a satchel on his back. (BBC1 main News, 13 October 2000)

There were also criticisms made of the level of force being used by the Israelis. As a journalist commented in another bulletin: 'The Israelis call this restraint but only about six of their men were wounded, compared to more than 300 Palestinians' (BBC1 early evening News, 30 September 2000). Later, on ITV it was reported that Israeli soldiers were 'showing absolutely no restraint, firing live ammunition into crowds from 20 metres' (ITV early evening News, 20 October 2000). Sometimes the references are more muted, as in these comments:

Serious questions are being asked about the use of live ammunition. (ITV early evening News 2 October 2000)

... Israel's lethal brand of policing. (BBC2 late News, 3 October 2000)

Israel still wielded a big stick – helicopters fired rockets killing at least one Palestinian. (BBC1 early evening News, 4 October 2000)

So another display of really tough tactics by the Israeli security forces. (BBC1 main News, 13 October 2000)

More severe criticisms emerged from within Israel itself when, for example, Shimon Peres, the Israeli foreign minister, was reported in October 2001 as trying to 'rein in' the Israeli army. It was clearly stated that elements of the army were trying to 'wreck' a ceasefire:

Aides of Mr Peres have accused the army of damaging Israel's image, and seeking to wreck the ceasefire he brokered last week with the Palestinian leader, Yasser Arafat, by opening fire on stone-throwing protestors. (*Guardian*, 2 October 2001)

The newspaper went on to report that:

Seventeen Palestinians have been killed since last week's truce ... two of them were shot dead on their way to work on Sunday when a convoy of Palestinian taxis came under fire from Israeli soldiers at an unmarked roadblock ... there are growing signs of disquiet with the army's operations in the West Bank and Gaza – including the use of live fire against unarmed protestors and 'surprise' checkpoints in the West Bank at which the two Palestinian labourers were killed. (*Guardian* 2 October 2001)

However, it was not suggested on television news at the time of our sample that the actions of the army might be linked to a political agenda (that is, to stop the peace process). But as we have noted above, the view put forward by the Israeli government at the time, that Yasser Arafat was encouraging violence for political ends, was in fact reported and discussed on TV news. There were also clear differences in the way in which deaths were reported for both sides. Although the Israeli army was reported as firing live ammunition into crowds, words such as 'murder' and 'atrocity' were not used by television journalists in our samples to describe the deaths of Palestinians.[14] Some emotive language was used in reporting Palestinian deaths. For example, a Palestinian is said to have 'died in the most horrific circumstances' when his mutilated and burnt body is reported to have been found. But it is noteworthy that this brief report appears only on the BBC and then the circumstances of the death are reported as a 'claim' made by Palestinians:

Outside a morgue in Ramallah, his children are grieving their father, it is claimed he was kidnapped by Israelis tortured and beaten to death. The children asked to go in and see their father's corpse, they are told they should remember him as he was because Isaam Joda was mutilated. Inside the morgue doctors examining the body say he was burnt with cigarettes and an iron before he died. (BBC1 main News, 10 October 2000)

In the same bulletin, the BBC also reports the death of an Israeli settler, Rabbi Leiberman. This death and the subsequent funeral service receives about twice as much coverage as that of the Palestinian. It is described as a 'savage, cold-blooded killing' and there is no use of the word 'claim' in referring to its circumstances. The account, which, according to press reports, came from the Israeli authorities, is simply endorsed and reported by the journalist:

And there is grief too in this Jewish settlement. Children are in mourning on both sides of the divide, this family has also lost a husband and a father. Rabbi Leiberman was kidnapped and shot dead as he tried to get to a Jewish shrine being ransacked by Palestinians.

This is followed by an interview with an Israeli:

This is the way it is going at the moment, it shows that there is no way we could live together. Because the Arabs don't want to, not because we don't want to, because the Arabs don't want to. We've given them every chance to be able to live together and they don't want to accept it.

The journalist then continues:

Rabbi Leiberman's body was found here in a cave. This was a savage cold-blooded killing in a remote and isolated area and the tragedy is that even if there's a lasting deal to end this crisis it may not be enough to prevent random acts of sectarian violence like this one. (BBC1 main News, 10 October 2000)

There are two points to be made here. The first is on language. On the same day that these stories appeared, the BBC had also reported that 'almost one hundred people have died in the past twelve days, almost all of them Palestinians' (BBC1 early evening News, 10 October 2000). Despite the very large number of Palestinians who had died, words such as 'savage cold-blooded killing' had not been used to describe their deaths. The second point is that there are differences in the way in which statements from Palestinian and Israeli sources are treated. In practice this means that Israeli definitions and the use of specific emotive words can become the 'normal' language of news. We can see this in the reporting of the death of the twelve-year-old Palestinian boy, Mohammed al-Durrah, on 30 September 2000. This death was widely reported and was presented as a tragedy. The boy was reported to have 'wept with fear as his father tried to shade him' (BBC1 main News, 30 September 2000), and that they 'cowered terrified in no-man's land' (ITV early evening News, 2 October 2000).

But it is clear that there are competing explanations of the circumstances surrounding the death. The Palestinians regarded it as a deliberate killing. This view appears very infrequently. On one BBC bulletin the boy's parents are interviewed. The journalist begins by reporting the views of the boy's mother:

'This was an outrage', she said 'and I want the whole world to know how it happened. Miraculously his father survived but his body is punctured with eight bullet holes. "They shot at us until they hit us", he told me, and I saw the man who did it – the Israeli soldier. The Israelis haven't admitted responsibility.' (BBC1 main News, 1 October 2000)

The Israeli view was that the boy was caught unintentionally in crossfire and that they had not seen him. It is quite clear from other bulletins that this view predominates and is sometimes endorsed by journalists, while the view that the boy and his father were deliberately targeted is absent. We can see this in the following examples:

Newscaster: Palestinians have been mourning the death of a twelve-year-old boy *killed in the crossfire*.
Journalist: The Palestinian death toll is rising steadily, among them a twelve-year-old boy, Mohammed al-Durrah, who, with his father, got *caught in the crossfire*. Israeli soldiers should open fire only when their lives are in danger but they killed the child who clearly posed no threat whatsoever. (ITV early evening News, 1 October 2000 – our italics)

The worst clashes have been in Jerusalem, the Gaza Strip and the West Bank, where a twelve-year-old boy was *killed in the crossfire*. (ITV main News 1 October 2000 – our italics)

One death more than any other has inflamed Palestinian passions, that of this twelve-year-old boy filmed over the weekend, cowering with his father before he was shot and killed. (BBC1 main News, 2 October 2000)

... the fatal shooting by Israeli soldiers at the weekend of twelve-year-old Mohammed al-Durrah as he cowered with his father. Israel says the boy was *caught unintentionally in crossfire*. (ITV lunchtime News, 2 October 2000 – our italics)

Newscaster: Children were again caught up in the clashes today in a repeat of the scenes in which a twelve-year-old Palestinian boy was shot and killed yesterday.

Journalist: The Israelis are fully aware of the worldwide abhorrence at the death of twelve-year-old Mohammed al-Durrah, who, with his father, got pinned down during a *gun battle*. For 45 minutes they cowered terrified in no-man's land, but eventually the Israelis killed the boy. *They said afterwards they hadn't seen him.* (ITV early evening News, 2 October 2000 – our italics)

Journalist: Twelve-year-old Mohammed al-Durrah with his father pinned down during a *gun battle*. For 45 minutes they cowered terrified. But then the Israelis killed the boy. *They said afterwards they hadn't seen him ...*

President Clinton: 'It was a heartbreaking thing to see a child like that *caught in a crossfire.*' (ITV main News, 2 October 2000)

Journalist: Nearby I met the mother of twelve-year-old Mohammed al-Durrah, the Palestinian boy killed on Saturday *in the middle of a ferocious gun battle*. Mohammad's last moments alive were captured on film, his father telling him not to be afraid, a few seconds later he was shot dead. (BBC1 main News, 3 October 2000 – our italics)

It is clear that the journalists are sympathetic and do say that it was the Israelis who killed the boy, but it is the Israeli explanation of this event which is most frequently referenced. These patterns in the use of language and the adoption of 'official' Israeli definitions are also shown in the news coverage of a sequence of deaths in October 2000 in which Israeli soldiers and Israeli Arabs were reported as having been killed by angry crowds.

Between 8 and 11 October 2000, there were a series of reports in the press and on television of attacks on Israeli Arabs by Jewish Israelis, in Tel Aviv, Tiberius, Jaffa and Nazareth. Israeli Arabs make up 20 per cent of the population of Israel.[15] Many believe that they are treated as second-class citizens within Israel and in the early days of the intifada they had been reported as protesting/rioting in 'support for their Palestinian cousins' (BBC1 early evening News, 1 October 2000). On 10 October 2000, the *Guardian* reported an attack on the Arab community in Nazareth as follows:

In Nazareth, in the heart of Israel, hundreds of Jewish extremists attacked an Israeli/Arab neighbourhood overnight. When the police arrived they fired rubber bullets at the local Arabs – not their assailants, killing two men. (*Guardian,* 10 October 2000)

On the same day, the *Independent* reported attacks in Tel Aviv and Jaffa: 'in the seaside community of Bat Yam, just south of Tel Aviv, two Israeli Arabs were stabbed'. They also reported that 'in nearby Jaffa, three Arab-owned apartments were burned' and that some Jews were chanting 'death to the Arabs' (*Independent,* 10 October 2000). On the following day the *Guardian* reported that 'mosques and Arab businesses in Tel Aviv were besieged by Jewish mobs in a night of mayhem', and that 'on two consecutive nights this week, Jewish mobs attacked the two-hundred-year-old Hassan Bek mosque in central Tel Aviv' and that those who did it were screaming 'death to Arabs' (*Guardian,* 11 October 2000). On the same day the *Independent* reported that:

A Jewish mob wrecked one of Israel's most famous restaurants and tried to kill its Arab waiters by blocking them inside and torching the place ... outside a young man gazed happily at the mess. 'We want to cut all the Arabs throats; we want to kill them all' he said. (*Independent,* 11 October 2000)

In all, thirteen Israeli/Arabs were reported to have been killed in these events. The *Guardian* reported that the clashes in Nazareth had been described as a pogrom by an Israeli peace group:

... what is happening in Nazareth today is a pogrom, bearing all the hallmarks which were well known to Jews in tsarist Russia, that is collusion between the racist attackers and police. (*Guardian,* 10 October 2000).

The television news reporting of these events was rather muted by comparison. The following references were made within our sample:

Some Israeli civilians are taking matters into their own hands. Last night a Jewish mob attacked a mosque in the city of Tiberius. It seemed to be an act of revenge, following a Palestinian assault on a Jewish holy shrine on the West Bank. (BBC1 early evening News, 8 October 2000)

Some Israelis are taking it upon themselves to respond. In Tiberius on Saturday night a Jewish mob attacked a mosque and beat up Arabs. It seemed to be an act of revenge following a Palestinian assault on a Jewish shrine on the West Bank. Tonight Jews are again attacking Arabs, in the northern city of Nazareth. (BBC1 main News, 8 October 2000)

Inside Israel itself Jews have taken to the streets to show their anger. This is a mosque being attacked in Tiberius last night. (ITV main News, 8 October 2000)

A second Israeli Arab was killed in Nazareth and a Jewish settler died near Nablus in the West Bank. (BBC1 lunchtime News, 9 October 2000)

As the national mood in Israel darkens, these were the rare scenes in Tel Aviv, it may be far removed from the West Bank but even here the conflict is spilling out onto the streets. Two Israeli Arabs were stabbed and Arab homes were set alight as Jews staged running battles with the police. (ITV lunchtime News, 10 October 2000)

Passions on all sides are still running high. Even in Tel Aviv violence has now hit the streets. These were angry Jews last night looking for Arab victims. (ITV early evening News, 10 October 2000)

Overnight violence flared again inside Israel. In Acre, Israeli Arabs clashed with the police. (BBC1 lunchtime News, 11 October 2000)

On the following day, two Israeli soldiers were reported on TV news to have been killed by a crowd of Palestinians. According to these reports, four Israeli soldiers in a civilian car were arrested by Palestinian police in Ramallah. The Israelis stated that they were simply reservists who had taken a wrong turning into the town. The Palestinians believed them to be part of the Israeli undercover units. A crowd gathered outside the police station where they were being held. Some of these Palestinians gained access to the station, where two of the soldiers were then killed and the body of one of these was thrown from a window. The other two soldiers who had survived were later handed over to the Israeli authorities.

There are three points to be made about the TV news coverage of these events. The first is that the deaths of the two Israeli soldiers receive over five times as much coverage as that of the 13 Arabs who had been killed in 'mob' violence. Second, the deaths of the Israeli soldiers are highlighted in the coverage, receiving headlines such as 'Swift retaliation after Israeli soldiers are lynched' (ITV early evening News, 12 October 2000). Third, there is a very clear difference in the language used to describe the two sets of events. For example, 'lynch-mob' is not used in relation to the Arab deaths. We can see these very sharp differences in the structure and tone of coverage if we consider the following accounts from our sample of the deaths of the Israeli soldiers. In this BBC News from 12 October 2000, a 'frenzied mob' is reported as 'baying for their blood':

A *frenzied mob* of Palestinians besieging the police station in Ramallah. It was here that several Israeli soldiers had been arrested by Palestinian police and the mob were *baying for their blood*. Eventually they burst into the police station surging through the gates and clambering into the windows. Israel says the soldiers inside were just reservists who lost their way. The Palestinians insist they were members of a plain-clothes undercover unit. Whatever the truth, two of them were about to die. With cameras filming from the outside, young Palestinians could be seen in this window *savagely beating and stabbing soldiers to death*. Victory signs to indicate the deed had been done. The *frenzied crowd could hardly contain their glee*, especially when one of the bodies was thrown down to them from the window. Israel was outraged and promised vengeance. It was almost immediate. Just after noon prayers, Israeli helicopter gunships swarmed over Ramallah. People ran for their lives for they knew what was coming. They had incurred the wrath of Israel.

From a nearby rooftop we watched wave after wave of rockets rain down on Ramallah. First target, the police station where the soldiers had been *so barbarically killed*. (BBC1 main News, 12 October 2000 – our italics)

There are a number of words which were used specifically to describe the deaths of the Israeli soldiers, such as 'atrocity', 'murder' and, as we have seen, 'lynch-mob' and 'barbarically killed'. None of these were used in our samples for Arab/Palestinian deaths. The following examples are all from the first day on which the deaths of the two soldiers were reported:

> The [Israeli] attack is precise and repeated. Rocket after rocket slams into the police station destroying the very rooms where the *murders* took place ... Israel said it would take drastic action and it has, for the brutal *murder* of its soldiers this morning it has now traded a direct assault on the heart of the Palestinian city ... The Israelis are saying these are symbolic, if you like, pinprick attacks against, first of all the scene of this morning's *atrocity*. (BBC1 early evening News, 12 October 2000 – our italics)

> Palestinian police seized four Israeli soldiers and took them to a police station, but two were apparently *lynched by a mob*. (ITV lunchtime News 12 October 2000 – our italics)

> This was the trigger [for Israeli attacks]. The *murder* of two Israeli soldiers inside a Palestinian police station in Ramallah. The Palestinian security forces could not keep a *lynch-mob* of their own people at bay. In a first-floor room the soldiers were beaten and stabbed to death. Their bodies were later dumped out of this window. (ITV early evening News, 12 October 2000 – our italics)

There is also some discussion of the implications of the killings and a journalist refers to the Israeli view that they are a justification to 'abandon restraint':

> On Monday night Ehud Barak had withdrawn his ultimatum and threat of a crackdown but clearly he felt that the brutal killing of the two soldiers here was a step too far – *justification for abandoning restraint*. (ITV early evening New, 12 October 2000 – our italics)

Some might question the uncritical use of the word 'restraint' – since, as the previous bulletin had noted, 'the violence has left about one hundred people, mainly Palestinians dead' (ITV lunchtime News, 12 October 2000). It is also noteworthy that while the Israeli attacks after the killing of the soldiers are consistently referred to as a 'retaliation' and 'a response', the same links are not made to Palestinian actions. In other words, the killing of the soldiers is not routinely described as a response to the large number of Palestinian deaths. In analysing such points we are not seeking to justify or legitimise any killings in the conflict. But as we will see, such linkages in the structure of coverage are very important in how viewers understand the origins and causes of violence.

The language of 'lynching', 'brutal murder' and 'slaughter' continues over the days which follow:

This is the Ramallah police station where two Israeli soldiers were *brutally murdered*. (BBC1 lunchtime News, 13 October 2000 – our italics)

Today they buried one of the Israeli soldiers who was beaten and stabbed to death by a mob of Palestinians and whose *murder* triggered a wave of Israeli reprisals. (BBC1 late News, 13 October 2000 – our italics)

On this BBC bulletin we are then given details of the personal and tragic circumstances of the victim. We are told that 'he married his sweetheart only last week. She is expecting his baby.' The Palestinians are then said to 'show no sign of remorse':

In Ramallah Palestinians have been marching past the police station where the two soldiers died such horrific deaths. It has now been reduced to a pile of rubble by Israeli gunships. But these Palestinians show no sign of remorse. Instead they chant Islamic revolutionary slogans and protest about the Israeli attacks on their town. (BBC1 late News, 13 October 2000)

On the same day ITV news describes the deaths of the soldiers using words such as 'brutal slaying' and 'slaughter' (ITV lunchtime News, 13 October 2000). A later bulletin also notes that 'It was here yesterday with the mob violence that the Israeli-Palestinian conflict reached its lowest moment, exposing a raw and brutal enmity' (ITV late News, 13 October 2000).

It is perhaps significant that the 'lowest moment' in the conflict is seen as the mob violence which killed Israeli soldiers rather than the killings of Israeli Arabs or other Palestinian deaths. People on both sides of the conflict suffered terrible fates, but there were some clear differences in the manner in which these were described on the news. These differences in the use of language to describe deaths and killings are part of a much wider pattern in which some views, explanations and ways of understanding the conflict are given prominence. It may of course be argued that news which is balanced and impartial should not endorse any perspective but should report the views of both sides. However, we did find many departures from this principle, both in the sense that Israeli views were sometimes endorsed and highlighted, and that Palestinian/Arab perspectives were more likely to be downgraded or simply absent. In the section which follows we will examine a series of later samples of news coverage to identify possible similarities or changes in the patterns of coverage to which we have pointed so far.

ADDITIONAL CONTENT SAMPLES:
OCTOBER–DECEMBER 2001, MARCH–APRIL 2002

Here, we analyse a series of additional content samples of TV news using the same methods as above. The purpose is to examine whether the trends which we have identified thus far are continued in later coverage. There were a number of specific areas of news content which we wished to identify and analyse for purposes of comparison with the earlier samples. These included news on the origins and history of the conflict, the reasons for the fighting, the rationales of the two sides, descriptions of motives and coverage of casualties. We chose these additional samples of news from periods where there was extensive media coverage of the conflict and analysed early evening and late bulletins from BBC1 and ITV. The sample dates from which the bulletins came were 17 October to 13 December 2001 (47 bulletins), 2–9 March 2002 (21 bulletins) and 9–16 April 2002 (30 bulletins). We also wished to identify any new themes or issues which had emerged in these periods. These later samples came after the events of the 9/11 attack on the US, which changed the international climate in which acts of violence and 'terrorism' were discussed. Within Israel, Ariel Sharon, the right-wing politician who had played such a role at the outset of the intifada, was now prime minister. There were also changes in the manner in which the Israeli-Palestinian conflict was fought. In 2001, the Israelis had begun a series of military incursions into areas which had been under local Palestinian administration, and some Palestinian groups were engaging in the extensive use of suicide bombs. The incursions were reported as involving attacks on refugee camps and the demolition of Palestinian homes as part of a new plan announced by Ariel Sharon to deal with the revolt against the Israeli occupation. As we have noted, this was a period of extensive settlement and military development in the occupied areas and it was reported that the Israeli army had 'uprooted thousands of olive trees and vast tracts of farmland in Gaza' (*Guardian*, 12 April 2001). In our analysis of news content above we noted the dominance of Israeli perspectives and how this in part reflected the success of their public relations output. In on-screen appearances/interviews, Israelis had twice as much coverage as Palestinians. To develop this analysis further in these samples, we analysed all reported statements as well as interviews. We counted all the coverage given to statements from each side and found that the Israeli dominance was sustained, notably in BBC coverage.[16]

In our first sample, we found that there was very little coverage of the history and origins of the conflict or discussion of the nature of the relationship between the two sides – that one was subject to military control by the other. The same was true of our later samples – we found nothing on the history and origins of the conflict. As before, there was extensive coverage of the violence and there was sympathy expressed for those caught up in it, but very little analysis of its nature and causes. We did, however, find that such issues were discussed more directly in other media and interestingly within Israel itself. In March 2002, Michael Ben-Yair, the Israeli Attorney General between 1993 and 1996, wrote in the Israeli newspaper *Ha'aretz*:

> The intifada is the Palestinian people's war of national liberation. We enthusiastically chose to become a colonialist society, ignoring international treaties, expropriating lands, transferring settlers from Israel to the occupied territories, engaging in theft and finding justification for all these activities ... we established an apartheid regime. (quoted in the *Observer*, 31 March 2002)

Because such perspectives on the history and nature of the conflict were substantially absent from TV news, the practical effect was to remove the rationale for Palestinian action. Much of the news implicitly assumed the status quo – as if trouble and violence 'started' with the Palestinians launching an attack to which the Israelis 'responded'. The lack of commentary on the nature of the occupation is clearly one dimension to this. Another is that there is little discussion of the possibility that actions by some Israeli groups might be designed to provoke a Palestinian response. We did, however, find that this was a subject taken up in the Israeli press. For example, in November 2001 the *Guardian* reported that Israeli newspapers were being very critical of the assassination policy pursued by Ariel Sharon's government. In November 2001 the military commander of Hamas in the West Bank had been killed shortly before the arrival of two US peace envoys. This, said the Israeli commentators, had increased the threat of suicide bombing. As one noted in Israel's largest daily paper, *Yediot Ahronot*:

> Whoever gave the green light for the assassination operation knew full well they are actually breaking, with a single blow, the gentleman's agreement between Hamas and the Palestinian Authority of refraining in the coming days from perpetrating terror attacks.

The Israeli paper also criticised the army for planting an explosive device which had killed five Palestinian children, noting that

> The act of revenge now hovering in the air has complete legitimacy, both on the Palestinian street and in the Palestinian Authority, in the light of the deaths of five children by an Israeli Army bomb. (quoted in the *Guardian*, 26 November 2001)

Other Israeli commentators have suggested that the policy of 'targeted killings' by the Israelis was being used to provoke the Palestinians. A spokesman from Courage to Refuse, an organisation of dissenters from the Israeli Army, commented that:

> Any suicide attack within Israel, deplorable as it is, is used by Sharon as a pretext for inflicting ever-increasing misery on the 3.5 million inhabitants of Palestine. And if suicide attacks are not forthcoming, you can count on Sharon to provoke them with his so-called 'targeted killings'. (*Guardian*, 5 July 2002)

It has also been argued that the reason for such 'provocation' is that some powerful political and military groups did not want a peace with the Palestinians, which involved an independent Palestinian state. They would prefer a completely subordinate Palestinian population or another diaspora in which Palestinians move into other countries. The Israeli peace activist Uri Avneri has commented on Ariel Sharon that

From the day he took power, his agenda has been to erase the Oslo accords and dismantle the Palestinian Authority and its armed forces. He believes that ultimately the Palestinians will flee, as they did in 1948, or agree to be herded into a few isolated bantustans. (quoted in the *Guardian*, 11 January 2002)

David Hirst makes a similar point in an extended analysis of the Middle East crisis:

Ostensibly [Ariel Sharon] wants to return to the peace process. In reality he never did. For this was a war, which he and like-minded soldiers and politicians long anticipated; and once he got this war he did everything to fuel and perpetuate it. It was never a secret: he always opposed the Oslo Accord, and the historic compromise it involves, a Palestinian state on 22 per cent of original Palestine. From the outset, this was his war to destroy any idea of Palestinian self-determination on any portion of Palestinian land, and any legitimate institution in power to bring it about. (*Guardian*, 22 February 2002)

It can be seen that from a Palestinian perspective, the issue is not simply that the Israeli authorities may be acting 'first' in the sequence of violence, it is also that the Israeli 'response' is less about catching 'terrorists' than about destroying the possibility of a Palestinian state. The Israeli historian Avi Shlaim has argued that Ariel Sharon pursued this objective by linking his own actions to the American 'war against terror':

Ever the opportunist, Sharon was quick to jump on the bandwagon of America's "war against terror" in the aftermath of September 11. Under this banner Sharon has embarked on a sinister attempt to destroy the infrastructure of a future Palestinian state. His real agenda is to subvert what remains of the Oslo Accords, to smash the Palestinians into the ground and to extinguish hope for independence and statehood. (*Observer*, 14 April 2002)

As we will see, the news coverage in our samples was not normally informed by such perspectives. It tended rather to focus on the narrow reporting of violent events within a framework of Palestinian 'action' and Israeli 'retaliation'.

SAMPLE TWO: OCTOBER–DECEMBER 2001

Motives, retaliation and response

In analysing what we call the rationales of action, it is not our intention to legitimise or justify any killings. It is clear that people from both sides in this conflict met terrible fates. But in explaining the constructiõn and development of public understanding, it is important to show any differences that exist in descriptions of the motives of different parties and in the consequences of their actions. As we have indicated, there are very distinct and different perspectives, which exist on the nature of this conflict and the motives of those involved. The Israeli authorities and much of the Israeli population see the issue in terms of their security and indeed the survival of the state in the face of threats from terrorists and hostile neighbours. They present their own actions as a response or retaliation to attacks. In contrast, the Palestinians see themselves as resisting or responding to a brutal military occupation by people who have taken their land, water and homes and who are denying them the possibility of their own state. Our analysis suggests that the news framework and presentational structure, which was most frequently used in reporting events, tended to favour the Israeli perspective.

In this sample we found that Israelis were said to be 'retaliating' or in some way responding to what had been done to them about six times as often as the Palestinians.[17] This was a period of very intense conflict, including Israeli incursions into Palestinian towns and villages, suicide-bombs and other attacks. In summarising the period on BBC *News 24*, a journalist commented that: 'This cycle of violence began six weeks ago when an Israeli cabinet minister was shot' (BBC1, *News 24*, 2 December 2001). This is also how the Israelis presented the sequence of events. The Palestinians, however, regarded the killing of the Israeli minister as a 'response' to the assassination of one of their political leaders. The *Independent* described the sequence as follows:

> The most notorious assassination came at the end of August when Israeli helicopters hovering over the West Bank town of Ramallah fired two missiles through the office windows of the leader of the Popular Front for the Liberation of Palestine, Abu Ali Mustafa, 64, decapitating him as he sat in his swivel chair. As the leader of an established PLO faction, who according to Palestinians, was a politician rather than a member of the PFLP's military wing – he

was the most senior figure to be picked off by the Israelis. Seven weeks later the PFLP sought revenge by infiltrating a Jerusalem hotel and assassinating Israel's tourism minister, Rehavem Ze'evi, whose support for ethnically cleansing the West Bank and Gaza of Arabs had long made him an enemy of the Palestinians. (*Independent*, 9 November 2001)

The Israelis frequently referred to the killing of their own minister and gave it as their reason for the incursions/attacks on Palestinian towns and villages. The news then commonly reported this view without commenting on the Palestinian perspective on the sequence of events:

Israel has been under intense pressure from the Americans to pull out of Palestinian areas it occupied last week *following the killing of the* Israeli tourism minister. (BBC1 late News, 26 October 2001 – our italics)

A tribute to the minister assassinated one week ago today, Ariel Sharon says he has now captured some of the men involved, the reason he gave for his incursions into the West Bank. (BBC1 late News, 24 October 2001)

The assassination of an Israeli cabinet minister *led to the reoccupation* of Palestinian areas. (BBC *News 24*, 3 November 2001 – our italics)

Israeli forces have withdrawn from the town of Ramallah. Ramallah was one of six Palestinian towns which were occupied *after the killing of an Israeli cabinet minister.* (BBC Radio 4, 7 November 2001 – our italics)

The Israeli incursions/attacks were reported to have resulted in the deaths of 79 Palestinians in three weeks and other casualties plus the extensive destruction of homes and property (*Guardian*, 8 November 2001). Yet the pattern is persistent, that Palestinian attacks are rarely referred to on TV news as a 'response' or 'retaliation' to Israeli action. This structure can be seen clearly in the reports of a Palestinian attack and an Israeli 'retaliation':

Ten people have been killed and 30 injured after Palestinian gunmen opened fire on an Israeli bus travelling to a Jewish settlement in the West Bank. The bus was attacked as it approached Immanuel, north of Jerusalem. Tonight, *Israeli warplanes have retaliated* with air strikes against Palestinian targets in Gaza and Nablus. (BBC1 main News, 12 December 2001 – our italics)

Ten Israeli settlers were killed and up to 30 wounded in an attack by the Palestinian terrorist group, Hamas, on a bus in the West Bank. *Israel responded with air raids* on the West Bank and Gaza. (ITV main News, 12 December 2001 – our italics)

There is a much smaller number of references from journalists to the possibility of Palestinian counter-attacks and future action, as in the following reports:

The Israeli cabinet is meeting tonight and are planning more tough action but the lesson from the past is that Israeli strikes are met by Palestinian counter-attacks. The future is already written here and it holds a lot more blood. (BBC1 main News, 12 December 2001)

The bitter experience of the past 15 months suggests that the Palestinians will not regard this strike as a salutary lesson, but as a provocation. (ITV main News, 4 December 2001)

The BBC also describes how the actions of both sides are generating more hatred. A report notes that Israeli tanks have moved in on the headquarters of Yasser Arafat 'following the latest attacks on Jewish settlers'. A journalist then goes on to describe the attitudes on both sides:

If Arafat falls, his successors could be more extreme – the UN warning of chaos. Israel isn't listening; it's consumed by rage and grief. This woman, burying her husband today, one of ten people killed near a Jewish settlement last night by men Arafat did not jail. Israel now punishing innocent Palestinians. We found troops stopping May, her sister Rena, and sick mother from driving to their home. Israel generating more hate. (BBC1 early evening News, 13 December 2001)

Such references suggest that one reason for the continuing violence is its self-perpetuating nature – that it is a cycle of 'tit-for-tat' action. We saw this explanation in the first weeks of the intifada. There is, however, an apparent move in this later period towards the Israeli perspective that it is Palestinian action which is driving this cycle. The assumption is revealed in an extraordinary exchange between a journalist and an MP interviewed on Radio 4 about his recent visit to Egypt. The MP is asked: 'What can the Egyptians do to stop the suicide bombers – because that in the end is what is cranking up the violence at present?' The MP then replies: 'Well that is one view, the Israeli view' (Radio 4, 5.00 p.m. News, 1 April 2002). One consequence of the adoption of this view by journalists was that of the dominant pattern of action–retaliation which we have described. This was especially so in the headlines and in the introductory phrases of news stories. On 1 and 2 December 2001, there were reports of suicide-bomb attacks in Israel which killed 25 people and left hundreds injured. On 3 and 4 December, the BBC News reported Israeli attacks on Palestinian areas as follows:

Headline: No mercy – the Israelis *hammer the Palestinians after the weekend bombs.* The West Bank and Gaza under attack tonight, a moment of truth says Israel.

Israel *has hit back* with maximum force against Palestinians after the bomb attacks at the weekend which left 25 dead and hundreds injured.

Israel's *payback* to Yasser Arafat – at sunset Apache helicopters move in ...

Palestinians claim two were killed during Israel's *retaliation.*

Sum up: Israeli missiles have pounded Gaza city and the headquarters of Yasser Arafat, the Palestinian leader, *after the bomb attacks of the* weekend which left 25 dead and hundreds injured. The Israeli cabinet meeting in emergency session this afternoon said the attacks were a clear message to Mr Arafat to deal decisively with the problem of Palestinian terrorism. (BBC1 early evening News, 3 December 2001 – our italics)

Headline: Second day of *Israeli's retribution* – Palestinian targets are hammered again.

It's the second day of raids *in retaliation* for the Palestinian suicide-bomb attacks in Israel over the weekend.

Two people were killed and many injured. This is all part of Israel's *furious response* to the weekend's suicide bombings, which killed so many Israelis.
Interview question: We're into the second day of *retaliation*, is there any end in sight to this series of attacks that we've seen? (BBC1 early evening News, 4 December 2001 – our italics)

On ITV news it was reported that

Israel gave the Palestinian Authority another humiliating reminder of its military power today with more attacks *in response* to the weekend's suicide-bombings.
Sum up: Israel launched more attacks *in response* to the suicide bombings of the weekend. (ITV main News, 4 December 2001 – our italics)

This is a pattern which was apparently used quite extensively. The following are from programmes outside our main samples:

Dozens of Palestinians and Israelis have been killed in a relentless round of suicide-bombings and *Israeli counter-attacks*. (BBC2 *Newsnight*, 10.30 p.m., 13 December 2001 – our italics)

The Israelis had carried out this demolition *in retaliation for* the murder of four soldiers. (Channel 4 News, 7.00 p.m., 10 January 2002 – our italics)

Five Palestinians have been killed when the Israeli army launched new attacks on the Gaza Strip *in retaliation for* recent acts of terrorism. (Radio 4, 7.30 a.m., 6 March 2002 – our italics)

Such formulaic reporting excludes at least two key 'alternative' perspectives on the motivations of those involved in the conflict: (1) that Palestinians may be seen as resisting or responding to Israeli military control and the occupation as well as reacting to specific events such as attacks and assassinations; (2) that Israeli actions may be designed to destroy the possibility of a Palestinian state as well as to attack the 'terrorist infrastructure'. At one point the BBC does touch on the future of the Palestinian Authority, which is responsible for the local administration of the Palestinian areas. On 13 December 2001 there was a report on Israeli attacks on the Authority's buildings in Gaza and the West Bank. Israelis are said to be 'smashing [Arafat's] institutions one by one, bulldozing his territory into rubble ...'. A UN Middle East envoy says on camera, 'if the Palestinian Authority crashes, then Oslo is over' (meaning that the peace process is over). But what is the rationale for the destruction of these institutions? We do not hear the view that Sharon has always been against the Oslo agreement or the suggestion that he has provoked Palestinian action to make sure that it fails. Following the comments of the UN envoy, we hear only that 'Israelis say it's over already, they are consumed by rage and by grief' (BBC1 late News, 13 December 2001). This does not mean that the rage and grief are not genuine, but to see the destruction of the potential Palestinian state simply as a 'grief-stricken response' is only one view of what this conflict is about.

Arafat and Sharon

Our research suggests that the Israeli perspective is highlighted in terms of causes, motives and preferred outcomes. The Israelis present themselves as confronted by an unreasoning terror – the preferred solution is therefore simply to catch the terrorists. Within this way of understanding the conflict, the only problem is that Arafat will not co-operate sufficiently in arresting the 'extremists'. There is no comparable criticism of Sharon on television news at this time. In our earlier sample from the first weeks of the intifada, he had been referred to as a 'right wing enemy of the peace process' and his role at the inception of the intifada had been discussed. By the time of this sample, however, Sharon was prime minister of Israel, and criticism of him is more muted. In contrast, the view that Arafat is to blame is more extensively featured and pursued on the news. In the wake of the suicide-bombs of 1 and 2 December 2001, Sharon was able to develop his account of Arafat's responsibility and to do so with some help from journalists who reiterated his views:

Newscaster: And within the past minutes the Israeli prime minister, Ariel Sharon, has addressed the nation on television. He said that Israel had been dragged into a war of terror. He said that Yasser Arafat was the biggest obstacle to peace in the Middle East.
Ariel Sharon: Arafat is responsible for everything that is happening here. Arafat chose a strategic decision; he chose a terrorism strategy. He chose to try and achieve political achievements through murder by killing innocent civilians. Arafat chose the way of terror.

We are then given more detail on these views by the correspondent in Israel:

> Well the prime minister has been speaking on television as you say, saying that Israel is going to use new methods and old in the fight against terrorism, insisting that it will not be stopped by the militants who *he says are trying to drive the Israelis out of their land.* He's also claiming basically as we had suspected that the Americans had effectively given him carte blanche. He's been saying that George Bush told him that the United States and Israel stand together side by side in the war against terrorism. (BBC1 early evening News, 3 December 2001 – our italics)

There are no comments here by the journalist on international law, on the legality of the occupation, on Sharon's policies, or questioning the issue of who has been driven from what land. On the following evening, the Israeli views are developed further:

> *Journalist*: For months, Israelis have said that he must do more to crack down on Palestinian militants. Now, they argue, his failure makes him personally responsible for this weekend's acts of terrorism.
> *Israeli spokesman*: Yasser Arafat can't have it both ways. He can't be a statesman and give harbour to the PFLP, to Hamas, to Islamic Jihad.
> *Journalist*: The bombs were the worst suicide attacks for years, but part of a terrible pattern. Before long, Hamas activists had released a video of one of the suicide-bombers. Arafat seemed unable or unwilling to stop it. His Palestinian police did then swoop in to arrest more than 100 suspected militants. But for the Israelis it was too little, too late ... (BBC1 early evening News, 4 December 2001)

The Israeli view is also reported on ITV news:

> Israel has warned that its military will resume the bombardment of Arafat's power base unless he proves he can control the extremists among his people. (ITV early evening News, 6 December 2001)

The Israelis continue to take matters into their own hands because they believe Yasser Arafat is simply not doing enough to rein in the Palestinian extremists. (ITV early evening News, 10 December 2001)

On 6 December 2001, ITV news interviewed Arafat. There was no criticism of Sharon or his policies in this, and little on the history or nature of the Israeli military occupation other than to report Arafat's comments that the Israeli measures were 'humiliating' him and his people. The main focus of the interview was on Arafat's attitude to 'terrorism' and on the 'crackdown' which he was supposed to be pursuing on 'terrorist activities'. The interview ends with the journalist equating the success of this with being committed to 'peace':

> The general verdict on Yasser Arafat's crackdown appears to be so far so good, but the Palestinian leader will have to do much more in the days ahead to convince the sceptics that he is, as he said tonight, truly committed to peace. (ITV late News, 6 December 2001)

There is no commentary here on what the Israelis might have to do in order to be seen as 'committed to peace'. On the following day BBC news interviews Yasser Arafat and focuses on Israel's claim that 'Yasser Arafat isn't doing enough to arrest militants'. Before speaking with Arafat, the BBC is taken through the backstreets of Gaza to meet members of Hamas. The point they are making is that 'Yasser Arafat says it's a struggle to hunt down the extremists of Hamas, but it didn't take us long to find them.' The reporter notes that 'the men who believe in suicide-bombings are all senior militants, the kind Arafat has promised to arrest'. We hear that these men do not expect to be rounded up any time soon and one states that Arafat 'can't stop us resisting the Israeli occupation'. The subsequent interview with Arafat then focuses on whether he will make arrests, as in this interview exchange:

> *Journalist*: There are many still out on the streets. We ourselves found one of the men on Israel's wanted list.
> *Yasser Arafat*: I arrested now 70, what they are asking beside who I had arrested before.
> *Journalist*: Will you arrest them all?

The journalist then notes finally, 'those excuses not good enough for the Israelis' (BBC1 late News, 7 December 2001). There is nothing here on the role of Sharon or the Israelis in the continuing violence. But without this it is very difficult to understand the perspective or the motivations of the Palestinians. The journalist goes on to note the difficulties which Arafat has in arresting the wanted men. The problem is apparently that they enjoy wide popular support:

> The extremists are heroes to many Palestinians, more popular every time they kill. Few want to see them behind bars, so Yasser Arafat is trapped between the wrath of Israel and the wrath of his own people. (BBC1 late News, 7 December 2001)

We can see why viewers might be confused by such coverage or have difficulty in understanding why the violence is so intractable. ITV news asks in one, more critical, bulletin: 'What is driving this succession of bombings by Islamic terrorist groups and can Yasser Arafat or anyone else stop the perpetrators?' The answer it gives is as follows:

> The majority of Palestinians now back the hard-line groups. They're demanding Israel leaves territory in the West Bank and Gaza Strip that was promised to their people in a peace deal. (ITV late News, 3 December 2001)

The question was an important one to ask, but the above answer shows the problems which we identified earlier. There is nothing to indicate the relationship which exists between the two sides. It sounds rather like an argument over a piece of land, which is how some viewers understood it. In the same bulletin, there are then two brief comments from Middle East experts, who indicate that Arafat cannot control Hamas and Islamic Jihad because they are opposed to him, but there is little to explain why all these events are occurring. Viewers might also ask what is the sense of using a word such as 'extremist' if it is the majority position? Why would 'ordinary' Palestinians support such action? One BBC News programme in our sample had attempted to answer some of these questions by going to interview the family of a suicide-bomber. The action of the bomber is referred to as 'a reply to Ariel Sharon's devastating air strikes' and the bomber's family is described:

We found the bomber's family in their modest house near Bethlehem, not militants or gunmen, just ordinary people, but such is the hatred now between the two sides that they wished more blood had been spilled. (BBC1 late News, 5 December 2001)

This report is noteworthy in that it attempts to situate suicide-bombing in the context of Palestinian society. It makes the point that the bomber was a 'quiet family man' who was 46 years old:

Relatives showed me a picture of the bomber, not the typical young militant but a quiet family man of 46. 'He got up at four this morning', his wife Fatima said, 'prayed and read the Koran. He told me to look after our sons and our daughters, and he said goodbye.' (BBC1 late News, 5 December 2001)

One explanation of such an action, suggested in the report, is that it is part of the cycle of violence – of constant attack and counter-attack. But the report leaves open the issue of why this cycle continues. The only clue to this is given in a reference to 'political progress':

Suicide-bombings are a source of pride and Palestinians say they won't stop without *political progress*. However many militants Yasser Arafat puts behind bars, others are waiting to take their place. (BBC1 late News, 5 December 2001 – our italics)

This is the limit of the presentation of the Palestinian perspective. The phrase 'political progress' is used to cover the whole relationship of the Palestinians to the Israelis – the loss of homes, land and water, the occupation and military rule. The phrase equates to those in our first sample of news where Palestinian actions were explained by references to 'frustrations with the peace process'. Such phrases act as a form of euphemism, and effectively avoid raising some of the more controversial aspects of this conflict. There has, however, been criticism that such interviews are conducted at all. Some pro-Israel groups have argued that to discuss the motives and personal histories of suicide bombers is to 'sanitise' them or give them legitimacy (see, for example, Phillips, 2003). But it is clear that to understand the conflict requires an analysis of motivations and historical causes. This does not imply approval of violent actions. Indeed, the consequences of such actions were made perfectly clear on television news, as can be seen in the very graphic accounts that were given of the aftermath of suicide-bombings and other killings.

Terrorists, gunmen and defenders: words and perspectives

The choice of a word to describe a social action can have a crucial influence on how the action is understood and the legitimacy which is granted to it. This is in part the traditional debate about the difference between calling someone a 'terrorist' or a 'freedom fighter'. In describing the Israeli-Palestinian conflict, journalists are obviously aware of how different words relate to different perspectives. In this example from ITV news, a journalist identifies the two viewpoints:

> The Palestinian people regard these gunmen as the defenders of Bethlehem. However, Israel views them as terrorists who should be arrested by Yasser Arafat's police force. (ITV early evening News, 24 October 2001)

There is nothing in the commentary to explain why the two sides would see their world so differently or the nature of the relationship between them. It is, however, an attempt to distinguish two ways of speaking about the participants. But although the journalist is consciously presenting the Palestinian view, his sentence still uses the word 'gunmen'. In our culture, this word has very negative connotations – it is usually used to describe armed bank robbers or those involved in other criminal activity, and is also used interchangeably with the word 'terrorist'. We can consider an actual example of its use in a different political context. In the following case a report from the *Daily Telegraph* about Northern Ireland discusses a proposed amnesty as part of the peace process. The headline for the report is: 'Amnesty for *Gunmen* still on the Run' (our italics). The first line of the report then reads: '*Terrorists* who are still at large and wanted for offences ... will be given an amnesty' (*Daily Telegraph*, 25 October 2001). In a report from the Israeli-Palestinian conflict, ITV news also uses the words interchangeably. This report is about the deaths of five Palestinian children killed by an Israeli bomb, which was apparently triggered as they walked to school. We are told initially that 'Israel is investigating whether a bomb meant for *terrorists* may have been to blame' (our italics). A few lines later in the report we hear 'Such a bomb would have been intended for Palestinian *gunmen*' (ITV early evening News, 23 November 2001 – our italics).

It is clear from our work that negative words such as 'terrorists' and 'gunmen' were typically applied to Palestinian actors rather than to Israelis. We also found a number of examples in periods before our samples, which apparently indicates a long-term trend – for example, 'a Palestinian terrorist hurled two grenades into a bus queue' (BBC1 early evening News, 19 October 1998), and 'tougher Palestinian measures against Islamic terrorists' (BBC2 *Newsnight*, 23 October 1998). We have already seen how the word 'terrorist' was used in Israeli criticism of Arafat. There were a number of other references to Israeli views on terrorism in our sample, such as:

[Ariel Sharon] used every opportunity he could to attack the Arabs as terrorists, and to make it clear that there would be absolutely no room for compromise at all until all the terrorist problem was solved. (BBC1 early evening News, 1 November 2001)

For them [the Israelis], it is their war against terrorism. (BBC1 early evening News, 4 December 2001)

[Ariel Sharon] said that Israel had been dragged into a war on terror. (BBC1 early evening News, 6 December 2001)

The Israeli army says the intended target was a known Islamic terrorist. (BBC1 early evening News, 10 December 2001)

There were also references to the views of the US government, which in practice tended to reinforce the Israeli perspective, as in the following examples:

President Bush: Once again I call upon Chairman Arafat to make maximum efforts to *end terrorism* against Israel. (BBC1 late News, 7 March 2002 – our italics)
Colin Powell: As we have responded to terrorism we know that Israel has the right *to respond to terrorism*. (ITV early evening News, 12 April 2002 – our italics)[18]

There are also occasions when journalists endorse the use of the word 'terrorist' by using it directly in their own speech without attributing it as part of a reported statement:

Israel unleashed its pent-up anger against Palestinians today after a weekend of deadly suicide-bombings by Islamic *terrorists*. (ITV late News, 3 December 2001 – our italics.)

Ten Israeli settlers were killed and up to 30 wounded this evening in an attack by the Palestinian *terrorist* group, Hamas, on a bus in the West Bank. (ITV late News, 12 December 2001 – our italics)

Journalist: The Americans know that they can hardly tell the Israelis that they cannot use all the means at their disposal to go after *terrorists*, when of course that's exactly what the Americans are doing in Afghanistan. (BBC1 late News, 2 December 2001)

The Israeli army launched new attacks in the Gaza Strip in retaliation for recent acts of *terrorism*. (BBC Radio 4, 7.30 a.m., 6 March 2002 – our italics)

Five Israelis were killed in attacks by Palestinian *terrorists*. (ITV late News, 5 March 2002)

[The Jenin refugee camp in the West Bank] the target of Israel's most determined efforts to *root out potential terrorists*. (BBC1 early evening News, 12 April 2002 – our italics)

Headline: Deadlock still on the West Bank. Israel stays *until the terrorists are beaten*. (BBC1 late News, 14 April 2002 – our italics)

Interview question: If Arafat can't arrest members of Hamas, can't arrest the *terrorists* ... (BBC2 *Newsnight*, 9 August 2001 – our italics)

He [Israeli reservist] had to search hundreds of Palestinian homes, *rooting out terrorists*. (BBC1 Breakfast News, 8.30 a.m., 11 June 2002 – our italics)

There is one occasion in our sample when a BBC reporter refers to the Israelis as 'state terrorists', while reporting the views of President Assad of Syria. The British prime minister, Tony Blair, was visiting the country shortly before travelling to Israel. The journalist notes that 'Tomorrow's hosts are the very same people that today's hosts regard as bloody state terrorists, and of course the Israelis think much the same thing of the Syrians, the Palestinians and others.' He also notes that 'Syria's President Assad ... regards Palestinian suicide-bombers and assassins as freedom fighters' (BBC1 late News, 30 October 2001). Journalists are unlikely to take their lead from the president of Syria, given the nature of the Syrian regime, but this is hardly a reason for not representing the Palestinian perspective in other news coverage. There are many people apart from the president of Syria who view the conflict very differently from the perspective offered by the Israeli authorities. As Max Hastings has pointed out, writing in the *Daily Mail*:

> It may be argued that Israeli action represents a rival terrorism, rather than a counter-terrorism. Yet the Israelis have been largely successful in persuading the Bush administration that Palestinian suicide bombers represent a common foe, in the same league as the September 11 hijackers. To most outsiders, however, it is plain that what is happening in Israel and the West Bank must be addressed primarily as a political issue, rather than a military one. (Hastings, 2002)

The key point is that the use of a label such as 'terrorist' can actually obscure the proper consideration of causes and possible solutions. On the news, confusions over how people are described are symptomatic of a larger problem in explaining the motivations of those involved and the history and the nature of the conflict. The sheer number of terms used to describe Palestinians does seem to indicate this. Israeli forces were described as 'soldiers', 'troops', and in one case 'brothers in arms', but were most frequently referred to as 'the Israelis'.[19] Words applied to Palestinians included 'activists', 'followers [of Hamas]', 'guerrillas', 'militants', 'extremists', 'assailants', 'gunmen', 'bombers', 'terrorists', 'killers', 'assassins', 'fundamentalist groups', 'attackers', 'self-styled Palestinian martyrs' and 'fanatics'.

As far as the Palestinians are concerned, such labels can obscure what for them is central, that this conflict is a war of national liberation against what they see as a brutal military occupation. This is a long way from the perspective that the key issue is to 'catch the terrorists'. It does seem that there is a reluctance or an inability in TV news to talk about the nature of the occupation and Israeli military control and a reluctance to discuss these issues as motives for Palestinian action. This is not to say that there is no sympathy expressed by journalists for Palestinians, or indeed for those who are presented as the 'innocent victims' on both sides of the conflict.

The issue of casualties and victims is an important area of coverage in terms of potential impacts on public understanding, and we turn to this now.

Victims and casualties of the conflict

We noted in our first sample that there was sympathy expressed for victims and especially for children who were injured or killed. In this sample, such casualties now included Israeli children because of the growing use of the tactic of suicide-bombing. There was also sympathy expressed for those who were displaced by this new phase of the conflict. This BBC bulletin describes an Israeli military incursion into Bethlehem and the effect on those who lived there. It begins with a description of a march by church leaders, calling for the troops to go, and comments that the protesters are walking 'straight into a battleground'. It then describes a family trying to escape the danger:

> The disruption caused by Israeli troops is what lined the road to Bethlehem today ... Outside a brother and sister reunited, Esa told me he slipped into Bethlehem behind the march to get his sister and her children away from danger ... Their ordeal wasn't over yet, we followed as they set off with their car, but then a warning from down the street, it wasn't safe. As they ran back to the church more gunfire but in the end this one family did get out, leaving this behind. (BBC1 late News, 23 October 2001)

The image of victims caught up in violence beyond their control is continued in this description of a suicide-bombing by the same journalist:

> Another night of death in Israel. Emergency workers sift through the wreckage left behind by one more Palestinian suicide-bomber. More families who will grieve, more damage to America's bid for a truce. The wounded being brought in, passengers who had just been trying to get home, like this woman who stared the bomber in the face, but saw no hint of what he had in mind. (BBC1 late News, 31 October 2001)

When children are involved, the theme of their innocence as victims can be very powerfully expressed, as in the next three examples. The first is from when five children were killed by an

Israeli bomb on the way to school, the second is a description of suicide-bomb attacks on 1 and 2 December, and the third is of Israeli 'retribution' after these attacks:

> Yet more child victims of the lethal stalemate bedevilling the Holy Land. The young innocents this time were five Palestinian boys, all from the same extended family. The youngest just seven, two were ten years old, the other two 14. (ITV early evening News, 23 November 2001)

> At the hospital, more families in mourning, Israel is bleeding ... The terror began last night in downtown Jerusalem, the victims were the young teenagers, maimed and killed on the street's pedestrian mall. Two suicide-bombers had struck, causing carnage. (BBC1 late News, 2 December 2001)

> The bombs were aimed at a Palestinian security base, but the base is close to a school. Dozens of children were on the streets. Two people were killed and many injured ... Yet again the innocent are caught at the centre of the conflict. (BBC1 early evening News, 4 December 2001)

In the following example, a BBC journalist describes the effects of a suicide-bomb detonated on a bus:

> Yet another deadly strike and a return to chaos and carnage ... Israeli soldiers and civilians on board had little chance. They were caught in a hail of metal; explosives had been packed with nuts and bolts. Those not killed were injured – in Haifa's hospital, the agonising wait to find out who lived and who died. (BBC1 early evening News, 10 April 2002)

A young girl had been terribly injured in the blast. The journalist translates the mother's words:

> 'She used to be a beautiful girl,' her mother says, 'now she is burned, her hair is gone. I wish I'd taken a picture of her before this happened.' Long after the blast, the mobile phones of the victims were still ringing – family and friends hoping to hear voices that are gone forever. (BBC1 early evening News, 10 April 2002)

However, we did note in our earlier sample that there were some differences in the manner in which the casualties on each side were reported. To explore this further here, we will compare the reporting of two incidents which occurred on 10 and 12 December 2001. The first was an attack by Israeli helicopters using missiles in Hebron, which killed two Palestinian children. The second was an attack by Palestinians on a bus carrying Israeli settlers, cars and a military vehicle, in which ten people were reported to have been killed. In both cases there is an emphasis on the suffering of the casualties and the involvement of children:

Israeli helicopters on a mission to kill. Smoke rising after they fired their missiles. Israel trying to kill a leading militant, but while he was sitting in traffic on a busy street. This, the wreckage left behind by the botched assassination. The target, Mohammed Satr, is expected to recover but Israel's missiles killed a boy called Sha'adi and a child still in nappies, Puram, who was only three. (BBC1 late News, 10 December 2001)

A journey home that ended in death. Bus number 189 ambushed as it neared a Jewish settlement. The attack, brutal and sophisticated, first a roadside bomb just off the bus, then gunmen firing on the passengers as they tried to flee. Flares lighting up the hillside as troops chased the attackers, one was killed at the scene. Shocked survivors rushed to hospital, ultra-orthodox Jews who live on occupied Palestinian land. They'd taken their children out to celebrate a Jewish holiday. This father managed to escape with his baby. *'It was a massacre'*, Israel said, promising a severe response. (BBC1 late News, 12 December 2001 – our italics)

There were, however, differences in the reporting of these two events which relate to systematic patterns in news coverage. The first is the difference in the words used to describe them. The Palestinian action is referred to as 'a horrific attack' (BBC1 early evening News, 12 December 2001). In a later news on ITV, the Israeli description of this event as a 'massacre' is taken up and used by journalists when describing a subsequent Israeli action:

The trigger for the Israeli offensive *was a massacre on the West Bank*. Funerals took place today for ten Israelis shot dead when Hamas

gunmen ambushed a bus. (ITV early evening News, 13 December
2001 – our italics)

This statement again illustrates the point noted above that Israeli
actions are frequently presented as a response, in this case as being
'triggered' by the Palestinian 'massacre'. There is no similar link made
in the case of the bus attack by the Palestinians. There is no reference
to the Israeli missile strike of two days before, or to any other Israeli
attacks. A third point of difference is that in discussing the missile
strike, the Israelis' rationale for their action is very clearly expressed.
We are told the following:

> The Israelis say the intended target was a known Islamic terrorist.
> (BBC1 late News, 10 December 2001)

> The intended target, a member of Islamic Jihad, survived the
> strike, although he was among nine people injured. A suicide
> attack that wounded eight Israelis today brought orders for more
> military action against the Palestinians. (ITV early evening News,
> 10 December 2001)

> The Israelis continue to take matters into their own hands because
> they believe Yasser Arafat is simply not doing enough to rein in
> the Palestinian extremists. (ITV early evening News, 10 December
> 2001)

The journalists do not always sound happy about the Israeli
rationales that are given, but they were none the less included:

> Israel says the main target here was planning further attacks.
> Maybe so, we have only Israel's word for that, but whatever his
> crimes may be, innocent lives have been taken. (BBC1 late News,
> 10 December 2001)

> Today's missile strike may have prevented an impending suicide
> attack, but children were killed in the process. (ITV early evening
> News, 10 December 2001)

There is no comparable inclusion or discussion of the reasons for
Palestinian action. This does not mean that the Israelis escape without
criticism – an Israeli spokesman is interviewed and asked: 'Is it

acceptable for Israel, a democracy, to kill two children?' (BBC1 late News, 10 December 2001).[20] But the fact remains that it is the Israeli rationales that are routinely present in the coverage, both in the form of reported statements and in interviews with their spokespeople.[21]

These differences between the coverage of the two sides are partly a result of Israel's very developed public relations output and its practised ability to supply information and speakers to the media. We also found in other news stories that the Israelis were able to affect the structure and content of coverage by placing limits on the movements of journalists. This particularly affected TV reporting, since cameras were sometimes not allowed into 'sensitive' areas. We can see this more clearly if we look in detail at the reporting of an Israeli incursion into the village of Beit Rima in October 2001. The BBC report begins with an account of the deaths of Palestinians, followed immediately by an Israeli statement:

At least nine Palestinians were killed after Israeli tanks, helicopters and ground troops forced their way into Beit Rima, a village north of Ramallah. The Israelis say they arrested two people over the assassination last week of the Israeli tourism minister. (BBC1 late News, 24 October 2001)

The report then gives two versions of the events and the journalist notes the limits on what they were allowed to see. There was then a brief interview with an Israeli soldier:

The dead of Beit Rima, Israel sent them back for burial. It says there was a gun battle in the village. Palestinians say a bloodbath. Israeli tanks still prowling the outskirts of Beit Rima today, that's all we were allowed to see, but we found these soldiers on their way out, brothers in arms embracing, some faces still blackened from combat, all proud of their part in the assault, but not saying much.
Journalist: Well what was it like last night?
Israeli soldier: Intense, it was intense. (BBC1 late News, 24 October 2001)

There are two accounts of what has happened. There is no evidence offered as to which is correct, and the journalist notes that it is impossible to take the camera in. The problem is outlined in the report:

One soldier stopped ... maybe thanking God for his survival. Israel hasn't lost any troops in the past six days, but the Palestinians say they have more than 40 dead. But these Israeli soldiers have just come out of the village, having finished their mission, but they are making sure we can't go inside. Beit Rima was sealed by the army when it began its operation and it remains sealed still. So, it's impossible for us to take our camera in, speak to the villagers and get their accounts of what happened. (BBC1 late News, 24 October 2001)

The journalist also notes that the material which they are showing was recorded by the Israeli army and supplied to the BBC:

The first pictures from inside Beit Rima, the Israeli army apparently helping the wounded, though Palestinians claim they kept ambulances out for hours. It was the army which recorded this material and supplied it to us. (BBC1 late News, 24 October 2001)

ITV news on the same night also notes the limits on movement imposed by the Israeli forces and is left, as with the BBC, in the position of simply reporting the statements of both sides:

At least six more Palestinians died today in fierce fighting on the West Bank after Israeli forces moved into the village of Beit Rima. Troops sealed off the village, preventing ambulances and reporters from entering. The Palestinians accused them of carrying out a massacre, but the Israelis insisted they were hunting for the killers of Israeli cabinet minister, Rehavam Ze'evi. (ITV late News, 24 October 2001)

On the following day, the media gained access to Beit Rima. The BBC showed pictures of demolished houses and reported local people as saying 'it was a night of hell'. A local Palestinian and relatives of a wanted man are spoken to amidst the rubble of their homes. There is no doubt that this bulletin shows the consequences of the war on the Palestinians, but there is no questioning of Israeli claims which are reported as follows:

'We'll have to bring out mats', Amallah told me 'and sleep on the rubble tonight.' Everything is gone. Beit Rima was in mourning today, Israeli sources say the troops didn't find the man they wanted most. He's free but the five policemen are dead. *Israel claims there was a gunfight.* They're going now to bury the dead. *Whatever the truth of what happened here,* Israel is claiming the heavy assault on this village as a military victory. (BBC1 main News, 25 October 2001 – our italics)

The use of the phrase 'Israel claims' may imply a note of doubt, but later reports in the press give a much more critical account. The *Guardian* reported that at least five Palestinians were killed in the first moments of the assault. These were policemen and other local militia working for the Palestinian Authority. The *Guardian* quoted the director of emergency services for the Palestinian Health Ministry as saying 'They did not have time to put on their shoes.' It also commented on the scale of the operation:

> For a village the size of Beit Rima, just four thousand people, the scale of the Israeli operation was astonishing. Witnesses say as many as thirty tanks and army vehicles drove in under covering machine gunfire from helicopters in the dark early hours of Wednesday. (*Guardian*, 26 October 2001)

Interestingly, a journalist from the *Observer* also interviewed Israeli troops leaving the village but used their account to explicitly criticise the official Israeli version of events. As their reporter notes:

> One thing seems certain. The Palestinian account of a lethal ambush on Beit Rima launched without warning by a massively superior force equipped with tanks, helicopters and elite combat troops against half a dozen men, is given credence by the stories of the assault troops of the Nahal Brigade, who attacked them. (Observer, 28 October 2001)

The *Observer* report in some way parallels the BBC's description of the troops leaving the village:

> We met them at dusk on Wednesday walking out of the village, two lines of young Israeli soldiers, heavily armed, their faces blacked up for night fighting. Reaching the Israeli checkpoint that blocked the entry of reporters into the village, they hugged and cheered each other. (*Observer*, 28 October 2001)

The newspaper journalist then makes two specific points: (1) that resistance had been light, contrary to Israeli claims, and (2) according to Palestinians, some people were killed while they slept:

> What had they done? we asked. 'We killed some Arab terrorists', the young men replied. It was, they told us an, 'easy operation' despite some Israeli injuries. Combat, they added, had been short – resistance light after the first assault by the undercover soldiers. This contradicted the claims of army spokesmen that the gunmen had been killed during 'fierce fighting'. Was the fighting fierce? we asked. They laughed and shook their heads. It was not fierce say Palestinians because some of those who died were executed as they slept. (*Observer*, 28 October 2001)

The *Observer* report also notes disquiet in the Israeli press about the raid on Beit Rima. It quotes a report in *Ha'aretz* that the raid on Beit Rima was planned two weeks before the killing of the Israeli cabinet minister. The *Observer* report also notes that a distinguishing feature of the village is that it is easily cut off at the end of a solitary road, and makes the following point:

> The suspicion that is emerging is that Beit Rima was selected for no other reason than it was an easy target for Israeli forces to make a lethal demonstration. Next time – the warning is explicit – it will be the Palestinian state, not just a village, which will be the target. (*Observer*, 28 October 2001)

Some of these differences between the TV and press coverage arose because of the difficulties experience by TV journalists in the limited time which they have and in the restrictions that can be put upon the movement of cameras and equipment. But it is also clear that some press accounts speak much more directly about the effects of what Palestinians experience as the military occupation and clearly articulate the view that Israeli policy is directed against the whole Palestinian population. As the *Observer* notes:

> The military operations against six Palestinian cities in the past week became a vast reprisal raid against the entire Palestinian people. In Ramallah and in Bethlehem, in Tul Karm, Jenin, Qalqilya and Beit Rima, it is ordinary civilians who are being given a brutal lesson in the exigencies of the overwhelming nature of Israeli

military power and being punished simply for existing. (*Observer*, 28 October 2001)

This account differs sharply from that given later by a BBC journalist who summarised the sequence of events. In this BBC account, there is no mention of the possible Israeli motive being to 'mount a lethal demonstration' or the Palestinians being 'punished for existing'. This report simply repeats the Israeli view that they moved in 'to catch the gunman':

> This current cycle of violence may be beyond control. It began six weeks ago, an Israeli cabinet minister, a right-winger, was shot dead in Jerusalem. That day, Israeli forces moved into Palestinian areas to catch the gunman (BBC1 late News, 2 December 2001)

As we have seen, while there is extended criticism and commentary in television news on the policy and actions of Arafat, there was nothing in this sample which offered a comparable critique of Ariel Sharon or his policies. The main focus of the television account is to present the conflict as between two warring parties caught in a cycle of violence. This cycle is shown as propelled mainly by Palestinian action, and a key issue is whether Arafat will be able to stop this and 'catch the extremists'. The result of this tragic cycle as portrayed on television news is that innocent civilians suffer. Within this account, as we have indicated, there were also clear differences in the manner in which the casualties of both sides were featured. It was Israeli casualties who were described by TV journalists using words such as 'atrocity', 'murder' and 'horrific attack'.

In our earlier samples we had also found an emphasis on Israeli casualties in terms of the amount of coverage which was devoted to them. In this sample from October to December 2001 we found that there was significantly more coverage of Israeli casualties than Palestinian.[22] To investigate this further we took an additional sample from March 2002.

SAMPLE THREE: MARCH 2002

Coverage of casualties

This sample ran from 2 March to 9 March and included a total of 21 bulletins (ITV: 11 and BBC1: 10). This was a period of relatively high casualties on both sides. On 9 March 2002 the BBC reported that 'for the Palestinians it's already the bloodiest week of this conflict: 140 dead, one-tenth of the casualties since the uprising began' (BBC1 late News, 9 March 2002). Israeli deaths were just under one-third of this number. When we analysed the text of the news bulletins, we found that there was actually more coverage of Israeli deaths and casualties, than of Palestinian' (120.25 lines covering Israeli deaths and casualties, compared to 46 lines covering Palestinian deaths and casualties).[23] We can see this pattern in the following examples. The first is headlined as a story about Israeli 'hitting back' at the Palestinians:

> *Headline*: Avenging their dead, Israel hits back against the Palestinians. The West Bank under attack. Tanks and warplanes hit Palestinian targets. (BBC1 late News, 3 March 2002)

The story which follows then focuses very largely on the casualties of the Israeli side. There was a sharp contrast between the non-specific language of 'tanks and warplanes hit Palestinian targets' and the very detailed account given of Israeli deaths and injuries. The report goes on as follows:

> Good evening. Israel's prime minister Ariel Sharon is facing mounting pressure to stop the escalation of violence in the conflict with the Palestinians. More than 20 Israelis have been killed in the past 24 hours. Israel has retaliated with a renewed offensive against Palestinian targets. Tonight the Israeli security cabinet is holding an emergency meeting to discuss its strategy.
> *Journalist (in Israel)*: Behind the barbed wire, the dead lined up in a row. Ten Israelis killed this morning at this lonely checkpoint. Seven of them soldiers. A Palestinian sniper shot them one by one. And just a few hours later this – burying last night's victims. Nine Israelis killed in a suicide bombing. This is the final farewell for an entire family. Here they were in life, Shlomo and Nechmad and their daughters Larin and Sheraz. Ambulances full of young victims last night. 'Evening the score', Palestinian militants said, after Israel's push into refugee camps killed more than 20. So revenge was taken on babies like Shimon. Today his grandmother Hannah was at his bedside. She wants tougher action against the Palestinians. (BBC1 late News, 3 March 2002)

As we have seen above, the deaths of children tend to be treated with special sympathy. On the following day, the BBC reported on an Israeli attack:

Among the dead, a doctor in his ambulance and five children killed after school. Three taken from this family leaving Hafaz behind – today he lost his mother, his sister and his two brothers. 'Poor children', their Aunt Najah told us, 'What were they guilty of?' she wants to know. Here on the right, the children's father, a militant called Hussein Abu Quik. Israeli security sources say he was the target but he's alive, clutching this photo of a family that's gone. (BBC1 late News 4 March 2002)

On ITV News, the report is introduced as follows:

Israeli missiles destroy a Palestinian security building in Bethlehem tonight causing explosions that could be heard in Jerusalem six miles away. But what has angered the Palestinians more is the death of five children, among 16 Palestinians killed on the West Bank today. (ITV late News 4 March 2002)

But overall there is a continued emphasis on Israeli deaths and injuries, both in terms of the amount of coverage which they receive and the consistently detailed accounts which are given of them.

On 8 March 2002 it was reported that more than 40 Palestinians died when Israel launched raids by land, sea and air on the West Bank and Gaza (BBC *News 24*, 7.00 p.m., 8 March 2002). On the BBC main news that night, the headline is: 'More than 40 dead in the Middle East on the intifada's bloodiest day.' The news item then initially mentions the casualties on both sides:

The bloody violence in the Middle East reached a new level of intensity today. More than 50 people have been killed in less than 36 hours, making this the worst day since the start of the Palestinian intifada 17 months ago. The total number stands at more than 1,300. The killing accelerated last May with the Palestinians suffering the highest casualties, but the number of Israeli civilians dead has been rising too [*bar graph on screen showing number of deaths*]. (BBC1 late News, 8 March 2002)

The item then continues with a report from a journalist in the Middle East, which focuses very largely on Israeli casualties:

Journalist: The bloodiest day yet began with 19-year-old Mohammed Farhad. He's dead now but death came only after he had killed five young Israelis and injured many more. It was mayhem, Farhad acted alone, infiltrating a Jewish settlement before using his assault rifle and grenade to maximum effect. The victims were religious students, young men being groomed to become officers in the Israeli army. Most of the casualties were hit as they sat together during Bible studies. Today the Jewish settlers who live on this occupied Palestinian land were retracing the steps of the attacker. After cutting the perimeter wire, he raced up the sandbank. At the top there was nothing between him and the settlement school. The killing only stopped when he too was gunned down. It is this kind of incident which incenses Israeli public opinion and guarantees a massive and bloody response. Standing here amid all of this, international diplomacy seems frankly irrelevant. The violence on the ground has reached a new level of intensity and in many ways, it feels that it's beyond the control of the politicians. And so the Israelis are determined to continue their crushing assault against the Palestinians. This is the West Bank city of Tulkarem, the population of some 20,000 is under a second day of Israeli military occupation. The fighting here and in the Gaza Strip means that today alone the Palestinians are counting by their dead by the dozen. The deadliest 24 hours in all these months of conflict. (BBC1 late News, 8 March 2002)

The report then goes on to give the Israeli rationale for their actions:

Journalist: Tonight there is no question about the Israelis' ability to inflict pain. They continue to insist that this is their war against terrorism, that they are rounding up extremists. But the bitter experience here is that even all of this cannot stop the Palestinian attacks, which have provoked such furious retaliation. (BBC1 late News, 8 March 2002)

Here again we see that it is the Palestinians who 'attack' and the Israelis who 'retaliate'. The Israeli intention is given as being to round up 'extremists' and the only criticism of this strategy is whether it will work to stop Palestinian attacks.

Motivation and rationales for action: March 2002

Much of the coverage in this sample follows the well established patterns which we have already identified. Israeli 'retaliation' continues to be a persistent theme, as we can see in the following examples:

> Israel has *retaliated* with a renewed offensive. (BBC1 late News, 3 March 2002 – our italics)

> Predictably, the Israelis launched fierce military *reprisals*. (ITV late News, 3 March 2002 – our italics)

> Headline: Blood for blood; Palestinian suicide attacks *trigger* more Israeli raids. (BBC1 late News, 5 March 2002 – our italics)

Such patterns have clear implications for the manner in which the rationale and motives of the two sides are presented. There are very clear differences in the manner in which the actions of both sides are described. On 4 March, BBC1 reports on the deaths of Palestinian children in a family. A mother, sister and two brothers were killed when Israel attempted an attack on a Palestinian 'militant'. This Israeli rationale is given and the dead are referred to as having been 'killed in a wave of reprisals for the deaths of more than 20 Israelis over the weekend' (BBC1 late News, 4 March 2002). On the following day the BBC lunchtime News reports Palestinian attacks which have killed Israelis, but there is no reference here to past Israeli action. The headline speaks of murder: 'The killing goes on in Israel. Nine more are murdered in twelve hours' (BBC1 lunchtime News, 5 March 2002).

There are also references to other themes which we have seen before, such as the cycle of violence in which both sides are referred to as being involved in a constant sequence of attacks, as in these references: 'Bloodshed here always guaranteed more bloodshed' (BBC1 late News, 4 March 2002) and 'There have been more violent revenge attacks by both Palestinians and Israelis' (BBC1 late News, 5 March 2002). There are occasional references by journalists on the ground to the Palestinian 'response' and, in this example from ITV, to a 'strike back':

After a week that had seen scores of Palestinians killed in towns and refugee camps across the West Bank and the Gaza Strip, it was the strike back that all had feared and in the end none could prevent. (ITV late News, 9 March 2002)

But this view does not appear in the headline and overall, there is an emphasis on Palestinian action and Israeli 'retaliation'. In this sample there are over three times as many references describing the Israelis as 'responding' as the Palestinians.[24] There are other respects in which this sample follows previous patterns of news content. There is almost nothing on the origins or history of the conflict. There is little analysis of the role of Ariel Sharon or his policies. There are brief references from interviewees, such as 'He promised the Israelis that he will make peace and he made war' (BBC1 late News, 3 March 2002) and 'I hold Mr Sharon solely responsible for the escalation of violence' (BBC1 lunchtime News, 5 March 2002). In our earlier sample of the first days of the intifada Ariel Sharon had been referred to by a BBC journalist as a 'right-wing enemy of the peace process' (BBC1 late News, 3 October 2000). His role in the outbreak of the intifada was also described, but by the time of this sample, Sharon was prime minister of Israel and such commentary from journalists had disappeared. Indeed, one BBC journalist, while referring to his attacks on the Palestinian areas, noted that there was 'still no sign that Mr Sharon can bomb the Palestinians back to the negotiating table' (BBC1 lunchtime News, 5 March 2002). Such a comment implies quite clearly that Ariel Sharon's purpose is to negotiate and it is the Palestinians who are somehow holding the process up.

We have indicated that the Israeli perspective was simply assumed in some accounts by journalists. There was also what sometimes appeared to be an identification with the Israelis. On 8 March 2002, when five Israeli military students were reported to have been killed at a settlement in occupied territory, they were described as 'preparing to defend their country'. The commentary on ITV News was as follows:

Here four other teenagers were preparing to defend their country at a military training camp when they were killed. The Palestinian gunman caused panic by throwing several grenades before opening fire and students were gunned down as they tried to escape the flames. But there was no remorse from the gunman's father, who said he was proud of his son. That attack only reinforced Israeli determination to drive further into the towns and camps where Palestinians live – *ripping up roads around Bethlehem as part of the ongoing fight against terror.* (ITV early evening News, 8 March 2002 – our italics)

There are dreadful deaths on both sides in this conflict, but it is clear that there are differences in how the actions and motives of each side are described. The above commentary refers to 'Israeli determination' in the 'fight against terror'. We do not hear of the Palestinians or their actions being described in this fashion. There are no commentaries such as 'the Israeli attacks have reinforced the determination of Palestinian fighters to defend their land against Israeli terror'. There are other examples to which we can point. We do not hear of Palestinian attacks as sending 'a tough message to the Israelis to end military rule'. But an Israeli attack with bombs and missiles was described on BBC Radio 4 as 'the Israelis are sending the toughest possible message to the Palestinians' (6.00 p.m., 19 May 2001). In TV news there is sometimes an assertion of Israeli action and its rationale which is not present for the Palestinians. On 7 March 2002, the BBC described Israeli incursions into locally controlled Palestinian areas with these words:

The Israelis have vowed to hit the Palestinians hard and that's exactly what they're doing ... The commanders insist this is an anti-terror mission – the Israeli army is in good spirits, its political leaders determined to press on with the offensive. (BBC1 late News, 7 March 2002)

It is unlikely that an attack by Palestinians would be presented in this way.

The example below from ITV News offered a different perspective, suggesting that both sides were equally aggressive and that both justified their actions as 'legitimate defence':

Mr Sharon has predicted that the current army offensive will be both aggressive and continue, but so too is the campaign being waged by Palestinian militants ... Neither the Israelis nor the Palestinians accept any of the blame for this situation. Instead both sides justify their actions as legitimate defence. (ITV early evening News, 6 March 2002)

This suggestion of an 'equivalence' between the two sides is of course one possible perspective on the conflict. It does not, however, say anything about the origins or history of the conflict or that one side is subjecting the other to military occupation, or international opinion on the legality of this.

We have suggested that the Israeli perspective tends to predominate in news accounts, but it does not do so exclusively. As we have noted, journalists do show the effects of the war and the suffering it causes for both sides. In the above BBC report, the journalist notes that 'the Palestinians are facing desperate times' (BBC1 late News, 7 March 2002). In the following ITV News, a journalist describes the terrifying experience of waiting for bombs to fall:

Israeli air raids have become a daily hazard for the Palestinians of the overcrowded Gaza Strip. The sight of warplanes overhead may be familiar, but it is none the less a terrifying experience to be on the ground waiting for the bombs and missiles to land. (ITV early evening News, 6 March 2002)

The news also shows how Israelis feel 'vulnerable' and 'threatened' as, in the following example. In addition it illustrates the emphasis on Israeli casualties, to which we have already pointed. Although the headline for this story is about Israeli attacks on Palestinian areas and the report notes that there is violence across Israel and the Palestinian territories, the bulk of the text features events in Israel:

It feels like war on all fronts. A day of bewildering, widespread violence across Israel and the Palestinian territories; a day of bloodshed and death. During morning rush hour a Palestinian suicide attack in the northern town of Rapullah – one Israeli killed, many injured. At about the same time near Jerusalem, an Israeli woman was shot dead in her car as she drove to work, and all of this came hours after yet another Palestinian gun attack, this time in a Tel Aviv restaurant. Three more Israelis died here. *It's all left many Israelis feeling threatened and vulnerable*, especially the Jewish settlers, who live on land regarded by the outside world as occupied Palestinian territory. Many are frightened, but determined they will not be driven out. (BBC1 late News, 5 March 2002)

A female settler is then interviewed:

Even though I'm scared, I still go out on the streets and I send my
kids to school and I go shopping and I continue my daily life. But
I do ... the fear is getting worse.

The report then mentions the 'Israeli response' to Palestinian
attacks:

An Israeli response to Palestinian attacks has been predictable.
Panic in Nablus and destruction in Bethlehem. Devastating, yes,
still no sign though that the Palestinians can be bombed back
to the negotiating table. (BBC1 late News, 5 March 2002 – our
italics)

The BBC1 early evening news on the same night had featured an
interview with a different settler, but again made the point about
settlers being 'frightened but determined to stay'. This report also
included an interview with a Palestinian and did in some respects
feature the views of both sides. The report was introduced with the
words 'the Jewish settlements in the West Bank are blamed by many
for provoking the fighting'. A journalist in the Middle East then
describes the settlement, referring to it as a 'Jewish neighbourhood in
the outskirts of Jerusalem'. He then notes that its families are 'deeply
religious' and have the 'unshakeable belief that this is their land by
the will of God'. The views of the outside world are mentioned and
a settler then speaks on camera:

Journalist: They know that the outside world regards this as an
illegal settlement built on occupied Palestinian territory. But for the
people here that is irrelevant. Many are frightened but determined
to stay.
Male settler: Sometimes I think I just want to go back to my family.
I came here and I am by myself and all my family is back in New
York but then I love this country so much and I feel it is such a
beautiful country that I just will not leave.
Journalist: From his apartment balcony, Seth Clayman has a clear
view of neighbouring Arab villages. He remembers when there was
a peace, even co-operation between the communities and even in
these violent times he has hope for the future.
Male settler: There is a lot of room for everyone. I guess if we can
get along – it is not beyond our reach. Not beyond our reach.

The journalist then goes on to note that there are Palestinian flats and apartments just a few metres away from the Israeli homes and that a fence has been built between the two sides, which he refers to as 'a physical symbol of the hatred and distrust which now separates these two neighbouring communities'. He then comments on how the Palestinians view the settlements, and a Palestinian teacher appears briefly on camera:

> For many Palestinians, the Jewish settlements are clearly visible from their homes. On this side of the divide the settlements are a gross provocation, a symbol of occupation and repression. Mohammed is a teacher and a bitter man. 'The land they live on was my grandfather's and now it's mine', he says. 'They took it in ways God only knows and when someone takes our land that is death for us.' There is much anger here and that promises still more violence. (BBC1 early evening News, 5 March 2002)

This report offers an image of a frightened but friendly settler who wants peace and co-operation. The Palestinians, we are told, see the settlements as a symbol of occupation and repression. But since the nature of the occupation and its history are barely discussed on the news, viewers might well ask, 'What repression?' It is not surprising if many are puzzled over the relationship between the settlers and the Palestinians. There is no mention in this BBC report of the religious settlers as described in the Amnesty International and B'Tselem reports, noted above. These referred to a series of attacks, attempts to take Palestinian land and to how 'violent groups of settlers...fire at olive pickers, killing and wounding them, steal their crops and destroy their trees (B'Tselem, 2003d). The point is that from the Palestinian perspective and indeed for some Israelis the settlements are a key factor in exerting military and economic control. It is not hard to explain the Palestinian position. As they see it, when Israel was created, they were driven from their homes and had to live as refugees. The Israelis then took over the land that they had moved to and they have had to live under variations of Israeli economic and military control ever since. Without the knowledge of such perspectives and their links to motivation, it can be very difficult to understand why the conflict is so intractable. The question which must be asked about TV news journalism is why it has such difficulty in explaining the Palestinian perspective, when it can so readily feature that of the Israelis.

SAMPLE FOUR: JENIN, APRIL 2002

On 29 March 2002, the Israeli army launched a new offensive on locally controlled Palestinian areas, including Jenin, Nablus and Bethlehem. These conflicts, and particularly the attack on Jenin, attracted widespread media coverage and were the subject of bitter controversy. This focused on the conduct of the Israeli forces and also on the manner in which their actions were reported. There were claims that Palestinians had been 'massacred' and then counter-accusations that the media were reproducing propaganda and a distortion the truth. The access which journalists had to Jenin was severely controlled by the Israeli authorities while the fighting was in progress. This raised further questions about how journalists should cover a conflict in which one side could restrict the flow of information by virtue of its military dominance. To shed some light on these issues and on how TV news did actually cover Jenin, we took a further sample of 30 early evening and late news bulletins from BBC1 and ITV News between 9 April and 16 April 2002.

Restrictions on coverage and effects on news content

Both BBC1 and ITV News made it clear that there were severe restrictions on their reporting. As the BBC noted on 11 April:

> Israel has been very careful to keep the international media out. Today is the first opportunity that we've had to have even a limited freedom to go around and talk to people and ask them to tell us their stories. And there is no way we can prove what they're saying is true. (BBC1 early evening News).

ITV also noted the intimidation of journalists in enforcing these limits:

> When they saw us filming, the Israelis made clear they didn't like it. We're just on the edge of the Jenin refugee camp, taking some cover, as Israeli snipers have been firing warning shots over our heads. (ITV late News, 11 April 2002).

When the restrictions were briefly lifted, the TV news included critical reports on Israeli actions. But as this BBC bulletin notes, the journalists cannot pursue the stories or verify them, and before they can film very much, the Israeli army 'ushers them away':

Itadel is grieving for her husband Mohammed. She claims he was killed by soldiers as he tended his sheep. This boy told us he saw Mohammed being shot once, then left to bleed to death. His word against the army's. It denies killing innocent civilians. The relatives are struggling home to mourn now, it's only an hour since the dead man was shot. Israel says its troops are here to crush the militants, to stop the suicide-bombers but Palestinians in Jenin say civilians are paying a high price. A whole city being punished for what the militants have done. Before we could film too many more scenes like this, the army ushered us away. (BBC1 early evening News, 11 April 2002)

One consequence of the inability to pursue stories was that journalists were frequently reduced simply to repeating the claims and counter-claims of both sides, as in these examples:

For now, there are two conflicting accounts. The Palestinians call it a massacre, a war crime. They say that many hundreds of Palestinians in the camp have been killed, including many civilians ... But Israel's version is very different. It says no massacre, no mass graves and no cover-up ... and it says that the attack on Jenin is part of Israel's legitimate war against terror. (BBC1 early evening News, 12 April 2002)

The Palestinians accuse the Israelis of a massacre here and of bulldozing bodies under the rubble. The Israelis, who continue to patrol the streets of Jenin in strength, deny that. (ITV early evening News, 12 April 2002)

Channel 4 News apparently gained better access by going into Jenin by a back route, travelling through olive groves. Lindsey Hilsum described to us how they were able to do this, because they were led by a guide who had military experience. Their report raised some additional issues such as allegations of looting by Israeli troops and the use of a Palestinian as a human shield. They carried this interview:

Journalist: Like many others, Ali Abu Sereh was initially imprisoned in his house but then the soldiers decided they had a better use for him.

Interviewee: [caption: 'Ali Abu Sereh, teacher']: After two days they took me with them, I had to go knock on my neighbours' doors, so that the soldiers could enter the houses, each time a door was opened, they would rush in. They searched five or six houses while I was with them. Whenever I entered they would make me lay on the floor and tie me up until they had finished the search, but when I was knocking on the door of one house, another Israeli patrol shot me.

Journalist: A mistake presumably, he says they left him on the street. The next morning a neighbour rescued him, but it was five days before they were able to get him to hospital, which is why his wound has gone septic. (Channel 4 News, 7.00 p.m., 11 April 2002)

There were other areas in which Channel 4 News differed significantly from BBC1 and ITV News. The following extracts from interviews show that it raised very clearly the issues of the legality of Israel's action and also asked whether the Palestinians could be seen as resisting 'terror' imposed by Israel. The first interview is with Mark Sofer, the Israeli ambassador to Ireland:

Journalist/presenter: Ambassador, what you have surely shown us is that violence begets violence. The terror that you are visiting upon the refugees in the Palestinian camps, gunmen there may be in there, they regard as resistance, you regard them as terrorists. Its one man's terrorist and another man's resistance.

Mark Sofer [caption: 'Israeli Government Spokesman']: When I ask you if placing a bomb in a synagogue, or blowing yourself up next to little babies in pram and their mothers is anything but terror, is that resistance? The terror has affected us even prior to the '67 war, prior to the fact that the time that we were actually in the territories, it affected us during the peace process itself in the 1996 and 1997 period, it's affecting us today, terrorism and peace cannot exist.

Journalist/presenter: Ambassador, I must ask you the same question in return. When you sent massive hardware, tanks, into refugee camps, where again there are babies in prams, and you fire your shells into areas in which there are women and children living, let alone gunmen, who regard themselves as resisters, what can you expect? (Channel 4 News, 7.00 p.m., 10 April 2002)

On the following night the same journalist interviewed Gideon Meir, introduced as a spokesman for the Israeli government:

Gideon Meir: We must understand this was a war, this was a war against terror.
Journalist/presenter: But there has clearly been terror on both sides. And I mean, you have also got to expect that if you are illegally in someone else's territory, they are going to resist and that is what happened. (Channel 4 News, 7.00 p.m., 11 April 2002)

We might ask why such arguments are clearly made on Channel 4 News, but not on BBC1 or ITV News. There does seem to be a reluctance to raise such issues. This, together with the limits imposed on coverage, can give a very constrained view of the conflict. We have already noted how Israeli casualties are disproportionately covered relative to actual numbers of deaths and injuries.[25] We discussed the issue of the restrictions of coverage imposed by the Israeli military with three very senior journalists: Paul Adams and Tim Llewellyn, who had both covered the Israeli-Palestinian conflict for the BBC, and Lindsey Hilsum from Channel 4 News. Paul Adams suggested that it might have been better, if possible, to have gone into Jenin with mini-cameras. In fact, it does seem that there were journalists who were present in Jenin during the attack. Marie Colvin from the *Sunday Times* described to us how she was there when the assault started and then had to stay because it was too dangerous to leave. Another suggestion made in these discussions was that there were now sufficient numbers of young journalists who would be prepared to take the risk of living for extended periods in the occupied territories. This would in some way reverse the imbalance of having the bulk of the journalistic community based in Israel. The difficulty would be in getting the newsrooms in London to use such reports from the occupied territories. As we have seen, there seems to be even less interest in featuring informed accounts of the nature and origins of the conflict.

TV News and propaganda

At the time of the attack on Jenin, Palestinians described it as a massacre by the Israelis and claimed that hundreds of people had been killed. The Israelis, on 12 April 2002, gave the figure as 100 dead and more injured (BBC1 early evening News, 12 April 2002). They later revised this figure and a UN report published on 1 August 2002 gave the figure of 52 confirmed Palestinian dead, of whom between 14 and 22 were civilians (the Israelis gave the figure of 14, Human Rights Watch gave it as 22). In part, the variations in these figures emerge from the confusion which normally characterises reporting of war and disasters. However, in the case of Jenin, it was argued by some that the claims of a massacre of hundreds of people were part of a propaganda effort by the Palestinians to discredit the Israelis. It was also suggested that the BBC had reported the Palestinian claims as 'fact'. Thus Stephen Pollard, writing in the *Guardian*, criticised both the original BBC coverage of Jenin as well as a later BBC2 news item on the UN report when it was published:

> *Newsnight's* coverage of the UN report into Jenin was typical. The BBC had faithfully reported the Palestinian claims of a massacre as fact. So how would they deal with an inquiry which confirmed that there was no massacre? Easy: change the attack. The opening film by David Sells signed off with this impartial thought, which summed up the tone of his report: 'What happened in Jenin was no massacre but it was appalling in its own right'. (*Guardian*, 24 September 2002)

The first of these arguments that Palestinian claims had been reported 'as fact' seems clearly to be incorrect. In the extensive body of coverage which we have analysed, the BBC did not endorse the Palestinian view but merely reported it. It is also clear that at the time of Jenin, Palestinian claims were very directly questioned, as in this exchange between two BBC journalists:

> *Newscaster:* A lot of claims are being made by the Palestinians, how can we be sure those claims are genuine?
> *Journalist:* I think at this point the simple answer is, we can't. (BBC1 early evening News, 11 April 2002)

Journalists seem to have been quite scrupulous in this. Lindsey Hilsum, for example, from Channel 4 News, told us that she very carefully avoided employing the word 'massacre' in her reports. It is important to distinguish between two types of statements – those which simply report a source and those which endorse or assume a perspective. In this case, the difference is between a journalist stating that 'Palestinians call it a massacre' and a direct statement such as 'there was a massacre'. We saw above that when a bus carrying settlers, a military vehicle and cars were reported to have been attacked by Palestinians, the killing of ten people was described by the Israeli authorities as a 'massacre'. The description was then taken up and endorsed in this reference on ITV News: 'The trigger for the Israeli offensive was a massacre on the West Bank' (ITV early evening News, 13 December 2001).

Although the BBC apparently avoided using the word 'massacre' to describe Palestinian deaths in Jenin, soon after they did endorse its use, in this headline about a bombing: 'Arafat warns his people after the latest massacre of Israelis' (BBC1 early evening News, 8 May 2002). Another suicide-bomber at the time of Jenin, who killed six people, was described as a 'mass murderer'. In this BBC report, '[She] made herself a martyr and mass murderer in yesterday's suicide attack in Jerusalem' (BBC1 early evening News, 13 April 2002).

We found no evidence that the BBC unduly accepted Palestinian claims. There were, however, occasions where they clearly endorsed Israeli perspectives. Consider these two descriptions from the BBC and ITV of the aforementioned suicide-bomber and her origin in Jenin. On ITV we hear that 'The bomber was a woman from the *beleaguered* Palestinian town of Jenin' (ITV early evening News, 12 April 2002 – our italics). In this description she comes from a 'beleaguered' place which is under attack. In the BBC's description, however, Jenin is the place where the Israelis are making 'determined efforts' to 'root out terrorists': 'The suicide-bomber is believed to have come from the Jenin refugee camp in the West Bank, the target of Israel's most determined efforts to root out potential terrorists' (BBC1 early evening News, 12 April 2002).

The second claim made by Stephen Pollard is that the BBC misreported the conclusions of the UN report. The quote from David Sells, which he criticises, does, however, include a clear statement that there was 'no massacre' and it is not greatly different from the commentary on the UN report which appeared in other media. The *Daily Telegraph*, for example, is a newspaper which is often thought of as being sympathetic to Israel. It stated that:

A United Nations report on the April 'battle of Jenin' has dismissed claims that Israel massacred hundreds of civilians but it cited copious evidence that the army violated international law by using human shields, failing to protect civilians, shooting at ambulances and denying medical aid to the wounded. (*Daily Telegraph*, 2 August 2002)

Other press reports gave further accounts of civilian deaths. The *Independent* noted the cases of

> Fadwa Jamma, a Palestinian nurse who was shot through the heart while trying to tend a wounded man ... fourteen-year-old Faris Zeben, who was shot dead by an Israeli tank when he went shopping for groceries when the curfew was lifted ... Afaf Desuqi, who was killed when Israeli soldiers blew open the door of her house as she tried to open it for them ... Kemal Zughayer, shot dead as he tried to wheel himself up the road in his wheelchair. (*Independent*, 2 August 2002)

The *Guardian* noted that 'the civilian toll in Nablus was perhaps double that in Jenin', and quoted the UN report as revealing that 497 Palestinians were killed and 1,500 wounded in the period of the Israeli actions between 1 March and 7 May 2002. It also noted that during the same period there had been 16 bombings and suicide attacks in Israel in which more than 100 people were killed and scores wounded (*Guardian*, 2 August 2002). A report by Amnesty International in November 2002 noted the case of a 38-year-old severely disabled man who was in a house in Jenin which Israeli soldiers were preparing to demolish. According to the Amnesty report, his family showed the soldiers the man's ID, indicating his disabilities. The soldiers refused to help and the house was then bulldozed with the man 'trapped inside', killing him, despite appeals from his family (*Guardian*, 4 November 2002). It seems to us distasteful to argue over whether 'enough' civilians were killed in Jenin or elsewhere to justify the use of a word such as 'massacre'. As we have seen, it was in fact used to describe the killings of smaller numbers of Israelis than of Palestinians who died in Jenin. However, the key point is that journalists should report such killings by either side and should make it clear when international law is violated. Both the UN report and another report by Amnesty International in fact pointed to the illegality of the actions of both sides. Amnesty particularly highlighted the killing of children, noting that 'Israel had killed 250 Palestinian youngsters since the beginning of the Palestinian uprising in September 2000' and that 'Palestinian groups had killed 72 Israeli children in "direct and indiscriminate" attacks' (*The Times*, 1 October 2002).

As we have seen, in practice on TV news the coverage of deaths and casualties had a very disproportionate emphasis on those of Israel and different language was sometimes employed by journalists to describe these. There is no evidence from our analysis to suggest that Palestinian views were given preferential treatment on the BBC. The opposite is really the case.[26] This is part of a consistent pattern on TV news in which Israeli perspectives tended to be highlighted and sometimes endorsed by journalists. The next chapter examines possible relationships between such structures in news content and the development of public belief and understanding of the conflict.

3
Audience Studies

INTRODUCTION

Television news remains the main source of information on world events for a large majority of the population. A recent study by the Independent Television Commission of viewing habits found that in 2002, 79 per cent of the population regarded television news as their main source of world news (ITC, 2003). We have shown above the patterns of explanation which exist in news coverage and the manner in which some perspectives on the conflict are dominant. We will now explore the possible links between these structures in news content and the nature of audience belief. This will cover issues such as the role of visual imagery and how the inclusion or exclusion of different types of explanation may influence audience understanding. We will also examine the manner in which the structuring of reports may influence belief, for example, that one side in the conflict is often presented as initiating action while the other 'responds'. We also analyse links between audience understanding of stories and the effect of this on levels of interest – if people do not understand, do they simply switch off ? Another key area is to examine how it might be possible to increase audience comprehension in this very complex area of news output.

SAMPLES AND METHOD

For this work we used both questionnaire and focus group techniques. The focus groups consisted of seven to eight people on average, who engaged in activities and discussion with a single moderator. They were selected on the basis of income, age and gender. Thus they included ten groups of middle-class and low-income men and women (aged around 25–50), plus one group of elderly people (aged over 65) and three further groups of young people aged 17–23, who were students. This was a total of 100 people. A list of the groups is given below. As far as is possible we selected 'normally occurring' groups, that is, people who would meet and speak with each other in the normal course of their lives. Thus some groups were drawn from parents at a school in London, and were local residents; others met for social activities, such as a group of women who went to dance classes together; others worked together, such as groups of teachers, cleaners and office workers, and some groups included family members.

Participants in focus groups

1. Low income male and female cleaners/janitors, Glasgow (six people).
2. Low-income females, residents, Hammersmith, London (five people).
3. Low-income males, residents, Hammersmith, London (ten people).
4. Middle-class males, residents, St Albans (four people).
5. Middle-class females, office workers, Glasgow (four people).
6. Middle-class females, dance class, Paisley (eleven people).
7. Middle-class males, residents, Glasgow (four people).
8. Middle-class male and female teachers, Paisley (six people).
9. Middle-class females, residents, Hammersmith, London (six people).
10. Middle-class males, residents, Hammersmith, London (eight people).
11. Young male and female students, Glasgow (ten people).
12. Young male and female students, Glasgow (eleven people).
13. Young male and female students, Glasgow (five people).
14. Elderly/retired males and females, Glasgow (ten people).

This project was designed with the help of journalists and broadcasting professionals. One of its key features was that we invited journalists to sit in on focus groups, to take part in the discussions and to raise issues as they wished. Those who took part in the study included George Alagiah and Brian Hanrahan of the BBC, and Tim Llewellyn, a former BBC Middle East correspondent; Lindsey Hilsum from Channel 4 News; Ken Loach, independent film-maker, and Adrian Monck and Gaye Flashman from Channel Five News. Others who helped and gave advice and comments include John Humphrys, Sian Kevill, Fran Unsworth, Sue Inglish, Evan Davis, Paul Adams and Nik Gowing from the BBC; John Underwood from Clear Communications; Alex Graham from Wall to Wall Television and Sandy Ross and Paul McKinney from Scottish Television.

We also had a specific interest in the responses of young people since there is a considerable contemporary debate on their usage of news and on whether this relates to how well they are informed on politics and world affairs and to their level of interest in these. Part of the work for the focus groups involved the detailed discussion of a series of questions about the Israeli-Palestinian conflict. We developed an abbreviated version of these and asked them in questionnaire form to two separate groups of British students (one of 300, the other 280) aged between 17 and 23. These two groups were asked the same questions one year apart, in October 2001 and October 2002. For purposes of comparison we also asked the same questions to two groups of students from Germany and the United States (114 from Germany who were High School students aged 16–18, and 49 from the US who were Journalism/Communications students aged 20–21). Thus our total sample was 100 in focus groups and 743 who answered the questionnaire.

FOCUS GROUP METHODS AND QUESTIONS ASKED

A key feature of this work was to identify the nature and sources of audience belief. The media are a key source of information, so one dimension of the study was to analyse how people respond to messages and to examine the conditions under which they accepted or rejected what they heard or saw. At the beginning of each focus group, the moderator explained to those present that they would be asked questions about the conflict, but it was also stressed that this was not a 'quiz'. The group were told that we were only interested in what each person knows and understands and that it did not matter to us if their answers were 'right' or 'wrong'. We are studying the judgements they have made about the information they have received and the processes by which beliefs are formed. It is an important part of this method to explain very carefully what we are doing and to establish a level of trust with the participants so that they are not afraid to say what they are actually thinking.

The method and sequence of activities in the focus groups were as follows. First, we asked nine questions about the conflict and sources of information which had been used. Each member of the groups gave written answers to these questions:

1.   What comes into your mind when you hear the words 'Israeli-Palestinian conflict?' It might be a picture, it might be something

someone has said, it might be something you have read or seen, or even somewhere you went on holiday – but what comes into your head?

2a). What is the source of what came into you head when you heard 'Israeli-Palestinian conflict'?

2b). Are there any other sources which you have ever used to find out information about that particular conflict?

For questions 3 and 4 the groups were read a phrase from television news which used the words 'occupied' and 'settlers'. The phrase was 'the settlers who have made their homes in occupied territory' (BBC1 early evening News, 9 February 2001). They were then asked:

3.   Who is occupying the occupied territories?

4.   What nationality are the settlers?

5.   In the period since the intifada began (September 2000), which side would you say has had the most casualties? Is it a lot more Israelis, a few more Israelis, about the same for each side, a few more Palestinians or a lot more Palestinians?

6.   Why are they fighting? What is the conflict about?

7.   There have been a number of wars in that region since the Second World War which involved Israel. Can you name any of them and give dates?

8.   What land or countries were occupied in these conflicts?

9.   Do you know of any United Nations resolutions or any criticisms that have been made by the UN about the actions of anyone in the conflict?

Following this, we then gave each group member a set of 16 photographs that were taken from TV news coverage. The photographs showed the main areas of reporting as revealed in our content analysis. They included images of fighting, stone-throwing, the aftermath of a suicide-bombing and pictures of past peace talks and negotiations (for example, of Yasser Arafat meeting President Clinton and Ehud Barak). The group members were then asked to imagine that they were journalists and to write a brief news story using the pictures as a stimulus. The purpose of this was to examine whether they were able to reproduce news language and the explanations of the conflict which were prominent in news accounts. This was then followed by a discussion about the pictures they had used and their understanding of them. For example, one picture featured a group of Palestinians burning an American flag. We asked the group members what they understood from this and what the motive for this action might be. An important element of this procedure was to establish what information group members were taking from news accounts and whether they believed what they were told. Some people who were well informed about the conflict could write very good versions of the news but were also quite critical of it, so the ability to reproduce a news programme is not the same as actually believing the news. However, the news writing exercise and the questions provided an excellent starting point for extended discussions about what the group members did understand and believe about the reasons for the conflict and the manner in which they were informed.

After the news writing exercise, the moderator initiated a further discussion by going through each of the questions and asking in detail about how the group members had arrived at their answers. In practice the participants often joined in spontaneously to offer their own personal histories and accounts of how they had come to understand the conflict. This then led to a more extended discussion on the origins and causes of the conflict. The moderator then raised other specific issues such as whether the group had heard of the Palestinian refugees or knew their history. They were also asked about how they 'saw' the conflict, for example, as 'religious' or 'economic' or simply as a dispute between bad neighbours. How did they see the 'trouble' as starting, and had they heard of other issues such as disputes over water and how it was controlled?

Finally we discussed the general issue of how understanding related to levels of interest. In the group sessions, many questions were addressed to the moderator and to the journalist present by group members who simply wanted to know more and to increase their own understanding. We will discuss this further in our results section, but it was clear that a major reason for viewers 'turning off' from the news was simply that they had little understanding of what they were watching.

QUALITATIVE AND QUANTITATIVE APPROACHES

'Qualitative' methods imply a concentration on processes of meaning and understanding. There are several advantages in using the qualitative techniques of focus group work (so called because they offer a higher qualitative integrity of data). The first is that they enable the investigator to check that the respondents have really understood the questions and that the answers given do reflect what is actually believed. A second advantage is that the detailed discussion often throws up other related issues which can be pursued. For example, when we asked questions about the reasons for the conflict, a frequent response was that it was over 'land'. But we did not realise until the discussions that some people understood this to mean that it was a form of border dispute in which two countries fought over a piece of land which separated them. Another advantage of such discussions is that, as people hear more arguments and information with which they are unfamiliar, it is possible to see how beliefs are modified and develop. A further very important element of the focus group approach is that it enables a rapport or level of trust to develop between those taking part and the moderator, so that people become less guarded and more prepared to say what they really believe. It takes time for people to think carefully about the origins of their own understanding and to be clear about what they are being asked to do. We can see this if we consider an actual exchange of views in a focus group. In this example, the moderator asks about the issue of who is seen to be 'starting' the violence and how this is shown on the news. The difficulty with this for the group was that some of them were sympathetic to the Palestinians. As it turned out they did think that the news presented the Israelis as responding to Palestinian 'action'. But they were reluctant to acknowledge this because they themselves rejected this way of seeing the conflict. It took some time to separate their beliefs about what was 'really' happening from what they were 'seeing' on the news. The moderator began by asking if the news gave the impression of one side starting the fighting while the other 'retaliates':

> *First speaker*: It depends what you call fighting because they are depriving them of the things they are depriving them of and that's an aggressive act in itself.
> *Moderator*: But do you get the sense that one side is starting the actual …
> *First speaker*: Yeah, the Israelis.
> *Moderator*: You get the sense that the Israelis are firing the guns first …
> *First speaker*: Not firing the guns but they're doing things that are leaving the Palestinians thinking they have no choice.
> *Moderator*: I just wonder if from the news you get the sense that one side is starting it and the other side retaliates …

First speaker: Usually what we see on the news is the Palestinians doing something and the Israelis overreacting.

Moderator: How many people think it comes across as the Palestinians doing something like a suicide-bomb and the Israelis retaliate? [*No response*]

Nobody sees this thing about retaliation? Because a minute ago you were saying you did see it as the Palestinians starting it and the Israelis retaliating.

First speaker: But you're assuming that I trust what I see on the news.

Moderator: No, I'm not saying do you believe it, that's separate. I'm saying do you think it comes across as that?

First speaker: Maybe to other people, yeah.

Moderator: Let me make that point again, I'm asking you does it come across as that – whether you believe it or not is another matter – does it come across as one side doing something and then the other side retaliating? How many people think that? I'm not talking about whether you believe it or not. Before, you said it did come across as that.

First speaker: Well that's obviously what we are led to believe and what most people believe.

Moderator: I'm not sure that it is.

Second speaker: In reality, you could have half a brain like me, but you wouldn't believe it – you could see the falsehoods in it.

Moderator: That's a separate question – whether you believe it or not, I'm only interested in what you think the news is saying.

First speaker: It does seem the way they report it on the news.

Second speaker: It's being portrayed that way, yes.

First speaker: It does seem that the Israelis are retaliating to something the Palestinians did.

Third speaker: Yes.

Moderator: How many people think that? [*General nods*] How many, one, two, three, four ... eight. (Low-income group, London)

Establishing what people do actually believe can take time. As the first speaker commented after this exchange: 'I just think we're a lot of paranoid people.'

Another advantage of the focus group discussion is that participants can reproduce the everyday speech and interaction with each other in which they might 'normally' discuss TV or what they have seen or read about current events. This can show how the assumptions of cause and the relationships presented in the media become part of everyday speech. For example, in the following exchange one participant explains why he thinks most casualties are Israeli, and then a second person spontaneously introduces the 'retaliation' theme which he expresses with the words 'getting their own back':

> *First speaker*: Because of the indiscriminate attacks. It seems like there's been more Palestinian attacks.
> *Second speaker*: But if you watch the news you know that they always get their own back. (Middle-class male group, St Albans)

The focus group can also be combined with other qualitative techniques such as the personal interview, in which participants may be spoken with individually after the main session, to clarify specific points and to enable people to say anything which they were reluctant to comment on in the context of a group. This is important in areas of great personal sensitivity, for example, where we have investigated issues such as media coverage of child abuse or mental distress. The disadvantage of focus groups is the amount of time and resources they consume to establish such a high level of qualitative integrity of data. The corresponding advantage of questionnaire methods is that they enable very large numbers of people to give replies relatively quickly. Such quantitative techniques can give a snapshot of what people know or believe at any one time. But to examine in detail the processes by which such beliefs are formed really requires qualitative approaches such as the focus group.

THE QUESTIONNAIRES

We gave an abbreviated version of the questions which we used with the focus groups to our two groups of British students. The questions were:

1. When you hear the words 'Israeli-Palestinian conflict', what comes into your mind? What do you see in your head?
2a. What is the source of what you have just thought of, where did it come from?
2b. Are there any other sources which you have used to find out information about this conflict?

The same phrase from TV news ('the settlers who have made their homes in occupied territory') was read to them as with the focus groups. They were then asked:

3.   Who is occupying the occupied territories?
4.   What nationality are the settlers?
5.   Since the beginning of the intifada, which side has had the most casualties? Is it a lot more Israelis, a few more Israelis, about the same for each, a few more Palestinians or a lot more Palestinians?
6.   Where did the Palestinian refugees come from? How did they become refugees?
7.   TV news has shown pictures of Palestinians burning the US flag, why would Palestinians do this?

We also took two groups of seven to eight students from this main sample and met them separately to discuss their answers, in a similar way to a normal focus group. The intention was to identify any problems which might have existed in answering the questions.

We also gave the same questionnaire to groups of American and German students, since we had a specific interest in the knowledge which young people had of world and political events. For the same reason we asked a series of additional questions which were not about the Israeli-Palestinian conflict. These questions related to a range of historical and contemporary events. The British, American and German students all gave answers to these. Some related to wars such as the Second World War and Vietnam, others to the history of the Soviet Union and the slave labour camps about which Solzhenitsyn wrote. We also asked about US interventions in Latin America: Nicaragua, where a private army was financed by the Reagan administration, and Guatemala, where the US was involved in the so-called 'dirty war'. The questions were as follows:

8.   What were the Gulags in the Soviet Union?
9.   In the Vietnam War how many casualties were there on each side, was it a lot more Americans, a few more Americans, about the same, a few more Vietnamese or a lot more Vietnamese?
10.   Who were the Contras in Nicaragua?
11.   In 1999 President Clinton made a public apology in Guatemala – why?

12. In the Second World War, which country of the Allies defeated the most German divisions?

These questions also offered an interesting point of comparison with the Israeli-Palestinian conflict, since many of the subjects to which they related were not covered at all in recent news reporting. Others such as the Second World War and the Vietnam War have been featured in fictional accounts such as Hollywood films and made-for-TV dramas. It was therefore interesting to examine any differences in knowledge or understanding which might emerge from these variations in media output. The replies to these questions and a fuller account of this part of the research are given in Appendix 3.

RESULTS

The replies to the questionnaires and the responses and discussion in the focus groups fell into seven categories. These were:

1. Memories, images and associations that group members had of the conflict.
2. The sources of information used.
3. The origins, history and causes of the conflict.
4. The news writing exercise.
5. Beliefs about casualties.
6. Cultural identification and empathy.
7. Understanding and interest in news.

We will discuss each of these in turn.

MEMORIES, IMAGES AND ASSOCIATIONS

The first question was on what came into people's minds when they heard the words 'Israeli-Palestinian conflict'. The responses overwhelmingly referred to images of war, conflict and violence, such as 'war, death, children dying'; 'bombings, people dying'; 'gunmen, suicide-bombers' and 'children throwing stones at Israeli soldiers'. In our two large samples of British students 71 per cent and 79 per cent of them gave such answers (for the German students 82 per cent and US students 74 per cent) and for the focus groups it was 75 per cent. Others named general issues such as 'religious conflict' or political figures, and a few cited personal experiences. A detailed breakdown of the responses is given in Appendices 1 and 2. There was one very noticeable difference between the British students interviewed in 2001 and the second group a year later in 2002. In 2001, 2 per cent of the first group named suicide-bombings, but this rose to 24 per cent in the second group a year later, which may be a result of the increased emphasis on Israeli casualties which we noted in our content analysis.

SOURCES OF INFORMATION USED

The participants mostly linked their answers for question 1 to TV news as the key source. For the two groups of British students, 82 per cent and 85 per cent cited the news, while for the focus groups the figure was 84 per cent. This corresponds with other research, including the findings of the ITC 2002 study (ITC, 2003) we cited above. For the German and American students the figures were lower at 61 per cent and 58 per cent respectively. The American students were more likely than the British to cite newspapers as a source, but this probably reflects the fact that they were studying media and journalism. Other sources included books, journals, radio, personal experiences and the comments of other people. Peace rallies appeared as a source in the British sample of 2002. For more information on the use of sources see Appendices 1 and 2.

In the focus groups middle-class males and professional groups tended to be the best informed about the conflict and also to cite the widest range of sources. It was also apparent that where people were well informed, the main sources were often not TV news. Middle-class males tended to be heavy consumers of news, but this consumption was indicative of a high level of interest which was being fed by other sources such as books, the quality press or further study in higher education. In fact such groups could be rather disparaging of TV news as a source. As one participant commented:

There is no depth to it – television news more or less covers anything superficially. I think we are dumbing down. Someone has told the BBC that the average person has an attention span of less than two minutes and that is rubbish but they are buying into it. More and more it's 'How can we keep them watching – whether we are giving information or not?' I certainly wouldn't rely on BBC television news for anything I thought was really important. (Middle-class male group, Glasgow)

The statement on attention span seemed to be confirmed by George Alagiah from the BBC who commented in another focus group that

> In depth it takes a long time, but we're constantly being told that the attention span of our average viewer is about 20 seconds and if we don't grab people – and we've looked at the figures – the number of people who shift channels around in my programme now at six o'clock, there's a movement of about 3 million people in that first minute, coming in and out. (At low-income male group, London)

None the less, for many viewers, TV news was still a key source of information about events in the conflict. The news apparently affected beliefs even amongst those who watched very little or claimed to be non-watchers. In the following example a woman comments on how she avoids the news:

> I don't ever watch the news. They are normally not particularly happy incidents that have gone on in the world throughout the day, so I avoid it. (Middle-class female group, London)

But her written answers had apparently been affected by the news, which became clear as they were discussed:

> *Moderator*: [As reasons for the conflict] you had territory and religion.
> *Female speaker*: It vaguely came from listening to the news when I was doing something else.
> *Moderator*: It sort of seeped in?
> *Female speaker*: While doing something else, yes. (Middle-class female group, London)

There was also some concern expressed in the groups as to the quality of the information and explanations given on the news. Some believed they were not being given the whole story:

> *First speaker*: There's too many gaps, if you are being shown a partial picture, you are obviously not being shown a whole picture … they are showing you what they want you to see, and it shows

that they are showing you what they want you to see, what we are seeing is what we are being fed.
Second speaker: They never really tell you the in-depth reasons about it – 'This guy went into bomb a pizza restaurant' – why? 'The Israelis are going to attack' – why?
First speaker: What pushes them to that extreme? (Low-income male group, London)

One reason for this criticism of television news was that the first speaker had alternative sources of information which offered a different version of events. This focus group took place in a very busy multi-ethnic part of London. The first speaker commented on how he had met people with direct experience of events that he had seen reported on television:

[I was] meeting people who were refugees who were actually in the country and [them] saying 'You're watching this on the news but I was actually there on the day this took place.' (Low-income male group, London)

As we will see, such access to alternative accounts had a strong influence on the beliefs of some participants about the nature of the Israeli-Palestinian conflict and its causes.

ORIGINS, HISTORY AND CAUSES OF THE CONFLICT

Most of the participants in this research had little idea of the history or origins of the conflict. In the large sample groups of British students in 2001, 4 per cent wrote that the Palestinians had been forced from their homes on the formation of Israel. In 2002 the figure was 8 per cent (for the German and American students the figure was 26 per cent and 19 per cent respectively – see Appendices 1 and 2). For the British students there were an additional 14 per cent in 2001 and 22 per cent in 2002 who suggested that the Palestinians had in some way lost their homes because of Israel, or who mentioned the occupation as a factor – they used words such as 'kicked out', 'deported', 'evicted' or 'excluded'. The majority simply did not know or made general references to the problems of refugees, such as 'driven out by fear of war and hunger' or 'through armed conflict, bombing'. It was also clear from the focus groups that most people had very little detailed knowledge. The British students were studying social sciences, arts and history at university and the focus groups contained a strong representation of middle-class males/professionals who are high consumers of news. Even so, in the focus groups as a whole just 19 per cent mentioned the formation of Israel in relation to the Palestinian refugees and most could not name any wars in the region. The level of public knowledge as a whole is probably even lower than this.

The majority also had no knowledge of the link between the wars of 1948 and 1967 – that Palestinians who were displaced from what became Israel in 1948 moved to areas such as Gaza, the West Bank of the Jordan and East Jerusalem and were then subject to military occupation after 1967. In the focus groups, the moderator was sometimes asked by the participants about the origins of the conflict. In response they were given a very brief account of the events of 1948 and 1967, based on the work of the Israeli historian Avi Shlaim (2000), and sometimes helped by the comments of journalists who were present. Although the account given was extremely brief, it could have a very dramatic effect on the understanding of group members as this exchange indicates:

> *Moderator*: Would it help you when you are watching the news, if you knew that history?
> *First speaker*: Yes.
> *Second speaker*: A lot more.
> *Third speaker*: Absolutely.
> *Second speaker*: If they did refer more to the history, the whole thing would mean a hell of a lot more for a lot of people.
> *First speaker*: That's right, we need to know more.
> *Third speaker*: It's so fragmented and vague, I mean to try and explain it to my children, I found it difficult – I'm not the sharpest tool in the box anyway, but having said that, on what I was given by the media, a great deal of it was blank, and you just filled in the blanks that I didn't have a clue about – 1948? Was there a war in 1948? Well now I know there was. (Low-income male group, London).

Lindsey Hilsum from Channel 4 News put the question directly to a group of middle-class women as to whether they would like more background information:

> *Lindsey Hilsum*: I want to know whether you want to know more about it or not. Would you like there to be more background

information on the Middle East or do you think there's plenty ...?

First speaker: Yeah I absolutely agree with that. I always think if only they'd give just us the quick potted history of what brought us to this point. Sometimes when the Israeli-Palestinian conflict kicks off again I become really interested and I follow it day by day to see what's going up, who's retaliating and what's happening with the suicide-bombers. But I think, God, if anybody just turned on their television or their radio now, they wouldn't have a hope in hell of following what was happening.

Lindsey Hilsum: Yes.

First speaker: You want somebody to say, this is all because in 1948, that happened and that happened.

Lindsey Hilsum: A sort of 'New readers start here' ...

First speaker: Yes, yes, something like that. (Middle-class female group, London)

Tim Llewellyn, a former BBC Middle East correspondent, then goes on to describe how he has sometimes found it hard to follow news which is outside his area of expertise:

Tim Llewellyn: I know a lot about the Middle East, but I was watching BBC World the other night, which is supposed to be better on foreign coverage ... I was amazed to see, I remember one story was about presidential elections in Brazil. Now I watched very closely on this, I don't know much about Brazil, I knew there were elections, but I haven't been following it in the newspaper – what the background is, who's running for office and why. I thought [the item] was dreadful. You were given no background information, it was extremely glib, it took a lot for granted, it took a lot of knowledge for granted on the part of the viewer.

First speaker: Yes, that's right.

Moderator: Is that a feeling that you quite often have, that you don't feel you've got enough background knowledge to actually understand what's going on?

First speaker: Yes.

Second speaker: Definitely, with home news and American news you're very conscious and you do know, but even with European news you don't get that much – in the Bosnia war there wasn't a great lot of background. (Middle-class female group, London)

One BBC journalist actually told us that he had been instructed not to do 'explainers' by his own editor. As he put it: 'It's all bang bang stuff.' In another focus group, one participant specifically raised the issue of how the news is dominated by images of atrocity and horror to the exclusion of material on background and origins:

> *First speaker*: One of the problems with most of the news is that you get the atrocity, the horror but it's the background that is the key bit. *Newsnight* does go some way to filling one in a bit on that but I'm pretty ignorant of it really and that's the more important, more interesting, important stuff, the background, the origins rather than the latest [action].
> *Second speaker*: I'm drawn to background and overview articles rather than the latest bus being blown up.
> *Moderator*: Is that a general feeling, that there is too much emphasis on immediate action and image?
> *Third speaker*: I think that characterises all news coverage.
> *Moderator*: That is your view?
> *Third speaker*: Yes, absolutely. (Middle-class male group, London)

Yet as the first speaker also pointed out, there is clearly an important role for powerful images since they may have a strong emotional influence and can affect the commitment to watch a particular story:

> When that boy and his dad were shot by Israeli soldiers, unfortunately the British TV cut the pictures, but even so it's still fairly shocking and that re-energised, reawakened my interest. Just because that brought it home to me as a parent. If I was in that situation with my son ... that did make me realise just what it must be like. (Middle-class male group, London)

There were some other reservations expressed in this and other groups as to how much historical detail could be included in news and whether longer historical accounts should be shown in dedicated current affairs programmes. A small number of people indicated that they were not interested in the subject or were just too busy – 'it goes in one ear and out the other', as one participant said. Another questioned whether audiences would want more in-depth accounts (middle-class males, London), but overall there was a strong feeling in the groups that it was difficult to understand the present without some knowledge of the past. As a young male from Glasgow put it:

> I've not heard any historical context from the news at all. They don't tell us that – they don't say – they leave it on the short scale. 'This fighting was due to yesterday's fighting, which was due to the day before.' But they don't go back to all that, I don't know anything about that [history]. The reporter will say 'The Israelis fired into a Palestinian refugee camp today in response to a Palestinian suicide-bomber yesterday', but they won't say why the Palestinians are fighting or why the Israelis are fighting – it doesn't go back any length of time. (Student group, Glasgow)

The lack of historical knowledge made it very difficult for people to understand key elements of the conflict. For example, some had written that 'land' was an issue but there was a great deal of confusion over what this meant. Another participant described how his understanding included no sense of the Palestinian case that land had been taken from them:

> The impression I got was that the Palestinians had lived around that area and now they were trying to come back and get some more land for themselves – I didn't realise they had been actually driven out, I just thought they didn't want to live as part of Israel and that the places they were living in, they decided they wanted to make self-governed – I didn't realise they had been driven out of places in wars previously. (Student group, Glasgow)

Some people saw the conflict as a dispute between two countries or peoples, who had a strip of land between them that they both wanted, as in this exchange:

> *Moderator*: How did this land conflict come about?
> *Male speaker*: They are right next to each other and they are trying to get a bit more off each other.
> *Moderator*: Do you see it as two countries, two groups and two countries and they are both fighting over this bit of contested land?
> *Male speaker*: That is it, yes.
> *Moderator*: So something in the middle of it all?

Male speaker: It is like the border and they are trying to take a bit off each other. (Low-income group, Glasgow)

The same point is made in another group:

I didn't realise – I didn't know all the geography of Palestine being occupied. I thought there was Palestine, then there was Israel and then there was the border in between that they were fighting over. (Office workers, female, Glasgow)

Another sees the conflict as a 'nice piece of land' that they are both fighting over, without any sense that land has been taken:

Female speaker: I just thought it was disputed land, I wasn't under the impression that the Israeli borders had changed or that they had taken land from other people. I just had the impression that it was a nice piece of land that both, to put it simplistically, that they were fighting over and I thought, it was more a Palestinian aggression than it was Israeli aggression
Moderator: Did anyone else see it this way?
Answers: Yes, yes [five out of ten people in this group assented]. (Student group, Glasgow)

There were similar problems in understanding terms such as 'occupied territories'. Because many in the groups did not understand that Palestinians had been subject to military occupation after 1967, there was some confusion over what the word 'occupied' meant.

The nature of the occupation and limits to understanding

In our questions we had asked, 'Who is occupying the occupied territories and what nationality are the settlers?' In our main samples of British students only 9 per cent in 2001 and 11 per cent in 2002 knew that the Israelis were occupying and that the settlers were Israeli. In the first of these samples there were actually more people who believed that the Palestinians were occupying the territories and that the settlers were Palestinian. In the German and US groups there were more people who knew the correct answer to both questions (26 per cent of the German students and 29 per cent of the American students). In the focus groups the figure was 39 per cent. The figure for the American students probably overstates the level of knowledge amongst young Americans since these were journalism and media students and some had done projects on the Israeli-Palestinian issue. Even so, there was a good deal of confusion amongst them. For example, over half of those who had written that the Palestinians became refugees on the formation of Israel or were 'forced from their homes by Israel' also thought that the Palestinians occupied the occupied territories. We found similar confusion in the British focus groups over who was occupying and what this signified. One woman from a London group commented on her reply as follows: 'I put "not sure", then I thought it was the Jews, then I thought maybe it was the Palestinians moving into Jewish occupied territory' (low-income female group, London).

Given that so many did not know that there was a military occupation, it is not surprising that the consequences of it for the Palestinians were little understood. Even in groups that were comparatively well informed, such as middle-class males in Glasgow, there was little knowledge of economic consequences such as those caused by the Israeli control of water. In the focus group sample as a whole only 9 per cent were aware of this issue. There was little understanding of areas such as human rights – only two people in all the focus groups raised these as an issue. Even in groups that tended to be sympathetic with the Palestinians (such as low-income males in London) there was some surprise when they heard that there were pass laws and identity cards which restricted movement. There was almost no knowledge of the large number of UN resolutions which have been passed, either those relating to the legality of the occupation or to human rights abuses in the territories. These absences in public knowledge very closely parallel the absence of such information on the TV news. The issue of what people were not told was sometimes raised in the groups. In this exchange, Brian Hanrahan from the BBC asks whether reporters are seen to be taking sides in the conflict:

> *Brian Hanrahan*: Do you think the reporter is telling you to believe one side rather than the other?
> *Female speaker*: I don't think it is always just the reporters telling you what side to believe. There's information that you get and also a lot of information that you don't get, so in that sense I feel what I'm being given is quite limited or selective. (Low-income female group, London)

This participant then speaks about the limited coverage of dissent within Israel. She describes how she had seen a very small article about this issue and compares it with very large headlines on other subjects:

> I remember seeing in the newspaper a tiny little article and it was about some young students in the Jewish army who refused to fight: 'This isn't fair' [they said] and they refused. They were supposed to be forcing some Palestinians out of some territory and they refused to do it and they put down their arms ... but it was only like a tiny little piece of information, so in that way, when you get a small piece of information, a tiny article and it's further down the newspaper it's very, very easy to miss. I feel as though in other [subjects] you get big headlines and even those are choosing.
> (Low-income female group, London)

The perception audiences had of Israeli settlers in the occupied territories was also significant. On the news as we have seen, the settlers were presented as vulnerable and under attack. Yet as we noted above, the settlements have a key role in the occupation. As the Israeli historian Avi Shlaim (2000) put it, they were part of a policy of exerting strategic and military control. Many were built on hilltops to give them a commanding position with the explicit encouragement of Ariel Sharon. Established settlements were strongly fortified and their occupants were often heavily armed. One of the very few people in the focus groups who knew this actually wrote that 'the word "settler" is a euphemism' (male teacher, Paisley). But it was more common to see the issue in the terms adopted by the news. The 'occupied territories' were not seen as having been subject to military occupation and the settlements were not understood as being part of this. The army was there simply to keep the Palestinians back:

> *Moderator*: Do you get the impression watching the news that it is a military occupation by Israel?
> *Male speaker*: A military occupation? No, it's to give the Israelis land to work on, to live on and the army backs them up and keeps back the Palestinians in my opinion. (Middle-class male group, Glasgow)

Another participant described his impression of TV news:

> I think you sometimes get the impression from the news that these are people who happen to want to live there ... and the military

backup is in pursuit of their peaceful wish to just go and live there, and I think that's the impression I get from the news, rather than that it is a military occupation. (Teachers group, Paisley)

With this perception of the conflict it is not hard to see how the Palestinians appear as the aggressors. As a Glasgow student put it:

I had no idea why they were fighting, I just thought it was the Palestinians trying to claim more land. I didn't know it was kind of like back [had a history]. I knew it was disputed but I didn't know the Israelis had taken land.

Two other students from Glasgow described the influence on their beliefs of seeing a documentary by John Pilger, which showed the power and reach of the settlements:[1]

First speaker (male): The all-Jewish roads, I'd not seen that before.
Second speaker (female): It made it look much more like an invasion and not just a bunch of poor benighted people trying to find somewhere to live.

Even people who were sympathetic to the Palestinians had absorbed the message of the settlers as small embattled communities. A middle-class male from Glasgow described his surprise when he heard that the settlements controlled over 40 per cent of the West Bank:

I had absolutely no idea it was that percentage – I was gobsmacked when I heard it. I saw them as small, embattled and surrounded by hostile Palestinians – that's entirely thanks to watching the television news.

And there were other areas where the absence of explanation made it difficult to understand the motives of those involved.

The United States, Israel and the Palestinians

We asked the participants why the Palestinians might wish to burn the American flag. Some thought it might be for religious reasons or because of extreme support for Islamist opponents of the US. A middle-class woman in London wrote that it was 'to show support for Taliban hijackers'. But there was also considerable confusion over the relationship between Israel and the US. In the two British groups of students, just over a third wrote that the US gave 'support' or military/monetary aid to Israel (37 per cent and 38 per cent). For the Germans, the figure was 69 per cent and for the American students, 46 per cent (see Appendices 1 and 2). In the focus groups 34 per cent of the participants knew of support or military/monetary aid. There were also a number of comments that the US was 'not welcome' (office workers, Glasgow), that they were 'sticking their noses in' (low-income group, Glasgow), and that the US was seen as 'interfering with the situation' (Paisley teachers). In a group of middle-class women in London it was said that the Palestinians had 'lost faith in American intervention', but none of these women knew that the US supplies arms and money to Israel. There was also a sense that the US was involved in brokering between the two sides, but why they might not be trusted in this was, for most people, very unclear. What was missing from many people's understanding were more direct explanations for Palestinian hostility, such as that the armaments being used to attack them were paid for by the US. There was a clear feeling in the groups that such information should be given. Even those people who were concerned about how much explanation could be included in news programmes said that this was 'the least' they should be told (middle-class males, London).

Without any understanding of the origins or history of the conflict or the rationales of those involved, the dispute could be seen simply as an argument between 'bad neighbours' or just an undifferentiated mess of inexplicable violence: 'We don't actually listen to what's going on, it's all kind of like shock value, "Oh my goodness, look at all the nightmares with what is happening over there".' (student group, Glasgow). A middle-class woman in London described it as 'a big mish-mash area'. A woman from Glasgow suggested that the fighting would stop 'if they kept their children in the house and stopped them throwing stones'. Others thought that there were probably deep reasons for the conflict but that they just did not know what they were. A minority were comparatively well informed, often by sources other than TV news. We can see this mixture of responses in a typical student group of ten people which met in Glasgow. In this group five saw it as a fight over land between 'conflicting neighbours'. None of them had heard of the economic issue of water and none had any idea that the occupation was widely seen as illegal. Two members of this group knew that the US gave aid and money to Israel and one of these knew that the US also supplied them with arms. We have already commented on the lack of historical knowledge of members of this group who did not know that Israel had taken any land. This lack of knowledge of origins and causes had another important effect on some participants in this and other groups, in that the conflict and fighting was seen as being initiated by the Palestinians.

Response and Retaliation: Who Starts the Violence?

We showed in our content analysis of TV news that a consistent pattern existed which emphasised Palestinian action and Israeli response and retaliation. This apparently affected how some people saw the conflict and how they allocated 'blame' for the violence. As one student from the above focus group commented:

> *Female speaker*: You always think of the Palestinians as being really aggressive because of the stories you hear on the news. I always put the blame on them in my own head.
> *Moderator*: Is it presented as if the Palestinians somehow start it and then the Israelis follow on?
> *Female speaker*: Exactly, I always think the Israelis are fighting back against the bombings that have been done to them. (Student group, Glasgow)

Another student answering a questionnaire believed that 'a lot more Israelis' had been killed than Palestinians and wrote that 'The Palestinians trigger every incident which makes the Israelis retaliate.' The news presentation of Palestinian action and Israeli response was clearly seen within the groups, as in these comments:

> *First speaker*: They [the Palestinians] killed that minister earlier in the year and that sparked reprisals ...
> *Second speaker*: There was bombing today of the Palestinian areas and the linkage was made absolutely with that bombing by the Palestinians. (Middle-class male group, St Albans)

The second of these speakers commented of the Israelis 'they are so vulnerable'. But another speaker in the same group questioned the relationship as portrayed on the news: 'You hear it is always the Israelis holding back a bit and then they do the reprisal, but it has been going on so many years it could be anyone starting it.' In another group, a middle-class male from Glasgow offered this critical view of TV news:

The Palestinians are always regarded as terrorists, Israel is the ideal state which is being attacked by the terrorists ... if it wasn't for the Palestinians and their suicide-bombs, the thing would run perfectly well.

There were often mixed views within the groups. For example, in the group of women from Paisley, three stated that they did see the Israelis as 'responding' to what was done to them by the Palestinians, but then a fourth women used the phrase 'retaliate' while speaking and then paused, saying that she was surprised at herself as she did not see the Israeli actions as justified.

Another participant raised a further important point. He argued that although the structure and language of news might favour the Israelis, the visual images of Israeli dominance may lead viewers to criticise them:

The reporting of the Palestinians, of the atrocity of the car bombs, of suicide-bombings by Hamas, is clearly reported as being a dreadfully wrong thing and an atrocity. I think the reporting of the Israeli army in the Palestinian territories is not so clearly put across as Israel are in the wrong, but just the repetition, the sheer volume of images of Israeli dominance in Palestinian territories puts across the idea that Israel is wrong in that context. (Middle-class male group, London)

Another person from the same group thought that the news was biased against Israel exactly because it did show images of boys throwing stones against soldiers and tanks. He thought that these would necessarily prejudice the viewer against Israel: 'How anybody could think that the images of tanks smashing down buildings, of Israeli soldiers armed against boys throwing stones is sympathetic to the Israelis defies logic.' This does raise an interesting question which the moderator noted, which is that if such events are occurring in the conflict, then what would constitute 'bias' on the part of the broadcasters? Would it be to show the images or to avoid transmitting them, so that audiences could *not* see them? Another speaker in the group raised a more crucial point, that images alone are unlikely to convince an audience on the legitimacy of either side in a dispute. As he pointed out, in the case of Northern Ireland, British audiences became accustomed to seeing young people throwing stones at troops, but it did not follow that the audience sympathised with the stone-throwers. As he said: 'We generally believed that the British Army and the British government was right.' In the same way, in the Gulf War of 1991, the Iraqi army was clearly the 'underdog' in terms of military power but audiences in the West did not identify with the cause of Saddam Hussein. In the Israeli-Palestinian conflict, Israel argued that Palestinian children were being deliberately exploited by mendacious leaders and had been incited to attack the troops. For people who believe this, it might well affect how they perceive the actions of the Israeli army and the causes of the violence. In a Glasgow group, some participants had accepted the TV account of the sequence of the violence and concluded that the problem could be resolved if the children stayed in their houses and did not throw stones:

> *Moderator*: Did you ever see one side as starting the trouble and then the other one … ?
> *First speaker (female)*: All the wee guys with all the wee bricks.
> *Moderator*: All the wee guys with the wee bricks?
> *First speaker*: They are usually the ones that are usually standing there flinging them and then the army comes in.
> *Moderator*: They start it?
> *First speaker*: Yes, and then the army comes in.
> *Moderator*: OK, anybody else have that image, that it started with the people throwing the stones and bricks and then the others retaliate?
> *First speaker*: I think it starts that way. They fling the bricks and then they start flinging them and before you know it a fight breaks out.
> *Moderator*: When you watch that do you ever think that they oughtn't to be throwing the bricks in the first place?
> *First speaker*: Yes.
> *Moderator*: You do think that?
> *Second speaker (Male)*: Yes.
> *Moderator*: You have that feeling?
> *First speaker*: Oh aye, if they went into the house and never minded, there wouldn't be any fighting. It wouldn't be so bad. (Low-income group, Glasgow)

The important point here is that the image of inequality in the conflict does not necessarily result in the audience identifying with one side or the other. It might be that there are some images from war and conflict that are so grotesque that it would be difficult to find any way of justifying them. But as can be seen, the bulk of what we are shown is contested in terms of what it is to mean and signify about the actions of the two sides. In this country much of what the TV news audience hears is dominated by the official Israeli perspective and this does seem to have had some effect on audience beliefs. There was little knowledge of alternative accounts of the origins or causes of the conflict which might have been used in questioning such a perspective. The key source of what was known about the conflict was very often the television news. As we will see next, group members sometimes showed a remarkable ability to reproduce what they have seen.

THE NEWS WRITING EXERCISE

For the news writing exercise, each member of the focus groups was given a set of 16 photographs which were taken from TV news footage of the conflict. They were then asked to write a short news item using the pictures as a stimulus. They were not constrained to focusing on these pictures but in practice could write anything they wished. As a method this was designed to show what audiences have retained from news programmes. The pictures they were given included the aftermath of a suicide-bombing, an image of a dead Israeli soldier being pushed from a window, groups of Israelis rioting, a Palestinian boy being sheltered by his father as he was shot, and other images of stone-throwing, Palestinians in masks with guns and Israeli tanks. There were also pictures of prominent leaders and of peace negotiations showing Ehud Barak, Yasser Arafat and Bill Clinton, and a picture of Palestinians burning the American flag.

We found in this, as with other research using the same method, that many participants had a remarkable ability to reproduce both the content and structure of news bulletins. These are examples of 'news items' written by participants:

In response to yesterday's attack on the settlers' camp at Yashmin, Israeli tanks again battered [Palestinian] refugee camps. The Israeli tanks destroyed seven buildings. Palestinian sources reported 14 casualties including four children. The Israeli commander denied that any Palestinian civilians had been involved. Palestinian crowds stoned Israeli soldiers through the night. During the day a suicide-bomber blew himself up. This was the first such attack outside the occupied territories for some months. The Israeli

Premier said that the Israeli army would continue to take a hard and aggressive line while attacks on Israeli citizens continued. (Middle-class male, London)

Here in the Middle East guerrilla warfare rules. As you can see from our pictures the streets are a war-zone. Young men as young as twelve are involved in brutal slayings. Tanks and heavy artillery patrol at the West Bank and young men are seen in victorious mood as each tank hits its target. Yasser Arafat meets with President Clinton to try to find a solution but as this meeting takes place, Palestinians are seen burning the American flag in an act of defiance. (Low-income male, Glasgow)

Yasser Arafat, head of the PLO, is still being bombarded by artillery and heavy shelling by the Israeli army today. Arafat has been under siege in his compound for ten days now with no signs of a let-up from the Israelis. Ariel Sharon is insisting that the four men wanted for "terrorist activities" who are still in Yasser Arafat's compound give themselves up or the bombing will continue. Meanwhile in Gaza itself the stone-throwers are still on the streets with a determination that will not end until their leader is free. (Low-income female, London)

Not all showed such high levels of ability in writing the news. Some were vague over who was doing what and why it was significant:

The conflict between Israel and Palestine has been very violent, lots of guns and tanks. It has been caused by one of the parties invading land owned by the others. This land is currently unused but still does not belong to them. Leaders have tried deals to bring the fighting to an end but they have been futile. The fighting continues; it is the people themselves that are involved not just armies. (Young female student, Glasgow)

Another participant gave this account of the outbreak of the intifada:

Yasser Arafat has tried to get peace for his people for years. He has met Bill Clinton so that they can speak about what is happening. This time a leader went onto holy ground that he should not have been near and sparked more fighting. (Low-income female, Glasgow)

One of the reasons for the 'vagueness' amongst viewers is perhaps that the news itself is unspecific. We noted above in our content analysis that in reports of the onset of the intifada, Ariel Sharon was not named in many news bulletins and the significance of him as a figure to the Palestinians was not explained. Another participant in a Glasgow focus group made an important point about the nature of news reporting. She argued that the news effectively conveyed a series of emotional sequences (such as violence and its innocent victims) which characterised war reporting. As she comments, although the news had not conveyed 'the facts' to her she could still write the 'emotional' story:

> When I wrote about the pictures, I could have been writing about any war because obviously the facts have not been communicated to me there on the news, but the emotion of it all has, so I wrote about it in an emotional way. So it's like emotional reportage rather than factual reportage. (Female office worker, Glasgow)

This is the news she had written:

> Looking back over the Arab-Israeli conflict, moments of hope have emerged from the despairing gloom, only to be overshadowed by the ongoing bloodiness of the conflict. Hands have been shaken, alliances/agreements made, but lurking behind the politicians' gestures are more scenes of violence, townships being destroyed, innocent victims hiding behind their protectors – all being shot to pieces. Rebel forces are burying their dead as martyrs to their cause; meanwhile US influence is being rejected as unwelcome interference in a domestic conflict which is not theirs. (As above, female office worker, Glasgow)

Another participant from the group of elderly people also saw the images as representing the desolation and fear of war: 'These pictures represent the horror of warfare. Desolation, fear, hatred and two intractable leaders' (elderly male, Glasgow).

A lack of knowledge about events and why they happened was apparently no bar to being able to write the news. This became very apparent in the next example. Here a student noted that he was interested in the news on the Israeli-Palestinian conflict and watched items on it. He was able to produce a very competent and quite plausible news programme. Yet he is the same student who was quoted above as saying that he, 'just thought the Palestinians wanted to get some more land for themselves' and 'didn't realise they had been driven out of places in wars previously'. He had no knowledge of the origins of the conflict and misunderstood its causes, yet he could still write the following 'news':

> There is still much fighting close to the Israeli border with Palestinian territories with innocent children known to be among the victims. Yasser Arafat will not demand less than full control over the West Bank and Gaza and the Muslim quarter of Jerusalem but the Israelis are no longer willing to negotiate since the change of government. Despite the efforts of the US and Clinton in particular, what progress has been made was soon lost when Barak left office, replaced by the more hard-line Sharon. Hezbullah remain a threat to Israel which Palestine seems unable to control or unwilling to, as Israel claims. Both sides seem intent on attacking, with each attack causing more damage than the last – Israel has used the most advanced planes in its air force while there are repeated warnings of more suicide-bombers being ready to strike. (Young male student, Glasgow)

This is a clear account of some of the key themes in news content – of innocent children as victims, the threat to Israel from Hezbullah and suicide-bombing and Israel's use of advanced weaponry. Other participants reproduced in their stories the structure of TV news accounts – notably the sequence of Palestinian action and Israeli response to which we have pointed in our content analysis. In the first example below, the cause of Palestinian discontent is vague, the Palestinians then act by coming out in mass protests and riots and the Israeli army 'retaliates and fires':

> President Bush meets Arafat and new Israeli PM to encourage talks to find a peaceful solution. *Something sparks discontent/aggression toward Israel government* and Palestinians come out in mass protest with riots on the streets. *Israeli army retaliates* and fires on Palestinians. (Female office worker, Glasgow – our italics)

In the following examples the sequence is simply of Palestinian action and Israeli response:

A new, more hard-line leader has come to power in Israel *who has retaliated with* force on attacks by the Palestinians on Israel. (Young male student, Glasgow – our italics)

There has been continuing conflict between the Israeli authorities and the Palestinians on the West Bank over borders and security. Bomb outrages and atrocities have been swiftly followed by *government reaction* from Israeli tanks. (Male teacher, Paisley – our italics)

Palestinian snipers and suicide-bombers attacked Israeli targets and the Israeli army *retaliated with tanks*. (Female teacher, Paisley – our italics)

Today on the West Bank the conflict between the Israelis and Palestinians was renewed as Arafat supporters burned the American flag *and Israelis responded*. (Middle-class female, Paisley – our italics)

In response to Palestinian attacks on Israeli settlements, coupled with suicide-bombings in Israel, Israeli forces have destroyed large amounts of Palestinian homes. (Middle-class male, London – our italics)

One participant wrote that both sides were 'retaliating' to each other; another mentioned the 'cycle of violence', and two mentioned that Palestinians were responding/retaliating to Israeli action. But it is noteworthy that the common theme of Palestinian action and Israeli response had a significant effect on how some people remembered events. The picture of a young Palestinian boy being sheltered by his father was used in some of the stories. The boy's death occurred in the first days of the intifada. In the following 'news stories' this death is linked to the killings of Israelis by Palestinians, including that of the soldier thrown from the window of a police station and that of a newly-wed couple killed in a suicide-bombing. These events actually happened after the death of the Palestinian boy, but the use of the action-retaliation formula effectively reverses the sequence of events so the Israelis are seen as responding to something that has been done to them:

> An Israeli soldier was taken hostage and thrown to his death by Palestinians on the rampage. The scene was witnessed live on TV by a shocked nation who took to the streets to protest ... the Israeli people vowed to revenge this act and in the fighting that followed a ten-year-old Palestinian boy was shot dead in his father's arms. (Female teacher, Paisley)

> A young boy was killed as his father helplessly tried to shield him from Israeli bullets. The Israeli onslaught came as a direct retaliation to a newly-wed Israeli couple being killed by a Palestinian suicide-bomber in the latest Palestinian terrorist attack. (Middle-class female, London)

Many of the 'news stories' repeat the familiar themes of violence, confrontation and death. Some specific instances such as the deaths of the Israeli soldiers are described using the words 'mob' and 'lynching', as in the actual news:

> The violence continues – two Israeli soldiers were captured by a Palestinian mob, beaten then killed and their bodies defiled. (Middle-class male, Glasgow)

> The most heinous act to date was the lynching of Israeli policemen in Ramallah. (Middle-class male, Glasgow)

There were no stories written about the killing of Arabs by 'mobs' in Israel, although we had included the pictures of 'angry' Israeli crowds that had been briefly shown on TV news. As we have seen, the story of the young Palestinian boy being sheltered by his father was featured in the participants' 'news stories'. As we noted in the content analysis, the Palestinian view was that he had been deliberately killed, but this was very rarely featured. The Israeli statement that he had been 'caught in crossfire' was more commonly reported. This language is used in a number of the groups' 'news stories':

> Today there was yet another casualty of the Israeli-Palestinian conflict. A young boy was *caught in the crossfire* as Israeli troops

opened fire in the West Bank. (Middle-class female, London – our italics)

Israeli soldiers return fire and a father and son are *caught in crossfire* – the boy is fatally wounded. (Middle-class male, Glasgow – our italics)

The fatal shooting of an eleven-year-old Palestinian boy *caught in the middle of another clash* between the Israeli army and Palestinians liberation extremists raised tension in the current intifada campaign against Israel. (Middle-class male, London – our italics)

The American flag has been publicly burned by the Palestinians following the death of a young child who had been *cornered in crossfire* between the Jewish soldiers and Palestinians in Jerusalem. (Middle-class female, Paisley – our italics)

Audience members appear to have absorbed both the language and the structure of news accounts, although it does not follow that they always believe what they are told. To investigate this further, we asked specific questions about casualties.

We showed in our content analysis in Chapter 2 that there is sometimes a difference in the language employed in television news to describe casualties from the two sides, and also that there was an emphasis on Israeli casualties in terms of the amount of coverage they received. We will now examine how this might affect audience understanding and beliefs.

BELIEFS ABOUT CASUALTIES

We asked the participants: 'Which side has had the most casualties? Is it a lot more Israelis, a few more Israelis, about the same for each, a few more Palestinians or a lot more Palestinians?' In the period of our analysis the Palestinians had a casualty rate which was in fact much higher than that of the Israelis, (with a ratio of 2–3:1 in terms of deaths). Yet, if we look at the sample of British students from 2002, just 35 per cent knew that the Palestinians had significantly more casualties, while 43 per cent stated that there were more Israeli casualties or that the figures were the same for each side (for the German students the figures were respectively 24 per cent and 51 per cent, and for the US students, 18 per cent and 47 per cent).

In the focus groups we found that 42 per cent of the participants believed either that Israel had the most casualties or that the numbers were about equal. The key factor in the first of these beliefs appeared to be the extensive coverage of attacks on Israelis and in particular of suicide-bombings:

> I couldn't remember any figures, but then I thought it was the one, I remembered it was the suicide-bombers. They are the ones who go in and take maybe a whole busload and I thought it would be more Israelis. I don't remember anything showing me the amount of Palestinians who have been killed – I don't remember that, but when it's something about Israelis being killed that has more effect on me – maybe there's more publicity about that. (Middle-class female, Paisley)

> Because of the indiscriminate attacks – it seems like there's been more Palestinian attacks. (Middle-class male, St Albans)

The view of Israeli casualties was also linked to the perception about the Palestinians as being 'more hostile':

> *Moderator*: Who thought that the Israelis had the most casualties, what made you think that?
> *Male speaker*: I just assumed the Palestinians were hurting [them] and they had a bigger army and they were trying to wade in there to Israel ...
> *Moderator*: What are the images in your head that gave you that idea then?
> *Male speaker*: Just seeing people in Israel getting shot in the streets and getting thrown out windows and things like that. It seemed as if it was the Palestinians that were taking over. (Low-income group, Glasgow)
> *Female speaker*: I thought the Palestinians were being quite hostile and that was basically the only theory behind it. I heard the word Palestinian more on the news, I think, I assumed. (Student group, Glasgow)

Some people stated simply that they had seen more coverage of Israeli casualties: 'I thought I'd heard more about Israeli casualties on the news' (female student, Glasgow). One speaker believed the casualties were about equal, but commented that 'Usually the images you see are wounded Israelis. They show Palestinians but not as often or as powerfully' (male student, Glasgow). Another student commented on how she had 'picked up' her view that most casualties were Israeli: 'It must have been something I picked up from watching the news – you are surrounded by the media and you're not consciously taking it in but you do take it in and get a perspective' (female student, Glasgow).

There was another key factor in the formation of belief which related to the manner in which news accounts were structured. The presentation of violence as a constant sequence of attacks by each side had led some people to believe that casualties would be about equal. A participant from a group of elderly people commented that he thought the casualties were the same because 'first of all it would be some of the Israelis being killed then it would be the Arabs being killed'. A student also noted that 'you hear stories about Israel bombing camps and stories about suicide-bombers in Israel' and this had led him to believe that the casualties were 'roughly the same'. The phrase 'tit for tat' which had been used on the news was used by some participants in explaining their beliefs:

Moderator: Why did you see [casualties] as even?
Female speaker: Because usually it is a case of you go in and shoot somebody and then the next thing somebody else is dead on the other side – it is usually a tit for tat. (Low-income group, Glasgow)

It's always portrayed as tit for tat – I believed that the numbers are about level. (Male student, Glasgow)

The strong influence of TV imagery is very apparent. In the following exchange the first speaker says that there are more Palestinian casualties, but thinks there is not much difference between those of the two sides and cites the frequency of attacks on Israelis. The second speaker believes that there were 5,000 Israeli casualties and 1,000 Palestinian casualties, and then directly relates this to what she has seen on television:

First speaker: I would have thought more Palestinians within the past two years. I wouldn't have thought it was that many more. There's been quite a lot of attacks that have involved a lot of Israelis

– you know big groups, buses, restaurants, and so on, so I would imagine there's not that much difference ...

Second speaker: Well basically on the news coverage they do always seem to make the Palestinians out to be the ones who are the suicide-bombers, so it's like, I would imagine it's going to be more casualties on the Israeli side, but it is purely from television, that's where I'm getting my info from, that's how it's been portrayed to me on television. (Low-income female group, London)

In the group of teachers from Paisley, it was thought that the news did feature more Israeli casualties, but they used logic to deduce that there would be more Palestinian casualties. They focused on the imbalances in weaponry and differences in the manner in which casualties were inflicted:

First speaker (male): Mine was the Palestinians suffer more casualties at all levels of severity. The nature, the way the casualties are inflicted is different. They ... the big news story of a suicide-bomber usually happens to the Israelis and Jews in Tel Aviv. Whereas the kind of reprisals and shootings of the military actions against people in the West Bank is ongoing all the time virtually.

Moderator: So what was your view about how many were on each side?

First speaker: I think the Palestinians suffered most casualties. I'm not entirely certain about that ... the impression the news gives you is there is higher Jewish casualties.

Moderator: The impression the news gives you is there are higher Jewish casualties?

Second speaker (male): It certainly seems to get mentioned more – any Jewish casualties ...

Moderator: Is that ...

Third speaker (male): You hear more of the Israeli atrocities.

Fourth speaker (female): Again by virtue of the nature of the Palestinians, I always seem to see them throwing stones, with Israelis with weapons and from that I would assume. (Teachers group, Paisley)

One of this group mentioned the 'brutality' of Israeli retaliation as a factor in his belief, but the most common reason given for seeing most casualties as Palestinian was simply the disparity in the military capacity of the two sides:

Images of tanks pounding Palestine – it just seemed to make more sense ... mainly just from that one image – that if they're using heavy artillery, then it is probably going to cause more casualties. (Male student group, Glasgow)

They show that the Palestinians are young boys with sticks and stones trying to fight the Israelis with their guns and tanks. If that's all they've got to fight with, presumably they are killed more often than someone with a gun. (Middle-class female group, Paisley)

They are much less armed, one side is fighting with stones ... Yasser Arafat headquarters – the Israelis were just like crushing everything. (Low-income male group, London)

Very few people in the groups cited any specific information from TV news on relative casualty figures. Some people had information from alternative sources, such as newspapers, leaflets, documentaries and the Internet. But an important factor seemed to be the logical deductions which were made. These were sometimes extended to take in other areas such as care of the wounded – the assumption here was that the Israelis had more funds and therefore more of their people would survive:

The Israelis have more money and they can take better care of people who are injured. (Low-income male group, London)

When you do see something like the suicide-bombers and what happens in Israel because of that, Israeli casualties, I'm always amazed at the number of ambulances and the support system that's rushing to deal with that crisis, and whenever you see the other end of it, the Palestinian casualties, they are there on their own with nothing. I get the feeling there isn't the backup system in Palestine to deal with those casualties that there is in Israel. (Middle-class female group, London)

There were some people in the groups who had connections with Israel either through friends or through having stayed there. Two of these stated that most casualties were Palestinian but at the same time said that there was more 'fuss' made about these casualties on the TV news or that Palestinian deaths were treated with more sympathy. It may be that they simply watched different bulletins from those in our samples, but their view is not supported by the material which we analysed. An alternative explanation might be that they were sympathetic to Israel and that coverage of Palestinian casualties in some way upset or contradicted their preferred view. They were comparatively well informed about events in the conflict and any sympathies which they had did not affect their judgement about the number of casualties. Interestingly, as we have seen above, viewers who were informed by the TV news and had apparently no great interest in the area were more likely to believe that the casualties were about equal or that most had been sustained by Israel.

CULTURAL IDENTIFICATION AND EMPATHY

Identification can be conditional on personal relationships – for example, contacts with friends or on cultural or family history. One student told us how she had attended an Arab school and how this had affected her understanding of the conflict. Such cultural histories can also affect the 'facts' and versions of causes of disputes which are heard by the individual. It was also made clear to us that for some members of the Jewish community, memories of the Holocaust had a powerful influence on how the Israeli-Palestinian conflict was seen. In a one-to-one discussion outside the groups, a Jewish woman described her experience of visiting Auschwitz and the appalling sight of piles of children's shoes. She then said that 'Sharon is a thug', but commented that there are times when someone like that is needed. The conflict was seen through the prism of the Holocaust – as she said, 'We cannot go quietly into the gas chambers again.'

Another woman in a focus group expressed her view that the history of the Jewish people had affected how the Israeli-Palestinian conflict was understood. She saw Israeli actions as being motivated by fear and thought that public perceptions were influenced by feelings of guilt:

I felt that [the Israelis] had tried to enlarge their area, but I could understand because there is a lot of fear from the Israeli point of view. They feel very frightened where they are, and also, because of the past history of the Jewish people, we feel quite guilty as well. (Middle-class female group, Paisley)

It is also possible for audiences to identify at a more general cultural level – for example, to see one side of the conflict as being 'people like us' with manners, customs and lifestyles which are readily understood and recognised. As one participant from London put it:

It's much easier for those of us in the West to imagine that a car bomb in the middle of a city is a tremendously terrifying thing ... when you see a car bomb go off in the middle of a sophisticated city, the experience is much closer to one we can 'imagine'. (Middle-class male group, London)

An additional factor to which this speaker pointed was that London had experienced being attacked during the IRA campaigns and he and another participant described being close to bombs when they went off. The issue of cultural identification was raised by other participants – Israel was referred to as 'an island of democracy' in the Middle East (middle-class male, London). At the same time, some aspects of Muslim culture were seen as strange and difficult to identify with. A female participant, who was actually quite sympathetic to the Palestinians, gave her own rather mixed feelings on this:

I feel there are lots of images I have of Muslim women that I find it very hard to see them beyond my own sort of white Western perspective because they're all covered up. And when you hear them mourning – because I know that my voice goes 'What's that noise?' and I know that that must be my Western culture that makes me think [that], but it does come across as alien to me, and I'm aware that it is my perspective, but that doesn't make me get any closer, if you know what I mean. (Low-income female group, London)

These comments then stimulated a further discussion between Brian Hanrahan from the BBC and the film-maker Ken Loach who were present in this group. They focused on the issue of whether journalists should intervene to help audiences 'see through' cultural difference by appealing to more universal values;[2] for example, concern for human suffering or loss – and should this be done in the name of balance?

Ken Loach: That seems a very reasonable response that people do empathise with situations that match their own. Do you consciously try to counteract that effect when you are interviewing people who don't speak English or who are speaking Arabic or some language we don't understand. Is there an attempt to re-balance that and should there be?

Brian Hanrahan: Erm, no.

Ken Loach: Should there be, do you think if we are even-handed to both sides?

Brian Hanrahan: Re-balance in the sense of trying to deliberately skew the scales so that you feel more sympathy for this person, no; re-balance if you mean, do we try and present that person in their own, so that their argument or their background comes across clearly?, yes. I certainly wouldn't try if there was someone who looked alien, was in an alien culture in an alien setting, I wouldn't try to do something that made them seem more like us, because I would feel that I was then intervening too much.

Ken Loach: It's a question more of not to skew it, but to elucidate it ...

Brian Hanrahan: I'd certainly try.

Ken Loach: ... in a way that the audience would identify with the person because of their motherhood or because of their plight which is universal, so that you are not distracted by the veil ...

Brian Hanrahan: We would go looking for common themes so you could understand, 'this is a mother', 'this is a teacher'. (At low-income female group, London)

The predominant response in the groups was that in practice people did 'see through' cultural difference and they spoke in terms of universals. As one woman put it, 'suffering is suffering'. There were also references to other values such as a concern with the abuse of power and the perception of the Palestinians as the 'underdog'. One young male participant commented on how the Israelis had 'built up' their country – while the Palestinian areas were 'not very good'. The Israeli towns were Westernised, with discos – but this did not affect how he identified with the two sides. As he put it, 'I would support the Palestinians, I'd support the underdogs' (low-income male group, London). As we have already noted, visual imagery of the Palestinians as the underdog does not necessarily produce a sympathetic response. A key factor is how such imagery is contextualised through explanations of cause and how these affect understanding of the legitimacy and rationale of the two sides. In the above case, the speaker had also been influenced by Palestinians he had met, who had been giving out leaflets at the local shopping precinct.

We also found cases in the groups where the visual imagery of war was simply too much for some people and they said that they turned away. Ken Loach explored this response and asked why they would not feel empathy with those involved:

> *Ken Loach*: Obviously everyone here is very caring and thoughtful in general in the way that we are talking about it, and yet I was very struck by what you said, when you said 'I can't bear to watch it.' Now sometimes you'll see pictures of mothers and their dead children and grandparents with children who have died or sons who have died and you as parents, daughters or whatever, I would think that you would, all things being equal, you would identify with that person's suffering. What is it that stops you, stopping in front of the television and saying: 'I absolutely understand what that person is going through, I have a sense of what that person is going through', because if news is to work that is what sharing a story is. What is it that stops you feeling that empathy? (Low-income female group, London)

One speaker replies that such images may be 'emotionally exhausting'. And then Ken Loach asks: 'Is it also to do with feeling you have no control, no say in it?' To which a female participant replies: 'Oh yes, because there is a thing that nothing is going to change, there are so many of those images, it's depressing and futile' (low-income female group, London).

One dimension in this sense of powerlessness is the lack of understanding about why the events are occurring. As we have found in this and other research, the world can appear to people as an inexplicable mess. Of course a greater understanding does not necessarily mean that something can be easily done by viewers to solve the problem. But in principle, to see events as having causes can be a first step towards understanding the possibilities for change, and to engaging with what is shown and to having opinions about it. As another participant put it:

> There is definitely an absence of explanation which causes an absence of feeling because I can quite easily sit and I say I feel no way about it whatsoever. Because I haven't been there it's got nothing to do with me whatsoever, so I have a lack of feeling about it. But I also have a lack of understanding about it – maybe if I

knew a lot more about it, I'd have more feeling and more opinions on it. (Low-income male group, London)

There was a strong feeling in the groups that the news should explain origins and causes and that journalists should speak more directly to viewers about was happening and why. The participants in the groups did not want news that was in any way biased or inaccurate, but the desire for clear, straightforward accounts was very apparent. It was also the case that when viewers did understand the significance and relevance of what they were watching, then this could strongly affect their level of interest in the news.

UNDERSTANDING AND INTEREST IN NEWS

We asked the participants in the focus groups whether, when watching the news, they felt that journalists assumed a level of knowledge or understanding which they did not have. A clear majority assented to this. Not all agreed – the middle-class males were more likely to say they understood the news very well. But for many there was a problem and examples were given of how the lack of understanding impacted on the interest which viewers had on the news:

> Every time it comes on [the Israeli-Palestinian conflict] it never actually explains it so I don't see the point in watching it – I just turn it off and go and make a cup of tea or something. I don't like watching it when I don't really understand what's going on. (Female student, Glasgow)

> It's like the Kosovo conflict, I don't want to watch it, I don't understand it – I switch it off. (Middle-class female group, Paisley)

Others pointed to their feeling of complete incomprehension:

> It is all mumble-jumble and you don't understand. (Low-income male group, Glasgow)

> I hear them waffling on and it's all so quick and he knows what he's talking about but I just don't have a clue what they're going on about … you could be sitting there listening to it but it's going to have less interest to you if you don't understand it. (Middle-class male group, St Albans)

Another problem which some participants identified was that explanations may have been given at the beginning of a story, on the first day of being reported. But since they frequently came into stories 'halfway through' a cycle of events, they could not understand what was happening:

> *Moderator*: Do you ever have the feeling that the journalist expects you to have a background knowledge that you don't actually have?
> *Female speaker*: Yes definitely, there's loads of times when like, there's just the background stuff that I don't really know anything about.
> *Male speaker*: I think it's more of a case that they assume, kind of, it's part of an ongoing story. They assume that you've been there from the start and that you've constantly watched. (Student group, Glasgow)

In another group the same point is made:

> It's not like I watch BBC News every day. You might miss a couple of weeks of news; you might miss some developments happening. And it's not like *Newsround*, where they tell you why they are fighting, over what, what's happened recently. They assume that you actually know more – over the last three years of watching it. (Male student, Glasgow)

There was some concern in the groups as to whether the news could sustain long explanations. Yet we found in practice that a relatively small amount of new information could substantially improve understanding. In this exchange, the moderator mentioned the confusion over the phrase 'occupied territory' and had previously explained what it meant:

> *Moderator*: If they use words such as 'occupied territory' it's not clear from that phrase who is occupying what.
> *Female speaker*: By adding just a couple of words they could make that clear. (Middle-class female group, London)

In another group it was apparent that a relatively straightforward piece of information, such as that the Israelis controlled water supplies and how this affected Palestinian agriculture, had a strong effect on how a participant understood the intractability of the conflict: 'What was really important for me today was learning about the water because that's a real power point isn't it?' (low-income female group, London).

We found clear links between understanding and levels of interest, as in this exchange:

Moderator: Is there a link between you turning off and not being interested and that you don't actually quite understand what is going on?

First speaker: Sometimes if you are not up to speed ...

Second speaker: Sometimes things are more human and more real if you do understand the things that are behind it.

Moderator: I see you nodding [*to third woman who has previously said she does not watch the news*] ...

Lindsey Hilsum: [*To the same person*] Is there anything that would make you more interested in the news?

Third speaker: I can understand what you are saying and I think that is probably one of the things if I was to turn on the news, if I was forced to for whatever reason, it would help if I actually knew what I was listening to, if I understood where they were coming from. So take this war, I don't know how it started, I don't know the background behind it, so I'm actually listening in effect to gibberish, so that would make a difference. (Middle-class female group, London)

This also came across strongly in the following exchange from a student group. There was a very strong feeling within the group that their interest was linked to understanding, and the point was also made that the explanations should be contained within news programming:

Moderator: So when they talk about 'Palestinian refugees' and 'occupied territories' it really doesn't mean anything to you? Would you have found the news more interesting if you had understood those things?

First speaker (female): Yes.

Second speaker (male): Possibly, I wouldn't have switched off if I'd known the historical context. I would probably have had an emotional tie to it and got into it a bit more.

First speaker: It wouldn't have been just random facts, 'cos that's what it feels like, just random facts with no context at all really. And it's much preferable to see a short slot on the news, because obviously a documentary lasts half an hour or an hour and you don't want to watch all that.

Third speaker (female): It would change my perception of it, I would understand it. (Student group, Glasgow)

A clear majority in the groups as a whole stated that their interest increased when they understood more. This was very marked in the responses of group members to discussions in which they took part. Some became extremely interested and stayed behind to ask extensive questions. In two groups it was suggested that they might meet again as informal discussion groups. Other participants told us subsequently that they had spoken for long periods with friends about the issues that were raised, and others told us that they would now watch the news with more interest. This was not true of everyone. A minority said that they understood the news or that they preferred it as it was or that they thought the subject matter of news was intrinsically boring and it would not make any difference if they understood it more. But for the bulk of the people in this study the relationship between understanding and interest in news was very marked. This did suggest the need for change in the current structure and content of news programmes to address the problem that so many people are apparently not well informed by the news services which they see as their primary source of information.

4
Why Does it Happen?

FACTORS IN PRODUCTION?

We look here at key factors which affect the production and structuring of news accounts in this area. As we have seen, there is in general a dearth of in-depth, analytic and explanatory material included in news reports. Journalists in our focus groups pointed to the problems in producing a constant flow of news items and to pressures of time. Newsroom discussions do not focus very often on issues of audience comprehension or the overall effect of news programming on public understanding. As Adrian Monck pointed out to us, the main concern of news producers is often the logistics of how to get the job done in the time available. As he noted, there are a limited number of ways in which news stories are currently told. These include the standard news package with video inserts, or a studio discussion or a live piece to camera by an expert journalist. As he put it, which format is used and what goes into the story is often dominated by the pressure to deliver a sequence of programmes lasting exactly 24 minutes and 36 seconds (timed to the second). He believed that it was now very important for journalists and broadcasters to reorient their concerns and think about how news output could be restructured to improve its capacity to inform. Others also pointed to factors in the current organisation of news programming which limit the ability of journalists to explain and analyse. One participant in the focus groups was a professional photographer and he commented that

> Part of the problem is just the way the news medium works nowadays – where you are geared up to having constant 24 hour news and you get the feeling that some of the journalists on the spot are spending more time in front of a camera because they have to do 15 different TV news programmes and four different radio programmes, than they are actually finding out what's happening in the story, and that means we do not get as much analysis, as much colour, as much depth in what's going on. You get moment-by-moment repetition. (Middle-class male group, London)

244

Lindsey Hilsum also noted the pressures of time but linked this to the specific difficulties of covering the Israeli-Palestinian conflict, with its long complex history in which explanations are intensely contested:

> There are two problems ... how far back do you go is one and the other is with a conflict like this, nearly every single fact is disputed ... I think, 'Oh God, the Palestinians say this and the Israelis say that' and I have to, as a journalist, make a judgement and I say this is what happened and it's quite clear and there are other things where I wasn't there and I didn't see it with my own eyes. I know it's a question of interpretation so I have to say what both sides think and I think sometimes that stops us from giving the background we should be giving, because I think 'Well, bloody hell, I've only three minutes to do this piece in and I'm going to spent a minute going through the arguments.' (Middle-class female group, London)

But, as she notes, the journalists should be giving the context, and our study suggests that the removal of it has important consequences. As we have indicated, the absence of key elements of Palestinian history makes it difficult to understand their perspective. Their actions could appear without context and in consequence they may be seen as 'initiating' the trouble. In contrast, when the Israelis acted, the news often gave an explanation which could legitimise what they were doing. Israeli views on terrorism and the rationale for their actions were clearly included on the news, and Israelis were more frequently quoted and featured than Palestinians. One reason for this disparity was the more efficient public relations machine which the Israelis operated to supply information to journalists. At the same time it was sometimes difficult for journalists to obtain information from the Palestinian side about current events. We interviewed a US journalist who had headed a Jerusalem-based news agency in the period before the intifada. As he noted, most journalists actually lived in Israel and were regularly supplied with information:

> Nearly all [the journalists] lived in Israel or West Jerusalem, rather than in Palestinian areas. The Israelis were very nice to them. They speak their languages, they dress like us, for the most part they act

like us. They press the right buttons. The other thing is the Israeli efficiency, 'You want these documents, I'll get them for you', miles of statistics![1] (Interview, June 2002)

He believed the Palestinian operation was far less effective:

Palestinian spokesmen are their own worst enemy. They often come across as boorish, the message is often incoherent. Official Palestine does have a method problem. They miss the essential points. Arafat is a one man show, he is almost always incoherent. (Interview, June 2002)

He also noted the difference in that the Israeli approach was essentially proactive while the Palestinians were essentially reactive:

Palestinians don't have a clear public relations approach. They [Palestinians] start from a reactive approach. I get 75–100 emails a day from official Israeli sources and organisations which support [Israel] (about 15 per cent from government, the rest lobbyists and supporters). I get perhaps five a week from Palestinian sources. (Interview, June 2002)

In contrast, some British Zionists with whom we spoke took the view that there were weaknesses in Israeli press and public relations, particularly in the Israeli Defence Forces (IDF). Joy Wolfe from the Women's International Zionist Organisation commented on the 'inexperience' of the IDF team who have 'very poor communication equipment and not even a proper English-speaking translator who can put out a decent and accurate press release' (23 October 2003). Overall, however, it does seem from our research that the Israelis achieved much more space for their views than the Palestinians (as shown, for example, in the relative amounts of reported statements/interviews).

British journalist Robert Fisk has also described how the regular supply of information and well organised public relations can set agendas in news:

The journalists' narrative of events is built around the last thing someone has said and the last thing, given the constraints of time and the rolling news machine that they have heard on the agency wire. So what you would find on television in the last few weeks is that every time an Israeli statement was made, it was pushed across at the Palestinians. So the Israelis would say: 'Can Arafat control the violence?' and instead of the television reporters saying: 'Well that's interesting, but can the Israelis control their own people?' the question was simply taken up as an Israeli question and became part of the news agenda. There seemed to be no real understanding that the job of the reporter is to analyse what's really happening, not simply to pick up on the rolling news machine, the last statement by one of the sides. And given the fact that the Israelis have a very smooth machine operating for the media, invariably what happened is, it was Israel's voice that came across through the mouths of the reporters, rather than [having] people who were really making enquiries into both sides and what both people were doing. (*The Message*, BBC Radio 4, 20 October 2000)

It has often been noted that it is easier for journalists to accept the routine supply of information than to undertake the difficult, expensive and sometimes dangerous path of generating independent material. Journalists who were working in the occupied territories complained of extensive intimidation and it has been suggested that this has worsened as the intifada gathered momentum. The veteran BBC correspondent Keith Graves has written in the *Guardian* that

When I was first based in the Middle East as a BBC correspondent thirty years ago, Israel was rightly proud of its position as the only country in the region where journalists could report freely. Not anymore. Under the Sharon government intimidation of reporters deemed 'unfriendly' to Israel is routine and sanctioned by the government. (*Guardian*, 12 July 2003)

Organisations such as the Foreign Press Association (FPA) in Jerusalem and Reporters Sans Frontiers have accused the Israelis of deliberately targeting gunfire at journalists, noting that eight had been wounded (*The Observer*, 17 June 2001).[2] A recent programme on Channel 4 television gave a detailed account by journalists of what they regarded as the deliberate killing of a colleague by Israeli security forces, when he had been filming the bulldozing of Palestinian homes.[3]

The Palestinian Authority has also made attempts to limit unfavourable coverage by, for example, trying to control what is filmed. But it seems clear that, overall, Israel's public relations and system of information supply is more sophisticated and well resourced. There are also powerful lobbies which support them in the US and to some extent in Britain. The *Independent*, for example, has reported that 'the Israeli embassy in London has mounted a huge drive to influence the British media'. The paper quoted the embassy's press secretary as saying that

> London is a world centre of media and the embassy here works night and day to try to influence that media. And, in many subtle ways, I think we don't do a half bad job, if I may say so ... We have newspapers that write consistently in a manner that supports and understands Israel's situation and its challenges. And we have had influence on the BBC as well. (*Independent*, 21 September 2001)

The *Observer* has also written of the intensity of this campaign, noting that:

> A new front is opening in the intifada. Faced with increasing international criticism of its handling of the Palestinian uprising, the Israeli government of Ariel Sharon and its allies in the powerful and influential pro-Israeli lobby, have stepped up their efforts against international media reporting of the current crisis. News organisations that fall foul of Israel are accused of being pro-Palestinian at best, and at worst anti-Semitic. (*Observer*, 17 June 2001)

Journalists spoke to us of the personal criticism and 'flak' which they had received. Lindsey Hilsum from Channel 4 News commented on 'the number of emails that I receive saying that I'm anti-Semitic because I've written something they don't like about Israel' (in focus group: middle-class females, London).

The *Observer* also noted the organised nature of letter writing campaigns:

> For many years, pro-Israel organisations have organised letter-writing campaigns to protest against articles and programmes

they dislike. With the development of email, this activity has grown enormously. Websites ... target individual journalists and provide ready-written letters of complaint for subscribers to send out. (*Observer*, 17 June 2001)

Pro-Israel groups often argue that both 'bias' in the media and physical attacks upon Israel are at root caused by anti-Semitism. There is certainly evidence of anti-Semitism in the speeches of some Muslim clerics and in the Arab media.[4] The Israelis have occasionally pointed to this as part of making their own case. We spoke in some detail about this with Nachman Shai, who was a key Israeli spokesman in the early period of the intifada. He was also Director General of the Ministry of Science, Culture and Sport and had been chief spokesperson for the IDF at the time of the Gulf War. His view was that Israel tended to avoid using anti-Semitism as an argument. He also noted that it was more significant as an issue to Jews living outside Israel: 'Anti-Semitism doesn't have the same significance to Israelis as to non-Israelis, since we are not exposed to it in our everyday life' (interview, 15 August 2003).

There was another very important issue which affected the contemporary development of Israeli public relations. After the events of 9/11 and the attack on the US, Israel had stressed its role as part of the 'war against terror'. This had much more 'general' connotations in terms of presenting Israel as one part of the Western Alliance. As Nachman Shai commented.

We selected the first [war on terror] instead of the second [anti-Semitism] because we are part of the Western world. We very much played the first argument. It worked better with governments, they gave us more support. It's like if you've run out of arguments, you're stuck with anti-Semitism. The first one is based on common interests. (Interview, 15 August 2003)

We might note that for Israel to present itself as part of a general 'war on terror' against those who dislike Western values also has the advantage of drawing attention away from specific actions by Israel which have contributed to the origins and development of the Middle East conflict. However, a final comment from Nachman Shai was on the quality of international media coverage, including that of Britain. He regarded it as having improved and cited the effect of suicide-bombings on how the conflict was seen:

It has gradually become more balanced than in the beginning – the media are now seeing more of the complicated issues than at the beginning, because of the indiscriminate violence of the suicide-bombers against the Israeli population. (Interview, 15 August 2003)

The essence of what Nachman Shai is saying is that the Israelis have stressed their role in the general 'war on terror' rather than the issue of anti-Semitism, and also that the coverage of suicide-bombing has improved the 'balance' of coverage, from the Israeli perspective. This is strikingly different from the arguments of pro-Israeli commentators in Britain who have stressed anti-Semitism and attacked media coverage.

CLAIMS THAT THE MEDIA ARE BIASED AGAINST ISRAEL

The *Observer* also pointed to the influence of lobby groups such as the Conservative Friends of Israel which invites senior journalists to lunches at the House of Commons. It commented that 'for those working for organisations perceived as being biased against Israel these can be uncomfortable affairs'. Such lobby groups often assert that the media is biased against Israel. The Conservative MP Gillian Shephard is quoted as saying:

Let's not forget that Israel feels under siege. And it literally is. That is what drives the feeling of ultra-sensitivity. They feel that there is bias and there is a conspiracy against them. There is a perception that Israelis are portrayed as instigating the problems and that the historical context of the threat against Israel is forgotten. There is a feeling too that Israel – which is a tiny island of democracy amid much less democratic neighbours – never gets enough credit for what it has achieved. (*Observer*, 17 June 2001)

As we have seen, our study does not support the view that Israel is portrayed unfairly. Yet Gillian Shephard points to the deep sense of persecution which some in the wider Jewish community still apparently feel at the hands of the media. In February 2003, for example, Melanie Phillips wrote in the *Jewish Chronicle* of a conference on anti-Semitism and the discussions and evidence which were presented at it. The recurring theme, she notes, was 'a nexus of anti-Jewish hatred between fanatical Islamists on the one hand and the British and European media on the other'. She argues that

> Europe has waited for fifty years for a way to blame the Jews for their own destruction. So instead of addressing genocidal Muslim anti-Semitism, the Europeans have seized upon a narrative which paints the Jews as Nazis and the Palestinians as the new Jews. (Phillips, 2003)

She notes how the conference 'was told about the way the British media describes Israel's "death squads", "killing-fields" and "executioners" while sanitising Palestinian human bombs as "gentle", "religious" and "kind"' (Phillips, 2003). While it is clearly true that vicious anti-Semitism exists in some Islamic groups and elsewhere, this description of the British media does not accord with what we have found. We were also puzzled by what some people in our focus groups believed about TV news. There is an interesting phenomenon well documented in psychological studies whereby a strong commitment can lead to an inability to see information that contests the preferred view or violates a preferred expectation. We did find in our study at least one case where a person found it difficult literally to see what was in front of him. The great majority of those in our audience groups did not process information in this way, but in this case the participant stated that the news was biased against Israel and that the photographs he had used in the news writing exercise were also 'pro-Palestinian'. We pointed out that they had been carefully chosen. They did in fact include a picture of the aftermath of a suicide-bombing, which showed an Israeli ambulance with the Star of David on the side. They also included the image of a dead Israeli soldier being thrown from the window of a Palestinian police station. But the participant focused his attention very largely on an image of an Israeli tank in a Palestinian area and expressed his concern about what people would think of this.

Overall, the results of our study suggest that it was Israeli perspectives which predominated in TV news and this is in part the result of a very well developed system of lobbying and public relations. Another key factor affecting media coverage is the very close political and communication links which exist between the US and Britain.

THE US CONNECTION

Our content analysis showed that speakers from the US were frequently featured on TV news and that they commonly endorsed or supported Israeli positions. There was no comparable referencing of the governments of other nations who were more critical of Israel.[5] Given the significance of the US as the world's sole remaining superpower and its relationship with Britain, it is not surprising that the views of its politicians would be featured but none the less it had a significant effect on the balance of TV news coverage. There is some evidence to suggest that the perspectives on the Middle East adopted by US politicians are strongly influenced by pro-Israel lobbies. A recent Radio 4 programme looked in detail at this and noted how the pro-Israel groups now included the Christian Right:

> *Journalist*: It's time to revive one of the oldest stereotypes in American politics, the power of the Jewish lobby. Today, it's not the Jewish lobby which counts, it's the pro-Israel and the difference is crucial. Two of the most formidable organisational networks in America, the Jewish Establishment and the Christian Right have joined forces. Together, they can penetrate deep into the body politic. (*A Lobby to Reckon With*, BBC Radio 4, 7 May 2002)

The programme visited the Cornerstone Church in San Antonio, Texas, 'a stadium-sized arena' with 10,000 worshippers, whose services are broadcast to millions of homes. The pastor's sermon is heard:

> God entered into an eternal covenant with Abraham, Isaac and Jacob that the nation of Israel would belong to the Jewish people for ever, and forever means 2002, 3002, 4002, forever is forever. Jerusalem is the eternal capital of the Jewish state. (*A Lobby to Reckon With*, BBC Radio 4, 7 May 2002)

The programme also pointed out the strength of Jewish American activism and the role of AIPAC (the American Israel Public Affairs Committee). It was also stated that there are smaller Jewish groups in the US who are opposed to Israel's current policies, but the influence of AIPAC is very noteworthy:

> *Journalist*: AIPAC's power has become the stuff of Washington legend. *Fortune* magazine consistently puts it in the top five special

interest groups. No other foreign policy based lobby group gets into the top 25. (*A Lobby to Reckon With*, BBC Radio 4, 7 May 2002)

The programme also interviewed J.J. Goldberg, an American author who has written on AIPAC and other pro-Israel groups. He comments on how the influence of 'political action committees' has developed through the financing of the opponents of those who speak against Israel:

> AIPAC has a lot of influence on foreign policy, they work hard to make sure that America endorses pretty much Israel's view of the world and of the Middle East. They do it partly by convincing, partly by implied threats. AIPAC does not raise money for candidates but there are Jewish PACs (Political Action Committees) that raise campaign funds for candidates. Four or five times over the last twenty years, these PACs have gone after members of Congress who voted in ways that AIPAC didn't like. They have flooded their opponents with money and enabled them to beat the incumbents. Sent a message that if you really go against AIPAC, you'd better know where you're next dollar is coming from. So that, as I've been told by a number of congressional aides over the last few years, if the congressman doesn't vote against Arafat they'll pay a price. If they do vote against Arafat, there's no price to be paid. There's no percentage for the member of Congress to stand up for peace, for compromise. Nobody is going to reward them, they'll be punished. (*A Lobby to Reckon With*, BBC Radio 4, 7 May 2002)

As the BBC programme notes, the strength of the lobby was shown at the annual conference of AIPAC which featured the attendance of half the US Senate and half the members of the lower house. It has also been argued that media coverage in the US is strongly influenced by the pro-Israel lobby. Michael Massing, writing in *The Nation*, noted that the activities of AIPAC are rarely analysed in the American media:

> Journalists are often loathe to write about the influence of organised Jewry. Throughout the Arab world, the 'Jewish lobby' is seen as the root of all evil in the Middle East, and many reporters and editors – especially Jewish ones – worry about feeding such stereotypes. (*The Nation*, 10 June 2002)

254 Bad News From Israel

But he also comments that the main obstacle to covering such groups is fear:

> Jewish organisations are quick to detect bias in the coverage of the Middle East and quick to complain about it ... As the *Forward* observed in late April, 'rooting out perceived anti-Israel in the media has become for many American Jews the most direct and emotional outlet for connecting with the conflict six thousand miles away.' Recently an estimated one thousand subscribers to the *Los Angeles Times* suspended home delivery for a day to protest what they considered the paper's pro-Palestinian coverage. The *Chicago Tribune*, the *Minneapolis Star Tribune*, the *Philadelphia Enquirer* and the *Miami Herald* have all been hit by similar protests. (*The Nation*, 10 June 2002)

Massing asks whether such protests have an effect and considers the experience of the *New York Times*. On 6 May 2002 the paper had run two photographs of a pro-Israel parade in Manhattan:

> Both showed the parade in the background and anti-Israel protesters prominently in the foreground. The paper, which for weeks has been threatened with a boycott by Jewish readers, was deluged with protests. On May the seventh the *Times* ran an abject apology. That caused much consternation in the newsroom, with some reporters and editors feeling that the paper had buckled before an influential constituency. 'It's very intimidating', said a correspondent at another large daily who is familiar with the incident. Newspapers, he added, are 'afraid' of organisations like AIPAC and the President's Conference. 'The pressure from these groups is relentless. Editors would just as soon not touch them.' (*The Nation*, 10 June 2002)

Ted Turner, the founder of CNN also famously ignited an international controversy by saying that both the Israelis and the Palestinians were engaged in 'terrorism'. As the *Guardian* reported:

> After the Turner interview appeared ... there were calls for the cable and satellite operators [in Israel] to pull CNN from their output. One of the main satellite operators in Israel, Yes, added CNN's arch-rival Fox News – perceived to be sympathetic to Israel – to its package of channels. CNN clearly had some talking to do, and its

most senior editorial executive got himself on the first flight out of Atlanta when he read Turner's comments. Eason Jordan, chief news executive at CNN spent the next week or so on a whirlwind damage-limitation exercise [in the Middle East]. (*Guardian*, 1 July 2002)

The *Guardian* also noted that Fox News had 'endeared itself' to the conservative right in its approach to the Middle East conflict: 'It now refers, for example, to Palestinian suicide bombers as "homicide-bombers". In Israel, it is held up as a model of "objective" reporting' (*Guardian*, 1 July 2002).

Fox is part of Rupert Murdoch's organisation which has extensive media interests in Britain, owning, for example, the *Sun, The Times,* the *Sunday Times* and the *News of the World*. Sam Kiley, a correspondent for *The Times*, resigned in September 2001, blaming its allegedly pro-Israeli censorship of his reporting. He spoke of Rupert Murdoch's close friendship with Ariel Sharon and heavy investment in Israel. Writing in the London *Evening Standard*, he commented that

> *The Times* foreign editor and other middle managers flew into hysterical terror every time a pro-Israel lobbying group wrote in with a quibble or complaint and then usually took their side against their own correspondent ... I was told I should not refer to 'assassinations' of Israel's opponents, nor to 'extra-judicial killings or executions'. (Quoted in the *Guardian*, 5 September 2001)

The *Guardian* also reported Kiley as saying that

> Murdoch executives were so scared of irritating the media mogul that when [Kiley] interviewed the Israeli army unit responsible for killing a twelve-year-old Palestinian boy, he was asked to file the piece without mentioning the dead child. (*Guardian*, 5 September 2001)

The *Daily Telegraph* has also been the subject of disputes over its Middle East coverage. The proprietor of the Telegraph group, Conrad Black, is strongly supportive of Israel and journalists complained that this was affecting editorial policy. In March 2001, The *Guardian* reported that:

Three prominent writers – all of them past contributors to Mr Black's Telegraph group have signed a letter to the *Spectator* accusing him of abusing his responsibilities as a proprietor. Such is the vehemence with which Mr Black has expounded his pro-Israeli held view, they say, no editor or reporter would dare write frankly about the Palestinian perspective. (*Guardian*, 16 March 2001)

On the same day in the *Guardian*, William Dalrymple, one of the authors of the letter, wrote:

A press baron is an immensely powerful figure. With that power, comes responsibilities, and those responsibilities are abused when he makes it clear that certain areas are off-limits to legitimate enquiry, and that careers will suffer if those limits are crossed. (*Guardian*, 16 March 2001)

The pressures of organised public relations, lobbying and systematic criticism together with the privileging of Israeli perspectives by political and public figures, can affect the climate within which journalists operate. There is no total control and there are areas of the media where the debate is relatively open. But these factors go some way to explaining why journalists sometimes have difficulty in giving a clear account of the Palestinian perspective, while they can apparently more easily facilitate that of the Israelis.

5
Conclusion

One of the key issues to emerge from this research is that for many viewers, their level of interest in news related very directly to their level of understanding of what they were watching. We found strong increases in interest when people understood more about the history, origins and causes of events. A parallel phenomenon was that incomprehension led to detachment and increased the sense of powerlessness some people felt when watching terrible events with which they could not engage or relate to. There was a strong demand for clear direct explanations from journalists which cut through 'waffle' and 'spin' and which explained why these events were happening.

We also examined the conditions under which some viewers did engage with news stories or identify with the people who were being represented. There was some evidence of identification with the Israelis as being 'people like us', who have similar customs or who were 'democratic', and some people with Arab connections or friends identified with the Palestinians. A much more widespread identification in our audience samples came with what were seen as common or universal values. These included a concern with human suffering or with value judgements on, for example, oppression or the use of power. But how such values were applied by viewers could depend very much on the manner in which events were explained and understood. Some group members had argued that images of tanks against poorly armed Palestinians would necessarily result in an identification with the 'underdog'. But it was also pointed out that in other circumstances such as Northern Ireland, images of troops versus crowds of stone-throwers did not result in audiences identifying 'against' the soldiers. The crucial issue is whether the use of force is understood to be legitimate and in this sense TV news did have an important role in establishing how what was seen was to be evaluated. The Israelis could be seen as 'bullies' or their actions could be understood as emanating from their own 'vulnerability'. The image of a Palestinian fighter in a mask with a gun might be seen as a fearful icon of terrorism or as symbolising heroic resistance against an illegal occupation – the mask might appear as sinister or simply as a necessary precaution against arrest. The key issue is what we know and understand of the relationships which underpin events and the manner in which such images are contextualised when they are shown. It is in this contextualisation that the partisan nature of much TV news is revealed. As we indicated, to understand the origins of the Israeli-Palestinian conflict requires a knowledge of at least two key historical events. The first is that when Israel was established in 1948, large numbers of Palestinians were displaced from their homes and land. Both sides have given their own account of this and have sought to legitimise and explain their own actions. But even if we leave aside the accounts of Palestinians, it is clear that some eminent Israeli historians have given documented descriptions of how Palestinian society collapsed under deliberate military attacks. A second key issue is that after 1967, Palestinians in the occupied territories lived under various forms of military control in which they were ultimately subject to the power of Israel. The land, water and economic resources of these territories were then extensively exploited by Israel. Again, both sides give their own accounts of the legitimacy of this. Some Israelis and the Christian Right in the US might, for example, argue that the land was given to the Jews thousands of years ago by God, so it all belongs to the Israelis anyway. But it is clear that the fact of the military occupation and its consequences is crucial to an understanding of the rationale of Palestinian action. Television news has largely denied its audiences an account of these relationships and their origins, and in doing so has both confused viewers and reduced the understanding of the actions of those involved. Many in our audience samples did not even understand that there was a military occupation or that it was widely seen as illegal. There was very little knowledge of the conditions of the occupation or its effects on the Palestinian economy. There is a great difference between understanding the Palestinian view that they are fighting a war of national liberation against an occupying power and seeing the conflict as a border dispute between two countries that happen to want the same piece of land (which is how many people did see it). We also found that the attitudes of those in our audience groups could change sharply when they did learn more about the origins of the conflict. One female participant had commented in a focus group that the fighting would stop if the parents just kept their children in and stopped them throwing stones. When she heard in the discussion that Palestinians had lost their homes, she said

'If you knew, you'd be flinging bricks yourself' (low-income group, Glasgow). The absence of the Palestinian rationale also meant that on the news they were frequently presented as 'starting' the trouble while the Israelis 'retaliated'. This had a measurable impact on audience understanding and even extended to participants reversing in their memories the sequence of actual historical events (so the Palestinians were seen to do the first action and Israelis responded).

In contrast, Israeli views such as their need to defend themselves against terrorism were very well represented on the news. Israeli perspectives were more frequently featured in headlines and were often highlighted to the exclusion of alternatives. A frequency count of the coverage given to interviews and reported statements also showed the Israeli dominance.[1] Journalists sometimes adopted the language of Israeli statements and used it as their own direct speech in news reports. On controversial issues such as the Israeli settlements in occupied territory, there was a tendency to present these as 'vulnerable' and under attack without indicating that many are heavily fortified and play a key military and strategic role. This had a clear effect on how some audiences members saw them, including people who were sympathetic to the Palestinians (for example, one described his surprise when he had heard how much land the settlements controlled). There were other areas where the news was apparently partisan. Through the period of our work, Palestinians consistently incurred the highest number of casualties. The number killed was greater than that of Israelis by a ratio of 2–3:1. But on the news there was an emphasis on Israeli casualties both in the amount of coverage they received and in the language used to describe them. One of our samples was of a week when Palestinians incurred the highest number of casualties since the intifada had begun, yet there was more coverage of Israeli casualties. In our samples of news content, words such as 'mass murder', 'savage cold-blooded killing' and 'lynching' were used by journalists to describe Israeli deaths but not those of Palestinians/ Arabs. The word 'terrorist' was used to describe Palestinians, but when an Israeli group was reported as trying to bomb a Palestinian school, they were referred to as 'extremists' or 'vigilantes' (ITV main News and BBC1 lunchtime News, 5 March 2002).

As we have also indicated, the level of pressure, lobbying and public relations which exists in this area is likely to affect the media climate in both Britain and the US. This has important implications for the clarity and impartiality of the information which is received by mass publics. Of course, there is propaganda on both sides. The BBC correspondent Paul Adams discussed this with us and commented on the arguments put forward by the Palestinians and Israelis at the time of Jenin. The Israelis had sought to present themselves as engaging in targeted operations against terrorists. But the Palestinians wanted to present the inhabitants as civilians under attack and thus argued that the Israeli actions constituted a 'massacre'. As Paul Adams commented: 'The argument disappears into sterile debate about what is a massacre.' What is missing is the view that this is an uneven war and that 'It is a war of national liberation – a periodic guerrilla war, sometimes using violent means, in which a population is trying to throw off an occupying force' (interview, 9 August 2002).

We have seen that this 'war' has sometimes drawn on other elements such as anti-Semitism and amongst some, an intense rejection of Western culture. But it seems unlikely that the bulk of the world's populations are intrinsically 'fanatical'. In the past, historical compromises have been possible to resolve the most intractable of conflicts. But a key factor in moving towards this is that judgements about how it might be resolved require clear and accurate information and the perspectives of those involved have to be properly understood. The dust-storms of propaganda, which are created by those seeking to defend their 'own side', will in the end do nothing more than prolong the conflict and the agony that the people of the Middle East are having to endure.

Appendix 1:
Answers to Questions on the Israeli-Palestinian Conflict by Student Groups

1. What comes into your mind when you hear the words 'Israeli-Palestinian conflict'?

Response	British sample 2001 (%)	British sample 2002 (%)	German sample 2002 (%)	American sample 2002 (%)
War/violence/fighting	69	55	60	46
Suicide-bombings	2	24	22	20
Conflict over land	4	1	2	4
Religious conflict	11	8	12	12
Personalities: Arafat, Sharon, Bush	2	3	–	8
Muslims/Arabs	1	–	1	2
Environment: sand, sun, etc.	1	1	–	–
Flags: Israeli, etc./maps	1	–	–	–
Poverty	4	–	2	–
World Trade Center: Bin Laden, Saddam Hussein	4	1	1	6
	–	2	–	2
Emotional statement: injustice, tragedy etc.	–	5	–	–
No response	1	–	–	–

2a. Source of images.

Response	British sample 2001 (%)	British sample 2002 (%)	German sample 2002 (%)	American sample 2002 (%)
Television news	82	85	61	58
Newspapers	13	9	8	27
General media	2	–	–	11
Documentaries	–	1	–	–
Internet	1	–	4	–
Personal experience	1	–	1	–
Indirect experience (friends/relatives)	–	1	2	–

Books/journals	1	–	–	4
Radio	–	1	4	–
Peace rallies	–	2	–	–
No source identified	–	1	20	–

2b. What additional sources have you used?

Response	British sample 2001 (%)	British sample 2002 (%)	German sample 2002 (%)	American sample 2002 (%)
Television news	6	7	17	23
Newspapers	48	47	18	39
Documentaries	1	3	–	–
Internet	3	5	–	1
Personal experience	1	1	–	–
Indirect experience (friends/relatives)	5	7	3	1
Books/journals	4	2	–	5
Radio	6	2	2	6
Peace rallies	–	2	–	–
University course/school	–	–	–	4
No source identified	26	24	60	21

3. Who occupy the occupied territories?

Response	British sample 2001 (%)	British sample 2002 (%)	German sample 2002 (%)	American sample 2002 (%)
Israelis	19	29	47	39
Palestinians	15	16	26	43
Don't know/other	66	55	27	18

British sample 2001

Within the 19 per cent (57) who stated Israelis, 1 per cent (4) specified Israeli army/soldiers; 15 per cent (45) thought that the Palestinians occupied the occupied territories. Of the 66 per cent (198) who noted an alternative answer:

- 15 per cent (45) stated refugees
- 11 per cent (33) simply stated army/military/soldiers:
    - military of some kind
    - US army (4)
    - foreign soldiers
    - invading army
    - troops from somewhere

- 14 per cent (42) 'other' answers included asylum seekers, Afghans, white South African farmers, Afrikaners, terrorists and Iraqis and Macedonians
- 26 per cent (78) did not offer an answer

British sample 2002

Within the 29 per cent (81) who stated Israelis, 5 per cent (15) specified Israeli army/soldiers; 16 per cent (46) thought that the Palestinians occupied the occupied territories. Of the 55 per cent (153) who noted an alternative answer:

- 9 per cent (26) stated refugees
- 8 per cent (22) stated army/military/soldiers
- 3 per cent (8) thought US armed forces or UN
- 11 per cent (31) 'other' answers included white South Africans (5), gypsies and Iraqis
- 24 per cent (66) did not offer an answer.

4. What nationality are the settlers?

Response	British sample 2001 (%)	British sample 2002 (%)	German sample 2002 (%)	American sample 2002 (%)
Israeli	20	35	44	55
Palestinian	29	38	27	22
Don't know/other	51	27	29	23

British sample 2001

20 per cent (61) noted the Israelis as being the settlers; 29 per cent (88) that the Palestinians were the settlers.

Of the remaining 51 per cent (151) the majority did not offer an answer. However, the following were suggested: Zimbabwean, Pakistani (3), mixed Races/nationalities (7), Asian/Indian (2), the Taliban (2), Iranian (2), Afghani (11) Albanians, Kurds (2), Dutch South Africans, Kosovan refugees (2), Croatians, Americans (3).

British sample 2002

35 per cent (98) noted the Israelis as being the settlers; 38 per cent (107) that the Palestinians were the settlers.

Of the remaining 27 per cent (75) the majority (59) did not offer an answer. However, the remaining participants suggested the following: Africans (white farmers), Afghanis (2), Americans (5) (they thought US forces were the occupiers), Asians (2), South Africans (2), Dutch, Turks, Iraqis, and 4 thought both the Palestinians and Israelis were the settlers.

Summary of questions 3 and 4

Response	British sample 2001 (%)	British sample 2002 (%)	German sample 2002 (%)	American sample 2002 (%)
The Israelis occupy the occupied territories and the settlers are Israeli.	9	11	26	29
The Palestinians are the settlers and occupy the occupied territories	11	8	12	12
The Israelis occupy the occupied territories but the Palestinians are the settlers	11	19	12	18
The Palestinians occupy the occupied territories but the Israelis are the settlers	6	9	8	23
The remaining participants answered either Q3 or Q4 or neither question	63	53	42	18

5. Which side has had the most casualties? Is it a lot more Israelis, a few more Israelis, about the same for each side, a few more Palestinians or a lot more Palestinians?

Response	British sample 2001 (%)	British sample 2002 (%)	German sample 2002 (%)	American sample 2002 (%)
A lot more Palestinians	8	35	24	18
A few more Palestinians	32	21	12	31
A lot more Israelis	2	6	9	8
A few more Israelis	9	14	7	27
About same on each side	22	23	35	12
No response/limited answer	27	1	13	4

6. Where did the Palestinian refugees come from? How did they become refugees?

Response	British sample 2001 (%)	British sample 2002 (%)	German sample 2002 (%)	American sample 2002 (%)
Displaced from homes on the formation of Israel	4	8	26	19

| Forced from homes by Israel/occupation | 14 | 22 | 3 | 16 |
| Don't know/general references to refugees/war | 82 | 70 | 71 | 65 |

British sample 2001

Of the 14 per cent (43) who wrote that the Palestinians were forced from their homes by Israel, a small number, 5 per cent (16) of participants used the term 'occupation', and a further 2 per cent (7) of participants noted that it was a military occupation. One participant stated 'when Israel extended to the East/Gaza Strip'. The remaining 7 per cent (21) used the following phrases: 'displaced', 'seized', 'taken', 'pushed out/off', 'forced out' (10) and 'conflict caused dispersion'.

82 per cent (246) either did not know or referred generally to war/conflict and the problems of refugees. Of these 30 per cent (91) referred generally to war and conflict in terms such as:

- fight between the two governments
- through armed conflict (bombing)
- fleeing from oppressive regime
- running away from war
- driven out by fear of war and hunger
- they fled from somewhere because they were Muslim
- Palestinians became refugees as they were trying to escape war/poverty in their own country

The remaining 20 per cent (58) referred to war and conflict in terms of Afghanistan, Iraq, Kosovo 'war torn regions', '[Came from] other Middle Eastern countries affected by war'. Three participants thought the refugees were Afghani and one thought they were Jews from Europe; 32 per cent (97) gave no answer.

British sample 2002

Of the 22 per cent (61) who wrote that the Palestinians were forced from their homes by Israel/occupation, 7 per cent (19) of participants referred to this in terms of the 'occupation', and a further 5 per cent (15) of participants described it as a military occupation. The remaining 10 per cent (27) used the following phrases: 'displaced', 'evicted' 'kicked out', 'taken over' (7) , 'pushed out/off', 'forced out' (9), 'deported'; 'excluded'.

70 per cent (196) either did not know or referred generally to war/conflict and the problems of refugees. Of these, 22 per cent (62) referred to war and conflict in a similar way to the 2001 sample; for example:

- homes ruined by war
- they're fleeing homes because of war
- refugees through war, left their country to seek a better lifestyle
- to escape the war zones
- driven away by conflict

48 per cent (134) gave no answer.

7. TV news has shown pictures of the Palestinians burning the American flag – why would Palestinians do this?

Response	British sample 2001 (%)	British sample 2002 (%)	German sample 2002 (%)	American sample 2002 (%)
Military/monetary support for Israel	13	15	9	8
Support for Israel (unspecified)	24	23	60	38
Alternative response/no response	63	62	31	54

British sample 2001

Of the 13 per cent who stated that the US was supplying Israel with military/monetary aid, 7 per cent (23) noted that the US also supplied Israel with arms and 6 per cent (19) noted monetary aid. Two of this number suggested the extent of the financial support:

- US gives $3 billion foreign aid to Israel each year. Over 40 per cent of US foreign aid ... [to] Israel, 16th richest nation in the world.
- $5 billion of US 'Aid' used a year by the Israelis against the Palestinians.

In this sample 24 per cent (71) were non-specific about US support for Israel and used terms which do not directly imply military/monetary support:

- Americans seen to be helpful towards Israelis
- Americans operate a pro-Israeli, anti-Palestinian policy
- The US has had a large part to play in the peace process and Palestinians view input as very pro-Israel and biased
- America totally biased in conflict towards Israel (3)
- US has strong connections with Israel (2)
- America is allied to Israel (2)
- The Americans sympathise with the Israelis (3)
- America favouring Israel
- America siding with Israel (12)
- American support of Israeli policy in the 'homeland'
- Americans support and protect their enemies [Israelis]
- America is a supporter of Israel (3)
- US support of Israel, anti-capitalist
- US supported the Jewish in their campaign against Palestine

Of the 63 per cent (187) who offered 'Alternative response/no Response':

- 15 per cent (44) stated the reason as being that the Palestinians oppose US intervention/interference/trying to take charge; 'Resent American intervention in what they see as their business'; 'They hate Americans for trying to take over and interfering'

- 6 per cent (17) thought the Palestinians burned the American flag because the US has not supported them or become involved/intervened in finding a solution to the conflict, 'not helping their economy and debts', 'American refusal to provide arms to Palestinians', 'America withdrew from peace talks', 'America stopped aid'
- 22 per cent (65) stated dislike/disrespect/hatred of US and ideals/way of life/power in the world.
- 7 per cent (21) noted support for the Taliban, 'Osama bin Laden supporters', religious differences, anti-Bush sentiment over proposal to attack Saddam Hussein, support of Iraq in first Gulf War , 'American occupancy of Holy Land'
- 8 per cent (25) noted anti-capitalist sentiment
- 5 per cent (15) did not offer a response

British sample 2002

Of the 15 per cent (42) who stated that the US was supplying Israel with military/monetary aid, 13 per cent (37) stated that the US also supplied Israel with arms and 2 per cent (5) stated monetary aid. One in this sample suggested the extent of the financial support: 'US gives Israel $3 billion military aid a year and supports the occupation'.

In this sample 23 per cent (65) were non-specific about US support for Israel and used terms which do not directly imply military/monetary support:

- US has a big Jewish population and tends to side with the Israelis
- Americans side with Jewish (9)
- US sympathetic towards Israelis (2)
- US is pro-Israeli ... they [Palestinians] believe they are anti-Muslim
- US prejudice in favour of Israel
- They see US as an ally of Israel (2)
- The 'special relationship' and continued support of Israel
- America favours the Israelis in this conflict
- The US comes down on the side of the Israelis
- US are friends with Israel
- US sticking up for Israel
- US supportive of Israel
- US supports Israel over conflict; more lenient to Israel because of strong lobbying in US from Jewish groups
- US supporting Israel and they hate all things Western
- US supports Israelis ... way of life [US] totally against their religion
- US supports Israeli government

Of the 62 per cent (173) who offered 'Alternative response/no response':

- 7 per cent (21) because the Palestinians oppose US intervention/ interference/trying to take charge/US dictate and responsible for the conflict
- 15 per cent (41) thought the Palestinians burned the American flag because the US has not supported them [Palestinians] or because they had become involved/intervened in finding a solution to the conflict

- 13 per cent (37) simply stated dislike/disrespect/hatred of US and ideals/ way of life/power in the world
- 13 per cent (36) of this number some noted support for the Taliban, 'celebrate World Trade Center "bombing"', US support for the Palestinians, anti-Bush sentiment over proposal to attack Saddam Hussein
- 9 per cent (25) noted anti-capitalist sentiment
- 5 per cent (13) did not offer a response

American sample 2002

Of the 8 per cent who stated that the US was supplying Israel with military/ monetary aid, 4 per cent noted that the US also supplied Israel with arms and 4 per cent noted monetary aid.

In this sample 38 per cent were non-specific about US support for Israel and used terms which did not directly imply military/monetary support:

- The US allies itself with Israel (6 per cent)
- America sides with Israel (14 per cent)
- US was too involved and supports Israel

Of the 54 per cent who offered 'Alternative response/no response':

- 17 per cent stated dislike/disrespect/hatred of US and ideals/way of life/power in the world:
  - because they are Muslim and against US ideals
  - US is evil and treating them unfairly
  - they don't like democracy or all our [US] freedoms
- 35 per cent because the Palestinians oppose US intervention/ interference/trying to takes charge/US dictate and responsible for the conflict because they introduced the immigrants:
  - US trying to interfere and help fix the problem
  - [Palestinians] detest pro-Israeli bias in peace-making diplomatic efforts
  - Palestinians think it is not the US's business to be involved, they [US] are merely an interference
  - they don't like how the Americans want the conflict resolved and their interference
  - dislike the West's intrusion into their lives
- one participant noted anti-capitalist sentiment
- 2 per cent did not offer a response

German sample 2002

Of the 9 per cent who stated that the US was supplying Israel with military/ monetary aid, 8 per cent noted that the US also supplied Israel with arms and 1 per cent noted monetary aid.

In this Sample 60 per cent were non-specific about US support for Israel and used terms which did not directly imply military/monetary support:

- political support for Sharon (2)
- friend of Israel
- solidarity with Israel (2)
- US allied with Israel (3)
- US sided with Israel (7)
- US supports Israel (44)
- because the US helped to form the Israeli State (9)

Of the 31 per cent who offered 'Alternative response/no response':

- 11 per cent stated dislike/disrespect/hatred of US and ideals/way of life/power in the world:
    - Palestinians don't want to be supported by American way of life
    - betrayed of their rights by American government
    - do not agree on US's political system
    - hate America and their mentality
- 6 per cent stated it was because they [Palestinians] object to American interference:
    - US is involving itself in the whole conflict
    - don't want the US to try and solve this conflict
- 14 per cent did not offer a response

Appendix 2:
Answers to Questions on the Israeli-Palestinian Conflict by Focus Groups

1. What comes into your mind when you hear the words 'Israeli-Palestinian conflict'?

Response	Student groups (26)	Elderly/ retired (10)	Low-income groups (21)	Middle-class male groups (16)	Middle-class female groups (21)	Middle-class mixed (6)
Conflict, war/violence	15	8	12	10	13	5
Suicide-bombings	4	–	4	2	2	–
Conflict over land	–	–	–	–	1	–
Religious conflict	4	–	2	1	1	1
Personalities: Arafat, Sharon, Bush	1	1	1	1	1	–
Non-specific: simply stated, Muslims/Arabs	–	–	–	–	–	–
Environment: sand, sun, etc.	1	–	–	–	–	–
Flags: Israeli, etc./maps	–	–	1	1	–	–
Poverty	–	–	–	–	–	–
World Trade Center: Bin Laden	–	–	–	1	–	–
Emotional statement: injustice, tragedy, etc.	–	–	1	–	3	–
No response	1	1	–	–	–	–

2a. Source of images.

Response	Student groups (26)	Elderly/ retired (10)	Low-income groups (21)	Middle-class male groups (16)	Middle-class female groups (21)	Middle-class mixed (6)
Television news	22	7	15	9	18	5
Newspapers	1	1	2	4	3	–
General media	1	–	2	2	–	1
Documentaries	–	–	–	–	–	–
Books/magazines	–	–	1	1	–	–
Personal experience	–	–	–	–	–	–
Indirect experience (friends/relatives)	1	–	1	–	–	–
Radio	–	1	–	–	–	–
Internet	–	–	–	–	–	–
Peace rallies	–	–	–	–	–	–
No source identified	1	1	–	–	–	–

270

2b. What additional sources have you used?

Response	Student groups (26)	Elderly/ retired (10)	Low-income groups (21)	Middle-class male groups (16)	Middle-class female groups (21)	Middle-class mixed (6)
Television news	–	2	4	1	3	–
Newspapers	12	1	5	7	15	–
Documentaries	2	–	1	–	–	1
Internet	2	–	–	2	1	–
Books/journals	1	–	–	1	1	–
Personal experience	–	–	1	2	–	1
Indirect experience: (friends/relatives)	2	–	1	2	–	2
Radio	–	–	–	1	1	2
Peace Rallies	–	–	–	–	–	–
No source identified	7	7	9	–	–	–

Student groups

Two stated indirect experience as being: 'sister over in Israel'; 'Jewish friend who has lived in Israel'. Of the two participants who stated documentaries as a secondary source of images/information, one specified *Blue Peter* documentaries. One participant noted BBC Online as a secondary source.

Low-income groups

One participant stated personal experience as being: 'visit to region – talking to the people'. One participant stated indirect experience as being: 'Arabic friends'.

Middle-class male groups

Two participants stated personal experience as being: 'have visited the region several times'; 'visited Israel, personal emails from contacts'. Two participants stated indirect experience as being: 'a friend in the army with some knowledge of the area'; 'verbal first-hand stories told to me' 'other photographers' experiences ... photo essays from Palestine/Israel'. A further two participants noted in addition to their responses: 'Dad visited recently'; 'talked to people of the states involved'. Two participants who noted Internet specified BBC Online News and Guardian Online.

Middle-class female groups

The majority of participants in this group used newspapers as a secondary source of images/information. One participant noted *Time* magazine as a secondary source of images/information. Two participants who stated newspapers as a secondary source noted that they only read them occasionally.

Middle-class mixed group (teachers)

One participant stated personal experience as being: 'been to Israel and West Bank a number of times (had an MA in Middle Eastern Studies)'. Two participants stated indirect experience as being: 'brother-in-law from the

Middle East'; 'corresponded with a missionary teacher in Tabetha school in Israel (Church of Scotland school)'. Two participants who noted the radio as a source of information referred to the BBC World Service.

3. Who occupy the occupied territories?

Response	Student groups (26)	Elderly/ retired (10)	Low-income groups (21)	Middle-class male groups (16)	Middle-class female groups (21)	Middle-class mixed (6)
Israeli	6	9	7	15	9	4
Palestinian	5	–	7	1	7	1
Don't know/other	15	1	7	–	5	1

4. What nationality are the settlers?

Response	Student groups (26)	Elderly/ retired (10)	Low-income groups (21)	Middle-class male groups (16)	Middle-class female groups (21)	Middle-class mixed (6)
Israeli	6	6	7	13	6	4
Palestinian	5	2	7	2	8	1
Don't know/other	15	2	7	1	7	1

Summary of questions 3 and 4

Response	Student groups (26)	Elderly/ retired (10)	Low-income groups (21)	Middle-class male groups (16)	Middle-class female groups (21)	Middle-class mixed (6)
Those who understood that the Israelis occupy the territories, and that the settlers are Israeli	4	6	5	13	7	4
Those who think the Palestinians are the settlers and occupy the occupied territories	2	–	3	1	7	1
Those who stated that the Israelis occupy the occupied territories but that the Palestinians are the settlers	2	2	1	1	1	–
Those who stated that the Palestinians occupy the occupied territories but that the Israelis are the settlers	1	–	2	–	–	–
Answered either Q3 or Q4 or neither question	17	2	10	1	6	1

5. Which side has had the most casualties? Is it a lot more Israelis, a few more Israelis, about the same for each side, a few more Palestinians or a lot more Palestinians?

Response	Student groups (26)	Elderly/ retired (10)	Low-income groups (21)	Middle-class male groups (16)	Middle-class female groups (21)	Middle-class mixed (6)
More Palestinians	8	5	10	13	9	5
More Israelis	5	–	5	2	4	–
About the same on each side	8	3	6	1	7	1
No response/limited answer	5	2	–	–	1	–

6. Why are they fighting? What is the conflict about?

Response	Student groups (26)	Elderly/ retired (10)	Low-income groups (21)	Middle-class male groups (16)	Middle-class female groups (21)	Middle-class mixed (6)
Palestinians displaced from homes on the formation of Israel	4	–	2	6	4	3
Palestinians forced from home by Israeli occupation	1	3	1	4	2	–
Dispute over land	15	5	11	5	11	2
Religious dispute	3	–	5	1	2	1
Other/don't know	3	2	2	–	2	–

7. Can you name any of the wars involving Israel since the Second World War?

Response	Student groups (26)	Elderly/ retired (10)	Low-income groups (21)	Middle-class male groups (16)	Middle-class female groups (21)	Middle-class mixed (6)
4 wars identified	–	–	–	2	–	2
3 wars identified	–	–	–	3	–	–
2 wars identified	2	2	1	6	1	1
1war identified	3	5	2	5	3	2
No response/other	21	3	18	–	17	1

8. What countries were occupied during these wars?

Response	Student groups (26)	Elderly/ retired (10)	Low-income groups (21)	Middle-class male groups (16)	Middle-class female groups (21)	Middle-class mixed (6)
4 countries identified	–	–	–	6	–	1
3 countries identified	2	–	–	3	–	3
2 countries identified	3	2	–	3	–	2
1 country identified	–	3	1	1	1	–
No response/other	21	5	20	3	20	2

9. Do you know of United Nations resolutions or criticisms made by the UN of the actions of anyone in the conflict?

Response	Student groups (26)	Elderly/ retired (10)	Low-income groups (21)	Middle-class male groups (16)	Middle-class female groups (21)	Middle-class mixed (6)
4 or more resolutions	–	–	–	–	–	–
3 resolutions	–	–	–	–	–	–
2 resolutions	–	–	–	1	–	–
1 resolutions	3	–	1	4	–	2
No response	23	10	20	11	21	4

10. Can you explain the image of the American flag being burnt?

Response	Student groups (26)	Elderly/ retired (10)	Low-income groups (21)	Middle-class male groups (16)	Middle-class female groups (21)	Middle-class mixed (6)
Military/monetary support for Israel	3	1	–	10	3	1
Support for Israel (unspecified)	–	3	5	5	1	2
Alternative response/ no response	23	6	16	1	17	3

11. Are you aware of any issues regarding water in the area?

Response	Student groups (26)	Elderly/ retired (10)	Low-income groups (21)	Middle-class male groups (16)	Middle-class female groups (21)	Middle-class mixed (6)
Aware of the significance of water	–	–	–	7	1	1
Some awareness of the significance of water	–	–	–	–	–	–
Not aware of the significance of water	26	10	21	9	20	5

Middle-class male groups

Seven participants had an understanding of the significance of water, for example:

- Israel uses the water supply in the West Bank ... while siphoning off large amounts for its settlers in occupied territories
- Israel controls the infrastructure of the occupied territories and so controls the supply of water necessary for the irrigation of crops in Palestinian territories
- have read Palestinian families having water cut off for hours each day ... Israeli settlements, people swimming in pools. Water is being used as a weapon by Israel
- Israel monopolising water supply for agriculture and domestic supply
- Arab states believe Israel is taking more than its agreed share from mutual sources
- Israel accused of cutting off water supplies

One participant referred to water as being significant during discussion session.

Middle-class female groups

One participant referred to water during discussion session.

Middle-class mixed group

One participant referred to water.

Appendix 3:
Black Holes of History:
Public Understanding and
the Shaping of Our Past

In March 1999, President Clinton made a public apology in Guatemala. It was an extraordinary event and we asked a group of 280 young people why he might have done this. We were engaged in a study of what people knew about the history of their world and this was one of a series of questions which we put to groups of students. Very few of them knew why Clinton had apologised. Three per cent wrote correctly that it was because of US involvement in 'dirty wars' in support of right-wing regimes; 10 per cent believed he was apologising for the Monica Lewinsky affair, a subject which people knew much more about; the majority simply did not know. Yet Clinton's apology was remarkable. It followed the publication of a report by an independent commission which concluded that the US was responsible for most of the human rights abuses during a 36-year-old civil war in which 200,000 people died. Clinton was reported as saying:

> It is important that I state clearly that support for military forces or intelligence Units which engaged in violent and widespread repression of the kind described in the report was wrong. (quoted in the *Guardian*, 12 March 1999)

At the same time the US government declassified documents which showed the US had 'initiated and sustained a murderous war conducted by Guatemalan security forces against civilians suspected of aiding left-wing guerrilla movements' (*Guardian*, 12 March 1999). The documents revealed that the US set up a safe house in the presidential palace in Guatemala City which became the headquarters for the 'dirty war'. A state department cable from October 1967 showed that security operations included 'kidnapping, torture and summary execution'. Twenty-five years later, a CIA cable confirmed that civilian villages were targeted because of the army's belief that the Maya Indian inhabitants were aiding guerrillas. As the *Guardian* also reported:

> A report released this month by the Guatemala Truth Commission confirmed that entire communities were massacred. It said children were killed, abducted, forcibly recruited as soldiers, illegally adopted and sexually abused. Foetuses were cut from their mothers' wombs and young children were smashed against walls or thrown alive into pits. (*Guardian*, 12 March 1999)

Such events are intensely controversial and their history is often contested. Yet in this case the source was the US president and the documentary proof came from the US government itself. We put the same question to a group of 49 American journalism and media students and to another group of 114 high school students from Germany. In these samples 8 per cent of those from the US knew the correct answer and 4 per cent of the Germans, but the great majority did not know or thought it was related to Monica Lewinsky.

The United States has been involved in many 'dirty wars' in Latin America and there have been extensive accusations of human rights abuses. Right-wing military regimes were supported in countries such as Brazil while some elected regimes were attacked or displaced as in Nicaragua and Chile. In another question we asked: 'Who were the Contras in Nicaragua?' These were the private army financed by the US in the 1980s to attack the left-wing Sandinista government. The great majority of the students had not heard of them. We also found that the abuses of the Soviet communist system had apparently vanished into a similar black hole. We asked: 'What were the Gulags in the Soviet Union?' These were the slave labour camps which were established under Stalin's regime and which Solzhenitsyn wrote of in his books, *The First Circle* and *The Gulag Archipelago*. Five per cent of the British students and 8 per cent of the Americans knew what they were. The German students were better informed and 30 per cent gave the correct answer.

Popular history is likely to be shaped by the priorities and interests of those who produce it. In controversial areas it may serve to legitimise past actions or to celebrate them. This is expressed in the phrase 'history is written by the victors'. When beliefs about historical events do exist they are likely to have been coloured by the cultural struggles which characterize the writing of history and its popular construction. Beliefs about a major conflict such as the Second World

War can also vary between different societies. This is partly because history is told from the side and perspectives of those involved. We are taught about the famous battles that involved 'our' soldiers and watch popular films and TV programmes about them. But such memories were also affected by a second level of cultural struggle which developed after the war. This was the Cold War between East and West, which provided another filter for our perception. In the Second World War, the Soviet Union was allied with the United States and Britain in a common struggle against fascism. But after the war, the West and East were divided as ideological enemies. This meant that the contribution of the Soviet Union to the winning of the Second World War was not only neglected but was actually obliterated in some popular accounts. We can look, for example, at the manner in which anniversaries of the war were conducted. The fortieth anniversary of D-Day was on 6 June 1984. The early 1980s was a period in which the American Right had become dominant under President Reagan. This signalled an intensification of the Cold War, an intention to increase defence expenditure and extensive rhetoric on the 'evil empire' of the Soviet Union. When President Reagan attended the D-Day ceremonies in Europe, the commemoration of what was actually a joint struggle against the Nazis was turned into a straightforward attack on the Soviet Union. This is an extract from President Reagan's speech that was shown on British television news:

> The Soviet troops that came to the centre of this continent did not leave when peace came. They are still there, uninvited, unwanted, unyielding almost 40 years after the war. (ITN/Channel 4 News, 6 June 1984)

The effect was to remove consideration of the role of the Soviet armies in the actual war. This was discussed at the time by an 'alternative' weekly news programme made by Channel 4, under the title *Diverse Reports* (27 June 1984). Its role was to highlight issues that were missing from other news programmes. It produced a feature on the D-Day story and began by pointing to gaps in national news coverage. For example, the programme showed a report by ITN/Channel 4 News that stated: 'The Union Jack rose under the Queen's proud and watchful eye, to join the flags of all the nations who fought and defeated Hitler' (7.00 p.m., 6 June 1984). The programme commented 'not quite all; the Soviet flag was missing' (*Diverse Reports*, 27 June

1984). The programme then went on to describe the decisive role of the Soviet Union in the combat. It noted that the Battle of Stalingrad in 1943 was a key defeat for the Nazis in which they lost an elite army of a quarter of a million men. This was followed by the Battle of Kursk Bulge which was reported to be the biggest tank battle of all time. The German army was again routed and a significant proportion of its ground armour destroyed. D-Day was still a year away. By 1945 the Western allies had defeated 170 German divisions; the Soviets had defeated 607. The Soviet losses were enormous, with an estimated 20 million dead (compared to around 1 million for the Western forces).

Ten years after Reagan's speech, President Clinton came to Europe for the fiftieth anniversary of the D-Day celebrations. By then the Soviet bloc had collapsed, but the US president's speech still highlighted the role of the Allies and spoke of them as 'beginning to end' the war: 'Here the miracle of liberation began ... the forces of democracy landed ... on beaches such as these an army landed from the sea to begin to end a war' (BBC1 5.45 p.m., 6 June 1994). We asked the students the question: 'In the Second World War, which Allied country defeated the most German divisions?' Just 18 per cent of the American students and 29 per cent of the British gave the answer as the Soviet Union (65 per cent of the American students and 48 per cent of the British put Britain or the US). Interestingly, the German students were better informed and 73 per cent named the Soviet Union.

We also asked about the war in Vietnam, which the Americans eventually withdrew from in 1975. It is believed that the US dropped 3 million tons of explosives in this war which would have been more than the total tonnage dropped by the US and Britain in the Second World War (including the atomic bombs). In Vietnam, just under 60,000 Americans were killed. Vietnamese deaths were estimated at over 2 million. The question we put to the students was: 'In the Vietnam War, how many casualties were there on each side. Was it a lot more Americans, a few more Americans, about the same for each side, a few more Vietnamese or a lot more Vietnamese?' To this, 37 per cent of the US students replied that it was more Americans or that the numbers were about equal. The same percentage replied that it was 'a lot more Vietnamese'. The remainder thought it was 'a few more Vietnamese' or did not know. For the British, 34 per cent though it was 'a lot more Vietnamese' and for the German students it was 36 per cent. In our popular culture, US films have portrayed American forces as involved in heroic and bloody action against a deadly enemy. They do not typically discuss the millions of Vietnamese – mostly civilians – who were killed or injured. When the British students were told of the actual casualties, an audible gasp came from them. What is clear is that many of these young people, including the Americans, had no idea of the scale of death which had been imposed on Vietnam. In conclusion, it is clear that a limited knowledge of history can produce great confusion about past conflicts and, as we have seen elsewhere in this volume, about the origins of those which are still with us. Another very obvious issue to emerge from this part of our study is the difference in levels of knowledge between the students of different countries. The German students were from a high school and were being asked (and were answering) the questions in English. Yet in many questions a higher proportion gave correct answers compared with older British and American students who were at universities. This perhaps reflects in part the fact that in Germany, history and political studies are compulsory subjects until the age of 17. It is a matter of real concern if young people understand so little of the world in which they live and their judgements are shaped by the distorted history they are given. The democracy and human rights which some in the world enjoy are still fragile and subject to challenge. They were fought for under the slogan 'Knowledge is Power'.

The tables below give a fuller account of these results.

8. What were the Gulags in the Soviet Union? (as a percentage)

Response	British sample 2001	British sample 2002	German sample 2002	American sample 2002
Slave labour/prison camps	7	5	30	8
Other answers				
Rebels/terrorists	6	10	6	2
The army	1	6	3	2
Secret police	1	4	2	4
Working class	–	2	–	–
No answer given	85	73	59	84

9. In the Vietnam War how many casualties were there on each side? Was it a lot more Americans, a few more Americans, about the same for each side, a few more Vietnamese or a lot more Vietnamese?

Response	British sample 2001	British sample 2002	German sample 2002	American sample 2002
A lot more Vietnamese	21	34	36	37
A few more Vietnamese	31	32	14	14
About equal numbers	7	6	3	11
A few more Americans	10	11	3	6
A lot more Americans	8	16	9	20
No answer given	23	1	35	12

10. Who were the Contras in Nicaragua?

Response	British sample 2001	British sample 2002	German sample 2002	American sample 2002
Anti-communist 'freedom fighters' funded by Reagan, trained by the CIA, to overthrow Sandinista government	1	1	–	6
Freedom fighters/ rebels/guerrillas	11 (4% stated freedom fighters, 7% guerrillas)	10 (1% stated freedom fighters, 8% rebels against government)	2 (Rebels)	16 (Rebels, guerrillas)
Other answers (For example, drug lords, political group, army, local tribal people, communist group, Dictatorship in country, farmers, peacekeepers, secret police, drugs	10	9	7	12
No answer given	78	80	91	66

11. In 1999 President Clinton made a public apology in Guatemala
– why?

Response	British sample 2001	British sample 2002	German sample 2002	American sample 2002
US gave support to a brutal military regime under which there was much abuse of human rights	4	3	4	8
Because he lied about affair with Monica Lewinsky	1	10	11	6
US military action against/ accidental bombing	9	10	3	–
America using country for nuclear testing	1	–	–	–
Other answers (slavery, regime change, exploited them, etc)	6	8	–	18
No answer given	79	69	82	68

British sample 2001

4 per cent (12) showed some understanding of US involvement in
Guatemala:

- the USA backed a dictatorship
- American sanctions and military presence which caused many
  deaths – domino theory
- the US supported a military regime and there was much abuse
  of human rights
- America supported an oppressive regime
- human rights violations in the country whilst under American
  guardianship
- American interference in a conflict there
- America had a large interference in Latin American countries
  over fruit companies
- American intervention, slaughtered lots of people
- atrocities in Cold War
- American war atrocities, war crimes
- US oppression of socialism
- American war crimes

The following are the 'other' answers (6 per cent) (17):

- US involvement in slavery: 'For the US using them as slaves in the past' (4)
- America financed Contra rebels
- for not letting the Cubans into America/revolutionary movement against the government
- gave aid to their opponents
- sanctions against their country and inhabiting their land
- for deserting them when they needed help
- for being campaigners to change political regime (4)
- the US quelled fighting, Guatemala wanted independence
- financial backing in the conflict went to rebel group to fight America's war for them
- because the Americans exploited them (2)

British sample 2002

3 per cent (8) showed some understanding of US involvement in Guatemala:

- the US installed a brutal dictatorship in the 1950s to protect United Fruit
- for US supporting the military dictatorship in that country
- US responsibility, involvement in loss of life there
- for 'involving' them in a conflict which killed many of their people
- for casualties due to US intervention
- admitting to atrocities committed by US in the country
- in the 1960s the US government brought down the democratically elected regime through subterfuge
- for trying to control their country with military presence

The following are the 'other' answers, (8 per cent) (21):

- for American history of mistreating the people there
- for American sanctions on Cuba
- Cuban missile crisis and American attitude to Cuba
- trade embargoes (3)
- lack of American support to the country in order to fight the guerrillas
- for enforcing regime change

- for loss of life during Vietnam conflict (2)
- for not helping the government avoid a military coup
- for not helping them with money and aid to the country/caused death of people by not assisting with aid (5)
- Americans using force during Cold War
- for Guatemalans being slaves/slave labour (3)
- supporting opposition

German sample

4 per cent showed some understanding of US involvement in Guatemala:

- because America contributed heavily to the civil war with weapons and undermined peace
- US troops invaded and tried to help a government and civilians died
- because of the US trade unification of whole American continent

American sample

Nine people gave the following comments:

- US involvement in their country's government affairs
- some conflict in which US became involved and it went bad
- for what happened in civil war – US failure to involve themselves in the genocide
- for loss of life in the revolution and US failure to assist
- failed to put down an uprising that threatened US investments in the banana industry
- ownership of the Panama Canal
- for US attack on country to put down an uprising that threatened US investments in the banana industry
- economic neglect (2)

12. In the Second World War, which Allied country defeated the most German divisions?

Response	British sample 2001	British sample 2002	German sample 2002	American sample 2002
Soviet Union	32	29	73	18
Other answers	68	71	27	82
Britain	31	31	6	49
US	16	17	16	16
France	9	16	2	10
No answer given	12	7	3	7

Notes

PREFACE

1. For a discussion of issues in popular culture and audience response, including the active audience, resistance and post-modern accounts see Philo and Miller (2001).

CHAPTER 1: HISTORIES OF THE CONFLICT

1. In a letter dated 24 October 1915 McMahon laid out the areas that Britain planned to grant independence: 'The two districts of Mersina and Alexandretta and portions of Syria lying west of the districts of Damascus, Homs, Hama and Aleppo cannot be said to be purely Arab, and should be excluded from the limits demanded. With the above modification, and without prejudice to our existing treaties with Arab chiefs we accept those limits. As for the regions lying within those frontiers wherein Britain is free to act without detriment to the interests of her ally, France, I am empowered in the name of the Government of Great Britain to give the following assurances and make the following reply to your letter: (1) Subject to the above modifications, Great Britain is prepared to recognize and support the independence of the Arabs in all the regions within the limits demanded by the Sherif of Mecca' (British Government 1939, Cmd. 5974, letter cited in Ingrams, 1972: 2).
2. According to the British census of 1922 the total population of Palestine was 752,048, comprised of 83,790 Jews, 589,177 Muslims and 71,464 Christians (United Nations, 1945).
3. In a memorandum to Lord Curzon on 11 August 1919, Balfour wrote: 'the contradiction between the letters of the Covenant and the policy of the Allies is even more flagrant in the case of the "independent nation" of Palestine than in that of the "independent nation" of Syria. For in Palestine we do not propose even to go through the form of consulting the wishes of the present inhabitants of the country, though the American [King-Crane] Commission has been going through the form of asking what they are' (British Government, Foreign Office, 1919b, cited in Ingrams, 1972: 73).
4. The Revisionist movement were a political rival of Ben-Gurion's Labour movement. They espoused a more militant attitude towards the Arabs and a more liberal economic policy. Much of their support came from Polish immigrants in the 1920s and 1930s. The Revisionists laid claim to all of Palestine and Transjordan and argued that conflict with the Arabs was inevitable. Their military wing Betar was formed in the 1920s. Some Betar members split away in the 1930s to form the Irgun paramilitary group who fought the British mandatory authorities in the 1940s. The

Revisionist movement later provided much of the constituency for the Herut and Likud parties.

5. The Oxford historian Albert Hourani described Joan Peters' book as 'ludicrous and worthless' in the *Observer*. Ian and David Gilmour described it as 'preposterous' in the *London Review of Books*. *Time Out* described it as a 'piece of disinformation roughly the size and weight of a dried cowpat', whilst the chair of the Philosophy department at the Hebrew University, Avishai Margalit, condemned Peters' 'web of deceit' (reviews cited in Finkelstein, 2001: 45–6). McCarthy argues that unrecorded Arab immigration into Palestine during the Mandate period was 'small' and that for it to 'have had a significant effect on the ethnic composition of Palestine it would have had to have been immense'. He concludes that the 'argument that Arab immigration somehow made up a large part of the Palestinian Arab population is thus statistically untenable' (1990: 34). For a discussion of the effects of improvements in sanitation and hygiene on population increase in Palestine see Friedlander and Goldscheider (1979).

6. The US Secretary of State, James Byrnes, wrote to the British Foreign Secretary, Lord Halifax, arguing that American Jewry was not interested in the plight of the refugees in Europe, their main concern was that Jews 'ought to have a country to call their own'. Harold Beeley in the British Foreign Office complained that 'the Zionists have been deplorably successful in selling the idea that even after the Allied victory immigration to Palestine represented for many Jews "their only hope of survival"' (both cited in Ovendale, 1999: 94).

7. The pressure to open up Palestine to the Jewish refugees worried the British who feared the impact on public order. Ovendale (1999) claims that the US War Department had estimated that it would have to send 300,000 troops to Palestine to keep the peace if the area was opened to Jewish immigration. He also suggests that the US State Department was also concerned that an Arab backlash would strengthen Russian influence in a vital geostrategic area and recommended that the British colonial Empire be maintained intact.

8. For a comprehensive overview of the case put forward by the Arab delegates see the Official Records of the General Assembly, Second Session, Ad Hoc Committee on the Palestine Question, pp. 276–9, cited in UN (1990).

9. A number of delegates including Lebanese representatives claimed, during debates at the UN, that representatives from the US and USSR had used bribes and threats of economic sanctions in order to coerce smaller states to vote for the partition of Palestine (Official Records of the General Assembly, Second Session, Plenary Meetings, vol. II, 124th meeting: 1310).

10. For an overview of the concept of transfer in Zionist thinking see Masalha (1992). This perspective is challenged by Karsh (2000).

11. In 1959 the Palestinian historian Walid Khalidi went through the official records of Arab governments as well as Arab newspapers and the radio monitoring reports of the BBC and CIA and could find no evidence of broadcasts urging Palestinians to flee. This research was also

independently corroborated by the Irish scholar Erskine Childers in 1961. For an overview and discussion of the controversy see Hitchens and Said (1988). Some historians such as Gilbert (1999) argue that many Arabs left voluntarily prior to the arrival of the Arab armies in May 1948 without mentioning the impact of the alleged broadcasts.

12. This controversial incident has been the subject of much debate. The Israeli authorities have always maintained that it was a 'tragic case of misidentification'. Bregman (2003: 120–2) notes that others have suggested that it was deliberately undertaken to prevent the *Liberty* from detecting Israeli troop concentrations amassing in Galilee as part of the next day's attack on the Golan Heights. He argues that recently declassified tapes of conversations between air force personnel support the conclusion that the attack on the American ship was deliberate.

13. Yitzak Rabin remarked after Israel's victory that 'I do not believe that Nasser wanted war. The two divisions that he sent into Sinai on May 14 would not have been enough to unleash an offensive against Israel. He knew it and we knew it' (*Le Monde*, 29 February 1968 cited in Hirst 1977: 211). In a 1982 speech at the National Defense College Menachem Begin stated that 'The Egyptian Army concentrations in the Sinai do not prove that Nasser was really about to attack us. We must be honest with ourselves. We decided to attack him' (*New York Times*, 21 August 1982).

14. Menachem Begin claimed that, in the penultimate Ministerial Committee on Defense prior to the war, military leaders 'had no doubt of victory' and 'expressed their belief not only in the strength of the army but also in its ability to rout the enemy' (Begin, cited in Finkelstein, 2001: 135). The former Commander of the Israeli Air Force, Ezer Weizman, has claimed in relation to the 1967 war that 'there was no threat of destruction' to the State of Israel but that the war was justified so that Israel could 'exist according to the scale, spirit and quality she now embodies' (*Ha'aretz*, 29 March 1972, cited in Chomsky, 1999: 100).

15. Norman Finkelstein alleges that Marshall Tito of Yugoslavia put forward a peace plan involving a 'full Israeli withdrawal from the occupied territories in exchange for full demilitarization and other security guarantees in the evacuated territories, as well as an end to the call for an Arab state of Palestine'. He alleges that this proposal was accepted by both Egypt and Jordan but rejected by Israel as 'one-sided' (Finkelstein, 2001: 154).

16. The British representative Lord Caradon denied any ambiguity in the interpretation of Resolution 242, claiming that 'in our resolution we stated the principle of the "withdrawal of Israeli armed forces from territories occupied in the recent conflict" and in the preamble emphasized "the inadmissibility of the acquisition of territory by war". In our view the wording of the provisions is clear.' The French delegate emphasised that 'on the point which the French delegation has always stressed as being essential – the question of the withdrawal of the occupation forces – the resolution which has been adopted, if we refer to the French text which is equally authentic with the English, leaves no room for any ambiguity, since it speaks of withdrawal "des territoires occupes", which indisputably corresponds to the expression "occupied territories"'. The Indian representative asserted that 'the principle of the inadmissibility of

territorial acquisition by force is absolutely fundamental to our approach' and 'it is our understanding that the draft resolution, if approved by the Council, will commit it to the application of the principle of total withdrawal of Israeli forces from all of the territories – I repeat, all the territories – occupied by Israel as a result of the conflict which began on 5 June 1967' (all cited in Finkelstein 2001: 146).

17. Finkelstein points to the memoirs of the American diplomat Dean Rusk who claimed that the United States favoured omitting the definite article in the withdrawal clause because 'we thought the Israeli border along the West Bank could be "rationalised", certain anomalies could easily be straightened out with some exchanges of territory, making a more sensible border for all parties' (Rusk, 1991: 388–9, cited in Finkelstein, 2001: 148). However, he stressed that 'we never contemplated any significant grant of territory to Israel as a result of the June 1967 war. On that point we and the Israelis to this day remain sharply divided' (Rusk, 1991: 388–9, cited in Finkelstein, 2001: 148).

18. See for instance Karsh (2002) or Singer (1997).

19. Chomsky points to an article by Yedidia Segal in the 3 September 1982 issue of *Nekudah*, the journal of the religious West Bank settlers, which stated that 'those among us who call for a humanistic attitude towards our [Arab] neighbours are reading the Halacha [religious law] selectively and are avoiding specific commandments'. Segal argues that the Gentiles are 'a people like a donkey' and that the scriptures insist that 'conquered' peoples must 'serve' their Jewish masters and must be kept 'degraded and low' and 'must not raise their heads in Israel but must be conquered beneath their hand ... with complete submission'. 'There is no relation', Segal insists, 'between the law of Israel and the atheistic modern humanism', citing Maimonides that 'in a divinely-commanded war [such as the 1982 Lebanon invasion] one must destroy, kill and eliminate men, women and children', there being 'no place for any humanistic considerations' (cited in Chomsky, 1999: 123–4).

20. United Nations General Assembly Resolution 54/37 adopted 1 December 1999.

21. Hirst claims that 'In Israel's Arab schools children have always had to see their own Arab culture, history and religion through Israeli eyes: they saw it deliberately mocked and falsified. Arab history became little more than a series of revolutions, murders feuds and plunderings, whilst everything in the Jewish past was ennobled and glorified. It was always the Arabs in decline they learned about, never in their greatness; the heroes of the past, the Prophet, the Caliph Harun al-Rashid and Saladin, got perfunctory mention. In four years of secondary education Arab children had 384 periods of Jewish history as against only 32 of their own. The study of Old Testament was compulsory, while the Muslim and Christian religions were not taught at all' (1977: 238).

22. For instance General Assembly Resolution 53/56 passed 3 December 1998 by 151 votes to 2, Resolution 52/67 passed 10 December 1997 by 151 votes to 2, Resolution 51/134 passed 13 December 1996 by 149 votes to 2, Resolution 49/36C passed 9 December 1994 by 145 votes to 2, Resolution 47/70D passed 14 December 1992 by 142 votes to 2.

23. In the late 1970s a *Sunday Times* report (19 June 1977) found that torture
     was so widespread and systematic that 'it appears to be sanctioned at
     some level as deliberate policy' perhaps 'to persuade Arabs in the occupied
     territories that it is least painful to behave passively'. More recently
     Amnesty International has issued annual reports cataloguing the use of
     torture by the Israeli authorities (for example, Amnesty International 1997,
     1998, 1999b, 2000, 2001a). A report entitled 'Flouting UN Obligations
     in the Name of Security' (Amnesty International, 1999a) concluded that
     Israeli 'interrogation methods, such as violent shaking, or hooding and
     shackling detainees to low chairs with loud music playing, constituted
     torture or cruel, inhuman or degrading treatment or punishment and
     thus contravened Article 1 of the Convention against Torture' and that
     torture is 'officially authorized at the highest level and indeed effectively
     legalized'. In the same report it was noted that the 1,600 Palestinians
     detained by Israeli security forces in 1998 were 'routinely tortured or
     ill-treated during interrogation'. The *Independent* journalist Robert Fisk
     has produced a number of reports from the Israeli-controlled Khiam
     detention centre in Southern Lebanon detailing the use of electric
     shock torture applied to the genitals (*Independent*, 20 May 2000). A BBC
     Correspondent documentary (4 November 2000) also reported from Khiam,
     claiming that torture had also been used against children and pregnant
     women, and that prisoners had been tortured to death, in what Amnesty
     International described as 'war crimes'.
24. The use of 'administrative detention' involved detaining Palestinians
     for long periods without trial or legal recourse. Hirst alleges that in the
     1970s many Palestinians suspected of involvement with opposition
     movements were interned in camps in the desert: 'At its worst it meant
     the establishment of veritable concentration camps buried in remote
     corners of the Sinai desert. Nakhl, Abu Zu'aiman, Kusseimah were the
     names of places where whole families were kept in isolation from the
     outside world. They were there because relatives of theirs were suspected,
     no more, of working for the resistance. Crowded into tents surrounded
     by barbed wire, they were denied radios, newspapers or the most basic
     amenities from their homes, which were frequently destroyed during
     their captivity. Women and children would be put in one camp, male
     relatives of "wanted persons" – brother, nephews, cousins – in another'
     (1977: 248). By 1980 the Israeli daily *Ha'aretz* estimated the number of
     security prisoners or detainees passing through Israeli jails since 1967
     at close to 200,000 people or 20 per cent of the population, leading to a
     situation of 'horrendous overcrowding' and 'appalling human suffering
     and corruption' (8 August 1980, cited in Chomsky, 1999: 128). For more
     recent reports on detention without trial see Amnesty International
     (1999a).
25. Collective punishment could involve curfews where the local population
     is not allowed out for more than an hour or two a day for weeks or
     months at a time, schools are closed and there is no employment.
     Israel has justified the use of curfews on the basis that confining the
     Palestinian population to their homes for long periods prevents militants
     from attacking Jews. The use of collective punishment is illegal under

international law and Israel has drawn repeated censure from the United Nations: 'The United Nations Commission on Human Rights calls upon Israel to cease immediately its policy of enforcing collective punishments, such as demolition of houses and closure of the Palestinian territory, measures which constitute flagrant violations of international law and international humanitarian law, endanger the lives of Palestinians and also constitute a major obstacle in the way of peace' (United Nations, 1999). A report by the Israeli journalist Aharon Bachar in the Israeli daily *Yediot Ahronot* described a meeting where Labour Alignment leaders presented Menachem Begin with 'detailed accounts of terrorist acts [against Arabs] in the conquered territories'. They described the collective punishment in the town of Halhul where 'The men were taken from their houses beginning at midnight, in pyjamas, in the cold. The notables and other men were concentrated in the square of the mosque and held there until morning. Meanwhile men of the border guards broke into houses beating people with shouts and curses. During the many hours that hundreds of people were kept in the mosque square, they were ordered to urinate and excrete on one another and also to sing Hatikva [Jewish National Anthem] and to call out 'Long Live the State of Israel'. Several times people were beaten and ordered to crawl on the ground. Some were even ordered to lick the earth. At the same time four trucks were commandeered and at daybreak, the inhabitants were loaded onto the trucks, about 100 in each truck, and taken like sheep to the Administration headquarters in Hebron' (3 December 1982, cited in Chomsky, 1999: 131). The report further alleged that prisoners were beaten, tortured and humiliated and that settlers were permitted into prisons to take part in the beatings. For more recent reports on collective punishments see Amnesty International (2001b, 2001c) or Human Rights Watch (1996).

26. Hirst cites evidence from the Israeli League for Civil and Human Rights that searches 'were often carried with great brutality and violence'. During night-time raids, Hirst claims that it was a 'regular practice to ... carry men off to prison without any good reason, beat them up and torture them' (1977: 249).

27. After 1967 there were numerous diplomatic efforts to break the deadlock, all of which were fruitless. King Hussein issued a six-point peace plan in early 1969 at the National Press Club in Washington. Speaking officially in conjunction with Egypt's Nasser, Hussein offered a comprehensive peace treaty and recognition of Israel in exchange for 'the withdrawal of its armed forces from all territories occupied in the June 1967 war, and the implementation of all the other provisions of the Security Council Resolution (242)', adding that 'Israel may have either peace or territory – but she can never have both' (*Washington Report on Middle East Affairs*, 2 April 1984). This proposal was rejected by Israel. In December 1969 the US Secretary of State William Rogers put forward another peace agreement based on UN Resolution 242, specifying that Israel would return to the pre-1967 borders (with minor border modifications) and a solution to the Palestinian refugee problem would have to be found in exchange for a comprehensive peace treaty. The proposals were rejected by the

Israeli cabinet who declared that 'if these proposals were carried out, Israel's security and peace would be in grave danger. Israel will not be sacrificed to by any power policy, and will reject any attempt to impose a forced solution upon it' (cited in Shlaim, 2000: 291). In 1971 the Swedish diplomat Dr Gunnar Jarring reported that Egypt had offered Israel a full peace treaty based on Resolution 242, with the stipulation that Israel also had to withdraw from the Sinai and Gaza Strip, settle the refugee problem in line with UN resolutions, and establish a UN force to keep the peace. Israel's reply though positive insisted that 'Israel will not return to the pre-5 June 1967 lines' (Shlaim, 2000: 300). This, Shlaim suggests, doomed the Jarring Initiative. It also drew repeated criticism from the United Nations. The Jarring Initiative was followed by attempts at achieving an interim solution which Shlaim suggests floundered on Israel's refusal to accept a timetable for a permanent settlement, and its desire for territorial revisionism (Shlaim 2000). In 1972 and 1973 there followed a number of openly annexationist pronouncements by Israeli leaders. Moshe Dayan told *Time* magazine in July 1973 'there is no more Palestine. Finished', and in an April 1973 interview he talked of 'a new state of Israel with broad frontiers, strong and solid, with the authority of the Israeli government extending from the Jordan to the Suez Canal' (both cited in Shlaim, 2000: 316). Shlaim suggest that this, together with the later publication of the Galilee document detailing a large expansion of settlement building in the occupied territories, left Sadat little choice but to use force to try and regain the Sinai.

28. Boyle (2002) argues that when the Israeli forces started advancing the Soviets had considered inserting their own force into the conflict leading the Americans to raise their nuclear alert to Def Con Three, the highest state of preparedness. He claims that in the face of this the Soviets backed down but that the world had come perilously close to a nuclear confrontation between the superpowers. Three Israeli and American analysts have also clamed that Israel threatened to use nuclear weapons against Egypt and in fact prepared to do so at the beginning of the 1973 war in order to force the US to provide a massive consignment of conventional weapons, which was forthcoming (Perlmutter et al., 1982).

29. In March 1977 the Palestinian National Council called for an 'independent national state' in Palestine and an Arab-Israeli peace conference. Prime Minister Rabin's reply was that 'the only place the Israelis could meet the Palestinian guerillas was on the field of battle' (*New York Times*, 21 March 1977). In 1977 the PLO leaked a 'peace plan' in Beirut that stated that the (explicitly rejectionist) Palestinian National Covenant would not serve as the basis for interstate relations and that any progression beyond a two state solution 'would be achieved by peaceful means' (*Manchester Guardian Weekly*, 7 August 1977). In November 1978 Tillman claims that Yasser Arafat, in requesting a dialogue with American representatives, issued the following statement: 'The PLO will accept an independent Palestinian state consisting of the West Bank and Gaza, with connecting corridor, and in that circumstance will renounce any and all violent means to enlarge the territory of the state. I would reserve the right, of course, to use non-violent means, that is to say diplomatic and democratic

means, to bring about the eventual unification of all Palestine ... we will give de facto recognition to the State of Israel' (Tillman, 1982: 215–18). In April 1981, after PLO acceptance of the Soviet peace plan, the PLO representative Issam Sartawi declared that 'from this it follows that the PLO has formally conceded to Israel, in the most unequivocal manner, the right to exist on a reciprocal basis'. A week later Sartawi issued a joint statement with the former Israeli general Mattityahu Peled: 'the PLO has made its willingness to accept and recognize the state of Israel on the basis of mutual recognition of each nation's legitimate right of self-determination crystal clear in various resolutions since 1977' (all references cited in Chomsky, 1999: 68–78).

30. Testimony of Dr Chris Giannou before the House Sub-committee on Europe and the Middle East, 13/7/1982 (cited in Chomsky, 1999: 229).

31. For other reports on the ill treatment of detainees see *Der Spiegel*, 14 March 1983; *Haolam Haze*,15 December 1982; or *The Times*, 18 March 1983.

32. On the subject of Palestinian weaponry see Ze'ev Schiff (*Ha'aretz*, 18 July 1982) or Hirsh Goodman (*Jerusalem Post*, 9 July 1982) who suggested the Palestinian 'army' and weapons posed no significant threat to Israel and that many of the claims regarding the scale of weaponry were exaggerated. With regard to ceasefire violations, the *Christian Science Monitor* (18 March 1982) reported that the PLO had observed the ceasefire despite many Israeli provocations. The Abu Nidal group who attempted to assassinate the Israeli ambassador were sworn enemies of the PLO leadership and had previously tried to assassinate Yasser Arafat. All above references cited in Chomsky (1999: 210).

33. All extracts taken from *Do Not Say That You Did Not Know*, a report by the Israeli Committee for solidarity with Bir Zeit, 5 June 1982, cited in Chomsky (1999: 60).

34. See, for instance, 'Report of the Special Committee to investigate Israeli Practices Affecting the Human Rights of the Population of the Occupied Territories', A/RES/38/79, 15 December 1983, or 'Report of the Special Committee to Investigate Israeli Practices Affecting the Human Rights of the Population of the Occupied Territories', A/RES/39/95,14 December 1984, or UN Commission on Human Rights, 'Question of the Violation of Human Rights in the Occupied Arab Territories, Including Palestine', E/CN.4/RES/1985/1, 19 February 1985.

35. A B'Tselem (Israeli human rights group) report on the treatment of children detained by Israeli forces found that 'illegal violence against minors ... many [of whom] are innocent of any crime ... occurs on a large scale'. It found that violence directed against minors, including 'slapping, punching, kicking, hair pulling, beatings with clubs or with iron rods, pushing into walls and onto floors', was 'very common'. It also detailed more severe forms of ill treatment: 'Beating the detainee as he is suspended in a closed sack covering the head and tied around the knees; tying the detainee in a twisted position to an outdoor pipe with hands behind the back for hours and, sometimes, in the rain, at night, and during the hot daytime hours; confining the detainee, sometimes for a few days, in the "lock-up" – a dark, smelly and suffocating cell one and

a half by one and a half meters [five by five feet]; placing the detainee, sometimes for many hours, in the "closet" – a narrow cell the height of a person in which one can stand but not move; and depositing the tied-up detainee for many hours in the "grave" – a kind of box, closed by a door from the top, with only enough room to crouch and no toilet.' The Israeli daily *Hotam* (1 April 1988) reported the beating of a ten-year-old during an army interrogation who was left 'looking like a steak', noting that soldiers 'weren't bothered' when they later found out that the boy was deaf, mute and mentally retarded. Reporting on the treatment of Palestinians as young as 14 arrested 'on suspicion of stone throwing' the Israeli daily *Hadashot* (24 February 1992) cited the testimony of a insider at the Hebron detention centre: 'What happened there ... was plain horror: they would break their clubs on the prisoners' bodies, hit them in the genitals, tie a prisoner up on the cold floor and play soccer with him – literally kick and roll him around. Then they'd give him electric shocks, using the generator of a field telephone, and then push him out to stand for hours in the cold and rain ... . They would crush the prisoners ... turning them into lumps of meat.' All above reports cited in Finkelstein (1996: 47–9).

36. For other references on Hezbullah's influence on Hamas see *Ha'aretz* (21 April 1994) or *Nida' al-Watan* (15 November 1996).

37. Amongst others, the poet Mahmoud Darwish; the PLO's Lebanon representative, Shafiq al-Hut (both of whom resigned from the PLO executive committee in protest); the leader of the Palestinian negotiating team and Gaza Red Crescent Society, Haidar Abd al-Shafi, the Palestinian negotiator, as well as other prominent Fatah and PLO officials.

38. Hezbullah, which also run a network of social services, claim they are trying to protect the local population, many of whom have been expelled from their home by Israel's proxy force the South Lebanon Army. Human rights groups have condemned the expulsions as 'war crimes' and demanded that they stop (Human Rights Watch, 1999). The organization has also condemned both Israel and Hezbullah for targeting civilians.

39. The day before the agreement was signed Human Rights Watch (1998) urged the United States and Israel not to pressure the Palestinian Authority to expand its security crackdown without all sides making a clear commitment to safeguard human rights. Human Rights Watch pointed out that the 'Palestinian Authority's human rights record is already deplorable', and that the 'U.S. doesn't condemn these violations now – will the U.S. condemn violations once it is formally part of the process that creates them?' The Israeli human rights group B'Tselem published a report a month after the signing, pointing to 'mass arbitrary arrests by both the Palestinian Authority and Israel', and alleging that 'the agreement merely pays lip service to human rights, with no intention by any of the parties – Israel, the Palestinian National Authority or the United States – to hold the sides accountable for human rights violations'.

40. Barak claimed that he would not allow the Syrians to reach the waters of the River Tiberias (where Israel draws much of its water); the Syrians claimed that Barak was trying to lure them into an 'Arafat-style' agreement, normalize relations, curb Hezbullah and then we might withdraw.

CHAPTER 2: CONTENT STUDIES

1. Ariel Sharon was subsequently elected as Prime Minister of Israel in January 2001.
2. Thus we quoted a report in the *Financial Times* which noted that 'Shop stewards tell hair-raising stories about managerial failings, and point at the moment to constant assembly track hold-ups caused by non-availability of supplier component parts' (quoted in Philo et al., 1995: 12).
3. The three soldiers were later reported to have been killed either during or shortly after the abduction (www.ujl.org). On 10 November 2003, it was reported that the Israeli government had approved an agreement with Hezbullah to swap hundreds of Palestinian and Lebanese prisoners in exchange for a captured Israeli businessman and the bodies of the servicemen.
4. There were a small number of news items or parts of them which were lost through machine failure or because of sudden changes in programme times. This would not affect our overall conclusions on trends in coverage because the losses were random and news items tended to be repeated with slight variations throughout each day.
5. As a percentage of the coverage they accounted for 1.5 per cent, as measured in lines of text.
6. Of the explanations given, 6.5 per cent of the coverage in this sample described the allocation of blame by one side or the other (including discussions on the roles of Arafat and Sharon). The conflict was explained as a 'cycle of violence' in 2 per cent of the sample (61 lines). Religion was referred to as a cause in 2 per cent of the coverage (80.5 lines). Land, water and economic discontent were referred to in 18 lines (0.5 per cent). Israeli perspectives on security needs were 3 per cent (104.5 lines). The 'occupation' as a cause was 1 per cent (37.25 lines). The remaining text was taken up with studio links (3.5 per cent) and references to associated events, such as the effect of the conflict on oil prices (3 per cent). There were 17.5 lines on the history and origins of the conflict.
7. The use of torture by Israeli forces was outlawed by the Israeli high court in 1999. But after the start of the intifada in October 2000 there were reports that it was again being widely used (*Guardian*, 13 June 2002).
8. See Mike Berry's PhD thesis (Berry, 2004).
9. A similar problem arose when the Israelis constructed what they termed their 'security fence' in 2003. The Palestinians rejected this term, seeing the construction as a new attempt by the Israelis to take more land. It was also referred to by some Palestinian groups as an 'apartheid' wall. The BBC and other media sometimes chose to use the Israeli definition. When BBC Online was questioned over this, the following remarkable reply was given: 'Thank you for your email. We feel we are right to use the term "security fence" as this is what Israel is calling it' (BBC News Online, 8 August 2003). Although, as the BBC notes, they have published the views of those who are critical of the fence, this does not address the problem of the adoption by journalists of the language and explanatory definitions of one side. It should be possible for journalists to include both views. We found this example from ITV news where this was done: 'This is

the Israeli response to the assassination: the checking of all Palestinians driving into the West Bank. *The Israelis call this a security precaution, but there is chaos here and the Palestinians call it collective punishment'* (ITV early evening News, 17 October 2001 – our italics).

10. For interviews and on-screen appearances, as expressed in lines of text, the figures were: Israeli – 105.5, Palestinian – 52.25.

11. Such measures require decisions about what is to be included or excluded from counts, which have to be consistent across all the samples. For this count we included: time, date, place; who or what inflicted the casualties; descriptions of who was killed/injured as given by the reporters and eye-witnesses' accounts/statements by families or others; treatment by emergency services; funerals and mourning and specific references to the events, for example, 'the killing of the soldiers'. We also included estimates of casualties over time, for example, numbers of deaths since the beginning of the intifada. We did not include damage to property rather than people (such as bomb damage to shops); non-specific references to suicide-bombings or attacks, for example, 'Yasser Arafat is under pressure to control the suicide bombers' or claims and counter-claims of killings or massacres, which cancelled each other out (that is, when both sides were represented saying the opposite of each other at the same time). We also excluded from this count general commentaries on the wider ramifications of military action or bombings on world opinion or the peace process.

12. The disparity in deaths and casualties continued through the conflict, though not at the level of the first two weeks. In December 2000, the Israeli human rights group B' Tselem reported that between 29 September and 2 December 2000, 231 Palestinians had been killed and 29 Israelis, while nearly 10,000 Palestinians had been injured and 362 Israelis, (B'Tselem, 2000).

13. As expressed in lines of text, the figures were: Israelis/Jews – 92.5 lines, Palestinians/Arabs – 195.75.

14. The word 'massacre' was used on one occasion but not in relation to events in the intifada. While interviewing a Palestinian who had been injured, an ITV journalist notes: 'Six years ago he took twelve bullets when a Jewish fanatic carried out a massacre'. (ITV early evening News, 4 October 2000).

15. The *Independent* described their position in Israeli society as follows: 'Israel's one million Arabs form a fifth of the population. They are waiters and factory workers, a cheap labour pool that serves a growing consumer society, slogging on, despite civil rights violations and prejudice' (11December 2000).

16. In the sample from October–December 2001 the figures (all measured as lines of text) were: on BBC1 – Israeli 140.75 and Palestinian 53.25, on ITV – Israeli 36 and Palestinian 35.5. In the sample from March 2002 the figures were: on BBC1 – Israeli 22.25 and Palestinian 9, on ITV – Israeli 15 and Palestinian 6. In the sample from April 2002 the figures were: on BBC1 – Israeli 89.25 and Palestinian 50.25, on ITV – Israeli 64.5 and Palestinian 35.5. Taken together the figures were: for the BBC1

- Israeli 252.25 and Palestinian 112.5, and for ITV – Israeli 115.5 and Palestinian 77.

17. Measured in terms of the references, the figures were: Israeli 41 and Palestinian 7. For Sample Three (March 2002) the figures were Israeli 28 and Palestinian 9 (both BBC1 and ITV together).

18. The link between the actions of Israel and the 'global war on terror' being pursued by the US was challenged in an ITN bulletin which we noted above as having posed some critical questions about the conflict. A journalist asked rhetorically: 'Does this have any connection to the wider global war on terror? ... the majority of Israelis certainly believe so, but most of the world considers it a decades old problem with no direct link to Osama bin Laden or his terrorist network' (ITV late News, 3 December 2001). Such referencing of 'world opinion' which is critical of Israeli perspectives is comparatively rare in our samples. US opinion is much more frequently referenced. Indeed, statements from US politicians far outweigh even those from Britain. In the coverage from 2001 and 2002, for example, there were 66 US and 33 British statements (both BBC1 and ITV together). The figures for each channel are: BBC1 – US 34 and British 19, and ITV – US 32 and British 14. In the following example from a later ITV bulletin 'world opinion' is simply equated with that of the US: 'The presence in Jerusalem today of New York mayor Giuliani is further evidence that for now it's the Israelis *who have the world's sympathy*' (ITV main News, 9 December 2001 – our italics).

19. On 5 March 2002, BBC and ITV carried a report that a bomb had been planted at a Palestinian school and this was attributed to 'Jewish extremists' and 'Jewish vigilantes' (ITV main News) and to 'Jewish extremists' (BBC1 lunchtime News). The word 'terrorist' was not used to describe them but was used in the ITV bulletin to describe Palestinians.

20. An Israeli minister was also challenged by the BBC journalist in the report of the five Palestinian children killed on their way to school. The minister states that 'civilians are not there', and the journalist replies: 'Minister, I stood there yesterday, this is an area where children pass to go to school, this is an area where people cultivate. I have stood there and I have seen it. Now is it appropriate that a roadside bomb should be planted in this place?' (BBC1 late News, 23 November 2001).

21. As we have indicated above, Israeli statements substantially outnumber those from Palestinians on the BBC in this sample. For on-screen comments and reported statements, measured as lines of text, the figures were: Israeli 140.75 and Palestinian 53.25.

22. As measured as lines of text, both BBC1 and ITV: Israeli 152.75 and Palestinian 102.75. Individually the figures were: BBC1 – Israeli 94 and Palestinian 64.5, and ITV – Israeli 58.75 and Palestinian 38.25.

23. The breakdown of these figures was: BBC1 – Israelis 61.25 and Palestinians 21.25, and ITV – Israelis 59 and Palestinians 24.75.

24. The figures were: Israeli 28 and Palestinian 9 (both BBC1 and ITV together).

25. In this sample the figures for the coverage of both sides' casualties were: Israeli 128 and Palestinian 117.25 (both BBC1 and ITV together, measured

as lines of text). The BBC had an equal amount of coverage for each side, for ITV the figures were: Israeli 44.75 and Palestinian 34.

26. We counted the on-screen appearances/interviews and reported statements in this period. The Israeli dominance was again apparent – the figures were: Israeli 153.75 and Palestinian 85.75 (measured as lines of text, both BBC and ITV together).

CHAPTER 3: AUDIENCE STUDIES

1. *Palestine is Still the Issue* – ITV broadcast, 16 September 2002.

2. Such values are not 'universal' in the sense that everyone believes in or subscribes to them. They are universal in as much as they have the potential to traverse cultural difference, but they do not always do so. They may be contested by other cultural and political values such as racism. A white colonialist, for example, might not think that the 'value' of universal freedom should be applied to black people.

CHAPTER 4: WHY DOES IT HAPPEN?

1. Relationships became more fraught after the outbreak of the intifada. Journalists accused the Israeli armed forces of deliberate intimidation. We were also told that it was especially difficult for journalists whose work was actually seen in Israel (notably CNN and the BBC). One journalist was said to have taken her name from the door where she lived because of the amount of hate-mail she received. Journalists who are based in Israel tend to live in West Jerusalem. Those who are passing through on short-term assignments often stay in the American Colony hotel in East Jerusalem – a place which Melanie Phillips suggests is often used successfully by Palestinians to establish contacts (*Jewish Chronicle*, 31 October 2003). She also complains that because of a mixture of arrogance and despair the Israelis are not sufficiently committed to their public presentation. She says they take the view that Jews 'are no longer prepared to justify their own existence'. Yet paradoxically she also notes that the Israeli government press office and other ministry spokesmen deluge journalists with information and offers of help (*Jewish Chronicle*, 31 October 2003) The consequence of what she sees as Israel's public relations failure is that those who support Israel are left to run a gauntlet of 'lies and vilification'. Both sides often accuse the other of lying. Joy Wolfe commented to us on 'all the lies' by Palestinians in the portrayal of Jenin. But we also had two very senior journalists saying to us independently that, 'the Israelis lie and lie' and 'the Israelis lie all the time' (August 2003). Other journalists have criticised the quality of Palestinian accounts. What emerges from all this is that both sides complain about the quality of their own public relations and about the actions of the other side, but Israel and its supporters do have a comparatively well-resourced system and their views are well featured on TV news.

2. The Israelis also accused the Palestinians of intimidating journalists, but the FPA was reported to have disputed this and to have laid the blame on the Israelis (*Observer*, 17 June 2001).
3. *The Killing Zone*, Channel 4, 18 May 2003.
4. See, for example, a recent article by David Aaronovitch noting that 'The amount of anti-Semitic literature, journalism and television in Arab countries is voluminous ... what on earth is the blood libel doing in a column in a respected Egyptian mass daily paper, *Al-Ahram*, in a book by the Syrian defence minister and in broadcast sermons from various Palestinian mosques?' (Aaronovitch, 2003).
5. As we have indicated above, in our samples from 2001 and 2002 there was a very strong dominance of reported statements and interviews/on-screen appearances from US politicians, outnumbering even those from Britain (66 US and 33 British).

CHAPTER 5: CONCLUSION

1. In the 2001 and 2002 samples, the figures were: Israeli 367.75 and Palestinian 189.5 (both BBC1 and ITV, measured as lines of text).

References

Aaronovitch, D. (2003) 'The New Anti-Semitism', *Observer*, 22 June

Aham, A. (1923) *Am Scheideweg* (Berlin)

Amnesty International (1996a) 'Israel/Lebanon Unlawful Killings During Operation Grapes of Wrath'. AI Index: MDE 15/042/1996

—— (1996b) 'Israel/Lebanon: Amnesty International Demands Effective Protection for Civilians, Calls for Proper Enquiry into Killings by Israel'. AI Index: MDE 15/049/1996

—— (1997) 'Annual Report 1997 Israel and the Occupied Territories'. AI Index: POL 10/001/1997

—— (1998) 'Annual Report 1998 Israel and the Occupied Territories'. AI Index: POL 10/001/1998

—— (1999a) 'Israel: Flouting UN Obligations in the Name of Security. Oral Statement to the UN Commission on Human Rights on Israel and the Occupied Territories'. AI Index: MDE 15/034/1999

—— (1999b) 'Annual Report 1999 Israel and the Occupied Territories'. AI Index: POL 10/001/2001

—— (1999c) 'Israel and the Occupied Territories: Demolition and Dispossession: The Destruction of Palestinian Homes'. AI Index: MDE 15/059/1999

—— (2000) 'Annual Report 2000 Israel and the Occupied Territories'. AI Index: POL 10/001/2000

—— (2001a) 'Annual Report 2001 Israel and the Occupied Territories'. AI Index: POL 10/001/2001

—— (2001b) 'Israel/OT: The International Community Must Act to End Israel's Policy of Closures and House Demolitions. AI Index: MDE 15/066/2001

—— (2001c) 'Israel/OT: Committee Against Torture Says Israel's Policy of Closures and Demolitions of Palestinian Homes May Amount to Cruel Inhuman or Degrading Treatment'. AI Index: MDE 15/105/2001

—— (2002a) 'Without Distinction: Attacks on Civilians by Palestinian Armed Groups'. AI Index: MDE 02/003/2002

—— (2002b) 'Israel and the OT and the Palestinian Authority. Killing the Future: Children in the line of fire'. AI Index: MDE 02/005/2002

Aronson, G. (1998) 'Palestinian Leadership Fails to Understand the Importance of Settlements', *Report on Israeli Settlement in the Occupied Territories*, July/August.

—— (2001) 'Deconstructing the Taba Talks', *Report on Israeli Settlement in the Occupied Territories*, March/April.

—— (2003) 'Sharon Government's Separation Plan Defines Palestinian Borders', *Report on Israeli Settlement in the Occupied Territories*, July/August

Bard, M. (2003) *Myths and Facts Online Israel and Lebanon* [Internet]. Available from: <www.us-israel.org/jsource/myths/mf11.html> [Accessed 6 September 2003]

Bauer, Y. (1970) *Flight and Rescue: Brichah* (New York: Random House)

Beilin, Y. (1985) *Mehiro Shel Ihud* (in Hebrew) (Revivim)

Berry, M. (2004) 'Television and the Israeli-Palestinian Conflict', PhD thesis, University of Glasgow

Bohm, A. (1935) *Die Zionistische Bewegung* (Berlin)

Boyle, W.J. (2002) *The Two O'Clock War: The 1973 Yom Kippur Conflict and the Airlift that Saved Israel* (New York: St. Martin's Press)

Bregman, A. (2003) *A History of Israel* (Basingstoke: Palgrave Macmillan)

British Government (1919a) Public Record Office. Foreign Office No. 800/215

—— (1919b) Public Record Office. Foreign Office No. 371/4183

—— (1930) 'Palestine: Report on Immigration, Land Settlement and Development', Cmd. 3686

—— (1939) 'Report of a Committee on Correspondence between Sir Henry McMahon and the Sherif of Mecca', Parliamentary Papers, Cmd. 5974

—— (1947) 'The Political History of Palestine under the British Administration' (Memorandum to the United Nations Special Committee on Palestine), Jerusalem

B'Tselem (2000) *Illusions of Restraint*, Report, December

—— (2003a) *Casualty Statistics 1987–2003* [Internet] Available from <www.btselem.org/English/Statistics/Total_Casualties.asp> [Accessed 6 September 2003]

—— (2003b) *Fatalities in the al-Aqsa Intifada, Data by Month* [Internet] Available from <www.btselem.org/English/Statistics/Al_Aqsa_Fatalities_Tables.asp> [Accessed 6 September 2003]

—— (2003c) *Behind the Barrier: Human Rights Violation as a Result of Israel's Separation Barrier.* B'Tselem Position Paper, April.

—— (2003d) Violence of settlers against Palestinians [Internet] Available from <www.btselem.org/English/Settlers_Violence/Settlers_Violence.asp> [Accessed 26 March 2004]

—— (2003e) Handling of complaints of settler violence. Available from <www.btselem.org/English/Settlers_Violence/Law_Enforcement.asp> [Accessed 26 March 2004]

Cattan, H. (1973) *Palestine and International Law* (London: Longman)

Childers, E. (1976) 'The Wordless Wish: From Citizens to Refugees', in *The Palestinian Issue in Middle East Peace Efforts*, hearings before the Committee on International Relations, House of Representatives, September, October, November 1975 (US Government Printing Office)

Chomsky, N. (1992) *Deterring Democracy* (London: Vintage Books)

—— (1999) *The Fateful Triangle: The United States, Israel and the Palestinians* (London: Pluto Press)

Cockburn, A. and Cockburn, L. (1991) *Dangerous Liaison: The Inside Story of the US-Israeli Covert Relationship* (New York: HarperCollins)

Cohn-Sherbok, D. (2001) 'A Jewish Perspective', in D. Cohn-Sherbok and D. El-Alami (eds) *The Palestine-Israeli Conflict: A Beginners Guide* (Oxford: One World Publications)

Crum, B.C. (1947) *Behind the Silken Curtain* (New York: Simon & Schuster)

Dodd, P. and Barakat, H. (1968) *River Without Bridges* (Beirut: Institute for Palestine Studies)

Eban, A. (1992) *Personal Witness: Israel through my Eyes* (New York: Putnam Publishing)

Eddy, W. (1954) *F.D.R. Meets Ibn Saud* (New York: American Friends of the Middle East)

Feingold, H.L. (1970) *The Politics of Rescue* (New Brunswick: Rutgers University Press)

Finkelstein, N.G. (1996) *The Rise and Fall of Palestine: A Personal Account of the Intifada Years* (Minneapolis: University of Minnesota Press)

—— (2001) *Image and Reality of the Israel-Palestine Conflict* (London: Verso)

Fisch, H. (1982) *The Zionism of Zion* (in Hebrew) (Tel-Aviv: Zmora Bitan)

Fisk, R. (2001) *Pity the Nation* (Oxford: Oxford University Press)

Flapan, S. (1987) *The Birth of Israel: Myths and Realities* (New York: Pantheon Books)

Foundation for Middle East Peace (1997) *Settler Population 1972–97* [Internet] Available from: <www.fmep.org/charts/chart9811_1.gif> [Accessed 6 September 2003]

Friedlander, D. and Goldscheider, C. (1979) *The Population of Israel* (New York: Columbia University Press)

Gabbay, R. (1959) *A Political Study of the Arab-Jewish Conflict: The Arab Refugee Problem* (Geneva: Librairie E. Droz.)

Gilbert, M. (1999) *Israel: A History* (London: Black Swan Books)

Glasgow University Media Group (2002) 'Media Coverage of the Developing World: Audience Understanding and Interest' [Internet]. See GUMG website: <www.gla.ac.uk/departments/sociology/media.html>. Another version of this article is published as Philo (2002)

Gush Shalom (1998) *Who is Violating the Agreements?* [Internet] Available from: <www.gush-shalom.org/archives/oslo.html> [Accessed 6 September 2003]

—— (2003) *Barak's Generous Offers* [Internet] Available from: <www.gush-shalom.org/generous/generous.html> [Accessed 6 September 2003]

Harris, W.W. (1980) *Taking Root: Israeli Settlement in the West Bank, the Golan and Gaza-Sinai 1967–1980* (Chichester: Research Studies Press)

Hastings, M. (2002) 'The Disturbing Truth About a War on Terror', *Daily Mail*, 28 October

Heller, Y. (1985) *The Struggle for the State: Zionist Diplomacy of the Years 1936–48* (in Hebrew) (Jerusalem: Jewish Agency Protocols)

Herzl, T. (1960) *The Complete Diaries of Theodor Herzl* (New York: Herzl Press and Thomas Yoseloff)

Hirst D. (1977) *The Gun and the Olive Branch* (London: Faber & Faber)

Hitchens, C. and Said, E. (1988) *Blaming the Victims* (London: Verso)

Human Rights Watch (1996) *Israel's Closure of the West Bank and Gaza Strip*, July, vol 8, no. 3 (E)

—— (1998) *Security Pact May Encourage Human Rights Violations.* Press Release, New York, 22 October 1998

Human Rights Watch (1999) 'Israel/Lebanon, Persona Non Grata: The Expulsion of Civilians from Israeli-Occupied Lebanon' [Internet]. Available from: <http://hrw.org/reports/1999/lebanon/Isrlb997.htm> [Accessed 13 January 2004]

Independent Television Commission (2003) *The Public's View* (London: ITC)

Ingrams, D. (1972) *Palestine Papers 1917–1922, Seeds of Conflict* (London: John Murray)

Israeli Defence Forces (2003) *Israeli Civilians Killed/Wounded on the Lebanese Border 1985–99* [Internet] Available from: <www.idf.il/english/statistics/civilian.stm> [Accessed 5 September 2003]

Israeli Ministry of Foreign Affairs (1996). *Israel's Settlements: Their Conformity with International Law* [Internet] Available from: <www.israel.org/mfa/go.asp?MFAH0dgj0> [Accessed 5 September 2003]

——— (1999) *Suicide and Other Bombing Attacks Inside Israel Since the Declaration of Principles, September 1993* [Internet] Available from: <www.mfa.gov.il/mfa/go.asp?MFAH0i5d0> [Accessed 5 September 2003]

Kapeliouk, A. (1984) *Sabra and Shatila: Inquiry into a Massacre* (Belmont, MA: Association of Arab-American University Graduates)

Karsh, E. (2000) *Fabricating Israeli History: The 'New Historians'* (London: Frank Cass)

——— (2002) 'What Occupation?', *Commentary*, July

Khalidi, W. (1971) *From Haven to Conquest: Zionism and the Palestinian Problem Until 1948* (Munich: KG Saur Verlag)

Laqueur, W. and Rubin, B. (1984) *The Israel–Arab Reader* (New York: Facts on File/Viking Penguin)

Lilienthal, A. (1978) *The Zionist Connection* (New York: Dodd, Mead & Co.)

Linowitz, S. (1957) 'The Legal Basis for the State of Israel', *American Bar Association Journal*, vol. 43

Lustick, I. (1980) *Arabs in the Jewish State: Israel's Control of a National Minority* (New York: University of Texas Press)

McCarthy, J. (1990) *The Population of Palestine* (New York: Columbia University Press)

Masalha, N. (1992) *Expulsion of the Palestinians: The Concept of 'Transfer' in Zionist Political Thought* (Beirut: Institute for Palestine Studies)

——— (1999) 'The 1967 Palestinian Exodus', in G. Karmi and E. Cotran (eds) *The Palestinian Exodus 1948–1998* (Reading: Garnet Publishing)

Mishal, S. and Sela, A. (2000) *The Palestinian Hamas: Vision, Violence and Coexistence* (New York: Columbia University Press)

Morris, B. (1989) *The Birth of the Palestinian Refugee Problem* (Cambridge: Cambridge University Press)

——— (1992) *Israel's Secret Wars: A History of Israel's Intelligence Services* (London: Futura Publications)

——— (1997) *Israel's Border Wars, 1949–1956 Arab Infiltration, Israeli Retaliation, and the Countdown to the Suez War* (Oxford: Oxford University Press)

——— (2001) *Righteous Victims: A History of the Zionist-Arab Conflict* (New York: Vintage Books)

Neff, D. (1985) *Warriors for Jerusalem* (New York: Smithmark Publishing)

Netanyahu, B. (2000) *A Durable Peace: Israel and its Place Among the Nations* (New York: Warner Books)

Ovendale, R. (1999) *The Origins of the Arab-Israeli Wars* (Harlow: Pearson)

Pappe, I. (1999) 'Were they Expelled? The History, Historiography and Relevance of the Palestinian Refugee Problem', in G. Karmi and E. Cotran (eds), *The Palestinian Exodus 1948–1998* (Reading: Garnet Publishing)

Perlmutter, A., Handel, M. and Bar-Joseph, U. (1982) *Two Minutes over Baghdad* (London: Vallentine Mitchell)

Peters, J. (1984) *From Time Immemorial: The Origins of the Arab-Jewish Conflict over Palestine* (New York: HarperCollins)

Phillips, M. (2003) 'New Threat, but Left with Their Blinkers On', *Jewish Chronicle*, 28 February

Philo, G. (2002) 'Television News and Audience Understanding of War, Conflict and Disaster', *Journalism Studies*, vol. 3, (2) (London: Routledge)

Philo, G., Hewitt, J. and Beharrell, P. (1995) 'And Now They're Out Again: Industrial News', in G. Philo (ed.) *Glasgow Media Group Reader*, Vol. 2 (London: Routledge)

Philo, G. and Miller, D. (2001) *Market Killing* (London: Pearson Education)
Pundak, R. (2001) 'From Oslo to Taba: What Went Wrong?' *Survival*, vol. 43, no. 3.
Randal, J. (1983) *The Tragedy of Lebanon: Christian Warlords, Israeli Adventurers and American Bunglers* (London: Chatto & Windus/Hogarth Press)
Rusk, D. (1991) *As I Saw It* (New York: Penguin (USA))
Sachar, H.M. (1977) *A History of Israel: From the Rise of Zionism to Our Time* (Oxford: Blackwell)
Segev, T. (1993) *The Seventh Million: The Israelis and the Holocaust* (New York: Hill and Wang)
—— (2001) *One Palestine, Complete. Jews and Arabs Under the British Mandate* (London: Abacus)
Shafir, G. (1999) 'Zionism and Colonialism', in I. Pappe (ed.) *The Israel/Palestine Question* (New York: Routledge)
Shahak, I. (1994) Israel's State-Assisted Terrorism: 'Settlers' as Armed Combatants, *Washington Report on Middle East Affairs*, February/March.
—— (1995) *Analysis of Israeli Policies: The Priority of the Ideological Factor*. Report no. 154, 12 May
Shahak, I. and Mezvinsky, N. (1999) *Jewish Fundamentalism in Israel* (London: Pluto Press)
Shlaim, A. (2000) *The Iron Wall: Israel and the Arab World* (London: Penguin)
Shonfeld, M. (1977). *The Holocaust Victims Accuse: Documents and Testimony on Jewish War Criminals, Part I* (Brooklyn: Neturei Karta of USA)
Singer, M. (1977) 'Right is Might', *Jerusalem Post*, 29 June
Tillman, S. (1982) *The United States in the Middle East: Interests and Obstacles* (Bloomington: IN: University of Indiana Press)
United Nations (1945) League of Nations. 'The Mandate System. Origin Applications Principles'. 30 April 1985. LoN/1945.VI.A.1
—— (1967) General Assembly Fifth Emergency Session, 5 July
—— (1988) 'Report of the Special Committee to Investigate Israeli Practices Affecting the Human Rights of the Population of the Occupied Territories'. Resolution 43/58A, passed 6 December
—— (1990) 'The Origins and Evolution of the Palestine Problem 1917–1988'. [Internet] Available from: <http://domino.un.org/UNISPAL. NSF/561c6ee353d740fb8525607d00581829/aeac80e740c782e48525611500 71fdb0!OpenDocument> [Accessed 6 September 2003]
—— (1994) Commission on Human Rights. 'Question of the Violation of Human Rights in the Occupied Arab Territories, Including Palestine'. E/CN.4/RES/1994/3 (A+B)E/1994/24E/CN.4/1994/132, 18 February
—— (1996) 'UN Report on Israel's Bombing of the United Nations Compound at Qana, Lebanon'. S1996/337, 7 May
—— (1997) 'Illegal Israeli Actions in Occupied East Jerusalem and the Rest of the Occupied Palestinian Territory'. Resolution A/RES/ES-10/2, passed 25 April
—— (1999) Commission on Human Rights. 'Question of the Violation of Human Rights in the Occupied Arab Territories, Including Palestine'. E/CN.4/RES/1999/5, 23 April
Weisgal, M. (1944) *Chaim Weizmann* (New York: Dial Press)

Index

Aaronovitch, David, 299
Abbas, Mahmoud (Abu Mazen), 80
Abd Al-Shafi, Haidar, 294
Abdullah, King of Transjordan, 21
Abu Dis, 82
Abu Jihad, 63
Abu Nidal, 59, 60, 293
Achille Lauro, 60
Action and response (Palestinian
    and Israeli), 229
Adams, Paul, 113, 195, 201, 260
Agha, Hussein, 84–5
Aham, Ahad, 2
Airline hijackings, 44–5
Al Durrah, Mohammed, 145, 148–50
Al Ezzariyye, 82
Al-Haram Al-Sharif, 86
Al-Husseini, Abdul Qader, 18
Al-Hut, Shafiq, 294
Alkalai, Judah, 2
Albright, Madelaine, 105
Alagiah, George, 201, 211
Allon plan, 34; Allon-plus, 78
Allon, Yigal, 31
Al-Madani Mahmud, 88
American Israeli Public Affairs
    Committee (AIPAC), 252ff
American flag, burning of, 106–7
Amman Declaration, 60
Amir, Yigal, 74
Amnesty International,
    on settlement building, 39;
    on Israeli human rights abuses,
    42, 290–1
    on Palestinian suicide bombings,
    72
    on Israeli attacks on civilians in
    Lebanon, 75–6, 294
    on Hezbullah attacks on civilians
    in Lebanon, 294
    on Jenin incursion/invasion
    2002a, 198
Annan, Kofi, 104

Arab–Israeli Wars
    The 1948 War, 20–2, 91
    The Suez War, 27–9
    The Six Day War, 1, 29–34, 92
    The War of Attrition, 35–6, 47
    The October War, 47–8
    The Lebanon War, 54–60
Arab Revolt, 9–10
Argov, Shlomo, 59
Arafat, Yasser,
    establishes Fatah and PLO, 43–5
    addresses United Nations, 49, 64
    meets EU representatives, 53
    issues Amman declaration, 60
    ends collaboration with King Of
        Jordan, 60
    pushes for mini-state, 49, 52,
        63–4, 292–3
    negotiates Oslo agreement, 69
    involvement in torture, extra-
        judicial killings and corruption
        scandals, 79–80
    criticised for not stopping
        settlement building, 80
    negotiates final status agreement,
        83–8
    role at start of second intifada,
        132
    critiques of, on news, 165ff
Argentina, 3
Aronson, Geoffrey, 73, 80, 87–8, 89
Assad, President of Syria, 172–3
Aswan dam project, 27
Audience studies (samples and
    methods), 200
Auschwitz, 236
Austria, 53
Avneri, Uri, 158
Ayad, Massoud, 88
Ayalon, Ami, 79
Ayyash, Yahya, 75

Bachar, Aharon, 291

Bad neighbours (as reasons for conflict), 125, 221
Balfour, Arthur, 5, 286
Balfour Declaration, 5, 37, 45
Bantustan model, 62, 70, 74, 83
Barak, Ehud, 63, 81–8, 93, 294
Barakat, Halim, 32
Bard, Mitchell, 58–9
Bar-On, Mordechai, 59
Bauer, Yehuda, 14
Begin, Menachem, 30, 53–4, 288, 291
Beeley, Harold, 287
Ben-Gurion, David, 10, 12, 14–15;
    reaction to UN partition vote 18
    role in Israeli War of
        Independence 20, 22
    position on Palestinian refugees 24
    role in Suez conflict 27–9
    designs on Jerusalem and West Bank, 31–2
Ben-Yair, Michael, 157
Beit Rima (Israeli incursion/attack, October 2001), 178
Bernadotte, Count, 20–1
Berry, Mike, 295
Betar movement, 286
Biltmore Resolution, 13
Black, Conrad, 255
Black September, 45
Blair, Tony, 172–3
Bohm, Adolf, 4
Boyle, Walter, 292
Brazil, 35, 277
Bregman, Ahron, 4, 7, 17, 18, 21, 23, 36, 288
B'Tselem, 69, 116, 122–4, 289, 293, 294, 296
Burg, Yosef, 54, 58
Burns, General, 31
Bush, George W., 37
Bushinsky, Jay, 78
Bypass roads, 73–4, 78, 79, 82, 85, 86
Byrnes, James, 287

Cairo agreement 72–3
Camp David agreement, 53–4

Camp David final status negotiations, 83–6, 94
Caradon, Lord, 288
Carey, Elaine, 55
Casualties and deaths,
    case studies, 144–56
    coverage of , 182ff
    audience beliefs, 231
    figures for coverage of each side, 297
Causes, explanations (in news, absence of), 101ff
Central Intelligence Agency (CIA), 30, 276, 287
Chamberlain, Joseph, 3–4
Chamoun militia, 50
Checkpoints, military, 117
Childers, Erskine, 288
Chomsky, Noam, 40, 52, 56–7, 65, 289
Chovevei Zion, 2
Christian Right (in United States), 252, 258
Christopher, Warren, 75
Clinton, Bill, 84, 87, 105, 276, 279
Coburn, Judith, 49
Cohn-Sherbok, Dan, 10–11
Collective punishment,
    as employed by British mandatory authority, 10
    as utilized by Israel, 42, 73, 290–1
    Amnesty International position on, 42
    United Nations Commission on Human Rights views on, 291
Colvin, Marie, 195
Congreve, General William, 8
Conservative Friends of Israel, 250
Content analysis methods, 94ff
Contras (in Nicaragua), 277
Cornerstone church, 252
Courage to refuse, Israeli dissenters, 158
Cultural identification and empathy, 236
Curfews, on Palestinians, 23, 42, 66, 71, 73, 74, 77, 124
Curtiss, Richard, 75–6
Curzon, Lord, 6–7, 286
Cyprus, 4

D-Day anniversaries, 278
Dalrymple, William, 256
Darcy, General, 18
Darwish, Mahmoud, 294
Davis, Evan, 201
Dayan, Moeshe, 28, 32, 38, 41–2,
   91, 92, 292
D'Estaing, Giscard, 53
Direct statements, 97
Dissent (within Israel), 218–19
Dodd, Peter, 32
Dreyfus trial, 3
Drobless plan, 38
Dull Blade, operation, 89

East Jerusalem, sovereignty of, 109
Eban, Abba, 30, 49
Egypt
   invades nascent Jewish state, 21
   offers to recognise Israel in
      exchange for land in Negev, 22
   occupies Gaza strip, 23
   negotiates with Israel following
      1948 war, 23
   persecution of Jews in, 25
   as source of infiltration, 26
   invasion of, by Israel in 1956,
      27–8
   clashes with Israel in Six Day
      War, 29–31
   accepts UN resolution 242, 34
   fights War of Attrition, 35–6, 47
   launches October War against
      Israel, 47–8
   signs peace treaty with Israel,
      53–4
Ehrlich, Eyal, 62
Eitan, Rafael, 28
El-Kawakji, Fawzi, 18
El-Sarraj, Dr Eyad, 72
European Union
   criticises settlement building, 39
   criticises Israeli moves to change
      demographic balance in
      Jerusalem, 39
   supports Palestinian statehood,
      53
   criticises Israeli attack on Tunis,
      60

endorses 'road map', 89
Explanations, as area of coverage,
   108ff
   history and origins of conflict,
      110
   cycle of violence, 112
   land, water and economic
      discontent, 113
   social consequences of
      occupation, 116
   religion, 126
   Israeli perspectives on security,
      terrorism and incitement, 128
   Yasser Arafat and Ariel Sharon,
      the instigation of violence, 130

Fatah, 43–4, 69, 70–1, 88, 294
Feingold, Henry, 15
Finkelstein, Norman, 19–20, 30, 35,
   47, 54, 288–9
Fisch, Harold, 36
Fisk, Robert, 55, 56, 246, 290
Flapan, Simha, 10, 21
Flashman, Gaye, 201
Focus groups, participants, 201
Force 17, 88
Foreign press association, 247
Fox News, 255
France
   involvement in dismemberment
      of Ottoman empire, 5
   colludes with Britain and Israel in
      attacking Egypt, 27
   position on UN resolution 242,
      288
   supports two state solution at
      United Nations, 52
Funerals (in news content), 103–4

Galilee document, 292
Galili Plan, 38
Gaza Strip, population density and
   control of water, 115–16
Gemayel, Bashir, 54, 59
George, Lloyd, 5
Giannou, Chris, 55, 293
Gilbert, Martin, 9, 18, 25, 50–1,
   55–6, 61, 288
Gilmour, David, 287

Gilmour, Ian, 287
Givat Ze'ev, 88
Glubb, Sir John Bagot, 18, 26
Golan Heights, 29, 30, 33, 34, 47, 54, 92
Goldberg, J.J, 253
Goldenberg, Suzanne, 114
Goldstein, Dr Baruch, 71
Goodman, Hirsch, 55, 293
Gowing, Nik, 201
Graham, Alex, 201
Graves, Keith, 247
Guatemala, 276
Guatemalan Truth Commission, 277
Gulags, 277
Gulf War 1991, 67, 224
Gunmen, (words and perspectives), 170-1
Gur, Mordechai, 35, 48
Gush Emunim, 38, 53-4
Gush Shalom, 79, 85

Hadar, Amos, 40
Haddad, General, 50-1, 57
Habash, George, 43-4
Halifax, Lord, 287
Halper, Jeff, 85-6
Hamas,
    formation of and aims, 65-6
    Rabin deports activists to Lebanon, 68
    influence of Hezbullah on, 68, 294
    reaction to the Oslo Accords, 70-1
    involvement in suicide attacks, 71, 75, 78, 89
    condemnation of, by Amnesty International, 72
    leaders assassinated by Israel, 75,
    · 78-9, 88, 89
    attempts to negotiate with Israel, 78
    activists attacked by Palestinian Authority, 79
    support for, amongst Palestinians, 80, 168
Hanrahan, Brian, 201, 218, 237-8

Har Homa /Jabal Ghneim settlement, 78
Ha'etzni, Nadav, 74
Hareven, Aluf, 58
Harris, William Wilson, 33
Hass, Amira, 133
Hastings, Max, 173
Haycraft Commission, 8
Headlines (in news content), 138-44
Hebron protocol, 77
Hecht, Ben, 16
Herzl, Theodor, 3-4, 19-20
Hezbullah, 67-8, 75-6, 81, 97, 143-4, 294
Hilsum, Lindsey, 193, 195, 201, 213-14, 245, 248
Hirst, David, 2-4, 8, 10-11, 16, 18-19, 25, 28, 31, 38-9, 43-5, 159, 290-1
Hitchens, Christopher, 288
Holocaust, 236
Holocaust survivors, settlement of, 13-16, 287
Hope Simpson Commission, 8
Hostages, 98
Hourani, Albert, 287
Human Rights Watch, 291, 294
Humphrys, John, 201
Hussein, King of Jordan, 34, 44, 60-1, 63, 78-9, 291
Hussein, Sharif, 5
Hussein, Saddam, 67, 224

Independent television Commission (ITC), 200
India, 288-9
Inglish, Sue, 201
International Court of Justice, 17
Interviews (in news content), 136-8
Intifada, 1987, 61-6, 69, 70
Iran, 61
Iraq, 25, 29-31
Ireland, 53
Irgun, 9, 286
Islamic Jihad, 70-1, 75, 80, 168
Israeli Arabs, 23; attacks on and killings of, in Nazareth, 150-2

Israeli Committee Against House
Demolitions, 85
Israeli Committee for Solidarity
with Bir Zeit, 62
Israeli League for Human and Civil
Rights, 65, 291
Israeli soldiers, killing of in
Ramaleh, 152–5

Jabotinsky, Vladimir, 7, 10
Jansen, G.H., 54
Jarring, Gunnar, 292
Jarring initiative, 292
Jenin, Israeli attack/incursion, 192;
claims of 'massacre', 195ff
Jerusalem
status under Peel proposals, 10
status under United Nations
plans, 17, 21
Israeli moves to change
demographic composition of,
39, 73, 77, 78, 82, 86
United Nations condemnation of
such actions 39, 78
Israel annexes, 54
as site of conflict over holy
places, 9, 18, 77–8, 86–7
Jordan (previously Transjordan)
creation of by Britain, 6
Britain suggests a union with an
Arab section of Palestine, 9–10
invades nascent Jewish state 21
United Nations suggests it form
union with Arab state in
Palestine, 21
annexes West Bank, 23
negotiates with Israel following
1948 war, 23
as source of infiltration, 26
clashes with Israel in Six Day
War, 29–31
accepts UN resolution 242, 34
expels Palestinian guerrillas, 44–5
attends Madrid conference, 67

Kach party, 71
Kahan Commission, 57
Kaiser, Wilheim II, 3
Kalischer, Zvi Hirsh, 2

Kalkilya, 87
Karameh, battle of, 43
Karsh, Efraim, 287, 289
Keren ha-Yesod labour agreements,
8
Kevill, Sian, 201
Khalidi, Walid, 10, 19, 287
Khartoum conference, 33–4, 288
Khiam detention centre, 290
Kiley, Sam, 255
Kiryat Shemona, 48
King-Crane Commission, 7, 286
Kiryat Arba, 87
Koenig memorandum, 42
Kristallnacht pograms, 15
Kursk Bulge, battle of, 279

Lausanne peace conference, 23
Lebanon
invades nascent Jewish state, 21
negotiates with Israel following
1948 War, 23
as source of infiltration, 26
as site for Israeli 'reprisal raids'
following Black September
killings, 45
as site of hostilities between Israel
and PLO in 1970s, 48–52
1978 Israeli invasion of, 50–1
1982 Israeli invasion of, 54–60
attends Madrid conference, 67
as site of conflict between
Hezbullah and Israel, 75–6, 93
Israel withdraws troops from, 81,
93
Levy, David, 66
Libya, 25
Leiberman, Rabbi, 148–8
Lewinsky, Monica, 276–7
Lilienthal, Alfred, 33
Llewellyn, Tim, 195, 201, 214
Loach, Ken, 201, 237–9
Lustick, Ian, 42

Ma'ale Adumim, 83, 88
MacDonald White Paper, 12
Madrid conference, 67–8
Malley, Robert, 84–5
Mapai party, 22

Margalit, Avishai, 287
Maronite militias, 50
Marshall, Rachelle, 71, 81–2
Martyr Abu Mahmud Group, 45
Masalha, Nur, 19, 32, 287
Mash'al Khalid, 78
Massing, Michael, 253
Mayan Indian, 277
McKinney, Paul, 201
McMahon, Sir Henry, 5
Media bias against Israel, claims of,
    250ff
Meir, Golda, 21, 46
Memories (of conflict), 209
Methods
    focus groups, 202ff
    qualitative, 204ff
    quantitative, 204ff
Mevinsky, Norton, 38
Miller, David, 286
Mishal, Shaul, 66, 68, 75
Moda'i, Yitzak, 66
Monck, Adrian, 201, 244
Morris, Benny, 20, 32, 36, 41, 61, 83
Moshav agricultural movement, 40
Motives (rationales of action)
    of participants in conflict,
        retaliation and response,
        160–5, 186ff
Moyne, Lord, 16
Mufti of Jerusalem, 9, 11–12, 18
Muslim Brotherhood, 65
Mustafa, Abu Ali, 160

Nahariya, 48
Nasser, Gamal Abd, 27–31, 291
Nekudah, 289
Neff, Donald, 31
Netanyahu, Binyamin, 20–1, 37–8,
    46–8, 52–3, 61, 64, 69, 76–81
News writing exercise, 225
Nicaragua, 277
Non-Aligned States, 88
Northern Ireland, 223
Nuclear Weapons
    Israel threatens to use against
        Egypt during October War, 47
    estimations of Israel's current
        stockpiles, 60

Occupation (audience
    understanding of), 217
Origins of/history of conflict (in
    audience responses), 212
Oslo Peace Process, 69–88, 133
Ovendale, Richie, 5, 8, 13, 16, 21,
    27, 53, 60, 287

Palestine Liberation Front, 60
Palestine Liberation Organisation
    (PLO)
    establishment of, 43–6
    attacks Israel from bases in
        Lebanon, 48–52
    recognised by United Nations, 49
    suggests mini-state in West Bank
        and Gaza, 49, 52, 63–4, 292–3
    recognised by European
        countries, 53
    attacked by Israel in 1982
        Lebanon war, 54–9
    Israel refuses to negotiate with,
        60–1, 66–7, 292
    kills Israelis in Cyprus, 60
    Israel bombs headquarters of, 60
    Israel assassinates leaders of, 63,
        88
    accepts Israel's right to exist and
        renounces 'terrorism', 64
    Israel recognises, 69
    reaction to Oslo agreement, 70–1,
        294
Palestinian Authority
    formation of, 69
    Netanyahu accuses of failing
        to control militants and
        incitement, 61, 79
    loses support amongst
        Palestinians, 80, 82–3
    involvement in torture and extra-
        judicial killings of Palestinians,
        82, 294
    attempts to limit unfavourable
        coverage, 248
Palestinian economy, decline of, 74,
    94, 113
Palestinian National (PLO) Charter,
    69, 79, 80, 292
Palestinian Mandate, 6–17

Pappe, Ilan, 19, 22–4
Passfield White Paper, 9
Peace negotiations/prospects (in news content), 104
Peace Now, 53, 58, 114
Peel Commission, 9–10
Peled, General Mattityahu, 30–1, 293
Peres, Shimon, 61, 66, 69, 74–6, 88, 146
Peters, Joan, 11, 287
Phalangist militia, 50–1, 57
Phillips, Melanie, 169, 250–1, 298
Philo, Greg, 286, 295
Pilger, John, 220
Plan Dalet, 19–20
Pollard, Stephen, 196
Popular Front for the liberation of Palestine (PFLP), 43–4, 49, 70–1, 160
Powers, Charles, 56
Prisoners, Palestinian, 117
Production factors, 244–57
Public relations (Palestinian and Israeli approaches), 246ff
Public understanding and history, 276
Pundak, Ron, 88

Qana refugee camp, 76
Questionnaire
    audience groups, 202
    questions asked, 202ff, 207–9
    answers by student groups, 261–9, 280–5
    answers by focus groups, 270–5
Quibya, 26, 130
Quray, Ahmad (Abu Ala), 80, 87

Rabbani, Mouin, 70–1
Rabin, Yitzak, 30, 61, 63, 68, 73–4, 288, 292
Rabinowitz, Danny, 82–3
Randal, Jonathan, 50–1, 59
Reagan, Ronald, 278
Refugees:
    Palestinian, of 1948 war, 19–24, 92, 111

Israeli, leaving Arab states after 1948, 25
Palestinian creation of during Six Day War, 32–3
Egyptian created during War of Attrition, 35
Lebanese created by Israeli attacks, 49, 51, 75–6
Reinhart, Tanya, 73–4, 79
Reported statements, 97, 297–8
Reporters Sans Frontiers, 247
Restrictions on coverage, 192ff
Retaliation and response (in audience understanding), 222
Revisionist movement, 7, 9–10, 15, 19, 286–7
Rhodes, Cecil, 3
Rida, Rashid, 5
'Road Map', 89
Rogers, William, 291
Roosevelt, Franklin, 13
Ross, Sandy, 201
Rothschild, Lord, 4
Rubinstein, Aryeh, 40
Rubinstein, Danny, 71
Rusk, Dean, 289
Russia
    as site of anti–Jewish pogroms, 1, 4
    involvement in dismemberment of Ottoman empire, 5
    endorses 'road map', 89
Rydbeck, Olaf, 56

Sabra and Shatila killings, 57
Sachar, Howard, 2, 11, 25, 28, 30, 40, 48
Sadat, Anwar, 47, 53–4, 291–2
Said, Edward, 70, 132, 288
Sartawi, Issam, 293
Samuel, Herbert, 6, 8
Saudi Arabia, 47, 52
Save the Children, 65
Schiff, Ze'ev, 48, 73, 293
Security requirements, Israel, 129
Segal, Yedidia, 289
Segev, Tom, 10, 12, 14–15
September 11 2001 attacks on America, 107

Sela, Avraham, 66, 68, 75
Sells, David, 196–7
Settlements,
    establishment of, following Six
        Day War, 36–9
    strategic and military function of,
        92, 119, 219
    Peace Now on development of,
        114
    Israeli justifications for 36–9
    Amnesty International and
        United Nations position on,
        39, 78, 122–3
    expansion of by Menachem
        Begin, 53
    Likud promises to increase prior
        to Madrid conference, 67–8
    Israel refuses to negotiate over,
        71
    Rabin increases construction of
        following Oslo agreement, 73
    Netanyahu approves new
        construction of, 78
    Hamas cites as justifications for
        attacks, 78
    Israeli reservists protest over, 79
    Arafat's failure to prevent, 80
    Netanyahu and Sharon urge
        increase in, 80–1
    Barak expands construction of,
        81–2
    future of in final status
        negotiations, 83–6
    expansion of, 111
    as 'Jewish neighbourhoods',
        190
San Antonio, 252
Sandanista government, 277
Second World War, 277–8
Settlers,
    as vulnerable (in news content),
        119–20
    as desiring peace, 191
    attacks on Palestinians, 122, 191
Shaath, Nabil, 43
Shabak, 79
Shafir, Gershon, 3–4, 12, 38
Shahak, Israel, 38, 62, 73, 123–4

Shai, Nachman, 249
Shamir, Yitzak, 22, 61, 63, 66, 68,
    84
Sharon, Ariel,
    involvement in 'reprisal' raids,
        26, 28, 130
    perspective on occupied
        territories, 27
    role in 1982 Lebanon war and
        Sabra and Shatila killings, 55,
        57–9, 130
    perspective on first Intifada, 66
    implores settlers to 'grab
        hilltops', 80–1, 119
    visit to Al-Haram Al-Sharif, 87,
        130ff
    premiership, 88–90, 295
    policy of assassinations/targeted
        killings, 158
    attitude to Oslo Accords, 159
    critiques of, on news, 165ff
Shavit, Ari, 76
Shaw Commission, 9
Shephard, Gillian, 250
Shin Bet, 41, 116
Shizaf, Menachem, 62
Shlaim, Avi, 6–7, 14, 18–22, 25–9,
    31, 33–5, 47, 54, 59, 61, 65–6,
    68, 74–7, 81, 91, 159, 292
Shonfeld, Moeshe, 15
Shultz, George, 64
Singer, Max, 289
Solzhenitsyn, Alexander, 277
Sontag, Deborah, 81
Sources of information (for
    participants), 210
South Lebanon Army (SLA), 50–1,
    57, 290, 294
'Spin', 257
Stalingrad, 279
Stern Gang, 16, 22
Suicide bombings, 59, 68, 71–2, 75,
    78, 82, 89, 168–9
    condemnation of by Amnesty
        International, 72
Sultan Abdul–Hamid II, 3–4
Swarah, 82
Sykes, Mark, 6
Sykes-Picot agreement, 5

Syria
  invades nascent Jewish state, 21
  negotiates with Israel following
    1948 war, 23
  persecution of Jews in, 25
  clashes with Israel in Six Day
    War, 29–31
  rejects UN resolution 242, 34
  offers base for Fatah guerrillas, 43
  launches October War against
    Israel, 47–8
  occupies part of Lebanon, 50
  clashes with Israel during 1982
    Lebanon invasion, 54
  accused of fermenting 1987
    intifada, 61
  attends Madrid conference, 67
  negotiates with Barak
    administration, 81, 294

Taba peace talks, 87–8
Tactics (as area of news content),
  107
Talmon, Ya'akov, 40
Temple Mount, 67, 84
Terrorists (words and perspectives),
  170–4
Thabet Thabet, 88
Thatcher, Margaret, 60
Thematic analysis, 95ff
  ideology, 95
  explanatory theme, 96
Thorn, Gaston, 53
Tillman, Seth, 292–3
Time Out, 287
Tito, Marshall, 288
Torture:
  as employed by British
    mandatory authority, 10
  as utilised by Israel, 42, 55–7, 65,
    116, 117, 290
  role in creation of suicide
    bombers, 72
  United Nations condemnation
    of, 65, 72
  Amnesty International
    condemnation of 42, 290
  use of by SLA, 290

use of by Palestinian Authority,
  80, 116, 132
Trade Unions (in Britain), media
  coverage of, 95
Transfer, concept of in Zionist
  thinking, 3, 10, 19–20
Truman, Harry, 15–16, 22
Tsomet party, 80
Turner, Ted, 254

Uganda, 4
Understanding and interest (in
  news), 240
Underwood, John, 201
United Nations
  resolution on partitioning
    Palestine, 17
  resolution on the return of
    Palestinian refugees, 23
  threatens sanctions after Suez
    conflict, 28
  debate over Israeli withdrawal
    following Six Day War, 33–4
  condemnation of settlement
    building, 39, 78
  condemnation of Israeli moves to
    alter demographic balance in
    Jerusalem, 39 condemnation of
    Israeli human rights violations,
    42, 62, 64–5, 67, 73, 289, 291,
    293
  support for Palestinian
    nationalism, 46
  Arafat addresses, 49
  condemns 1978 Lebanon
    invasion, 51
  resolution calling for two state
    solution vetoed by United
    States, 52
  condemns massacres at Sabra and
    Shatila, 57
  condemns attack on PLO
    headquarters in Tunis, 60
  Arafat renounces 'terrorism' at,
    64
  condemns operation 'Grapes of
    Wrath', 76
  endorses 'road map', 89

United Kingdom
  support for creation of Jewish
    homeland, 4, 6–7
  pledges support for Arab
    independence, 5, 286
  governs Palestine under the
    League of Nations mandate,
    6–20
  recommends the partition of
    Palestine, 9–10
  intervenes in support of Egypt
    under Anglo-Egyptian treaty,
    22
  colludes with France and Israel in
    attacking Egypt, 27
  position on UN resolution 242,
    35, 288
United Soviet Socialist Republic
    (USSR)
  involvement in build up to six
    day war, 29
  position on UN resolution 242,
    35
  supports two state solution at
    United Nations, 52
  puts forward 1981 peace plan, 52
  role in Cold War, 278
United States
  supports creation of Jewish
    commonwealth in Palestine,
    13–16
  criticised for not accepting
    Holocaust survivors, 15–16
  pressurises smaller nations to
    accept UN partition vote, 17,
    287
  pressurises Israel to withdraw
    from Sinai in 1956, 27–8
  position on UN resolution 242,
    35, 289
  vetoes two state solution at
    United Nations, 52
  threatens to veto UN resolution
    on Palestinian self-
    determination, 53
  promises to protect Muslim
    refugees in Beirut, 57
  involvement in aftermath of
    1982 Lebanon War, 59–60

  strengthens military ties with
    Israel, 60
  supports bombing of PLO
    headquarters in Tunis, 60
  pressurises Britain not to meet
    with PLO, 60
  pushes autonomy plans for
    Palestinians, 63, 66
  prevents United Nations
    replacing Israeli military
    government with UN force,
    67
  invades Iraq, 67
  involvement in Oslo process,
    66–8
  vetoes UN resolution
    condemning settlement
    building, 78
  vetoes UN resolution calling
    for UN force to be sent to
    occupied territories to protect
    Palestinian civilians, 88
  puts forward 'road map', 89
  supplies weapons to Israel, 107
  audience understanding of role
    in conflict, 220ff
  political links with United
    kingdom, 251ff
  and 'dirty wars', 277
Universal Declaration of human
    rights, 116
Unsworth, Fran, 201
USS Liberty, 29, 288
Value assumptions (in news), 97
Vanunu, Mordechai, 60
Victims and casualties, 174ff
Vietnam, (US and Vietnamese
    casualties), 279–80
Village Leagues, 62
Violence (in news content), 101–3
Visual images of conflict, effect on
    audience, 223

Wall, Security/Apartheid, 89, 295
Walsh, Edward, 57
'War on Terror', 296
Water resources, 92–4, 119
Weitz, Joseph, 19–20, 24
Weizman, Ezer, 30, 35, 51, 288

Weizmann, Chaim, 4, 6–7, 10, 22
Wolfe, Joy, 246, 298
Womens' International Zionist
    Organisation, 246
'World opinion' on the conflict,
    297
Wye Accords, 80–1, 93, 119

Yaron, Amos, 58
Yassim, Sheikh, 65, 66, 79
Yirmiah, Dov, 56

Zangwill, Israel, 4
Ze'evi, Rehavem, 161
Zionists (British), 246